Also in the Variorum Collected Studies Series:

DAVID AYALON
Islam and the Abode of War: Military Slaves and Islamic Adversaries

NEHEMIA LEVTZION
Islam in West Africa: Religion, Society and Politics to 1800

MAJID FAKHRY
Philosophy and Dogma in Islam and the Impact of Greek Thought

AMNON SHILOAH
The Dimension of Music in Islamic and Jewish Culture

ETAN KOHLBERG
Belief and Law in Imāmī Shī'ism

C.F. BECKINGHAM
Between Islam and Christendom

R.B. SERJEANT
Customary and Shari'ah Law in Arabian Society

FRANZ ROSENTHAL
Muslim Intellectual and Social History

GEORGE MAKDISI
Religion, Law and Learning in Classical Islam

WILFERD MADELUNG
Religious and Ethnic Movements in Medieval Islam

M.J. KISTER
Society and Religion from Jāhiliyya to Islam

GEORGES VAJDA
Études de théologie et de philosophie arabo-islamiques à l'époque classique

ANDREW S. EHRENKREUTZ
Monetary Change and Economic History in the Medieval Muslim World

NICHOLAS LOWICK
Islamic Coins and Trade in the Medieval World

COLLECTED STUDIES SERIES

Law and Legal Theory in Classical and Medieval Islam

Wael B. Hallaq

Law and Legal Theory in Classical and Medieval Islam

VARIORUM
1995

Published by VARIORUM
Ashgate Publishing Limited
Gower House, Croft Road,
Aldershot, Hampshire GU11 3HR
Great Britain

Ashgate Publishing Company
Old Post Road,
Brookfield, Vermont 05036
USA

ISBN 0-86078-456-8

British Library CIP Data
Hallaq, Wael B.
Law and Legal Theory in Classical and Medieval Islam.
(Variorum Collected Studies Series; CS 474)
I. Title II. Series
340.59

US Library of Congress CIP Data
Hallaq, Wael B., 1955–
Law and Legal Theory in Classical and Medieval Islam /
Wael B. Hallaq.
p. cm. — (Collected Studies Series: CS474)
Includes indexes. ISBN 0-86078-456-8 (alk. paper)
1. Islamic law—history. I. Title. II. Series: Collected
Studies: CS474
LAW ‹ISLAM 7 Hall 1994› 94–26872
340.5'9—dc20 CIP

The paper used in this publication meets the minimum requirements of the American National Standard for Information Sciences - Permanence of Paper for Printed Library Materials, ANSI Z39.48-1984. ∞ ™

Printed by Galliard (Printers) Ltd
Great Yarmouth, Norfolk, Great Britain

COLLECTED STUDIES SERIES CS474

CONTENTS

This volume contains viii + 329 pages

PREFACE

The twelve studies that make up this volume are among a larger group of articles on the subject written during the decade following 1982 and published between 1984 and 1993. They constitute explorations in a field of research that is still in its infancy, and as such they reflect the development of the author's own understanding of the subject. It should not come as a surprise therefore that in one article certain assumptions may be taken as valid while in another these very assumptions are modified if not wholly refuted. One obvious case in point is Shāfi'ī's legacy in the evolution of legal theory during the century or so after his death. In certain articles I follow conventional wisdom in taking Shāfi'ī to be the founder of the science of legal theory. In article VII, however, I challenge this thesis and argue that the image of Shāfi'ī as the 'master architect' of legal theory was a much later creation. Thus, the explanation of any seeming contradiction must be sought in the chronological sequence of these studies.

Nevertheless, the studies have not been arranged chronologically, but rather around themes which bestow unity on three groups of articles. The first is the group consisting of I–IV which expound the interrelated issues of legal reasoning, legal logic and the epistemology of the law. The second group, V–IX, contains articles that are all historical in nature, questioning, in one way or another, theses or assumptions widely prevalent in the field. This revisionist approach, I must add, is also characteristic of II and XII. Finally, the last three articles explore various substantive issues of legal theory, including questions of methodology.

Wherever possible, errors in diacritical marks have been corrected. It will be noted, however, that I have not attempted to add the missing macrons over long vowels at the end of Arabic names in articles I and VI. At the time I wrote these articles, I thought such an exercise to be superfluous.

It is my pleasant duty to thank the editors and original publishers of the journals for permitting the reproduction of my articles in this collection, and for their prompt response to my enquiries. I should also like to record my thanks to Dr John Smedley whose efficiency and patient cooperation ensured the smooth production of this volume. Last, but by no means least, I should acknowledge an immense and long-standing debt to Ghada Bathish-Hallaq who took a close interest in my work over the years. Perhaps there is not a single page in this collection that has not been affected by her perspicacious and constructive comments.

W. HALLAQ

McGill University, Montreal
February 1994

PUBLISHER'S NOTE

The articles in this volume, as in all others in the Collected Studies Series, have not been given a new, continuous pagination. In order to avoid confusion, and to facilitate their use where these same studies have been referred to elsewhere, the original pagination has been maintained wherever possible.

Each article has been given a Roman number in order of appearance, as listed in the Contents. This number is repeated on each page and quoted in the index entries.

References in the Addenda and Corrigenda are indicated with an asterisk.

I

THE LOGIC OF LEGAL REASONING IN RELIGIOUS AND NON-RELIGIOUS CULTURES: THE CASE OF ISLAMIC LAW AND THE COMMON LAW

I. Introduction

It is only reasonable to assume that dissimilar legal systems possess dissimilar patterns of legal reasoning. Inasmuch as two legal systems differ in their structure and function, they also differ in the types of arguments they employ in their service. It may well be argued that law is, in the final analysis, the product of the premises and methods from and through which it is derived. Two such legal systems which display a vast difference in their overall structure and function are Islamic law and the common law.[1] This paper proposes to shed some light on the logic of legal

[1] Islamic law and the common law are treated here synchronically rather than diachronically. The convenient point of departure, insofar as this paper is concerned, is the phase of intellectual maturity of both systems falling in Islamic law, in the period after the tenth century A.D., and in common law, in the end of the last century and the present one. It is not implied that common law could reach intellectual maturity only toward the end of the nineteenth century; the concern of this paper is with analytical jurisprudence and the role of logic in law. Therefore, one cannot speak of such mature theory in common law before the latter part of the past century.

reasoning in both orders as well as to analyze the reasons and background which give rise to differences and similarities in their methods of reasoning. This will be done with the intent of bringing out some of the major factors which operate on the level of the judicial process and which contribute to the creation of differences in legal orders. The focal comparison in such a study must be the relationship between the logic of the law and the amount of emphasis given to social change in secular and religious cultures.

This, it must be pointed out, is a preliminary investigation which awaits a more thorough and comprehensive study—primarily because legal logic in Islam has not yet been analyzed, and our knowledge of the methods of legal reasoning subsumed under what is commonly known as *qiyās* is still rudimentary. This is particularly evident from the fact that, with very few exceptions, modern scholars of Islamic law translate *qiyās* as analogy without realizing the existence of other arguments (e.g., *a fortiori* argument in both its forms, the *a minori ad maius* and *a maiori ad minus*, *reductio ad absurdum* and induction) which are comprised by that nomenclature. This paper is not aimed at arguing for the existence of these arguments in *qiyās*; rather, it presupposes them. This presupposition, however, is fully justified by the sources cited herein.[2]

By way of introduction, it must be noted that the general attitude of Islamic and common law lawyers[3] towards logic cannot be described as positive. Although lawyers from both systems find logic an indispensable tool for the systematization and consistency of legal concepts and doctrines, logic generally remains suspect.[4] Surely, in each case, this attitude is the result of different causes. The Islamic lawyer resists logic because he views it as an offshoot of Greek philosophy. For him the unqualified acceptance of logic entails the acceptance of metaphysical conclusions which run against the fundaments of his belief as Muslim. Only when logic is stripped from its theological implications and used merely as a tool does the Islamic lawyer consider it legitimate.

In common law, logic is also rejected whenever it is conceived as a

---

* [2] Subsequent to the submission of this Article to press, further investigation of the arguments subsumed under *qiyās* led to the conclusion that, to the exclusion of the *argmentum e contrario*, which was considered as a linguistic argument, *qiyās* encompassed the arguments enumerated above. For a documented account of this investigation, see the author's *Non-Analogical Arguments in Sunnī Juridical Qiyās* (forthcoming).

[3] For purposes of convenience, the terms "lawyers," "judges," and "jurists" will be used loosely in this paper. The judges are primarily responsible for the development of common law, while the jurists undertake such a responsibility in Islam. Islamic law, like Roman law, is jurists' law. Despite usages such as "the Islamic lawyer," this distinction must always be kept in mind. On Islamic law as jurists' law, see J. SCHACHT, AN INTRODUCTION TO ISLAMIC LAW 209 (Oxford 1964); Weiss, *Interpretation in Islamic Law: The Theory of Ijtihad*, 26 AM. J. COMP. L. 199, 201-03 (1978).

[4] H.J.M. BOUKEMA, JUDGING 180 (1980); Goldziher, *The Attitude of Orthodox Islam Toward the "Ancient Sciences,"* in STUDIES ON ISLAM 198-209 (M.L. Swartz ed. & trans. Oxford 1981); Guest, *Logic in the Law*, in OXFORD ESSAYS ON JURISPRUDENCE 176 (1961); Simitis, *The Problem of Legal Logic*, 3 RATIO 1, 94 (1960).

rigorous tool of inference. Of great concern are the results to which logic may lead against the constantly changing social reality. Law, Justice Holmes said, is "the resultant of a conflict at every point between logic and good sense—the one striving to work fiction out to consistent results, the other restraining and at last overcoming that effort when the results become too manifestly unjust."[5] By this statement, Justice Holmes implied that logic brings about formal consistency of concepts irrespective of the consequences when applied to concrete matters of fact. The heart of the problem, common law lawyers argue, is compromising the necessary logical deduction from non-contemporaneous premises with contemporary problems, while simultaneously taking into account social and ethical questions.[6] Although this is a major problem facing the common law lawyer, the question of the serviceability of logic in law as a normative system[7] constitutes yet another insurmountable difficulty. To this last point we shall return later.

II. Role of Logic

Although the notion of "high authority" as a source of law lingers in the background of the common legal tradition, it would be accurate here, for all intents and purposes, to state that common law is rooted in, or grafted to, sociology. As such, it is to be construed in sociological terms. Common law is an instrument of social control and its relevance to society is an ever-present element in the mind of counsel as well as of the court. On the other hand, law in Islam is conceived not as a means employed in the service of society, but, rather, in the service of God, who alone knows what is best for society. Islamic law delineates the dictates of divine will, and it is perceived as the ideal way in which man can worship his Creator. It is an all-encompassing law which covers every conceivable human act, from liturgical forms to neighborly conduct, to partnership and homicide. Its sources are the Quran, the Sunna of the Prophet, the consensus of the community and its scholars, and the method of inference known as *qiyās*. Through the latter, which is the primary concern of this paper, the law is derived from the former three sources. Whatever these sources dictate becomes the law governing all Muslims. The changing social reality, at least in theory, has no effect whatsoever on the process of judicial reason-

---

[5] Dewey, *Logical Method and Law*, 10 Cornell L.Q. 17, 20 (1924).

[6] J. Stone, Legal System and Lawyers' Reasonings 285-86 (1964); J. Stone, The Province and Function of Law 170 (1946).

[7] As a normative system, law contains propositions which function as major premises in syllogistics. Norms are not statements; therefore, they are neither true nor false. The difficulty stems from this very fact because the validity of deductive logic hinges on the necessary relation between the truth of the premises and the truth of the conclusion. *See* C. Wellman, *Deduction in Legal and Moral Reasoning*, in Reasoning on Legal Reasoning 193 (A. Peczenik and J. Uusitalo eds. Helsinki 1979); Guest, *supra* note 4, at 183-86. For a general discussion of the normative character of law, see F. Castberg, Problems of Legal Philosophy 24 (Oslo 1957).

ing. Only when these religious sources enjoin the protection of a certain human need does the law allow for that need and for those analogous to it. Should this need change because of new circumstances and conditions, the Islamic lawyer stands helpless in the face of the omnipotent sources. For example, one cannot alter a rule based on an explicit textual injunction and still characterize that rule as Islamic. Islamic law is not a law enacted by Muslims; rather, it is enacted by God, for Muslims. Human reason cannot make law; it only functions as the means by which law is discovered. Thus, instead of being organically tied to social exigencies, Islamic law is rooted in divine volition and authority, whether or not this authority takes cognizance of social reality.

Legal reasoning in common law thus differs from its Islamic counterpart in that it is bound by facts and norms which, while relevant to the conclusion, are not entirely intrinsic to the premises. Reasoning in common law recognizes the validity of a legal norm (conclusion) although such norm may not follow entirely from the given, established rules (premises). Admittedly, this somewhat lax procedure is often insisted upon in common law in exchange for a more mutable and flexible law. In Islamic law, on the other hand, the jurist is bound only by those premises which are prescribed by the religious sources, and, unless a certain ambiguity in the premises allows the inclusion or exclusion of certain material facts, nothing that does not follow from the premises can or should be joined to the conclusion.

Common law lawyers conceive logic as the organ by which one seeks to discover the conditions under which a conclusion follows from given premises. In other words, logic is viewed as concerned with the validity of the conclusion as it relates to the premises from which it is derived. Common law lawyers, interested as much in the truthfulness and validity of the legal premises and their relevance to changing situations, have always attempted to curb the overuse of formal logic in law. Although to a certain extent Muslim lawyers expressed their own reservations about logic, they have been considerably less successful in resisting the influence of logic on law.

III. Types of Arguments Used in Both Common Law and Islamic Law

A. Deduction

Admittedly, both legal systems use deductive logic, particularly when general principles and rules are laid down.[8] Under a broad principle, the

[8] O.C. Jensen, The Nature of Legal Argument 25 (1957); R. Cross, Precedent in English Law (3rd ed. Oxford 1977); Abu Ḥāmid al-Ghazāli, Mi^cyār al-^cIlm fī Fann al-Manṭiq 154 (H. Sharāra ed. Beirut 1966); Ibn al-Ḥājib, Mukhtaṣar al-Muntahā al-Uṣūlī 9-16 (Cairo 1326 H.); Abdel-Rahman, *La Place du Syllogisme Juridique dans la*

judge subsumes the case which needs a solution, and applies the general legal principle to that particular case. Such an operation, though purely deductive, seems so intuitive that one need not be thoroughly familiar with logic to conduct it. When it is established, for instance, that things intoxicating are forbidden in the Quran, little analysis is needed to reach the rule that whisky, vodka, etc., are forbidden by law. Similarly, it takes common sense to deduce from Quran V:96 which reads, "And I permit to you the catch of the sea . . .," that feeding on fish, shellfish, and other animals which inhabit the sea is permissible. Judge Cardozo has asserted that, when the Constitution or a statute supplies the rule which fits the case, "the judge looks no further."[9] In the works on Islamic legal theory and jurisprudence, the role of deductive logic in the process of legal reasoning is seldom discussed. Perhaps this is because Muslim jurists reckon that there is little mental endeavor involved in deductive-legal operations. For them it is simply a question of subsumption. In cases where deduction is used, however, the role of the judge is still significant. To reach a decision, the judge must first undertake the difficult task of establishing the exact meaning of the relevant law, and then ascertain its applicability to the new case from a purely legal standpoint.

Perhaps as a result of the impact of modern formal logic, common law lawyers, as well as other Western legal theorists, have gone well beyond their Muslim counterparts in discussing the relevance of deductive logic to law. An articulate treatment of this subject has not been undertaken in Islam,[10] although Western lawyers have dealt with it somewhat unsuccessfully. The judgment that *A* is guilty of offense *X* and must therefore be punished by *Y* can be a conclusion of a syllogism in which the major premise is a statute and the minor premise is a set of facts about *A*. This conclusion certainly differs from the conclusion in the classic syllogism "All men are mortal; Socrates is a man; therefore, Socrates is mortal." The latter conclusion is a factual statement, whereas the former's factuality hinges upon several conditions yet to be fulfilled. Such a distinction between legal and non-legal syllogism does not seem to disturb some common law lawyers. Sir Rupert Cross, for instance, has observed that "[o]ne allowance must certainly be made for this distinction, but it may yet be the case that there is a sufficient resemblance between the methods by which the conclusion is reached to justify the description of each of them as an example of deductive reasoning."[11] The acceptance of non-factual or

---

Méthode Exégétique chez Gazali, in LE RAISONNEMENT JURIDIQUE 185-94 (H. Hubien ed. Bruxelles 1971). *See also infra* note 43 (further on the deductive character of some *qiyās* arguments).

[9] B. CARDOZO, THE NATURE OF THE JUDICIAL PROCESS 14 (1964).

[10] Two of the few jurists who discussed this problem are Abu Ḥāmid al-Ghazāli and Taqi al-dīn Ibn Taymiyya. *See supra* note 8 and *infra* notes 37 & 48.

[11] R. CROSS, *supra* note 8, at 178.

normative statements in legal deduction is the result of the fact that the logic of norms has not yet been worked out.[12]

The lack of a practical solution for this and other problems[13] in deductive legal reasoning has prevented common law lawyers from dwelling too long on them. Deduction remains the most central, though by no means the only, method by which general legal principles are applied to questions of fact. Notwithstanding all difficulties, both legal systems find deduction an indispensable tool of legal reasoning.

In addition to syllogistics, both Muslim and common law lawyers use other arguments which take the form of deduction. The first is *reductio ad absurdum*, which is often used to reach a conclusion about a case by making a certain assumption and then proving that this assumption contradicts an established legal norm. The judge asserts, for instance, that *X* is a goal that the law *ought* to promote; but *Y* impedes, or would impede, the realization of *X*; therefore, *Y* ought to be prevented by law. Another instance of this argument may be the assertion that *X* is a goal which the law ought to promote; accepting *Y* as legal would defeat the realization of *X*; therefore, *Y* ought not be legally recognized. This argument abounds in both legal systems.[14] Also very common is the *a fortiori* argument by which a law governing a certain situation is extended to another more obvious situation. This is of two types: *a minori ad maius* and *a maiori ad minus*. An example of the first type is the inference from the Quranic injunction "Say not 'fie' to them (i.e., to parents) nor repulse them, but speak to them graciously"[15] that mistreating or beating parents is forbidden. Here the legal norm is transferred from a limited act to a more general one. The second type requires a reversal of this process, i.e., from the general to the particular. For instance, from the rule that the consumption of large quantities of wine is prohibited, it is ruled that the drinking of the smallest particle of wine is also prohibited.[16]

---

[12] Guest, *supra* note 4, at 185; Summers, *Logic in the Law*, 72 MIND 257 (1963).

[13] Following Aulis Aarnio, Carl Wellman has succinctly analyzed eight problems which arise in legal as well as moral deductive reasoning. *See* C. WELLMAN, *supra* note 7, at 193-98.

[14] M. GOLDING, LEGAL REASONING 55-60 (1984). Muslim jurists term this argument *qiyās al-ᶜaks*, and logicians *qiyās al-khulf*. *See* SAYF AL-DĪN AL-ĀMIDI, III AL-IḤKĀM FĪ UṢŪL AL-AḤKĀM 3 (Cairo 1968); ABU ḤĀMID AL-GHAZĀLI, *supra* note 8, at 118-19; IBN AL-ḤĀJIB, *supra* note 8, at 15; IBN ABI AL-ṢALT AL-DĀNI, TAQWĪM AL-DHAHN 48 (C.G. Palencia ed. Madrid 1915). The application of this argument is also evident in the formulation of the general principle of *maqāṣid* (or *maqṣūd*) *al-sharᶜ* (the aims of the law). *See, e.g.*, ABU-ISḤĀQ AL-SHĀṬIBI, II AL-MUWĀFAQĀT FĪ UṢŪL AL-AḤKĀM 127-28 (Cairo 1970); SAYF AL-DIN AL-ĀMIDI, III *al-Iḥkām fi Uṣūl al-Aḥkām* 71-76 (Cairo 1968); MUḤAMMAD B. ᶜALI AL-SHAWKĀNI, IRSHĀD AL-FUḤŪL ILĀ TAḤQĪQ AL-ḤAQQ MIN ᶜILM AL-UṢŪL 214 (Cairo 1909).

[15] Quran XVII:23.

[16] Later Muslim scholars often refer to the *a fortiori* argument as *bil-aḥrā*. Shāfiᶜi, the "master architect" of Islamic jurisprudence, uses it but under the general term *qiyās*. *See* RISĀLA, ISLAMIC JURISPRUDENCE 307-08(M. Khadduri trans. 1961) (It is to be cautioned that Khadduri consistently translates *qiyās* as analogy); IBN ḤABĪB AL-MĀWARDI, I ADAB AL-

The nature of law and its sources in the Islamic and common legal traditions make it difficult to work out legal concepts solely by means of formal arguments. Lawyers from both systems have acknowledged that deduction is only one of several arguments employed in legal reasoning.[17] Primarily, the lack of universal or general principles contributes chiefly to the relegation of strictly formal arguments to a secondary, often negligible, position. Despite the increasing entrenchment of the legislature on the common law, case law still constitutes the major segment of the common law system. Similarly, Islamic law is characterized by its concern with individual cases rather than with general precepts, a resultant manifestation of the material structure of its two primary sources: the Quran and the Sunna. The Quran was revealed to Muhammad piecemeal in order to fulfill and answer the specific needs which arose during the period of his Mission. Likewise, the Sunna, expressed in a collection of reports of the utterances and deeds of the Prophet, came to answer similar needs in later times. Characteristically, these two sources deal with specific issues and, strictly speaking, contain relatively few general legal principles. It is therefore clear that, like common law, Islamic law is, in a large measure, case law. This fact determines the type of argument and logic which best fits and serves common case law and Islamic law.

B. *Legal Analogy*

One of the most commonly used arguments in both systems, and one which answers most of the law's needs, is reasoning from part to part or case to case, an argument known as legal analogy.[18] The basic course of reasoning is the extension of a legal rule from one case to another due to a similarity which is deemed by the judge to be a material similarity. The form of this argument is as follows:

> A has the properties X, Y . . . .
> B has the properties X, Y . . . .
> A has the rule J.
> X, Y . . . are relevant properties in inducing J.
> ———————————————
> Therefore, B must have the rule J.

Such an argument gives rise to serious problems. For the logician, this argument, however meticulous it may seem, remains imperfect at best.

QĀḌĪ 587-92 (Baghdad 1971); IMĀM AL-ḤARAMAYN AL-JUWAYNI, AL-WARAQĀT (printed with the commentary of Jalāl al-Dīn al-Maḥalli, on the margin of SHAWKĀNI, *supra* note 14, at 199-200) (Cairo 1909)).

[17] C. WELLMAN, *supra* note 7, at 193. See the types of arguments as discussed by ABU ḤĀMID AL-GHAZĀLI, *supra* note 8, at 102-37.

[18] SAYFAL-DĪN AL-ĀMIDI, *supra* note 14, at 3-10; L. CARTER, REASON IN LAW 12 (1984); E. LEVI, AN INTRODUCTION TO LEGAL REASONING 1-2 (1949).

Muslim logicians and philosophers discard it because it is conjectural and merely leads to probable (*ẓannī*) knowledge. The Muslim and common law lawyers, while realizing its shortcomings, have no choice but to accept it. Undoubtedly, they have striven, within the limits imposed by the nature of such an argument, to strengthen it by supporting arguments with a view toward realizing its utmost potential. The crucial problem posed is determining the element of similarity which justifies the transference of the rule of one case to another. For it is this element which determines the validity of the conclusion.[19] How, in light of such considerations, the common element in analogy is decided in Islamic and common law is perhaps the most illustrative differentiation, not only of the legal reasoning in both systems, but also of their function and goal.

Whether it is taken to be "[t]he ground or reason of decision," or "[t]he point in a case which determines the judgment,"[20] or, as the Muslim jurist would put it, "that which induces the judgment,"[21] the *ratio decidendi* and the Islamic *ᶜilla* (the relevant similarity which justifies the transference of the judgment from the precedent to the new case) have remained the most illusive doctrines in common law and Islamic law. In Britain and the United States, this doctrine has been a major concern of a number of experts since the beginning of this century; in Islam, it occupied major portions of jurisprudential theories for several centuries. The first major attempt at defining the rules for finding the *ratio* of a case was made by Professor Goodhart in 1930. He concluded that the *ratio* is neither found in the reasons given in the judge's opinion nor in the rule of law set forth in that opinion. Nor is it necessarily found by a consideration of all the ascertainable facts of the case and the judge's decision. Rather, Goodhart argued, the *ratio* is to be found by taking account of (1) the facts treated by the judge as material, and (2) his decision as based on them. In finding the *ratio* it is also necessary to establish what facts are held to be material by the judge.[22] In other words, Goodhart proposes that a later court is bound by the presumably applicable precedent and its ruling, as an outcome of the judge's consideration of the material facts determined in the earlier case.

---

[19] The German scholar Urlich Klug properly remarked that the difficulty in using analogical argument lies in the obscurity of the distinction between essential and unessential respects. *See* J. HOROVITZ, LAW AND LOGIC 32 (1972).

[20] BLACK'S LAW DICTIONARY 1135 (rev. 5th ed. 1979). *See also* R. CROSS, *supra* note 8, at 76-79 (adopts any rule of law expressly or impliedly treated by the judge as a necessary step in reaching a conclusion and discusses means of ascertaining the *ratio decidendi* from a case).

[21] *See, e.g.*, ABU ḤUSAYN AL-BAṢRI, II AL-MUᶜTAMAD FĪ UṢŪL AL-FIQH 704-05 (Damascus 1964-65); MUḤAMMAD B. ᶜALI AL-SHAWKĀNI, *supra* note 14, at 207.

[22] Goodhart, *Determining the Ratio Decidendi of a Case*, 40 YALE L.J. 161 (1930). A summary of this article may be found in Goodhart, *The Ratio Decidendi of a Case*, 22 MOD. L. REV. 117 (1959).

After lengthy polemics in the *Modern Law Review* about the *ratio decidendi*,[23] Professor Julius Stone argued that Goodhart was attempting to set forth a prescriptive theory rather than a descriptive account for determining the *ratio decidendi*.[24] Stone found this unacceptable. He maintained that in each precedent there is implicit a number of *ratio decidendi*, and it is left to the deciding judges to determine, in light of current exigencies (e.g., public policy, ethics, justice), the "appropriate level of generality" in the precedent which must prevail in the new case.[25] It is not the material facts in the earlier case which must dictate the decision of the later court but rather "the analogical relevance of the prior holding to the later case," which requires "the later court to choose between possibilities presented by the earlier case."[26] Representing what may be termed "the sociological school of jurisprudence," Stone emphatically argued that the later court is the final arbiter of which *ratio* is applicable to the case in question.[27]

> In short a "rule" or "principle" as it emerges from a precedent case is subject in its further elaboration to continual review, in the light of analogies and differences, not merely in the logical relations between fact situations, and the problems springing from these; but also in the light of the import of these analogies and differences for what is thought by the later court to yield a tolerably acceptable result in terms of "policy," "ethics," "justice," "expediency" or whatever other norm of desirability the law may be thought to subserve. No ineluctable logic, but a composite of the logical relations seen between legal propositions, of observation of facts and consequences, and of value-judgments about the acceptability of these consequences, is what finally comes to bear upon the alternatives with which "the rule of *stare decises*" confronts the courts, and especially appellate courts. And this, it may be supposed, is why finally we cannot assess the product of their work in terms of any less complex quality than that of wisdom.[28]

Thus, "wisdom" and, as Justice Holmes stated, "good sense," must be employed in determining the *ratio* rather than a mechanical or fixed set of

---

[23] Some of the articles include: Goodhart, *The Ratio Decidendi of a Case*, 22 MOD. L. REV. 117 (1959); Montrose, *The Ratio Decidendi of a Case*, 20 MOD. L. REV. 587 (1957); Montrose, *Ratio Decidendi and the House of Lords*, 20 MOD. L. REV. 124 (1957); Simpson, *The Ratio Decidendi of a Case*, 20 MOD. L. REV. 413 (1957); Simpson, *Ratio Decidendi of a Case*, 21 MOD. L. REV. 155 (1958).

[24] Stone, *The Ratio of the Ratio Decidendi*, 22 MOD. L. REV. 597 (1959). For a useful summary of the main thesis of this article, see J. FARRAR, INTRODUCTION TO LEGAL METHOD 69-71 (1977).

[25] Stone, *supra* note 24, at 618.

[26] *Id.* at 604-05.

[27] *Id.* at 618.

[28] *Id.*

logical rules.[29] The lack of serious attempts in the Anglo-American legal tradition to "prescribe" methods by which a *ratio* of a case can be decided is an eloquent testimony to the disinterest of common law lawyers in a permanently defined and inflexible set of rules which might control and limit the ability of law to adapt itself to the changing reality.[30]

On the other hand, the Islamic lawyers, being acutely conscious of the religious character of their law, stress the dictates of the sources of law rather than the needs of the new cases to which they seek to find the "sound" solutions. Divinity has expressed its will in the Quran and sunna which are deemed not only the ideal guides in man's life but also the final revelation to mankind. Thus, insofar as deciding a new case is concerned, the Muslim jurist can operate on two levels which are determined by the nature of these two sources. On the first level, the jurist is bound by the explicit textual statements and commands. What determines the judgment in the new case is solely the explicit *ratio* in the original text, i.e., the precedent. There is little latitude for deciding the case in light of current exigencies. On the second level, however, the jurist is allowed a certain, although limited, freedom of interpretation in deciding the new case, due to the ambiguous nature of the textual precedents.

This paper is not concerned with the linguistic principles which come into play in determinating the *ᶜilla*; it focuses on the logical and perhaps semi-logical tools employed for this purpose. The first condition set forth for finding and establishing the *ᶜilla* is its efficiency, that is, its causal relationship with the judgment. The property or properties which constitute the *ᶜilla* must bring about a judgment. Joining an inefficient property to the *ᶜilla* will no doubt spoil that *ᶜilla*. Intoxication, for instance, is an efficient property which necessitates the judgment of prohibiting the consumption of wine. Should it be assumed that redness is a property which together with intoxication effects the judgment of prohibiting red wine, it must then always be assumed that in any judgment of prohibiting

---

[29] *Id.* at 619.

[30] The increasing concern with the flexibility of law brought about certain changes in the effect of precedent in the House of Lords. In 1966, Lord Gardiner, the Lord Chancellor, representing the Lords of Appeal in Ordinary, declared the following:

> Their Lordships regard the use of precedent as an indispensable foundation upon which to decide what is the law and its application to individual cases. It provides at least some degree of certainty upon which individuals can rely in the conduct of their affairs, as well as a basis for orderly development of legal rules.
>
> Their Lordships nevertheless recognize that too rigid adherence to precedent may lead to injustice in a particular case and also unduly restrict the proper development of the law. They propose therefore to modify their present practice and, while treating former decision of this House as normally binding, to depart from a previous decision when it appears right to do so.

M. ZANDER, THE LAW-MAKING PROCESS 104 (1980).

intoxicants the property of redness must be present in conjunction with the property of intoxication. Otherwise, the *ᶜilla* which is extended to a new case, say white wine, becomes invalid because the property of redness is inefficient due to its absence from white wine, while the same judgment of prohibition remains in effect. Since part of the *ᶜilla* has no efficiency beyond the case of red wine, the *ᶜilla* as a whole is rendered invalid.[31]

The second method is coextensiveness (the presence of the *ᶜilla* when the judgment is present) and coexclusiveness (the absence of the *ᶜilla* when the judgment is absent).[32] Like efficiency, this method seeks to emphasize the causal connection between the judgment and its *ᶜilla*. A valid causal relationship must have both the coexistence of the cause and its effect and the absence of one when the other is absent. This method also guarantees the exclusion of an additional, unnecessary *ᶜilla*. If two different *ᶜillas* are claimed to induce the judgment, it is inconceivable that when one *ᶜilla* becomes absent, the judgment becomes absent as well.[33]

In conjunction with these methods, Muslim jurists employ a third theory which may be termed the "joined method of difference and agreement."[34] By the method of difference, it is demonstrated that certain properties, say *A, B, C . . .*, constitute the only difference between the *ᶜilla* in the precedent and the *ᶜilla* in the new case. It is then proved that these properties are inefficient and irrelevant in inducing the judgment. In other words, such an analogy first assumes the total sum of differences between the *ᶜillas X* and *Y* are *A, B, C . . . .* The second premise is that *A, B, C . . .* have no weight insofar as the judgment, *J,* is concerned. Since *X* and *Y* are identical save for *A, B, C . . ., J* is the judgment.

As a prerequisite to the method of difference, the method of agreement must come into play. By this method, the similarity between *X* and *Y* is found. Then the judgment of the precedent is transferred to the new case.[35] The method of difference and agreement can be implemented only by use of what the logicians call disjunctive and conjunctive syllogism. Put schematically, the course of reasoning by analogy is as follows:

P has properties *A*, *B*, *C*, *D*, *E*, *F*.
Q has properties *A*, *B*, *C*, *D*, *E*.
P has the rule *J*.
F is not a property in *Q*.
A, *B*, and *C* are not relevant similarities.
D and *E* are relevant similarities and efficient in *J*.

---

[31] ABU ḤUSAYN AL-BAṢRI, *supra* note 21, at 789-90.

[32] ᶜALI SĀMI AL-NASHSHĀR, MANĀHIJ AL-BAḤTH ᶜINDA MUFAKKIRĪ AL-ISLĀM 111 (Cairo 1966).

[33] *Id.* at 112.

[34] This is reminiscent of Mill's methods of agreement and difference. *See* E. NAGEL, JOHN STUART MILL'S PHILOSOPHY OF SCIENTIFIC METHOD 211 (1974).

[35] MUḤAMMAD B. ᶜALI AL-SHAWKĀNI, *supra* note 21, at 213-14, 219, 220-22.

D and *E* are present when *J* is present and absent when *J* is absent.

———————————————————————

Therefore, *Q* has (or must have) the rule *J*.

The effort expended in establishing the *relevant* similarity which, in turn, determines the validity of transferring a judgment of one case to another must be seen in light of the conflict between formal logic and the actual needs of the law. Both Western and Muslim lawyers recognize the insuperable difficulties encountering conclusions by analogy. Some idealists in the West have gone so far as to say that a conclusion by analogy can be valid only after *modus barbara*.[36] The Muslim logician, Farabi, also argued that to be valid, analogy must be converted to the following syllogistic form: All *S*'s are *X*'s; all *A*'s are *S*'s; therefore, all *A*'s are *X*'s. This is so, he insisted, because valid analogy amounts to syllogistic inference. And when a syllogism cannot serve, analogy cannot be valid.[37] However, the imprecise nature of legal propositions and the law's actual requirements prevent jurists from accepting, much less adopting, such arguments. In real life it is rarely possible to ascertain conclusively the exact similitude between all aspects of two cases. Thus, to convert an analogy to strict syllogism would be tantamount to forging a link which is justified neither by the facts in the precedents or in the new case.

Another argument to which Muslim and common law lawyers resort is *argumentum e contrario*.[38] In analogy, the two cases possess a similarity which justifies extending the rule from the precedent to the new case. In the *argumentum e contrario*, the absence of such a link and the diametrical opposition of the two cases brings about a conclusion.[39] The argument may take one of two forms. The first is "*S* is a *P*; therefore, no non-*S* is a *P*." An example of this may be the following: From the rule that several legal residences are allowed for private persons, it is inferred that several legal residences are not allowed for corporations.[40] The second

---

[36] See the discussion in Simitis, *supra* note 4, at 70; Abu Naṣr al-Fārābi, *Kitāb al-Qiyās al-Ṣaghîr*, in 16 Revue de la Facultés des langues, d'histoire, et de géographie de l'Université d'Ankara 266-68 (1958); Al-Farabi's Short Commentary on Aristotle's Prior Analytics 93-98 (N. Rescher trans. 1963).

[37] Abu Naṣr al-Fārābi, *supra* note 36, at 267-68; Al-Farabi's Short Commentary, *supra* note 36, at 95. Also see the argument of Abu Ḥāmid al-Ghazāli, *supra* note 8, at 123-25; Abu-Ḥāmid al-Ghazāli, Miḥakk al-Naẓar 31 (Cairo ——). Urlich Klug also argues that in sound analogy the minor premise is subsumed under the major premise just as in any syllogism. Horovitz agrees and argues that analogical inference eventually reverts to syllogism and has no special logical structure of its own. *See* J. Horovitz, *supra* note 19, at 33.

[38] Sayf al-Dīn al-Āmidi, *supra* note 14, at 3; J. Farrar, *supra* note 24, at 50-51; J. Horovitz, *supra* note 19, at 44.

[39] Abu Ḥusayn al-Baṣri, *supra* note 21, at 698-99; Abu Ḥusayn al-Baṣri, Kitāb al-Qiyās al-Sharᶜī, printed with al-Muᶜtamad 1031-32.

[40] J. Horovitz, *supra* note 19, at 44.

form, often claimed to be the most important argument in Islamic law after analogy,[41] may be best illustrated by the well-known example about the purity—or impurity—of pets. The ruling that dogs are impure is reached on the basis of a Prophetic report making the Prophet refrain from visiting a residence in which a dog is present, but allowing him to visit another residence in which there is a cat. The Prophet then remarks that "(the cat) is not impure." This statement, coupled with the fact that he withheld his visit to the residence of the dog's owner, led to the conclusion that dogs are impure.[42]

C. Induction

The last of the major arguments common to both systems is induction[43] which, unlike deduction or analogy, bases itself more often than not on conclusions reached by other arguments. Except for a relatively few cases in the Quran and the Sunna where ready-made solutions are given, cases in Islamic law are ordinarily solved either through analogy from case to case, or by deduction through the subsumption of a case under a general

---

[41] ABU ḤUSAYN AL-BAṢRI, *supra* note 39, at 1031-32; SAYF AL-DĪN AL-ĀMIDI, *supra* note 14, at 3.

[42] ABU ḤUSAYN AL-BAṢRI, *supra* note 39, at 1036.

[43] Guest, *supra* note 4, at 188-90; ABU-ḤĀMID AL-GHAZĀLI, *supra* note 37, at 62-63. Notably, Muslim legal theoreticians do not always agree with regard to the types of arguments subsumed under *qiyās*. Only in a few works, such as those of Abu Naṣr al-Fārābi, Abu Ḥāmid al-Ghazāli, and Taqi al-Dīn Ibn Taymiyya is one presented with more or less a full account of these arguments. However, a close examination of the definitions of *qiyās* in the jurists' writings reveals that these definitions are left broad enough to allow the inclusion of many types of arguments. Some of the common definitions of *qiyās* are the following: (1) "predicating a known thing to another (known thing) on grounds of a common matter [i.e. cause] in order to establish, or negate, a rule for both of them" (*ḥamlu maᶜlūmin ᶜalā maᶜlūmin fi ithbāti hukmin lahumā aw nafyihi ᶜanhumā bi'amrin jāmiᶜin baynahumā min ḥukmin aw ṣifa*); (2) "applying the rule of the precedent to the new case on grounds of a similarity between the two cases" (*taḥṣīlu ḥukmi al-aṣli fi al-farᶜi li'shtibāhihimā fi ᶜillati al-ḥukmi*); (3) "the subsumption of a particular under a general" (*idrāju khuṣūṣin fi ᶜumūm*). MUḤAMMAD B. ᶜALI AL-SHAWKĀNI, supra note 14, at 198. *See also* ABU AL-WALĪD AL-BĀJI, AL-ḤUDŪD FI AL-UṢŪL 69-70 (N. Ḥammād ed. 1973). For other, but similar, definitions, see F. KHOLEIF, A STUDY ON FAKHR AL-DIN AL-RAZI 151-52 (1966) .

Such definitions are indicative of the inclusiveness of *qiyās*. In his chapter on legal reasoning, ᶜAbd al-Jabbār notes that the form of judicial *qiyās* does not differ from that of non-juridical *qiyās* (*wa-ṭarīqatu al-qiyāsi al-sharᶜiyi lā tukhālifu ṣūratuhā ṣūrata al-qiyāsi al-ᶜaqlī*). Ghazāli held the same view and added that the difference between the two is only in the premises. "The premises which are good for rational *qiyās* are good for juridical *qiyās*, but not all the premises which are good for juridical *qiyās* are good for rational *qiyās*" (*lā mukhālafata baynahumā fī ṣūrati al-qiyāsi wa'innamā yatakhālafāni fī al-mādati, bal mā yaṣluḥu an yakūna muqaddimatan fī al-ᶜaqliyyāti yaṣluḥu lil-fiqhiyyāti, walākin qad yaṣluḥ u lil-fiqhiyyāti mā lā yaṣluḥu lil-ᶜaqliyyāti*). ᶜABD AL-JABBĀR AL-ASADABĀDI, XVII AL-MUGHNI FI ABWĀB AL-TAWḤĪD WAL-ᶜADL 280 (Cairo 1963). *See* ABU ḤĀMID AL-GHAZĀLI, *supra* note 8, at 154. *Se See also* author's article *Non-Analogical Arguments in Sunnī Juridical Qiyās* (forthcoming).

principle. In induction, the common rule for a number of cases is extended to another case because this case is similar or identical in relevant aspects. Induction is then possible only when a number of identical cases exist. The form of the argument is: A, B, C, D . . . are cases which have the common characteristic X and the rule J; all cases which have the characteristic X must have the rule J; S has the characteristic X; therefore, S has (or must have) the rule J. A concrete example of induction from Islamic substantive law is the case of interest (*ribā*). The Prophet was said to have prohibited the exchange of gold for gold, silver for silver, date for date, wheat for wheat, and barley for barley unless they were equal in quantities and delivered immediately. The *ᶜilla* for this prohibition was determined (e.g., in the Ḥanafi School) to be their nature as fungible commodities sold by weight and measure. For this reason, exchange by unequal amounts was prohibited.[44] In accordance with this line of reasoning, all goods possessing this *ᶜilla*, such as raisins, must be subject to prohibition if exchanged under the aforementioned conditions.

The question then becomes: What differentiates induction from analogy in legal reasoning? The legitimacy of this question derives from the fact that the relevant similarity between the new case and the already solved cases is the same. This being so, an analogy between the new case and a single precedent would suffice. However, the common law lawyers would object that the extention of the rule by induction leads to a degree of certainty which is higher than that attained in analogy. The multiplicity of cases (instances) gives inductive support to the rule of the new case which analogical inference fails to provide. Thus, as in scientific induction, legal induction in common law belongs to a class of arguments superior to that of analogy; it stands in the middle position between analogical and deductive arguments.

In Islamic law, induction ranks even higher on the scale of certainty. It can be complete (perfect), leading to the same degree of certainty yielded by deduction. The entire corpus of common law is, as a practical matter, unlimited, making complete induction infeasible. In Islam, however, the sources of the law are defined and exhaustible. A complete enumeration of the instances supporting or negating a point of law yields the highest degree of certain knowledge about that point, provided counter-evidence does not exist. In the context of religion where a single explicit statement in the sources has a force of finality, it may be argued that multiple propositions should lead to a degree of certainty at least tantamount to that yielded by deduction. Such an inductive process would simply constitute a multi-deductive argument. For this reason a number of Muslim jurists hold complete legal induction to have a force equal to deductive arguments. However, even when incomplete, induction derives its force

---

[44] ᶜAbd Allāh b. Maudūd al-Mūṣili, II al-Ikhtiyār li-taᶜlīl al-Mukhtār 30-33 (Cairo 1951).

from the relative number of instances which can be observed with regard to a particular case. "The larger the number of pieces of textual evidence is, the stronger our knowledge becomes."[45]

In addition to its function as a method of reasoning, induction in Islamic law plays the significant role of reinforcing uncertain or weak premises. The equivalent of such a role is not to be found in common law. In the Islamic legal system, uncertain propositions from the Sunna (which alone constitutes the greatest bulk of the legal sources) may gain an added aggregate support by use of the inductive method, transforming them into certain premises.

How does this process work? To answer this question, it must first be observed that the dicta of sunna are divided into two basic categories: the *mutawātir* and the *āḥādī*. The *mutawātir* traditions are transmitted by countless persons who hear or see the Prophet say or do a certain thing. The large number of transmitters makes it inconceivable that the witnesses or the transmitters could have agreed on falsifying the report. Due to the authenticity of such a report and the certitude surrounding its transmission, the *mutawātir* traditions are said to lead to certain knowledge of what they contain. Traditions transmitted by fewer people than those who have witnessed and transmitted the *mutawātir* traditions are called *āḥādī*. The latter, when taken individually, do not lead to certain knowledge of the information they convey. Accordingly, when used individually as premises in an argument, a *mutawātir* tradition with an explicit meaning leads to certainty while an *āḥādī* tradition with the same clarity of meaning leads only to probable knowledge. Thus, rules based on individual *āḥādī* traditions are only tentative and experimental. Many Muslim jurists, however, argue that *aḥādī* traditions can lead to certain knowledge if they are supported by other pieces of circumstantial evidence (*qarā'in*) which may include other traditions of the same type and indecisive or ambiguous Quranic verses.[46] These textual pieces of evidence must, when interpreted, have the same meaning as the tradition which they purport to support. Another precondition for reaching certainty in such an arrangement is the number of supporting traditions and verses: They must be altogether as numerous as those in the *mutawātir* category. But unlike the latter which cannot, whether individually or collectively, be dubious, an *āḥādī* tradition can only be probable insofar as its authenticity is concerned. The aggregate of *āḥādīs*, however, cannot be

[45] *See* ABU ḤĀMID AL-GHAZĀLI, *supra* note 8, at 120.

[46] Indicisive or ambiguous (*mutashabihāt*) verses are capable of more than one interpretation. If an indecisive verse can be interpreted in such a way as to support the meaning of an *āḥādī* tradition, this verse is said to be a *qarīna*, a supporting piece of evidence. An unambiguous Quranic verse cannot be used as a *qarīna* to support an *āḥādī* tradition, because, by itself, it constitutes indisputable evidence which need not be supported by any *qarā'in* (plural of *qarīna*). However, a deductive or analogical argument based on an unambiguous verse can always become inductive if other ambiguous verses conveying the same meaning are available. *

dubious because Muslim jurists reason that a multitude of reports transmitted through so many channels and by so many transmitters who could not have known each other cannot possibly constitute a lie or a conspiracy in fabricating the report. In their multiplicity, the *āḥādī* traditions gain a strength tantamount to that of the *mutawātir*.[47]

The doctrine of inductive support is undoubtedly the product of a compromising approach to blend the elements of form and material substance in legal argument. Unlike the Aristotelian logicians who were primarily concerned with form, Muslim jurists paid equal attention to the material substance of the premises in relation to the degree of certainty to which they can lead. The emphasis that Islamic law places on the premises as the determinant of the degree of certainty of the conclusion may be illustrated by discussing the views of the influential Ibn Taymiyya on this subject.

Ibn Taymiyya's argument must be seen as a response to the traditional view which holds syllogistics superior to analogy. Against this view, he argues that syllogism and analogy are equivalent because any analogical argument can be converted to first figure syllogism.[48] Writing in the Islamic tradition, Ibn Taymiyya sees the analogical argument as consisting of four terms: (1) the *aṣl*, the precedent which is extracted from the scripture; (2) the *far*ᶜ, the new case requiring a solution; (3) the ᶜ*illa*, the similarity common to the *aṣl* and the *far*ᶜ; and (4) the *ḥukm*, the rule which is transferred from the former to the latter. The weakness of analogy does not lie in its form since it can be converted to syllogism. Rather, the weakness lies in the material substance of the premises and, more particularly, in the ᶜ*illa*. "If the subject matter (of the premises) is certain, whether the form of the argument is analogy or syllogism, then (the conclusion) is certain."[49] For instance, should the jurist conclusively establish that the consumption of wine was forbidden in the Quran because it is an intoxicant, he would be able to convert this possible analogy to a syllogism in which the major premise is "All intoxicants are forbidden;" the minor premise is "Vodka is an intoxicant;" the conclusion is "Vodka is forbidden;" with the middle term being the property of intoxication.[50]

---

[47] ABU BAKR AL-SARAKHSI, I UṢŪL 292 (Abu al-Wafa al-Afghāni ed. Cairo 1372 H.); BAYḌĀWI, II MINHĀJ AL-WUṢŪL 197-205, with Sh. Ismāᶜīl's II TAHDHĪB SHARḤ AL-ISNAWI (especially last paragraph of p. 205) (Cairo 1976). In fact, Shāṭibi went so far as to say that induction is the only method by which certainty can be reached in law. *See* SHĀṬIBI, I MUWĀFAQĀT 10-15 (1969).

* [48] TAQI AL-DĪN IBN TAYMIYYA, JAHD AL-QARIḤA FĪ TAJRID AL-NAṢIḤA (an abridgement by JALĀL AL-DĪN AL-SUYŪTI OF NAṢĪḤAT AHL AL-ĪMĀN FI AL-RADD ᶜALĀ MANTĪQ AL-YŪNĀN 289, 299-300, 328, 331 (Cairo 1947). *See also* N. HEER, IBN TAYMIYAH'S EMPIRICISM (unpublished).

[49] TAQI AL-DĪN IBN TAYMIYYA, *supra* note 48, at 289.

[50] On the classes of textual premises, see ABU ḤĀMID AL-GHAZĀLI, *supra* note 8, at 155-56. Examples cited are not those of Taqi al-Dîn Ibn Taymiyya but correspond perfectly to his arguments.

Here, the conclusion is formally and materially valid. Thus, whatever form of argument is used, a *certain* middle term will surely lead to a *certain* conclusion. In answer to the question of how one can know for certain whether or not a universal proposition is true, Ibn Taymiyya argues that statements derived from an infallible source (e.g., the Quran) are always certain.

The fundamental idea underlying Ibn Taymiyya's theory of logic in general, and legal logic in particular, is that the knowledge of the external world results from the observation of particular things.[51] Universal propositions are inferred by analogy and induction from particular propositions. If it is true that analogy and induction yield probable knowledge, our knowledge of the external world can only be probable. The only exception, however, is scriptural knowledge, which by virtue of being decreed by God, can only be certain.[52]

IV. Conclusion

This brief analysis of the logic of legal reasoning in Islamic law and common law has shown that the ultimate causes for difference between the two systems stem from the obvious fact that Islamic law is steeped in religion, whereas common law is a product of an essentially secular culture. The effect of this fundamental difference manifests itself in two main areas, the first of which is deductive and analogical reasoning. Law in the common legal tradition is conceived as a man-made instrument of social control which is in need of constant modification in line with social change. Accordingly, judges in common law have persistently endeavored to reason in keeping with the primal need of adapting law to current reality. Deductive logic, as one method of reasoning, is viewed as sufficiently stringent to disallow a gradual change in legal formulations. This is why deduction is often rejected and referred to as "dry logic." The ramifications of this attitude are even more evident in analogical reasoning. The similarity between two cases can justify an analogy on the basis of a *ratio* which the new case dictates, rather than on the basis of a *ratio* which the judge in the earlier case determined. Therefore, the similarity between the two cases becomes that similarity which the current policy of "ethics" and "justice" require. A change of this policy will most likely call for a change in the similarity which will result in a different rule.

Islamic law can be said to be more consistent in the application of logical principles, mainly because of the marginal importance of the element of change in Islamic law. Being strictly religious, law is bound by the letter and spirit of the fixed sources from which it is derived. In the

---

[51] Taqi al-Dīn Ibn Taymiyya can be said to have anticipated the theory of J. S. Mill. *See* E. Nagel, *supra* note 34, at 120-35. *

[52] Taqi al-Dīn Ibn Taymiyya, *supra* note 48, at 319, 341; N. Heer, *supra* note 48.

process of formulating the law, the Muslim jurist has no choice but to abide by the prescription of these sources. In accordance with this conception, the current needs of society have no particular importance in determining the similarity between the two cases. The material similarity is that which is dictated by the sources; any analogy to be drawn subsequently (which has been determined by scholars to be valid) must be based on the already established similarity. Thus, logical consistency takes priority over other considerations, including change.

Induction is the second area in which the difference between Islamic law as a religious system and common law as a secular system manifests itself. While induction serves as a method of legal reasoning in common law, Islamic law takes induction beyond this limited scope to employ it for the reinforcement of uncertain legal propositions. As demonstrated, induction can bring greater certainty into law because the bulk of the legal sources in Islam is defined and exhaustible.

All in all, Islamic law can be described as more "logical" than common law. This is clearly the result of the absence of the consideration for change in Islamic law. This seemingly positive characteristic of "logicism" has cost Islamic law a high price, manifesting itself in drastic reforms in the modern era, including the wholesale borrowings of European codes to replace the inoperative traditional laws. Common law, on the other hand, proved flexible enough to forestall the need for such radical reforms.

ADDENDA

p. 80, n. 2: see article II in this collection.

p. 93, n. 46: on *qarā'in*, see article X in this collection.

p. 94, n. 48: Nicholas Heer's article was published in *A Way Prepared: Essays on Islamic Culture in Honor of Richard Bayly Winder*, eds Farhad Kazemi and R.D. McChesney (New York: New York University Press, 1988): 109–115.

p. 95, n. 51: on Ibn Taymiyya's empiricism, see the Introduction to Wael B. Hallaq, trans., *Ibn Taymiyya Against the Greek Logicians* (Oxford: Clarendon Press, 1993), pp. xx ff., xxviii ff.; id., 'Ibn Taymiyya on the Existence of God', *Acta Orientalia*, 52 (1991): 51 ff., 62 ff.

II

NON-ANALOGICAL ARGUMENTS IN SUNNI JURIDICAL *QIYĀS**

I. Introduction

That the Sunnī juristic conception of arguments can generally be characterized as nonformal is due to the fact that the validity of arguments rests primarily upon the epistemological value of the revealed premises from which they are constructed[1]. The linguistic and legal structure of these premises determine the type of argument to be used in reaching the legal norm, the *ḥukm*. Accordingly, methods of reasoning employed in the construction of positive and substantive law range, as we shall see, from syllogistic to inductive arguments, including irregular deductions such as relational arguments[2]. These arguments, though often disguised by the seemingly impenetrable and unique formulations of the *uṣūlists*, can with the assistance of logic and dialectic be deciphered, and subsequently labeled with the corresponding designations given to them in these fields. Without such a procedure the identity of arguments prescribed in the works of *uṣūl al-fiqh* will remain in the realm of the obscure.

---

* A slightly shorter version of this paper was presented at the Center for Middle Eastern Studies, Harvard University, February 1986.

[1] This conception differs to a significant extent from the principles of formal logic where the validity of an argument is measured by the structure of premises and quality of the relationship between the propositions which justify the conclusion. On the centrality of the epistemological value of revealed premises in legal argument see, for instance, Muḥammad Ibn Idrīs al-Shāfiʿī, *Risāla*, ed. Muḥammad Sayyid Kīlānī, Cairo, 1969, par. 1482; Muḥammad b. Aḥmad Ibn Rushd (al-Ḥafīd), *Bidāyat al-Mujtahid wa-Nihāyat al-Muqtaṣid*, 2 vols., Cairo, 1329 H., I, 2; Abū Ḥāmid al-Ghazālī, *al-Mankhūl min ʿIlm al-Uṣūl*, ed. Muḥammad Ḥasan Haytū, Cairo, p. 336; idem, *Miʿyār al-ʿIlm*, ed. Sulaymān Dunyā, Cairo, 1961, pp. 155-156; Taqī l-Dīn Ibn Taymiyya, *Jahd al-Qarīḥa fī Tajrīd al-Naṣīḥa*, an abridgement by Jalāl al-Dīn al-Suyūṭī of *al-Radd ʿalā Manṭiq al-Yūnān*, ed. ʿAlī Sāmī l-Nashshār, Cairo, 1947, p. 289.

[2] On the logical properties of relational inferences see section IV below.

Muslim legal theoreticians conceive the material sources—the Quran, the Sunna and consensus[3]—as linguistically consisting of two basic categories: one encompassing clear premises, subject to only one interpretation, and the other ambiguous, capable of varying interpretations. Premises in the first category, unlike the second, yield necessary and thus certain knowledge (*ʿilm ḍarūrī qāṭiʿ*). Necessary or immediate knowledge is defined as the cognition which compels itself upon the mind without inference, such as the knowledge of the law of the excluded middle, the feeling of illness and the hearing of a particular sound[4]. Through the sense of hearing, for instance, knowledge of certain revealed 'clear speech' necessarily obtains in the intellect. Furthermore, necessary knowledge is said to obtain even with regard to matters unspecified by the sources, but matters which are tacitly subsumed under a categorical textual statement. An excellent case in point is Quran V:3 «forbidden to you are carrion, blood, pork (*laḥm al-khinzīr*)...». Sunnī jurists unanimously argued that the term *'khinzīr'*, though it was originally intended to mean only 'pork', covers all types of swine meat, including that of wild boars (*khinzīr barrī*). Though reasoning in this case can be clearly reduced to a syllogistic form, the jurists insisted that reaching the conclusion 'The meat of wild boars is forbidden' needs no inference since it is understood from the language of the Quranic statement itself (*min jihati dalālati al-lafẓ*)[5]. Thus matters specified in the material sources and those which can be immediately subsumed under them were considered to be purely linguistic and certainly outside the sphere of inferential reasoning. Only points of law and fact that were not covered by the sources were to be the object of reasoning through what is known as *qiyās*. The domain of the operation of *qiyās* was therefore predetermined to a significant extent by the volume of textual statements which were deemed to have been imbued with *dalālāt al-naṣṣ*. Admittedly, however, the constitution of such statements

---

[3] Although consensus cannot be considered as a revealed source of law, the great majority of *uṣūlists* argued that once a consensus has been reached on a case of law, the case itself becomes an authoritative precedent upon which a further *qiyās* can be based. See the introduction to my «On the Authoritativeness of Sunni Consensus,» in the *International Journal of Middle East Studies*, 18, 1986, pp. 427-454.

[4] Sulaymān b. Khalaf al-Bājī, *Kitāb al-Ḥudūd fī al-Uṣūl*, ed. Nazīh Ḥammād, Beirut, 1973, pp. 25-27; Muḥammad b. ʿAlī al-Tahānawī, *Kashshāf Iṣṭilāḥāt al-Funūn*, 2 vols, Calcutta, 1862, s.v. «*ḍarūrī*», I, 880 ff., especially p. 882, 11. 3 f.

[5] Ibn Rushd, *Bidāya*, I,3; Tahānawī, *Kashshāf*, s.v. «*mafhūm*», II, 1153, 11. 20 f.

amounted only to a fractional portion of the body of legal propositions[6]. The size of their portion was further narrowed down by the objections that were raised concerning those legal propositions which fell on the fine line between what is viewed as 'clear speech', capable of being applied intuitively to particular factual situations, and 'less clear speech', the latter's application being subject to legal analysis and inferential reasoning.

Consisting chiefly of the second category, legal propositions required the instrument of *qiyās* for extending the law embodied in them to unprecedented facts. But the linguistic and legal structure of these propositions was by no means uniform, a fact which had a significant effect on the evolution of varying types of arguments within *qiyās*. This essay seeks to explore these types to the single exception of analogy. The subsumption of analogy under *qiyās* is not only beyond dispute, but has been so predominant that the great majority of modern scholars conceive of *qiyās* as a term which exclusively denotes analogy[7]. Though unjustified, this conception is to a certain degree understandable, for analogy is the single argument that was unqualifiedly accepted by all mainstream Sunnī jurists[8]. That other arguments were not universally embraced in medieval jurisprudence must neither lessen from their importance nor be a cause for their neglect. In fact, one of the most vital discus-

[6] This is inferred from the *uṣūlists'* assertion that the great majority of the rulings of Sharīᶜa are reached through the medium of *qiyās*. See, for instance, Imām al-Ḥaramayn al-Juwaynī, *al-Burhān fī Uṣūl al-Fiqh*, ed. ᶜAbd al-ᶜAẓīm al-Dīb, 2 vols., Cairo, 1400 H., II, 743, par. 767.

[7] Hasan Abdel-Rahman and Joseph Schacht are among the very few scholars who observed the existence of other arguments in *qiyās*. However, they payed little attention to the logical strucτure of these arguments thereby confusing their identity and lumping them altogether under inductive arguments. See H. Abdel-rahman, «L'argument *a maiori* et l'argument par analogie dans la logique juridique musulmane,» *Rivista Internazionale di Filosofia del Diritto*, 98, Ser. 4, 1971, pp. 127-148, especially at 133; idem, «La place du syllogisme juridique dans la méthode exégétique chez Gazali», *Le raisonnement juridique*, ed. H. Hubien, Bruxelles, 1971, 185-194, at p. 186; Joseph Schacht, *The Origins of Muhammadan Jurisprudence*, Oxford, 1950, p. 99. See also Emile Tyan, «Méthodologie et sources du droit en Islam,» *Studia Islamica*, X, 1959, p. 82. It is noteworthy that in his later work *An Introduction to islamic Law*, Oxford, 1964, P. 208, 11.26-29, Schacht reverts to the mistaken assertion that «the method of ḳiyās.....is purely analogical.»

[8] The phrase «mainstream Sunnī jurists» is intended to exclude all those who rejected *qiyās* altogether, such as the Ẓāhirīs and some Muᶜtazilīs. On the opponents of *qiyās* see Muḥammad b. ᶜAlī al-Shawkānī, *Irshād al-Fuḥūl ilā Taḥqīq al-Ḥaqq min ᶜIlm al-Uṣūl*, Cairo, 1909, p. 199-200; Roger Arnaldez, *Grammaire et théologie chez Ibn Ḥazm de Cordoue*, Paris, 1956, pp. 165-194.

sions that arose in legal theory was with regard to methods of linguistic interpretation and legal reasoning in those cases which fell in the gray area between the explicit specification of revelation where reasoning was said to be superfluous, and the total absence of such revelation where analogy was deemed indispensable.

II. The *a fortiori* Arguments

Perhaps one of the most evincive arguments known to the *uṣūlists* is the *a fortiori* argument in both of its forms, the *a minori ad maius* and the *a maiori ad minus*. In expounding the modes of reasoning that come under the umbrella term *qiyās*[9], Shāfiᶜī (d. 204/820) remarks that the strongest form of *qiyās* may be illustrated by the following example: when God or his messenger forbids a small quantity of a certain matter, we conclude that a larger quantity of the same matter is also forbidden. Similarly, if, say, the consumption of a large quantity of a certain foodstuff is declared permissible, then a smaller amount of that foodstuff would also be permissible[10]. As an example of the first type of inference, known to Western jurisprudence as *a minori ad maius*, Shāfiᶜī gives Quran XCIX:7-8 «Whoso has done an atom's weight of good shall see it, and whoso has done an atom's weight of evil shall see it.» From this it is understood that the reward for doing more than an atom's weight of good and the punishment for doing more than an atom's weight of evil are more substantial than that promised for an atom's weight. An example of the second argument, the *a maiori ad minus*, is God's revelation permitting the killing of non-Muslims who engage themselves in war against Muslims. From this text one infers that acts short of killing, such as the confiscation of the property of non-Muslims, are allowed.

Some scholars, Shāfiᶜī remarks, refuse to term such inferences *qiyās*. They argue, he says, that the meaning of the texts encompasses these cases, that is, they come directly under the clear intention of revelation. The term *qiyās* must be used only to designate arguments in which the assimilated case (*farᶜ*) resembles, but is not subsumed under the meaning of the original, revealed case (*aṣl*)[11].

---

[9] Shāfiᶜī, *Risāla*, par. 1482.

[10] *Ibid*, pars. 1482-1485. Also see ᶜAbd al-Qāhir al-Baghdādī, *Uṣūl al-Dīn*, Istanbul, 1928, p. 18, 11. 7-10, who subsumes this argument under *qiyās*.

[11] Shāfiᶜī, *Risāla*, pars. 1492-1494.

Shāfiʿī is referring primarily to the Iraqi (Ḥanafī) jurists, who, together with the Syrians, were familiar with the *a fortiori* arguments[12]. As it will become clear, great many later Ḥanafī *uṣūlists* also advocated this doctrine. The eleborate defense of the Ḥanafī position can be found in numerous later Ḥanafī and non-Ḥanafī *uṣūl* treatises. An exponent of a common Ḥanafī doctrine is Abū Bakr al-Sarakhsī (d. 490 or 495/1096 or 1101) who treats of this issue as one which takes its premises from language, yielding a non-inferential, purely linguistic line of reasoning. In his quadrilateral division of textual legal propositions according to a hierarchical order of clarity, he assigns to the third category the designation *dalālat al-naṣṣ*, that which is understood from the language of the texts without rational inference.[13] In contradistinction to the first category, *ʿibārat al-naṣṣ*, which contains the types of statements that are expressly revealed to specify the ruling of a particular matter (*mā kāna al-siyāqu li-ajlihi*)[14], this category of propositions is intended to legislate in matters which have not been explicitly specified but are clearly understood from the language of these propositions. Legal questions in this category are denoted in the texts (*madlūlun ʿalayhā*) but not specifically stated (*ghayru manṣūṣin ʿalayhā*). The understanding of the meaning of such questions is the property of all laymen who have an adequate knowledge of the language, and not restricted to the reasoning lawyer. From Quran XVII: 23 «Say not 'Fie' to them (to parents) neither chide them, but speak to them graciously» one knows that uttering 'Fie' is prohibited because it signifies a disrespectful attitude towards one's parents. The language of this injunction makes it abundantly clear that all words denoting actions of the same meaning, and actions exceeding in strength the mild expression of 'Fie', such as insulting or beating one's parents, are prohibited. The purpose behind the prohibition of 'Fie' is to declare it forbidden for children to cause the least amount of harm to their parents. This, Sarakhsī insists, is not an inferential matter subject to the reasoning tool of *qiyās*, but only linguistic, because the full extent of the meaning of

---

[12] Abū Ḥanīfa (d. 150/767), Abū Yūsuf (d. 182/798), Shaybānī (d. 189/804), and Awzāʿī (d. 157/773) used the *a fortiori* argument in their legal reasoning. See Schacht, *Origins*, pp. 99, 110-111, 119.

[13] Shams al-Dīn al-Sharakhsī, *Uṣūl*, ed. Abū al-Wafā al-Afghānī, Cairo, 1372 H., I, 241: 1. 11, 243-247.

[14] Ibid, I, 236, 1.4.

'Fie' is in fact encompassed by the meaning of harm (*adhā*)[15]; it thus follows that harmful things which may range from expressing the mere sound of dissatisfaction to murdering one's parents are forbidden by the immediate, uninferred specification of the Quran. Of the same type of statements, Sarakhsī argues, is the Prophetic *ḥadīth* about cats: «It is (the cat) not impure; it is of those (animals) which wander about around you». On the basis of this *ḥadīth* it is reasoned that animals such as mice and snakes are also ritually pure because they possess the same property of wandering about around humans. This line of reasoning, Sarakhsī argues, is identical with the reasoning adopted in the question of beating one's parents in that its *ᶜilla*, or *ratio decidendi*, is so conspicuous in the language of the texts that the ruling can be grasped in the mind without the application of the method of *qiyās*. The only difference between the category under which the case of parents falls, and the second, more explicit category designated as *ishārat al-naṣṣ*, is that in the latter the injunction is understood through the medium of *lafẓ*, the immediate meaning of the letter of the text, whereas in the former through the *maᶜnā*, the implied but uninferred meaning of the text[16].

What Sarakhsī terms *dalālat al-naṣṣ*[17] the Shafiᶜī jurist Sayf al-Dīn al-Āmidī (d. 630/1232) calls *mafhūm al-muwāfaqa*, that is, the *a fortiori* correspondence (*bil-awlā*) of the rule in the original case to the assimilated case[18]. That from the prohibition, for example, of a small quantity of a certain matter one concludes that a larger quantity is even more prohibited, renders the ruling of the assimilated

---

[15] *Ibid*, I, 242, ll. 5-6: «*li'anna qadra mā fī al-ta'fīfi min al-adhā mawjūdun fīhi wa-ziyāda*».

[16] *Ibid*, I, 242, l. 17.

[17] This category of speech is also known as *faḥwā l-khiṭāb, mafhūm al-khiṭāb*, and *laḥn al-khiṭāb*. See ᶜAlī b. Muḥammad b. Ḥabīb al-Māwardī, *Adab al-Qāḍī*, ed. Muḥyī Hilāl Sarḥān, 2 vols., Baghdad, 1971, I, 588, n. 7; Sayf al-Dīn al-Āmidī, *al-Iḥkām fī Uṣūl al-Aḥkām*, 3 vols., Cairo, 1968, II, 210; Jamāl al-Dīn b. Ḥasan al-Isnawī, *al-Tamhīd fī Takhrīj al-Furūᶜ ᶜalā l-Uṣūl*, ed. Muḥammad Ḥasan Haytū, Beirut, 1984, pp. 240-241. In his *al-Kāfiya fī l-Jadal*, ed. Fawqiyya Maḥmūd, Cairo, 1979, p. 376, Juwaynī prefers the logicians' term *bil-awlā*. Tahānawī (*Kashshāf*, II, 1153) observes that Shāfiᶜī uses *faḥwā l-khiṭāb* and *laḥn al-khiṭāb* while the Ḥanafīs use *dalalāt al-naṣṣ*. This, however, seems anachronistic since Shāfiᶜī knows of no such technical terminology, although, as we have seen, he is familiar with the idea.

[18] Āmidī, *Iḥkām*, II, 210, ll. 7-8, 18-19. See also his observations in II, 98-99, 281-282.

case stronger and more relevant (*ashaddu munāsabatan*) to the intention of the Law Giver. It is on these grounds that Āmidī is more inclined to consider conclusions based on this category of propositions as linguistic and not inferential (*qiyāsiyya*). *Qiyās*, he insists, precludes the requirement that the *ʿilla* including the rule of the assimilated case be more relevant to this rule than to the rule of the original case. Such relevance, however, constitutes a fundamental element in *mafhūm al-muwāfaqa*. Also fundamental in this linguistic structure is the logical subsumption of the original case under the assimilated (in the *a minori ad maius*); e.g. the Quranic prohibition of uttering 'Fie' is part of the prohibition of harmful acts directed towards parents. Āmidī claims the existence of a consensus against the inclusion in *qiyās* of the principle of the subsumption of the original case under the assimilated. If there is to be any subsumption in *qiyās* it would be that of the assimilated case under the original[19].

Needless to say, this polemic against including in *qiyās* the *a fortiori* argument in both of its forms had its counter polemic, with the Shāfiʿīs as its chief exponents. Of these we find Abū Isḥāq al-Shīrāzī (d. 476/1083) and Abū al-Ḥasan al-Māwardī (d. 450/1058). The former, pinning the crux of the issue, pointed out that *a fortiori* conclusions involve an inferential line of reasoning because in this category the language of the texts does not explicitly state the ruling with regard to matters implied. Striking one's parents, which is obviously forbidden, cannot be understood from the very word 'Fie'. Only by implication that this term can be taken to mean 'any harm,' and such implication can be understood only through *qiyās*[20]. This type of *qiyās*, Māwardī states, is of the perspicuous (*jalī*) type, which, among other types, is the closest to the unambiguous, self explanatory texts. The ease with which *a fortiori* conclusions are reached derives from the fact that in such an argument the assimilated case, though unspecified by the texts, comes under the meaning (*maʿnā*) of these texts[21]. The lack of specification,

---

[19] *Ibid*, II, 211-212. See also the arguments of Abū l-Barakāt al-Nasafī, *Kashf al-Asrār*, 2 vols., Cairo, 1316 H., I, 252 ff.

[20] Abū Isḥāq al-Shīrāzī, *al-Lumaʿ fī Uṣūl al-Fiqh*, ed. Muḥammad al-Naʿsānī, Cairo, 1326 H., p. 30; idem, *al-Tabṣira fī Uṣūl al-Fiqh*, ed. Muḥammad Ḥasan Haytū, Damascus, 1980, pp. 227-228. Of those non-Shāfiʿī's who subscribed to this view is the Ḥanbalī Muwaffaq al-Dīn Ibn Qudāma, *Rawḍat al-Nāẓir wa-Junnat al-Munāẓir*, ed. Sayf al-Dīn al-Kātib, Beirut, 1981, p. 234.

[21] Māwardī, *Adab*, I, 588, pars. 1413.

Māwardī insists, draws the difference between the *naṣṣ*, the legally clear texts, and *al-qiyās al-jalī*. In the *naṣṣ* the case as well as its rule are *specified*, but in *qiyās* the rule is *derived* on the basis of another case. The word 'Fie' does not itself denote the meaning of 'striking' or 'insulting' and, conversely, 'striking' and 'insulting' are not used to describe the disrespectful act expressed by the term 'Fie'. The proponents of this conception argue that a king could order his guards to execute his father without uttering the expression 'Fie' before him[22]. Thus, the rule of prohibiting striking parents was deduced from the intention behind the prohibition of 'Fie', and not intuitively conceived from the very word itself[23].

The perception of the intent behind this injunction constitutes for the Shāfiʿī intellectual Abū Ḥāmid al-Ghazālī (d. 505/1111) the cornerstone in reasoning from the category of premises which have been revealed to prohibit acts diverting from or obstructing the performance of an obligation[24]. The full legal impact of such an injunction as «When the call for prayer is heard on the day of congregation, hasten to God's remembrance and leave your trading» (Quran LXII: 9) cannot be adequately appreciated if the command were understood to be only against practicing trade on Friday. The intent of the verse and the context in which it was revealed (*siyāqu l-āyati wa-maqṣūḍuhā*) makes it necessary to conclude that all other transactions and activities which divert from Friday's prayer must be taken to be of the same genus of trading, and thus prohibited[25].

Under the same typology, Ghazālī remarks, comes the verse about the treatment of parents. However, the much debated question that Ghazālī poses here is whether the conclusion 'It is forbidden to strike one's parents' is reached through the medium of language or through *qiyās*. The determinant in this question is the relation between striking and 'Fie'. If 'Fie' conveys in linguistic usage the meaning of striking, then this is not *qiyās*. On the other hand, if the prohibition of striking is understood from the *ʿilla* of the prohibition of saying 'Fie', then such an inference involves *qiyās ipso facto*. The fact that such a *qiyās* is quite intuitive and that its conclusion can be reached with little analysis, makes of it no less *qiyās*

---

[22] Āmidī, *Iḥkām*, II, 211, 11. 21-22.

[23] Māwardī, *Adab*, I, 589-590, pars. 1420-1421.

[24] Ghazālī, *Shifā' al-Ghalīl*, ed. Ḥamd al-Kabīsī, Baghdād, 1971, p. 50, 11. 6-7; *idem*, *al-Mustaṣfā min ʿIlm al-Uṣūl*, 2 vols., Cairo, 1324 H., II, 190.

[25] Ghazālī, *Shifā'*, pp. 50-52.

than other inferences subsumed under that term. Ghazālī excludes the first possibility, that is, the linguistic inference that from 'Say not Fie to them' the act of striking one's parents must be forbidden. In language 'say not Fie', as shown in the aforementioned example about the king, does not necessarily imply the negation of striking or other more brutal acts. Against the claim of some jurists that the prohibition of the abuse of parents is understood from the customary usage (*ʿurf*) of the language of the verse, Ghazālī retorts that the signification of textual premises may be grasped by making recourse to *ʿurf* only when the methods of causation (i.e. the method of establishing and verifying the cause, *taʿlīl*) and linguistic analysis have failed. In this case, however, Ghazālī asserts, the method of causation, which the jurist ought to consider first, must suffice. Thus the cause behind the prohibition in the verse is the necessity to respect parents, and the knowledge, which occurs through reason and custom, that uttering 'Fie' runs against such respect. And since striking obviously contradicts respect, the ruling of prohibition obtains. This, Ghazālī insists, is the very course of reasoning known as *qiyās*[26].

Responding to the opponent's contention that if this is deemed to be *qiyās* then the Anti-Qiyās folk[27] would have rejected the rule of the present case, Ghazālī states that they could not have done so because if they had rejected this *qiyās* and abided by the strict letter of revelation the rule would have been restricted to the mere prohibition of saying 'Fie' to parents. It would then also be argued that the texts of revelation contain no prohibition with regard to striking one's parents. To carry these assumptions to their logical conclusion would entail the paradox of prohibiting the uttering of 'Fie' in the presence of parents on the one hand, and allowing striking or insulting them on the other. That Qiyāsists and Anti-Qiyāsists reached the same conclusion is due to the fact that the premises as

---

[26] *Ibid*, pp. 56, 11. 1-11, 129, 11. 6-7. For a summary of this argument see his *Mustaṣfā*, II, 190-191. It is of interest to note that in his *al-Mankhūl*, pp. 334-335, which is perhaps his first *uṣūl* work, Ghazālī held the different view that *faḥwā l-khiṭāb* is not a *qiyās* inference nor a strictly linguistic one. The language of the verse about parents, for instance, contains nothing to the effect that striking parents is prohibited. But the context (*siyāq al-kalām*) and circumstantial evidence (*qarā'in al-ḥāl*) make the meaning of his prohibition quite clear. Therefore, Ghazālī asserted, *faḥwā l-khiṭāb* is not a *qiyās* inference.

[27] The reference here is to the Ẓāhirī school of law which rejected *qiyās* but accepted inferences which have clear textual support.

well as the course of reasoning in this particular case were easy to grasp. This, Ghazālī says, does not alter the fact that what is involved in this type of reasoning is *qiyās*[28].

Be it as it may, the fact remains that no small number of jurists held the view that the *a fortiori* argument is one of the arguments which come under *qiyās*. Even jurists like Āmidī, who considered it a linguistic inference, had in the final analysis to classify this argument as a type of *qiyās*, though he did mention that this matter was controversial[29]. Āmidī's classification is significant as it demonstrates that ignoring the substantial claims of the opponents was something unaffordable. Though it is difficult to establish precisely the identity of those who stood on both sides of the argument, it can be safely said that neither side was a minority. Drawing on earlier sources, the thirteenth/nineteenth century scholar

---

[28] Ghazālī, *Shifā'*, pp. 58-59. See also Shawkānī, *Irshād*, pp. 203, bottom line and 204. Ibn Ḥazm, the most important representative of the Ẓāhirī school of law, asserts that the prohibition of uttering 'Fie' to parents must by no means be taken to indicate that striking parents is prohibited. This particular Quranic sub-verse, he argues, does not by itself have any legal effect except for prohibiting the act of uttering 'Fie' before parents. Rather, the prohibition of striking and murdering parents is understood from the entire verse XVII:23: «The Lord had decreed that you worship none save Him, and that you show kindness to parents. If one of them or both of them attained old age with you, say not 'Fie' to them neither chide them, but speak to them graciously. And lower to them the wing of submission through mercy, and say: My Lord, have mercy on them both as did they care for me when I was little.» This language, together with *ḥadīths* related to this effect, render respect and kindness to parents an obligation. If 'Fie' were sufficient to establish the claimed prohibition, then, Ibn Ḥazm asks, why does God go in the same verse to the trouble of prohibiting other sorts of harmful attitudes and enjoining kindness and submission to parents? Furthermore, Ibn Ḥazm insists that linguistically the term 'Fie' does not mean nor imply striking or murdering. If a person strikes another and causes the breaking of his hands, etc., and if a witness who had seen the incident testifies that the former said to the latter 'Fie', then there would be no doubt that the witness is a liar. On the basis of all this, Ibn Ḥazm concludes that «the prohibition of saying 'Fie' is not a prohibition against murder or striking or defamation, but rather it is a prohibition against saying 'Fie' only.» See ᶜAlī Ibn Ḥazm, *al-Iḥkām fī Uṣūl al-Aḥkām*, ed. Aḥmad Muḥammad Shākir, 8 vols., Cairo, 1347 H., VII, 56-59.

[29] Āmidī, *Iḥkām*, III, 95. See also Ghazālī, *Mankhūl*, p. 333, 11. 3-5, who states that the *uṣūlists* rank the argument of *faḥwā l-khiṭāb* first in the classification of *qiyās* which consists of five categories. It may be worthwhile noting that earlier in the same work Ghazālī considers *faḥwā l-khiṭāb* the fifth category of knowledge (*al-khāmis min marātib al-ᶜulūm*). Ghazālī argues that although certainty does not occur in degrees and that in the final analysis all categories lead to the same indistinguishable degree of certainty, the process by which each category is understood to be certain varies according to whether it is attained through mediate or immediate means. See *Mankhūl*, pp. 46-48, especially p. 48, 11. 1-4.

Ibn ᶜAlī al-Shawkānī remarked that in his treatise *al-Nihāya*, al-Ṣafī l-Hindī (d. 715/1315) reported that the majority of jurists held the view in favor of subsuming the *a fortiori* under *qiyās*. On the other hand, Abū Bakr al-Ṣayrafī reported that the Mutakallims—the Ashᶜarīs and the Muᶜtazilīs—upheld the opposite view[30]. To these Shīrāzī added «some Ẓāhirīs»[31]. Although the accuracy of Ṣayrafī's classification can be instantly contested by bringing forth the example of Ghazālī who was an Ashᶜarī Mutakallim, there seems no reason not to accept it as well-nigh true.

III. The *reductio ad absurdum* Argument

A less controversial argument within the Sunnī legal circles was the *reductio ad absurdum*, known to *uṣūlists* as *qiyās al-ᶜaks*, and to logicians and philosophers as *qiyās al-khulf*[32]. Though we can cite Imām al-Ḥaramayn al-Juwaynī as one of its opponents[33], there is apparently little disagreement among jurists concerning its validity or its being a form of *qiyās*[34]. The eighth/fourtheenth century Ḥanbalī jurist Taqī l-Dīn Ibn Taymiyya declares it not only as a form of *qiyās* but also as legitimate as the indubitable analogy[35].

---

[30] Shawkānī, *Irshād*, p. 178, 11. 23-28. Ibn Qudāma reports that the Ḥanbalīs, like the Shāfiᶜīs, were divided among themselves on this question. See his *Rawḍa*, p. 234.

[31] Shīrāzī, *Tabṣira*, p. 227, 11. 6-7. The editor of *al-Tabṣira* remarks (p. 227, n. 6) that Ibn al-Subkī reported from Juwaynī that most *uṣulists* upheld the view that the *a fortiori* argument is not a form of *qiyās*. I could not, however, substantiate this claim in Juwaynī's *Burhān*.

[32] Ibn ᶜAlī Ibn Malkā Abū l-Barakāt al-Baghdādī, *Kitāb al-Muᶜtabar fī l-Ḥikma*, 3 vols., Ḥaidarabad, 1357 H., I, 184-188; Ibn Abī l-Ṣalt al-Dānī, *Taqwīm al-Dhahn*, ed. C. Gonzalez Palencia, Madrid, 1915, p. 48.

[33] Juwaynī, *al-Kāfiya*, pp. 225-226, states that *aṣḥāb al-ra'y* accepted *qiyās al-ᶜaks* while the Shāfiᶜīs rejected it. To the best of my knowledge, Juwaynī's assertion about the Shāfiᶜīs cannot be substantiated in the original sources. For instance, the Shāfiᶜī jurist Ghazālī, as we shall see, argued for the validity of this argument.

[34] Shīrāzī and Subkī, for instance, subsumed *qiyās al-ᶜaks* under *istidlāl* rather than *qiyās*. See Tāj al-Dīn al-Subkī, *Jamᶜ al-Jawāmiᶜ*, 2 vols., Bombay, 1970, II, 343; Shīrāzī, *Lumaᶜ*, p. 67. Under the broad category of *istidlāl* jurists subsumed a variety of arguments ranging from syllogistics to *istiḥsān* and *istiṣlāh*. It was therefore natural to consider the *reductio ad absurdum* an argument of *istidlāl*, for it manifested a logical property which is fundamentally deductive. On the role of *istidlāl* and syllogistics in Sunnī jurisprudence see my paper «Logic, Formal arguments and Formalization of Arguments in Sunni Jurisprudence» (forthcoming in *Arabica*).

[35] Taqī l-Dīn Ibn Taymiyya, «Fī Maᶜnā l-Qiyās,» in *Majmūᶜat al-Rasā'il al-Kubrā*, 2 vols., Cairo, 1323 H., II, 217, 11; 14-15; idem, *al-Qiyās fī l-Sharᶜ al-*

Qiyās al-ʿaks is defined as the course of reasoning in which the converse of a given rule of a case is applied to another case on the grounds that the *ʿillas* of the two cases are contradictory[36]. (This must not be confused with the *argumentum e contrario* which the Sunnī jurists almost unanimously considered as a purely linguistic argument, and was thus excluded from *qiyās*)[37]. The fundamental thesis of this type of *qiyās* is the establishment of a rule by demonstrating the falsehood or invalidity of its converse[38]. The argument presupposes a premise whose conclusion is to be established as true; a converse of this premise is adduced with the view of establishing that the conclusion to which it leads is false. Once it is established that the conclusion of the second premise is false, and that it stands in diametrical opposition to the conclusion of the first premise, we conclude that the conclusion of the first premise is true. A case in

---

Islāmī, translated to the French by H. Laoust, *Contribution à une étude de la méthodologie canonique de Takī-d-Dīn Aḥmad b. Taymiya*, Le Caire, 1939, p. 114. Laoust, however, mistranslates *qiyās al-ʿaks* as disjunctive syllogism, a term used for what Ibn Taymiyya and the *uṣūlists* knew as *al-sabr wa l-taqsīm*. See his *al-Radd ʿalā l-Manṭiqiyīn*, ed. by ʿAbdu ṣ-Ṣamad Sharaf d-Dīn al-Kutubī, Bombay, 1949, p. 205, 11. 10-12 and Ghazālī, *al-Iqtiṣād fī l-Iʿtiqād*, ed. I.A. Cubukcu and H. Atay, Ankara, 1962, pp. 15-16. See also Shīrāzī, *Lumaʿ*, pp. 67-68, who makes a clear distinction between disjunctive syllogism and *reductio ad absurdum*.

It must be mentioned here that certain jurists, while expounding *qiyās al-ʿaks*, as was the norm in the chapter on *qiyās*, insisted that the term «*qiyās*» is applied to the *reductio ad absurdum* metaphorically. According to Ibn al-Ḥājib, *Muntahā l-Wuṣūl wa l-Amal fī ʿIlmay al-Uṣūl wa l-Jadal*, ed. Muḥammad al-Naʿsānī, Cairo, 1326 H., pp. 122-123, especially p. 122, 11. 1-2, this was the view of Abū Ḥusayn al-Baṣrī.

[36] Abū l-Ḥusayn al-Baṣrī, *al-Muʿtamad fī Uṣūl al-Fiqh*, ed. Muḥammad Ḥamīdullāh et al., 2 vols., Damascus, 1964-65, II, 698, 11. 9-11; idem, *Kitāb al-Qiyās al-Sharʿī*, printed with *al-Muʿtamad*, p. 1031, 11. 11-12, read: «*huwa ithbātun yaqtaḍī naqīḍa ḥukmi l-shay'i fī ghayrihi*»; Āmidī, *Iḥkām*, III, 3, 11. 10-12.

[37] The *argumentum e contrario* stipulates that if an act is commanded it is concluded that any act to the contrary is prohibited. Conversely, it may be argued that the contrary of an act which is prohibited is recommended or obligatory. The Prophetic statement that «*zakāt* is owed on goats which are put out to pasture» is taken by those who espoused this type of inference to mean that goats which are maintained on fodder are not subject to *zakāt*. Further on this inference and its subdivisions see Shīrāzī, *Lumaʿ*, p. 30; Aboubekr Abdesselam Ben Choaib, «L'argumentation juridique en droit musulman,» *Revue du monde musulman*, VII (1909), pp. 70-86; A. Zysow, *The Economy of Certainty: An Introduction to the Typology of Islamic Legal Theory*, Harvard University, 1984 (unpublished dissertation), pp. 162 ff.

[38] Ghazālī, *Shifā'*, p. 450, 17-18; Kamāl al-Dīn Ibn al-Humām, *al-Taḥrīr fī Uṣūl al-Fiqh*, Cairo, 1351 H., pp. 418-419; Ibn al-Ḥājib, *Mukhtaṣar al-Muntahā l-Uṣūlī*, Cairo, 1326 H., p. 175.

point is the retaining of the profit resulting from *commenda* (*muqāraḍa*) contract. The agent in this contract must return to the investor the principal as well as a previously agreed-upon share of the profits. The agent receives the remaining share of the profits only as a compensation for his effort at investing. It is determined that the agent does not retain all the profit, but is entitled only to a part of it, by reasoning that if he does then he would be entitled to the profit accruing from the profit which had resulted from the investment of the principal. Since the agent cannot be the proprietor of the profit which results from the investment of the first profit because it creates an imbalance in the agreed-upon proportion, we conclude that the agent cannot exclusively retain the profit in the *muqāraḍa* contract[39].

Certain legal cases involving *qiyās al-ʿaks* take the jurist into a slight diversion from the strictly formal lines of the argument as is hitherto outlined. The standard and oft-cited case illustrative of such an argument is the case in which it is required to prove that fasting is a prerequisite for the performance of *iʿtikāf*[40]. Abū l-Ḥusayn al-Baṣrī, a Ḥanafī-Muʿtazilī jurist, puts it in these terms;

> We infer that fasting is a prerequisite for *iʿtikāf* by reasoning that if it were not a prerequisite it would not be necessary to perform *iʿtikāf* while fasting if [the Muslim has not] vowed to do so. And since prayer is not a prerequisite for *iʿtikāf* it would not be its prerequisite even if it were vowed to perform *iʿtikāf* while praying. The original case here is prayer, and its judgement is that it is not a prerequisite for *iʿtikāf*. We want to establish the converse of this judgement in fasting. The cause (*ʿilla*) in prayer is that it is not necessary for *iʿtikāf* by so vowing. The converse of the cause is thus established in fasting[41].

In other words, prayer in this case is not a prerequisite for *iʿtikāf*, as it has not been determined to be a necessary part in vowing to perform *iʿtikāf*. The *ʿilla* for which prayer is not a prerequisite is that it does not constitute a condition for the validity of *iʿtikāf* when

---

* [39] Ghazālī, *Shifāʾ*, p. 451, 11. 9-11.

[40] *Iʿtikāf*, or *ʿukūf*, is a recommended religious practice of retreat in a mosque. When the Muslim vows to perform *iʿtikāf* for a certain period of time, it is implied that he should fast as well. This practice becomes obligatory and his vow must thus be fulfilled. Differences between schools of law on this point are numerous owing to the lack of unequivocal evidence in the Quran or the Sunna. See, e.g., Ibn Rushd, *Bidāya*, I, 220 ff. See also ʿAḍud al-Dīn al-Ījī's commentary on Ibn al-Ḥājib's *Mukhtaṣar al-Muntahā l-Uṣūlī*, 2 vols., Cairo, 1973, II, 205-207, especially at p. 207, 11. 1-2.

[41] Baṣrī, *al-Qiyās al-Sharʿī*, pp. 1031-1032.

vowing. This *ʿilla*, however, is not found in fasting which is determined by consensus to be a prerequisite for *iʿtikāf* when the vow is made. Therefore, «had fasting been unnecessary in *iʿtikāf*, it would not have been necessary in vowing, as in the case of prayer[42].» (It is essentially the exclusive dependency of this mode of reasoning on diametrically opposing cases for deriving a conclusion that provoked the criticism of Juwaynī against this argument. Juwaynī finds it absurd to derive a matter from its opposite. For him, *qiyās* is reasoning on the basis of similarity and commonality not contradiction)[43].

While the *uṣūlists* are ordinarily satisfied with the aforementioned example as an illustration of the course of reasoning followed in *qiyās al-ʿaks*, jurist-logicians, such as Ghazālī, discerned in this *qiyās* another variation of *reductio ad absurdum*. The first step in this course of reasoning is reducing the proposition into its component elements, and then by invalidating these elements one by one, the entire proposition is proven invalid. One concludes that *īlā'* is not a type of divorce by reasoning that if it were a type of divorce it would require a direct statement (*ṣarīḥ*) or an indirect declaration of intent (*kināya*) to the effect that the husband is divorcing his wife. *Īlā'*, which merely involves a sworn testimony (*ḥilf*) to abstain from sexual intercourse for at least four months (after which divorce goes into effect) entails neither *ṣarīḥ* nor *kināya* declaration. Therefore, *īlā'* is not a type of divorce. This line of reasoning, Ghazālī notes, can be reduced to two premises and a conclusion[44]. If 'divorce' is D, *īlā'* is I, *ṣarīḥ* is S and *kināya* is K, the argument can be schematically put as follows:

If D is I then I is S and K
I is not S and K
Therefore, I is not D

In Ghazālī's view then, *qiyās al-ʿaks* as presented in this case seems to manifest the characteristics of conditional hypothetical syllogism in the *modus tollens*.

---

[42] Ghazālī, *Shifā'*, p. 452, 11. 12-13; Āmidī, *Iḥkām*, III, 3, 11. 12-18; Niẓām al-Dīn al-Anṣārī, *Fawātiḥ al-Raḥamūt*, with the commentary *Musallam al-Thubūt* by Ibn ʿAbd al-Shakūr, printed with Ghazālī's *al-Mustaṣfā*, 2 vols., Cairo, 1324 H., II, 247-248; Ibn al-Humām, *al-Taḥrīr*, pp. 418-419.

[43] Juwaynī, *Kāfiya*, p. 226.

[44] Ghazālī, *Shifā'*, p. 454.

IV. Syllogistics and the Logical Properties of the *argumenta a fortiori* and *reductio ad absurdum*

Āmidī, as we have seen, pointed out two objections against the inclusion in *qiyās* of the *a fortiori* argument, particularly the *a minori ad maius*. The second of these objections pertains to the logical property of the *a minori ad maius*, that is, the extention of the original legal precept to a larger situation by implication. This, Āmidī insists, violates the logical schemata of *qiyās*, which he understood to encompass inductive reasoning, chiefly analogy, as well as *reductio ad absurdum*. The unique structure of the *a fortiori* argument was acknowledged even by those who insisted that the argument is a form of *qiyās*. This raises the question concerning the nature of the logical property of the *a fortiori* argument, and the salient features which delineate the difference between this argument and the arguments of analogy and *reductio ad absurdum*.

It must be immediately stated here that the *a fortiori* argument had mystified the traditional logicians as much as it has eluded the modern ones. The latter have succeeded more than their predecessors in reducing the argument into a kind of asyllogistic inference while depending primarily on its crucial logical property of relational transitivity[45]. That the relation between the subject and the predicate of the premises is transitive, precludes the inference from being subsumptive and thus from being strictly syllogistic. In 'Hārūn is more generous than Charlemagne' the relation 'more generous' is transitive from Hārūn to Charlemagne. Such a relation is also said to be asymmetric, since there is no equation between the two as in 'Hārūn is as intelligent as Charlemagne', but rather a comparison in terms of 'more', 'greater', 'smaller', 'above', etc. It is this asymmetry which leads to the knowledge that striking parents is *stronger than* saying 'Fie' to them. Harm or harmful acts, being the common denominator, compels one to conclude that if 'Fie' is prohibited, then striking is at least equally prohibited. The absence of a necessary premise from the argument (which is in this case the harm in saying 'Fie') led a number of modern logicians to consider it an enthymeme[46].

[45] L.S. Stebbing, *A Modern Introduction to Logic*, 7th ed., London, 1950, p. 114; Morris Cohen and Ernest Nagel, *Introduction to Logic and Scientific Method*, New York, 1934, p. 78.

[46] J. Gregorowicz, «L'argument *a maiori ad minus* et le problème de la logique juridique,» *Logique et Analyse*, 17-18, Avril 1962, p. 69. For a criticism of

Muslim jurists, on the other hand, supplied the implied premise, which takes in a syllogistic the position of a middle term (i.e., harm). Thus, for Ghazālī the entire course of reasoning could be reduced to a deductive inference in which the major premise is 'All harmful acts (directed against parents) are prohibited'; the minor premise 'Striking is a harmful act'; and the conclusion 'Striking is prohibited.' Such an inference on the basis of the Quranic verse would have been impossible had it not been presumed that 'Striking is more harmful than saying 'Fie' to one's parents, and that 'Harmful acts are prohibited'. In this inference, however, the premises have not been originally stipulated but are themselves the conclusions of yet another inference. This fact precludes the *a fortiori* from being a regular deductive argument[47].

Nor can the *a fortiori* argument be considered inductive. Muslim jurists clearly ruled out the subsumption of the *a fortiori* under analogical inference. For them, the fundamental difference between the two arguments lies in the relationship between the original and the assimilated cases. In analogy the inference procedes from a particular to another particular, such as in the cases of date-wine and grape-wine. Once date-wine is determined to be prohibited because of its intoxicating property, the rule of prohibition is transferred to grape-wine, as it possesses the same property of intoxication. The original and the assimilated cases here stand on the same footing in that they are two equal particulars. This principle is the pillar of any sound analogy. In the *a fortiori* argument, on the other hand, there is no such parity between the cases. The original case always maintains a 'greater' or 'lesser' dimension than the assimilated case[48]. Added to this is the fact that in analogy the rule is inferred on the basis of a similarity which exists between the cases, whereas in the *a fortiori* the rule is *implied* without the prerequisite of drawing upon a similarity. This is precisely why the Ḥanafīs rejected the argument as a form of *qiyās*, and modern logi-

---

Gregorowicz's article see J. Horovitz, *Law and Logic: A Critical Account of Legal Argument*, Wien, New York, 1972, pp. 109 ff.

[47] See Gregorowicz, «L'argument *a maiori...*» for a useful summary of the views about the *a maiori ad minus* as an *a fortiori* argument, pp. 69-75; D.S. Robinson, *The Principles of Reasoning*, New York, 1924, p. 158. For attempts to reduce this argument to a syllogistic inference see R.M. Eaton, *General Logic*, New York, 1959, pp. 220-222.

[48] Āmidī, *Iḥkām*, II, 212, III, 95; Ibn Rushd, *Bidāya*, I, 3, 11. 24-26; Ghazālī, *Miʿyār*, pp. 203-205.

cians insisted on its irregularity as asyllogistic as well as an enthymeme.

The formal features of the *a fortiori* are less salient than those of the *reductio ad absurdum* argument, an argument which exhibits the classical form of indirect reduction of syllogism[49]. Indirect reduction «is a way of showing that if a certain syllogistic form is assumed to be valid, by assuming that its conclusion is false, a contradictory result follows, proved by a syllogism in the first figure. Hence, the original syllogism must be valid on pain of leading to a contradiction[50].» This method of proof rests squarely on a certain relationship between two syllogisms, and is itself deductive in character. «By combining the contradictory of the conclusion of a syllogism with each of the premises in turn, two new syllogisms can be constructed, each of which—taken *as a whole*—implies and is implied by the original syllogism[51].» Ghazālī, for instance, took the *reductio ad absurdum* as a valid form of syllogism. He recognized it, as we have seen in the example of divorce and *īlā'*, as a syllogism which logically stands on the same footing with conjunctive and disjunctive syllogisms[52].

That juridical *qiyās* encompassed irregular deductive and indirect syllogistic arguments must not come as a surprise. Muslim lawyers who dealt with legal logic have not only taken this for granted but went as far as to analyze analogy, the most dominant argument in *qiyās*, in terms of syllogistic logic. The Ḥanbalī jurist Taqī l-Dīn Ibn Taymiyya even argued that the syllogistic inference and analogy have, in the final analysis, the same force[53]. «This is why,» he continued, «many jurists use syllogistics in legal reasoning[54].» ʿAbd al-Jabbār al-Asadabādī and Ghazālī insisted that the form of rational *qiyās* (known to philosophers as *qiyās al-burhān*; demonstrative syllogism) does not differ from that of juridical *qiyās*[55]. Under

---

[49] Cohen and Nagel, *Logic and Scientific Method*, p. 88.

[50] Eaton, *General Logic*, p. 128.

[51] *Ibid*, p. 130.

[52] Ghazālī, *Miʿyār*, p. 131, 11. 7-9. This was also the attitude of logicians. See Ibn Malkā, *al-Muʿtabar*, pp. 184-188; Ibn Abī l-Ṣalt al-Dānī, *Taqwīm*, p. 48.

[53] Ibn Taymiyya, *Jahd*, pp. 259, 1. 10, 289, 331, *passim*.

[54] Ibn Taymiyya, *al-Radd*, p. 117, 11. 1-2 from bottom.

[55] ʿAbd al-Jabbār, *al-Mughnī fī Abwāb al-Tawḥīd wal-ʿAdl*, ed. Amīn al-Khūlī, 20 vols.(?), Cairo, 1962, XVII, 280, 1. 17, 282, 1. 4; Ghazālī, *Miʿyār*, pp. 202, 1. 11, as well as his introduction, p. 60, 1. 15; *idem, Shifā'*, p. 441, 1. 2. ʿAbd al-Jabbār remarked: «*wa-ṭarīqatu l-qiyāsi l-sharʿiyi lā tukhālifu ṣūratuhā ṣūrata l-qiyāsi l-ʿaqlī*». See also Ibn Taymiyya, *Jahd*, p. 233, 11. 2-8.

the term *qiyās* in law Ghazālī admitted both deductive and analogical arguments[56]. In addition to the common syllogism which consists of two premises and a conclusion (e.g., 'All intoxicating matters are forbidden'; 'All wines are intoxicating'; Therefore, 'All wines are forbidden') Ghazālī included analogy, or the *argumentum a simile*, in which the conclusion or the rule sought after is reached on the basis of a similarity between two particulars[57]. Like Ibn Taymiyya, Ghazālī asserted that in any sound analogical argument there must exist a middle term, a *ʿilla*, which justifies the transference of the characteristic property—the conclusion or the rule—from one particular to another[58]. But once it is determined that two premises are to be brought together on the grounds of a similarity, Ghazālī and Ibn Taymiyya deem such a relation—for different reasons to be sure—as potentially capable of acquiring both the analogical and syllogistic modes of reasoning. When the middle term is the efficient cause of the major term, the argument, Ghazālī declares, is termed by philosophers *burhān al-limā* and by jurists *qiyās al-ʿilla*. When the middle term is not causative, however, the argument is known to philosophers as *burhān li'anna* and to jurists as *qiyās al-dalāla*[59]. Thus, the essential structure of the form of juridical *qiyās* does not differ from that of demonstrative syllogism. The difference between them, Ghazālī observes, lies in the quality of material premises (*muqaddimāt*) used in each type of *qiyās*. «The premises which are good for rational *qiyās* (demonstration) are good for juridical *qiyās*, but not all the premises which are good for juridical *qiyās* are good for rational *qiyās*[60].» The acceptable premises in syllogistics are the certain (*yaqīn*) statements which, when molded into a pure deductive argument, yield certain (*yaqīnī*) conclusions. In addition to these premises, legal argument is also receptive of particular statements whose truthfulness is not absolutely certain or conclusive. But how is one to convert an analogical legal argument, which presupposes two particular

[56] Cf. R. Brunschvig, «Valeur et fondement du raisonnement juridique par analogie d'après al-Ġazālī,» in his *Études d'Islamologie*, ed. Abdel Magid Turki, 2 vols., Paris, 1976, II, 363-394.

[57] Ghazālī, *Mustaṣfā*, II, 229, II. 5-6.

[58] Ibn Taymiyya, *Jahd*, p. 292, 11. 3-6; Ghazālī, *Miʿyār*, p. 243, 11. 8-11.

[59] Ghazālī, *Miʿyār*, p. 243. For a further analysis of these syllogisms in light of Ghazālī's doctrine of causality see Michael E. Marmura, «Ghazali and Demonstrative Science,» *Journal of the History of Philosophy*, III (1965), 183-204, at 189 ff.

[60] Ghazālī, *Miʿyār*, p. 202.

statements brought together on the ground of a certain similarity, into a deductive inference? Ghazālī answers that to do so lawyers often convert the particular textual premise embodying the legal norm (*aṣl*) to a major universal premise in a deductive argument through the universalization of the *ʿilla* which induces, causally or otherwise, the ruling in the original case. This would transform analogy to a first figure syllogism[61]. A case in point is the Quranic prohibition of the consumption of wine. The jurist may argue that the reason for the prohibition is the intoxicating quality (*waṣf*) found in wine, and he may therefore formulate his findings in the categorical proposition: 'All intoxicating objects are forbidden' (or more precisely 'The consumption of any intoxicating object is forbidden'). Once he establishes the major premise, he will be able to set forth a syllogism in which the minor premise is, say, 'Vodka is an inoxicating object', and the conclusion 'Vodka is forbidden' (or 'The consumption of vodka is forbidden'). Though the same conclusion can be derived by the medium of analogy as well as syllogism, Ghazālī contends that when the conclusion is syllogistic it is certain, whereas a conclusion by analogy is only probable.

It is against the theory which assigns to syllogism a superior position over analogy that Ibn Taymiyya directed his piercing criticism when he wrote an impressive treatise in refutation of Greek logic[62]. His theory of logic and legal logic rests on the fundamental assumption that it is not the form of the argument but rather the material premises of that argument which determine the epistemological

---

[61] *Miʿyār*, pp. 165, 11. 18-19, 202, 11. 15-16: «*fa'inna l-muqaddimāti l-juz'iyyati fī l-fiqhi yutasāmaḥu bi-jaʿlihā kulliya.*» This is also the view of Abū Naṣr al-Fārābī, *Kitāb al-Qiyās al-Saghīr*, ed. M. Turker in *Revue de la faculté des langue, histoire, et de géographie de l'université d'Ankara*, vol. 16 (1958), 266-268, trans. Nicholas Rescher, *al-Farabi's Short Commentary on Aristotle's Prior Analytics*, Pittsburgh, 1963, 93-98. Some influential Western lawyers, such as Urlich Klug, argue that in sound analogy the minor premise is subsumed under the major premise just as it is the case in any syllogism. J. Horovitz agrees with him and asserts that analogical inference eventually goes back to syllogism and has no special logical structure of its own. Horovitz, *Logic and Law*, p. 33. See also Spiros Simitis, «The Problem of Legal Logic» *Ratio*, III, No. 1 (1960), pp. 60-94, especially p. 70.

[62] Ibn Taymiyya states in the introduction to *al-Radd ʿalā l-Manṭiqīyīn*, pp. 3-4, that his initial purpose was to refute the philosophers' metaphysics. He, however, realized that what led the philosophers astray was their methodology, i.e., their logic. On this in general see R. Brunschvig, «Pour ou contre la logique grecque chez les théologiens-juristes de l'Islam: Ibn Ḥazm, Al-Ghazālī, Ibn Taymiyya,» in his *Études d'Islamologie*, ed. Abdel Magid Turki, 2 vols., Paris, 1976, I, 303-327, at 321-326.

status of the conclusion. If the premises are certain, whether they are cast in the form of analogy (*tamthīl*) or categorical syllogism (*qiyās al-shumūl*), the conclusion must be certain. Conversely, uncertain premises necessarily yield an uncertain conclusion, irrespective of the argumentative form in which they are molded[63]. Ibn Taymiyya vehemently argues that like syllogism, analogy is not merely an inference in which a conclusion is derived from two particular premises. Rather, it is an inference based on two premises brought together by a middle term. If the middle term is established as the true *ᶜilla* of the major premise (i.e., the *aṣl*), then the conclusion must necessarily be certain, even though it is reached through analogical argument. Thus, if we are certain that the reason behind the prohibition of wine is its intoxicating quality, then the conclusion 'Vodka is prohibited' is absolutely certain. In the same vein, the certainty about the relatedness of the *ᶜilla* of intoxication to the prohibition of consumption allows us to convert the particular statement 'Wine is prohibited' to a more categorical statement 'All intoxicating objects are prohibited', which in turn permits a syllogistic inference in which the minor is 'Vodka is intoxicating' and the conclusion 'Vodka is prohibited'. «For people who possess sound reason», asserts Ibn Taymiyya, «*qiyās* encompasses both syllogism and analogy[64].»

The theories of Ghazālī and Ibn Taymiyya represent the culmination of the process in which logic had to be accounted for in the juridical methodology of *qiyās*, a methodology which goes beyond the simple procedure of reasoning by analogy[65]. *Qiyās* thus cannot be given the fixed definition of analogy. Instead, it should be regarded as a relative term whose definition and structure vary from one jurist to another. To Shāfiᶜī, for instance, *qiyās* denoted a different set of arguments than those found in the *qiyās* of a later Shāfiᶜī follower such as Āmidī. And Āmidī's *qiyās* encompassed arguments which the *qiyās* of the Ḥanafī Sarakhsī excluded. Ghazālī and Ibn Taymiyya, though they were in disagreement on

---

[63] Ibn Taymiyya, *Jahd*, pp. 289, 301, 331, *passim*.

[64] *Ibid*, p. 259, l. 10.

[65] In fact, the procedure of analogy was dependent on non-analogical arguments. The discovery and verification of the *ʿilla* in *qiyās* involved a number of methods that can easily be characterized as formal, such as conditional disjunctive syllogism (*al-sabr wa l-taqsīm*), the method of coextensiveness and coexclusiveness (*al-ṭard wa l-ʿaks*), etc. For a succinct account of these methods see Shawkānī, *Irshād al-Fuḥūl*, pp. 213-221.

methodology, bestowed on juridical *qiyās* a wider definition as to include formal arguments. Baṣrī, Ghazālī and Āmidī, among many others, recognized the *reductio ad absurdum* as an argument of *qiyās*. Furthermore, while some jurists included in *qiyās a fortiori* arguments, others excluded these arguments from the domain of *qiyās* and instead acknowledged them as purely linguistic inferences.

ADDENDUM

p. 298, n. 39: another illustrative example is provided by the Mālikī theorist Bājī: We maintain that the *'illa* behind the prohibition on taking out the organs of living animals is that the soul still resides in them. From this we conclude that the soul does not reside in animal hair, for if it did, the removal of this hair would have been, like the removal of organs, prohibited. Thus the absence of the *'illa* of prohibition in the case of hair (an absence which, in and by itself, amounts to a *'illa* that constitutes the converse of that found in organs) renders taking it out from living animals lawful. See Abū al-Walīd Ibn Khalaf al-Bājī, *Iḥkām al-Fuṣūl fī Aḥkām al-Uṣūl* (Beirut: Dār al-Gharb al-Islāmī, 1986), p. 673.

III

LOGIC, FORMAL ARGUMENTS AND FORMALIZATION OF ARGUMENTS IN SUNNĪ JURISPRUDENCE

*Part I. Logic and Formal Arguments**

SOME DECADES before the translation movement from Greek into Arabic began, a battle over the ultimate source of Law had already been fought and won by Traditionalist Islam, represented by the well-known Ibn Idrīs al-Shāfiᶜī (d. 204/820). The triumph of the theory of the divine origins of law compelled Islamic jurisprudence to dissociate itself from all rationalist tendencies involved in philosophical ventures. Chief among these tendencies were the discussions on metaphysics in which logic served as the guiding spirit of philosophical argumentation. Associated with such heretical enterprises, logic as an organon of philosophy could hardly be distinguished from substantive metaphysical doctrines, and in such an environment Traditionalist jurisprudence kept suspected logic at bay. It was not until the appearance of the Shāfiᶜī-Ashᶜarī intellectual Abū Ḥāmid al-Ghazālī (d. 505/1111) that logic as a method was sifted out of Aristotelian philosophy and thus cleared of its «non-theistic» tendencies. Ghazālī's endeavor in bringing logic into law, and the persistence of what may be called the Ghazālian thesis among some of his influential *uṣūlist* successors, will form the subject of this essay. While the following section attempts, in general terms, to analyze Ghazālī's attitude towards logic in the law, it is not until Part II of this essay that we will encounter, in the form of a translation, what may be described as one of the most revealing statements which Ghazālī made on the logic of legal argument.

I

Until the fifth/eleventh century, Sunnī jurisprudence succeeded to a significant extent in resisting the influences of Aristotelian for-

* Part I of this article is a revised version of a paper presented at the Twentieth Annual Meeting of the Middle East Studies Association, Boston, November 19-22, 1986.

mal logic. In Shāfiʿī's theory, for instance, no formal arguments were recognized; his typology of arguments was confined to analogy, *argumentum e contrario* and *a fortiori* arguments. Any rudimentary deductive arguments that may be discerned in his positive legal system were, for him as well as for his successors, but linguistic arguments.[1] Even towards the end of the fourth/tenth century, long after the translation of Greek philosophical works was undertaken, Sunnī jurisprudence was still little affected by the introduction of Greek formal logic. While several nonformal methods of legal inquiry seem to have been developed and refined in light of the new material that these translation offered, only one important formal argument was assimilated; namely, the conditional disjunctive syllogism, known to *uṣūlists* as *al-sabr wa l-taqsīm* or, briefly, *taqsīm*.[2] In this argument the possible effects of a legal fact are enumerated with the view of establishing the true effect(s), or the absence thereof. If P, for instance, is the legal fact, and Q and R are phenomena which we think to be the possible effects of

---

[1] In Sunnī legal theory, including that of Shāfiʿī, pure deductive arguments as well as *argumenta e contrario* were deemed necessarily linguistic, for the conclusion of such arguments was seen to be derived from the language of revelation rather than through the medium of rational inferences. In the background of this theory there lies the fundamental typology of certitude and probability, a typology which dominated and dictated the approach to legal analysis. Aside from considerations of authenticity, revelation was structurally and linguistically categorized into degrees of clarity, whereby the scale of certitude and probability could be applied. A Quranic text in which a rule is clearly specified needs no inference to deduce the legal norm therefrom. It was argued that the knowledge posited by such a text is necessary or immediate (*ḍarūrī*); the intellect, once exposed to it, has no choice but to comprehend it. Thus, when a genus is prohibited, for instance, it is *immediately* understood that each one of its species are also prohibited, even though the individual species are not specifically prohibited. This is why in the traditional exposition of legal theory deductive arguments are not recognized as such, but are instead identified as linguistic arguments. A glance at substantive and positive law books reveals the deductive character of arguments which are otherwise considered linguistic. For further discussion on this matter see my article «Non-Analogical Arguments in Sunnī Juridical Qiyās,» *Arabica* (1989), fasc. 3, pp. 286-306; Muḥammad b. Abī Sahl al-Sarakhsī, *Uṣūl*, ed. Abū l-Wafāʾ al-Afghānī, 2 vols., Cairo, 1372 H., I, 236-254; Abū l-Walīd Muḥammad Ibn Rušd, *Bidāyat al-Mujtahid wa-Nihāyat al-Muqtaṣid*, 2 vols., Cairo, 1329 H., I, 3-4.

[2] This method seems to have already been well established in the work of the *uṣūlist* and theologian Abū Bakr al-Bāqillānī (d. 403/1012), *Kitāb al-Tamhīd*, ed. R. J. McCarthy, Beyrouth, 1957, pp. 11-12. See also Abū l-Ḥusayn al-Baṣrī, *Kitāb al-Qiyās al-Sharʿī* (printed with his *al-Muʿtamad fī Uṣūl al-Fiqh*), ed. M. Hamidullah *et al.*, 2 vols., Damascus, 1964-65, II, 1037; Abū Isḥāq al-Shīrāzī, *al-Lumaʿ fī Uṣūl al-Fiqh*, ed. M. al-Naʿsānī, Cairo, 1326 H., p. 67.

P, then the course of reasoning may yield either of two conclusions:[3]

P is either Q or R
Not Q
———————
Then, R (Or not
R; then Q)

Or,

P is either Q or R
Not Q and R
———————
Then, Not P

In the fourth/tenth and fifth/eleventh centuries, this argument was subsumed under the broad category of *istidlāl*, generally conceived by jurists and theologians as an umbrella term for inferential methods of inquiry. Although *taqsīm* played an important role in the verification of the cause (*ᶜilla*) in the methodology of *qiyās*, Abū Isḥāq al-Shīrāzī (d. 476/1083), for instance, seems to have considered *taqsīm* as one of the *istidlāl* arguments which constitute an offshoot rather than an integral part of *qiyās*.[4] On the other hand, the theologian-jurist Abū Bakr al-Bāqillānī (d. 403/1012) subsumed the two separate sets of arguments *qiyās* and *taqsīm* under the heading *istidlāl*.[5] *Taqsīm* and *istidlāl* then were not unqualifiedly integrated into, or totally identified with *qiyās*.[5a]

The subsumption of non-*qiyās* arguments under *istidlāl* seems, as we can glean from later sources, to have contributed to the segregation of *istidlāl* from the traditional *qiyās* arguments. After the fifth/eleventh century, *istidlāl* comprised, in addition to *taqsīm* and other formal arguments, such principles as *istiḥsān, istiṣlāḥ*, and *istiṣḥāb al-ḥāl*.[6] Grouping these particular arguments and juridical

[3] Shīrāzī, *Lumaᶜ*, p. 67.
[4] *Ibid.*, p. 67, ll. 18-19.
[5] Bāqillānī, *Tamhīd*, pp. 11-12.
[5a] For a later distinction between *qiyās* and *istidlāl* see Ibn al-Ṣalāḥ, *Fatāwā*, in *Majmūᶜat al-Rasāʾil al-Munīriyya*, 3 vols., Beirut, 1346 H., III, 32.
[6] Muḥammad Aᶜlā b. ᶜAlī l-Tahānawī, *Kashshāf Iṣṭilāḥāt al-Funūn*, 2 vols., Calacutta, 1862, I, 498-499, s.v. «*istidlāl*»; Saᶜd al-Dīn al-Taftāzānī, *Ḥāshiya ᶜalā Sharḥ al-ᶜAḍud al-Ījī* (a commentary on Ibn al-Ḥājib's *Muntahā al-Wuṣūl wa l-Amal fī ᶜIlmayy al-Uṣūl wa l-Jadal*), ed. Shaᶜbān Ismāᶜīl, 2 vols., Cairo, 1973, II, 281, ll. 22-24. For *istiḥsān* (juristic preference) and *istiṣlāḥ* (public interest), see the *Shorter Encyclopaedia of Islam* by R. Paret. For *istiṣḥāb* (presumption of continuity) see Ghazālī, *al-Mankhūl min ᶜIlm al-Uṣūl*, ed. Muḥammad Ḥasan Haytu, Cairo, n.d., pp. 372-373.

principles together under one designation, namely, *istidlāl*, was not without significance. All of these shared an important characteristic; that is, they existed in the realm of the controversial within the systems of the four schools of law. But while *istiḥsān, istiṣlāḥ* and *istiṣḥāb* were always subject to discussion and potential approval of the opponent, formal arguments in *istidlāl* were either unqualifiedly embraced by the *uṣūlist* or totally ignored. Thus, unlike *istiḥsān*, for instance, formal arguments were expounded in certain *uṣūl* works without the usual mention of the opponents' claims or the proponents' vindication. They were briefly set forth in the manner logical principles were exposed in manuals of logic.

The inclusion of formal arguments in the chapter on *istidlāl* in a number of *uṣūl al-fiqh* works was, to be sure, a later development. At first, particularly during the sixth/twelfth century, it was in the introductory pages of those *uṣūl* works which admitted the Greek logical element that such arguments appeared. In other words, prior to incorporating formal arguments in the chapter of *istidlāl* (which was ordinarily placed towards the end of the treatise), there existed, and continued to exist, a preliminary attempt at introducing Greek, and especially Aristotelian logic, into legal theory in the form of an introduction to this discipline. This attempt can be clearly seen in such influential works as those of Ibn Qudāma (d. 620/1223), Ibn al-Ḥājib (d. 646/1248), Ibn al-Humām (d. 861/1456) and others.[7]

To trace this trend from its start, we must begin with Ghazālī, who was, as intimated above, the first jurist in Sunnī Islam to have integrated logic into legal theory to a large extent.[8] In the beginning

[7] Works on *uṣūl al-fiqh* are deemed influential when they are referred to frequently in subsequent works, and are subject to commentary by later authors. See further note 22 below.

[8] See Ibrahim Madkour, *L'Organon d'Aristote dans le monde Arabe*, Paris, 1934, pp. 262 ff. Some elements of Greek logic have already crept into *uṣūl al-fiqh* works prior to Ghazālī. The writings of Abū Bakr al-Jaṣṣāṣ (d. 370/980) and Imām al-Ḥaramayn al-Juwaynī (d. 478/1085), for instance, seem to reflect respectively some Stoic and Aristotelian influences. On Jaṣṣāṣ see Nabil Shehaby, «The Influence of Stoic Logic on al-Jaṣṣāṣ's Legal Theory,» in John E. Murdoch and Edith D. Sylla, eds., *The Cultural Context of Medieval Learning*, Dordrecht-Boston, 1975, pp. 61-85; on Juwaynī see I. Madkour, «La logique d'Aristote chez les Motakallimin,» in M. Mohaghegh and T. Izutsu, eds., *Collected Texts and Papers on Logic and Language*, Tehran, 1974, pp. 29-46, at 34; ʿAlī Sāmī Nashshār, *Manāhij al-Baḥth ʿinda Mufakkirī l-Islām*, Cairo, 1978, pp. 73, 83-84.

Over half a century before Ghazālī wrote on logic in law, the Andalusian Muḥammad Ibn Ḥazm (d. 456/1062) had already written at least one treatise on

of his *Mustaṣfā*,[9] he delivers a manual on logic, being the shortest in a trilogy whose other two parts are *Miḥakk*[10] and *Miʿyār*[11]. Although he makes the reading of this introductory treatise entirely voluntary, he asserts in the most unequivocal manner that he who has no knowledge of logic has, in effect, no knowledge of any science.[12] When he proceeds into the legal part of *al-Mustaṣfā*, however, no sign of any formal logical analysis can be detected and his treatment stands perfectly within the convention of classical *uṣūl al-fiqh*. What Ghazālī obviously intended in this treatise was not to revolutionize legal analysis but rather to insist on the necessity of logic as the only meaningful tool by which all inferences can be tightly molded according to a rational design. This is a remarkable retreat in comparison with his approach to the subject in his earlier works *al-Miʿyār* and, particularly, *Shifāʾ al-Ghalīl* in which he had analyzed legal arguments in terms of syllogistics.[13] It is instructive to note that the first of these two treatises is essentially an introduction to Aristotelian logic, and the second is a legal work treating of causation in law.

Apart from a number of brief notes made throughout *al-Miʿyār* on legal theory, Ghazālī illustrates the three figures of categorical syllogism together with their moods with examples drawn not only from philosophy and theology but also from law. This is also done in the case of conjunctive and disjunctive syllogisms, *reductio ad absurdum* and induction.[14] It is quite obvious that with these

---

logic with multiple legal examples. Such examples were not advanced merely for the purpose of illustration. Logic, Ibn Ḥazm asserted, is most useful in interpreting the Quran and the Sunna, and in drawing legal inferences. Those who do not comprehend such a simple fact have indeed distanced themselves from religion, and should not be allowed to decide in legal matters. See the significantly entitled *al-Taqrīb li-Ḥadd al-Manṭiq wa l-Madkhal Ilayhi bi-l-Alfāẓ al-ʿĀmmiyya wa l-Amthila l-Fiqhiyya*, ed. Iḥsān ʿAbbās, Beirut, 1959, pp. 9-10; A. Chejne, «Ibn Ḥazm of Cordova on Logic,» *The Journal of the American Oriental Society*, 104, 1 (1984), pp. 52-72, especially at 62-63.

[9] 2 vols., Cairo, 1322 H., I, 10-55.

[10] Eds. M. Naʿsānī and Muṣṭafā al-Qabbānī, Cairo, n.d.

[11] Ed. Sulaymān Dunyā, Cairo, 1961.

[12] Ghazālī, *Mustaṣfā*, I, 10, l. 17. This is reminiscent of Ibn Ḥazm's aforementioned assertion that those who do not come to grips with logic must not be trusted with religious and legal matters. See note 8 above.

[13] *Shifāʾ al-Ghalīl fī Bayān al-Shabah wa l-Mukhīl wa-Masālik al-Taʿlīl*, ed. Ḥamd al-Kabīsī, Baghdad, 1971, pp. 435-455, translated below.

[14] Ghazālī, *Miʿyār*, pp. 134-165. See also Hassan Abdel-Rahman, «La place du syllogisme juridique dans la méthode exégétique chez Gazali,» in *Le Raisonnement Juridique*, ed. H. Hubien, Bruxelles, 1971, pp. 187 ff.

examples Ghazālī was merely trying to bring closer to the mind of jurists an understanding of the structure of these inferences. There is no attempt at analyzing legal cases through the medium of these arguments. Nor is there any effort at identifying, in terms of the established theory of logic, the distinctive structure of legal logic. The sole exception, however, concerns analogy, which Ghazālī, following the tradition of Aristotle, insisted that in order for it to be logically valid, it must be converted to first figure syllogism.[15] In a chapter in *Shifāʾ al-Ghalīl* he goes further in this direction towards the formalization of legal logic and attempts an analysis of a wider variety of legal arguments in terms of syllogistics (see Part II).[16]

As it will become evident, Ghazālī's conception of the relationship between logic and law as expressed in his *Mustaṣfā* seems to have put the final stamp on the attitudes of a number of his successors towards the role of logic in law. These successors, however, exercised a great deal of caution in introducing to their *uṣūl* works the principles of logical theory as expounded by Ghazālī. While following Ghazālī faithfully, they have, with remarkable discretion, chosen the most relevant parts of the theory to introduce it to their jurisprudence. Despite Ghazālī's declared effort[17] at keeping the size of the logical introduction in the *Mustaṣfā* to a minimum, the end result remained a clearly independent treatise on logic. And like any standard Arabic manual on logic, this introduction begins with the exposition of the theory of definition (*ḥadd*)[18] and the rules governing its use and validity. The theory of syllogistics (*burhān*) is then stated with the familiar three figures and their moods, conditional hypothetical syllogism and finally conditional disjunctive syllogism (*al-sabr wa l-taqsīm* or *taʿānud*). In a later section of the treatise, he discusses the types of premises in demonstrative arguments with special emphasis on the criteria according to which a premise is determined to be certain or probable. And like any other standard manual on logic, the discussion of induction and analogy comes subsequent to the exposition of demonstrative arguments. In addition to the point which he already made in *al-Miʿyār* about the validation of analogy by means of its conversion

[15] *Ibid.*, pp. 165 ff.
[16] Ghazālī, *Shifāʾ al-Ghalīl*, pp. 435-455.
[17] Ghazālī, *Mustaṣfā*, I, 10, ll. 16-17.
[18] See note 25 below.

to the first figure, Ghazālī follows the Aristotelians in relegating induction to the ranks of inconclusive sciences. He asserts that when it is perfect, induction as such loses its identity since it necessarily reverts to categorical syllogism.[19]

The fundamental issue which Ghazālī does not fail to address in more than four of his aforecited works, particularly *al-Mustaṣfā* and *Shifāʾ al-Ghalīl*, is the differing terminology concerning two arguments common to both disciplines *uṣūl* and logic.[20] When the *ʿilla* is efficient in the major term, the argument is known to philosophers as *burhān al-limā* and to jurists as *qiyās al-ʿilla*. When the *ʿilla* is non-causal, the argument is known to philosophers as *burhān liʾanna* and to jurists as *qiyās al-dalāla*. The form of juridical argument is therefore identical to the logicians' formal argument. The difference between them, however, lies in quality of material premises (*muqaddimāt*) used in legal and rational arguments. «The premises which are suitable for rational *qiyās* (demonstration) are suitable for juridical *qiyās*, but not all the premises which are suitable for juridical *qiyās* are suitable for rational *qiyās*.»[21] The conversion of a probable legal premise to a conclusive one requires its 'universalization'; that is, the extention of the rule governing a particular case to the species in which this case is only an instance. This granted, the form of legal argument will be no different from the formally rational argument. In fact, aside from the thorny probelm of the logical validity of the 'universalized' major premise, this is the very process by which nonformal legal arguments are formalized (see part II and the introduction thereto).

II

Ghazālī's singular contribution to legal logic was certainly instrumental in bringing about certain structural changes in a good number of authoritative *uṣūl al-fiqh* works.[22] Just as he conceived of

---

[19] Ghazālī, *Mustaṣfā*, I, 51-52.

[20] *Ibid.*, I, 54-55; idem., *Shifāʾ*, pp. 435 ff., (part II below); *Miʿyār*, pp. 243 ff.; *Miḥakk al-Naẓar*, pp. 70 ff.

[21] Ghazālī, *Miʿyār*, p. 202. Further on *qiyās al-li'anna* and *qiyās al-limā*, see note 68 to the translation in Part II.

[22] Among these are the works of Sayf al-Dīn al-Āmidī and Ibn al-Ḥājib. On their paramount importance and popularity see the statement of Jamāl al-Dīn al-Isnawī, *Nihāyat al-Sūl fī Sharḥ Minhāj al-Wuṣūl*, printed on the margin of Ibn Amīr al-Ḥājj's commentary, *al-Taqrīr wa l-Taḥbīr*, 3 vols., Cairo, 1316 H., I, 3-4. The eighth/fourteenth century scholar Muḥammad b. Ibrāhīm Ibn al-Wazīr al-

logic as the valid organon of any inferential procedure, and thus prefaced his *Mustaṣfā* with a manual on formal logic and insisted upon the conversion of analogy into first figure syllogism, we find many of his successors employing logic to ground legal theory in what is fundamentally an Aristotelian conception of knowledge. The eighth/fourteenth century Ḥanbalī intellectual Taqī l-Dīn Ibn Taymiyya disapprovingly testified that those jurists and theologians who treated of law in this manner did so under the influence of Ghazālī.[23]

The Ḥanbalī jurist Muwaffaq al-Dīn Ibn Qudāma (d. 620/1223), a staunch advocate of Traditionalist Islam,[24] is the earliest legal theorist known to us to follow in the footsteps of Ghazālī in integrating logic into law. While Ghazālī makes the reading of his introduction optional, Ibn Qudāma, like many of his younger contemporaries and successors, incorporated the fundamentals of logic as part and parcel of his legal treatise. In his *Rawḍa*, logic is introduced into law in a manner bolder than that adopted by Ghazālī. Following the Aristotelian (-Stoic) division of knowledge into *taṣawwur* (*conceptio*) and *taṣdīq* (*verificatio* or judgment),[25] Ibn Qudāma briefly expounds in the first pages of his book the theory of definition (*ḥadd*) and categorical and conditional syllogism.[26] Perception of things, according to him, obtains either through definition or demonstration. The intellect first perceives individual

---

Yamānī observed that Ibn al-Ḥājib's *Mukhtaṣar* was the object of seventy commentaries. It is significant that Yamānī flourished only less than two centuries after Ibn al-Ḥājib. See his *Īthār al-Ḥaqq ʿalā l-Khalq*, Cairo, 1318 H., p. 200, ll. 11-12. For a similar statement see Ījī's *Sharḥ Mukhtaṣar Ibn al-Ḥājib*, ed. Sh. M. Ismāʿīl, 2 vols., Cairo, 1973, I, 5, ll. 2-17 (on the margin).

[23] Taqī l-Dīn Ibn Taymiyya, *Kitāb al-Radd ʿalā l-Manṭiqiyyīn*, ed. ʿAbduṣ-Ṣamad al-Kutubī, Bombay, 1949, pp. 14-15, 118, ll. 10-11; see also Jalāl al-Dīn al-Suyūṭī's abridgement of the same work entitled *Jahd al-Qarīḥa fī Tajrīd al-Naṣīḥa*, ed. ʿAlī Sāmī l-Nashshār, Cairo, 1947, pp. 286-287.

[24] See his *Taḥrīm al-Naẓar fī Kutub Ahl al-Kalām*, ed. and trans. G. Makdisi, London, 1962, as well as the introduction to the work by the editor.

[25] On these concepts and their origins in Greek philosophy see Harry A. Wolfson, «The Terms *Taṣawwur* and *Taṣdīq* in Arabic Philosophy and their Greek, Latin and Hebrew Equivalents» *The Muslim World*, XXXIII, 2 (1943), 114-128; Fehmi Jadaane, *L'influence du stoïcisme sur la pensée musulmane*, Beyrouth, 1968, 106 ff.; Nashshār, *Manāhij*, p. 37. Among other possible translations for the terms *taṣawwur* and *taṣdīq* are «assent» and «concept». See Charles E. Butterworth, *Averroes' Three Short Commentaries on Aristotle's «Topics,» «Rhetoric,» and «Poetics»*, Albany, 1977, p. 103, par. 1, nn. 1-2.

[26] Muwaffaq al-Dīn Ibn Qudāma, *Rawḍat al-Nāẓir wa-Jannat al-Munāẓir fī Uṣūl al-Fiqh*, Beirut, 1981, pp. 14, 18-19.

matters, such as the knowledge of the meaning of 'world', 'eternity' and 'createdness'. Further knowledge then obtains by predicating these individual matters on each other, thus formulating, for instance, the knowledge expressed in the statement 'the world is created,' or 'the world is eternal.' Unlike the knowledge of the meaning of 'world' and 'createdness' which is not subject to affirmation or denial, the knowledge which results in a judgement, e.g., 'the world is created', may be true or false. The first type, known as *taṣawwur*, is acquired through definition, and the second, known as *taṣdīq*, is acquired through demonstrative syllogism (*burhān*).[27]

In order to relate the inferences through which *taṣdīq* obtains to legal matters, Ibn Qudāma explains that the term *burhān* is used for inferences in which the two premises are certain, while probable premises make up what he terms *qiyās fiqhī* (juridical inference). He hastens to add, however, that assigning the term *qiyās* to legal argument is merely a metaphorical usage, for the form and structure of this argument does not differ from that of demonstrative syllogism in that they both require the subsumption of a particular under a general (*idrāju khuṣūṣin taḥta ʿumūm*). *Qiyās*, on the other hand, literally means measuring a thing by another, an inference which for Ibn Qudāma seems incapable of attaining the knowledge defined under the category of *taṣdīq*.[28] Thus, despite the given difference with regard to the certitude of the premises, the form of juridical inference is identical to that of demonstrative syllogism.

Syllogistics, Ibn Qudāma argues, stand as the methodological foundation of the knowledge of any science, be it rational or legal.[29] They are the only sound criteria for any inference. Accordingly, he proceeds to delineate these syllogisms, the conditions for their validity, and the manner in which they may serve in legal matters. For him then there are five types of syllogisms, three of which are categorical, one hypothetical and one disjunctive.[30] Using no

---

[27] Some scholars assigned to these concepts the terms *maʿrifa* and *ʿilm* instead of *taṣawwur* and *taṣdīq*. See Ibn Qudāma, *Rawḍa*, p. 14, ll. 9-10; Wolfson, «The Terms *Taṣawwur* and *Taṣdīq*...,» p. 114. On acquiring *taṣdīq* by means other than syllogism see the following note.

[28] Ibn Qudāma, *Rawḍa*, p. 22, ll. 15-19. Fakhr al-Dīn al-Rāzī (d. 606/1209), *Lubāb al-Ishārāt*, ed. ʿAbd al-Ḥāfiẓ Saʿd ʿAṭiyya, Cairo, 1355 H., p. 3, ll. 2-3, 30, l. 7, states that *taṣdīq* is obtained not only through syllogism (*qiyās*), but also through induction (*istiqrāʾ*) and analogy (*tamthīl*).

[29] *Ibid.*, p. 25.

[30] *Ibid.*, pp. 22-25.

technical terminology for categorical syllogism, Ibn Qudāma begins by casting an example of the first type of syllogism:

All intoxicants are forbidden
All wines are intoxicants

Therefore, all wines are forbidden

Explaining that the category of 'wine' is the thing being judged and prohibition is the judgement, he then excludes from the conclusion the term which is repeated in the minor and major premises. This term, he remarks, is known as the *ʿilla* which represents the answer to the question 'Why is wine prohibited?' An affirmative major and a universal minor are prerequisites for the validity of such an inference.

The second and third categorical syllogisms are in the second and third figures, respectively. As expounded by Ibn Qudāma, however, the first type of syllogism does not conform to the structure of the first figure. For, although the major and minor premises are universal, the position of the middle term in the premises follows the arrangement of the fourth figure. This poses the question of whether or not our author confused the first figure with the fourth. This is likely to have happened since the reducibility of figures was a common practice.[31] At any rate, the same argument can well be cast in the first figure as illustrated above.

In the second figure, the *ʿilla* plays the role of the predicate in both premises. The conclusion that 'A Muslim must not be given the death penalty if he kills a non-Muslim' emerges from the argument that non-Muslims are not equal to Muslims and that punishing by death a killer indicates that the man killed is a Muslim. For the validity of this mode, Ibn Qudāma observes, one of the premises must be negative and the other affirmative, and the major must always be universal. In such a syllogism the conclusion is necessarily negative.

The *ʿilla* in the third figure, known to jurists as *naqḍ*, is the subject of both premises. Ibn Qudāma gives the following example:

---

[31] Nicholas Rescher observes that from the standpoint of the Aristotelian construction of syllogism, there is no possibility of anything more or less than three figures. The fourth figure is simply part of the first. This may explain Ibn Qudāma's confusion. See his article «New Light from Arabic Sources on Galen and the Fourth Figure of the Syllogism,» *Journal of the History of Philosophy*, Vol. III, 1965, pp. 27-41, at 35.

All wheat is usurious
All wheat is an edible foodstuff

Therefore, some edible foodstuffs are usurious

The fourth argument in Ibn Qudāma's arrangement is conditional hypothetical syllogism, which he terms *talāzum*. Again without using the technical terminology of the logicians or the *uṣūlī*-logicians, he distinguishes two types, the *modus ponens* and the *modus tollens*. An example of the first type is:

If this prayer is valid then ablution was performed
This prayer is valid

Therefore, ablution was performed

In the *modus tollens* the consequent of the major premise is denied, i.e., 'Ablution was not performed,' thereby yielding the conclusion 'The prayer is not valid'. In this argument, the consequent, ablution, is predicated upon the validity of prayer; when ablution is performed prayer is valid, and when it is not performed prayer is invalid. Therefore, the consequent is a prerequisite for the antecedent; to have the second exist requires the existence of the first, and the absence of the first indicates the absence of the second, not vice versa. To argue that

If this prayer is valid then ablution was performed
Ablution was performed

Therefore, this prayer is valid

would be fallacious, for prayer may be rendered invalid by another factor unrelated to ablution. The same fallacy may be committed if the minor premise were 'This prayer is not valid'. Such an arrangement does not yield a valid conclusion. The governing principle of this syllogism is that the consequent must be inclusive of, or at least equal to, the antecedent. When the particular (antecedent) is affirmed the general (consequent) is also necessarily affirmed, and when the general is denied the particular is also denied. By the same token, the affirmation of the general does not lead to the affirmation of the particular. Nor does the denying of the particular lead to the denying of the general. In the statement 'All animals are corporeal,' affirming the existence of animality would necessarily affirm the existence of corporeality, and denying corporeality would certainly deny animality. An argument affirming the contrary cannot serve.[32]

The aforementioned *al-sabr wa l-taqsīm* ranks as the fifth and last syllogism in Ibn Qudāma's exposition. Having the characteristics of conditional disjunctive syllogism, *al-sabr wal-taqsīm* presupposes the decomposition of a given matter into all of its possible constituent elements, and by affirming one or a set of elements the rest of the elements are denied. For example, one may argue that the universe is either eternal or created. But the universe is created; therefore it is not eternal. Or that it is eternal; therefore, the universe is not created. To ascertain the validity of the conclusion about the given matter, an exhaustive account of all the possibilities which may constitute or affect that particular matter is deemed a prerequisite. In other words, leaving out of consideration a third possibility in the example of the universe may nullify the conclusion since the truth of the matter of creation may rest with the third excluded possibility.[33]

Arguments in all fields of knowledge, Ibn Qudāma asserts, must conform to the rules herein set. When they do not, it is only because the proper arrangement of the premises has been neglected, or because a premise has been suppressed. Suppressing a premise, Ibn Qudāma avers, is quite common in legal argument, because being so evident, the premise is taken for granted. A lawyer may thus argue that a man must be stoned to death because he committed adultery while enjoying the status of *muḥṣan* (being a free man and married, or having been married, to a free woman). Suppressed here is the major premise, viz., 'All *muḥṣan* adulterers must be stoned to death.' Similarly, lawyers often analogically argue that since grape-wine is intoxicating, it is forbidden, just like date-wine. Following in the footsteps of Ghazālī, Ibn Qudāma insists that analogy cannot be valid unless reduced to first figure syllogism.[34] This last observation must by no means be underrated, for it not only illustrates the persistence of the Ghazālian thesis of the paramount position of syllogistics, but also demonstrates that for Ibn Qudāma there are no valid arguments in law unless they can be

---

[32] Ibn Qudāma, *Rawḍa*, pp. 24-25. On the rules of conditional syllogism see Joseph G. Brennan, *A Handbook of Logic*, New York, 1957, pp. 79 ff.

[33] Ibn Qudāma, *Rawḍa*, p. 25.

[34] *Ibid.*, p. 26, ll. 8-10.

reduced to one or the other of the formal arguments which he has just expounded.

III

Though Ibn Qudāma went a step beyond Ghazālī in integrating the formal precepts of logic into the body of legal theory,[35] he remained within the general boundaries which Ghazālī had already set. We thus find no attempt on Ibn Qudāma's part to alter what is otherwise a conventional treatment of legal theory.

The early beginings of a somewhat different approach towards integrating logic into law can already be detected in Ibn Qudāma's younger Shāfiʿī contemporary Sayf al-Dīn al-Āmidī (d. 631/1233), who was heavily involved in the study of logic alongside the traditional sciences.[36] Āmidī begins his work *al-Iḥkām* by defining *uṣūl al-fiqh* and its relationship to the sciences upon which it draws. The absence of an exposition of formal logic in Āmidī's opening pages must not obscure the fact that espistemologically he was committed to the formal conception of legal science. This is evident even in the introductory pages where he asserts, in the tradition of Aristotle (and the Stoics), that knowledge of any science obtains either through *taṣawwur* or through *taṣdīq*.[37] Obviously it is by means of the latter that unspecified legal rulings are inferred from the revealed premises. An indispensable instrument in this process of inference is the legal indicant, the *dalīl*, which presents itself in three forms: rational, revelational and a combination of both.[38] The rational indicant, mostly used in theological discussions, leads to knowledge on grounds of rational premises, e.g., 'The universe is composite,' and 'All composite things are created'; therefore, 'The universe is created.' The revelational indicant is that which is derived either directly from the Quran, the Sunna or consensus, or indirectly through *qiyās*. But that which combines both the purely

---

[35] *Ibid.*, pp. 262 ff. for further analysis of arguments in light of formal logic.

[36] On Āmidī's career see the biographical notices in Tāj al-Dīn Ibn Taqī l-Dīn al-Subkī, *Ṭabaqāt al-Shāfiʿiyya l-Kubrā*, 6 vols., Cairo, 1906, V, 129-130; Shams al-Dīn Aḥmad Ibn Khallikān, *Wafayāt al-Aʿyān wa Anbāʾ Abnāʾ al-Zamān*, ed. Muḥammad ʿAbd al-Ḥamīd, 6 vols., Cairo, 1948, II, 455-456.

[37] Sayf al-Dīn al-Āmidī, *al-Iḥkām fī Uṣūl al-Aḥkām*, 3 vols., Cairo, 1968, I, 7, l. 11.

[38] *Ibid.*, I, 8, ll. 16-17.

rational and the purely revelational is what can be characterized as a formal argument taking its premises from revelation.[39]

The argument cast in the first figure about the prohibition of wine is a classic example of an inference grounded in a rational-revelational *dalīl*. This type of *dalīl* constitutes for Āmidī the basis of a category of inferences independent of *qiyās*, a category which he terms *istidlāl*.[40] Āmidī discusses several inferences under the heading of *istidlāl*, the third of which concerns itself with the *dalīl* that consists of propositions which, if admitted to be true, result in a true conclusion. Unlike Ibn Qudāma who does not use the technical terminology of the logicians, Āmidī freely employs such terminology in his discussion of formal arguments.

Following the Aristotelian division of syllogistics, Āmidī recognizes categorical conjunctive syllogism (*iqtirānī*), conditional disjunctive (*sharṭī munfaṣil*) and conditional hypothetical syllogism (*sharṭī muttaṣil*). Categorical conjunctive syllogism, consisting of two premises and a conclusion, must have one term repeated in both premises. This term, known as the middle term (*al-ḥadd al-awsaṭ*), determines, depending upon its position in the minor and major premises, the figure of syllogism. In the first figure, the middle term stands as the subject of the major and the predicate of the minor. In the second, it takes the position of the predicate in both premises, and in the third the subject. The fourth figure has the middle term as the predicate of its major and the subject of its minor. Āmidī finds the fourth figure superfluous, capable of providing nothing that is not already found in the first three figures.[41] In fact, just as Aristotle made his assertion that the first figure is the source of all other figures, and that the fourth is a mere variation on the theme of the first, Āmidī insists that the first figure is the most demonstrative (*abyanuhā*) and constitutes the real basis for the construction of all other figures.

The first figure, Āmidī states, lends itself to four moods (*ḍurūb*), the first of which has two universal affirmative premises and a universal affirmative conclusion. He gives the following example:

All acts of worship require intent (*niyya*)
[All] ritual ablution is an act of worship

Therefore, [all] ritual ablution requires intent

---

[39] *Ibid.*, I, 8, ll. 21-22. See also III, 175, l. 11, where he reintroduces the same concept under the category of *istidlāl*.
[40] *Ibid.*, III, 175.
[41] *Ibid.*, III, 177, ll. 1-2.

In the second mood, the major and the conclusion are universal negative. Thus:

No act of worship is valid without intent
[All] ritual ablution is an act of worship

Therefore, no ritual ablution is valid without intent

When the major, however, is universal affirmative, and the minor is particular affirmative, the syllogism acquires a different mood with a particular affirmative conclusion:

All acts of worship require intent
Some ritual ablution is an act of worship

Therefore, some ritual ablution requires intent

Āmidī's fourth mood consists of a universal negative major, a particular affirmative minor and a particular negative conclusion. Thus, using the same basic legal example:

No act of worship is valid without intent
Some ritual ablution is an act of worship

Therefore, some ritual ablution is invalid without intent

The four moods of the second figure have one quality in common, namely, a universal major. When the major is negative and the minor is universal affirmative, the conclusion is universal negative, as in the following example:

No sale is valid if the identity of the sold commodity is unknown
All sales of non-existent commodities are sales of commodities which are unknown

---

Therefore, no sale of non-existent commodity is valid

From a universal affirmative major and a universal negative minor of the above legal propositions, one reaches the same conclusion. But a particular negative conclusion, i.e., 'Some sales of non-existent commodities are invalid,' results in the third mood of the second figure, where the major is universal negative and the minor is particular affirmative. Likewise, the same conclusion may be reached in the fourth mood on the basis of a universal affirmative major and a particular negative minor.[42]

---

[42] *Ibid.*, III, 177-178.

The notable characteristics of the six moods of the third figure are their having in common an affirmative minor and at least one universal premise. Their conclusions are always particular, whether negative or affirmative. It suffices here to illustrate these moods by presenting examples of the first and the fourth moods, as these two share, respectively, the same conclusions as those of the second and third, and the fifth and sixth. The following is an example of the first mood which consists of two universal affirmative premises and a particular affirmative conclusion:

All wheat is an edible foodstuff
All wheat is usurious

Therefore, some edible foodstuffs are usurious

The fourth mood consists of a negative universal major and an affirmative universal minor with a particular negative conclusion:

No wheat can be bartered for an unequal quantity (of the same kind of wheat)
All wheat is an edible foodstuff

Therefore, no edible foodstuff can be bartered for an unequal quantity (of its own kind)

Premises structurally different from those used in categorical syllogism must, in order to be valid, be cast in a different type of syllogism. In Āmidī's arrangement, the next two important syllogisms after the categorical are the conditional conjunctive ('If ... then ...') and conditional disjunctive ('Either ... or ...'). Ibn Qudāma has already expounded the conditions for their validity.

IV

The Mālikī jurist Jamāl al-Dīn Ibn al-Ḥājib (d. 646/1248), a young contemporary of Āmidī, conceives the logical and epistemological foundation of the discipline of *uṣūl al-fiqh* in a like manner. In his legal works he firmly anchors the methodology of legal analysis and interpretation in the dichotomous conception of *taṣawwur* and *taṣdīq*. This, of course, is no innovation over his two predecessors Ibn Qudāma and Āmidī, but it appears from the extensive commentaries and super-commentaries on his *Mukhtaṣar* by Ījī (d. 756/1355), Taftāzānī (d. 791/1388), Jurjānī (d. 816/1413) and Harawī (probably died after the eighth/fourteenth century) that Ibn al-Ḥājib managed to secure a greater role for this dichotomy of the typology of the acquisition of knowledge in legal theory. The ultimate goal of this theory is the discovery of the law of God from the primary sources, and the means of such discovery, Ibn al-Ḥājib asserts, is the *dalīl*. The process of reaching the rule of a case which had not been stipulated in the sources belongs to the *taṣdīq* category of acquiring knowledge.[43] In this context of dealing with inferences from things known about the things unknown, Ibn al-Ḥājib expounds, in the same relative detail as Āmidī and Ibn Qudāma, the types of syllogisms, including the fourth figure of categorical syllogism which Āmidī deemed superfluous.[44]

Unlike Āmidī who touches only briefly on the concept of knowledge and the means of its acquisition in the beginning of his work, and who leaves syllogistics to be discussed later under the heading *istidlāl*, Ibn al-Ḥājib sets out by expounding syllogistics and the concept of knowledge while elaborating a different set of formal arguments in the chapter of *istidlāl*. Both Āmidī and Ibn al-Ḥājib generally define *istidlāl* as a means of inference other than *qiyās*, consensus or the two primary sources. But Ibn al-Ḥājib qualifies this definition by limiting *qiyās* here to the *qiyās al-ᶜilla*, that which is based on an efficient common cause. With this he asserts that *istidlāl* is the *fifth source* of Islamic law,[45] thus implying, as the commentator Taftazānī observes, that other types of *qiyās*, such as the *qiyāses* known as *nafy al-fāriq* and *talāzum*, come under *istidlāl*. (Like Āmidī, he also subsumes *istiṣḥāb* and the pre-Islamic laws—*sharᶜ man qablanā*—under *istidlāl*).[46] The *qiyās* of *nafy al-fāriq*, known to Ibn Idrīs al-Shāfiᶜī as *qiyās fī maᶜnā al-aṣl*, may be described as an analogical inference in which the differences between the two cases are shown to be irrelevant to the cause (*ᶜilla*) and the rule (*ḥukm*) of the case. The sexual difference between a concubine and a male slave, for example, must be dismissed as irrelevant in the case of contractual manumission (*ᶜatq*). Likewise, the impurity brought

---

[43] Taftāzānī, *Ḥāshiya*, I, 34-35; al-Sayyid al-Sharīf al-Jurjānī, *Ḥāshiya ᶜalā Sharḥ al-ᶜAḍud al-Ījī*, a commentary on Ibn al-Ḥājib's *Muntahā l-Wuṣūl wa l-Amal*, (printed with the *Ḥāshiya* of Taftāzānī), I, 36, ll. 11-13.

[44] Jamāl al-Dīn Ibn al-Ḥājib, *Muntahā l-Wuṣūl wa l-Amal fī ᶜIlmay al-Uṣūl wa l-Jadal*, ed. M. Naᶜsānī, Cairo, 1326 H., pp. 6-11, especially 8-10; the *Ḥāshiyas* of Taftāzānī and Jurjānī, pp. 84-115.

[45] Ibn al-Ḥājib, *Muntahā*, p. 33, l. 3.

[46] *Ibid.*, p. 151, last two lines; Taftāzānī, *Ḥāshiya*, II, 280.

about by a mouse falling in oil or clarified butter is effective in both foodstuffs in spite of the differences in their texture.[47]

The chief formal argument of *istidlāl*, however, is the *talāzum* (concomitance) between the rules of two cases without the specification of an efficient *ʿilla*. The inference of concomitance lends itself to a fourfold division, the first of which is what may be termed as coextensiveness (*ṭard*) and coexclusiveness (*ʿaks*), known together as the method of *dawarān*.[48] In the example of corporeality and compositeness it may be argued that all corporeal things are composite and all composite things are corporeal; likewise, it may be argued that whenever there is no corporeality there is no compositeness and whenever there are no composite things there are no corporeal things either. In the case of divorce and temporary separation (*ẓihār*), the course of reasoning is as follows: He whose divorce is valid, his temporary separation is valid and he whose temporary separation is valid, his divorce is valid. The argument gains additional strength by negatively reasoning that he whose divorce is invalid, his temporary separation is invalid and vice versa.[49]

The second consists of coextensiveness only, as in the example of created corporeality. Here, it is argued that all corporeal things are created, but not all created things are corporeal. Likewise, if *wuḍūʾ* (ablution) is accepted as valid without *niyya* (intent), then *tayammum* (ablution with soil or sand) is also accepted as valid without intent. The third is essentially the coexclusiveness of contradictions; what is true cannot be false and what is prohibited cannot be permissible. The fourth corresponds to the third but is negative in its postulate; e.g., what is not permitted is illicit.[50]

Although these inferences differ from the strictly syllogistic arguments expounded by Āmidī in the chapter of *istidlāl*, they can be reduced, as the commentator Ījī remarks, to disjunctive and conjunctive conditional syllogisms.[51] In fact, these arguments and the principles of coexistence and coexclusion according to which they

---

[47] Taftāzānī, *Ḥāshiya*, II, 280, ll. 5 from bottom and p. 281, l. 9; Ibn Qudāma, *Rawḍa*, p. 262, ll. 12-14.

[48] See Tahānawī, *Kashshāf*, s.v. «*dawarān*», I, 469.

[49] Ibn al-Ḥājib, *Muntahā*, p. 152, ll. 4-7; Taftāzānī, *Ḥāshiya*, II, 281-283 (for the example about divorce see p. 282, ll. 4-5 from bottom).

[50] Taftāzānī, *Ḥāshiya*, II, 283, ll. 13-19.

[51] Ījī, *Sharḥ*, II, 282, ll. 3-5.

operate are identical to the procedures employed in verifying the *ʿilla* of the original case (*aṣl*) in *qiyās*.[52]

V

All this goes to confirm Ibn al-Ḥājib's (and his commentators') commitment to formal arguments. In the long-standing tradition of *uṣūlists*, he affirms that *uṣūl al-fiqh* derives from the five legal norms (*al-aḥkām al-khamsa*), the established general principles of *kalām* and the Arabic language. Taftāzānī observes that Ibn al-Ḥājib, when dealing with *kalām* as one of the fundaments of *uṣūl*, had nothing to say about central theological issues such as belief, the truthfulness of the Prophet, miracles, etc. Instead, he discussed under *kalām* problems of knowledge and reasoning which are as pertinent to *kalām* as they are to any other science.[53] Jurjānī further explains that Ibn al-Ḥājib dwelled on logic under the guise of *kalām* because law, being a religious science, cannot be grounded in a science as alien as logic, and since *kalām*, the crown of religious sciences, has come to be inclusive of logic, it is used as a cover under which logic is subsumed. This, he says, makes obvious the fact that what is really at stake here is the need for logic in legal theory, a need which «al-Imām al-Ghazālī alluded to in the *Mustaṣfā*.»[54] In his super-commentary on Jurjānī, Harawī resents this play on words and seems to demand that the issue be addressed even more openly and directly. He remarks that

> These scholars went out of their way and placed restrictions on the principles of logic, restrictions which (aim at) removing these principles from the domain of logic. Furthermore, they claimed them to be part of *kalām*, in order that legal science, the chief of religious sciences, would not look as if it were in need of a non-religious science. But the fact is that all these (religious) sciences are in need of logic.
>
> Those who argue that the theological principles which are needed in *uṣūl* are (an intrinsic) part of *kalām* have erred, because these principles are of no service except in theological issues. But what is of service in legal theory is nothing (of these issues) but logic.[55]

This bold argument affirming the centrality of logic in legal theory is stated even more forcefully by the Ḥanafī jurist Muḥam-

---

[52] Taftāzānī, *Ḥāshiya*, II, 283, ll. 27-28.

[53] *Ibid.*, I, 38, ll. 10-14.

[54] Jurjānī, *Ḥāshiya*, I, 38-39. On Ghazālī see p. 38, ll. 25-26.

[55] Ḥasan al-Harawī, *Ḥāshiya ʿalā Ḥāshiyat al-Muḥaqqiq al-Sayyid al-Sharīf al-Jurjānī*, (printed with Taftāzānī's and Jurjānī's *Ḥāshiyas*), I, 39, ll. 30-34.

mad b. ʿAbd al-Wāḥid Ibn al-Humām (d. 861/1456) who insists that aside from the Arabic language and legal norms, *uṣūl al-fiqh* draws heavily upon logic. «Calling this a *kalām* principle is far-fetched.»[56] *Kalām* and *uṣūl al-fiqh* equally depend on logic. Logic is necessary for the knowledge of all sciences; it is the only tool for discerning the true from the false. The only question concerned with *kalām* in legal theory, Ibn al-Humām asserts, is perhaps that which pertains to whether good and bad acts are conceived as such by reason or by revelation.[57] Thus, what is termed by other theoreticians as *kalām* principles is not but principles of logic. In line with this conception, Ibn al-Humām, like Ibn Qudāma, Āmidī and Ibn al-Ḥājib, makes sure to delineate the theory of definition and the various types of syllogism (including the fourth figure).[58] In his commentary on Ibn al-Humām's *Taḥrīr*, Ibn Amīr al-Ḥājj follows suit.[59]

Similarly, the two later jurists Muḥammad b. Niẓām al-Dīn al-Anṣārī (d. 1119/1707) and Muḥibb Allāh Ibn ʿAbd al-Shakūr (d. 1225/1810) view logic as one of the three fundamental fields of knowledge upon which legal theory is founded.[60] Their predecessors, they note, have assigned the term *kalām* to this field,

---

[56] al-Kamāl Ibn al-Humām, *al-Taḥrīr fī Uṣūl al-Fiqh*, Cairo, 1351 H., p. 7, ll. 12-13.

[57] Ibn Amīr al-Ḥājj, commenting upon Ibn al-Humām's *Taḥrīr*, observes that in addition to this question there are two other *kalām* issues in *uṣūl al-fiqh*, namely, whether the *mujtahid* is rewarded if he errs and whether it is conceivable for an age to be devoid of a *mujtahid*. See his commentary *al-Taqrīr wa l-Taḥbīr*, I, 39, ll. 26-29. [It is worth mentioning that in my article «On the Origins of the Controversy about the Existence of Mujtahids and the Gate of Ijtihad,» *Studia Islamica*, 63 (1986), I have argued for a theological beginning of the debate about the possibility of the extinction of *mujtahids*. However, this is the first reference I have come across which explicitly states the origins of the debate].

[58] Ibn al-Humām, *Taḥrīr*, 1351 H., pp. 7-15.

[59] Ibn Amīr al-Ḥājj, *al-Taqrīr*, I, 39 ff., 52 ff., 55-65 (on syllogisms).

[60] Muḥammad b. Niẓām al-Dīn al-Anṣārī, *Fawātiḥ al-Raḥamūt*, with the commentary of Muḥibb al-Dīn Ibn ʿAbd al-Shakūr, *Sharḥ Musallam al-Thubūt fī Uṣūl al-Fiqh* (printed with Ghazālī's *Mustaṣfā*), I, 17, ll. 28-32. Commenting on Mullā Khusraw, al-Izmīrī observes that the derivation of solutions for individual legal cases from *uṣūl al-fiqh* is easily achieved through the first figure by applying the general principles of *uṣūl* to the particular cases of positive law. See his *Ḥāshiya ʿalā Sharḥ Mukhtaṣar Mirʾāt al-Uṣūl fī Sharḥ Mirqāt al-Wuṣūl*, 2 vols., Cairo, 1302 H., I, 39.

It is worth noting as well that Anṣārī and Ibn ʿAbd al-Shakūr were among those jurists who attempted to synthesize the Ḥanafī and Shāfiʿī *uṣūl al-fiqh* doctrines. Their work, as testified in the title page, is said to aim at harmonizing the theories of the two schools.

because logic is the tool through which theological conclusions are reached. Without elaborating much further on this point they proceed with a brief discussion of theological, epistemological and logical principles, including categorical and conditional syllogisms.[61]

VI

The infiltration of logic into an important strand of Sunnī jurisprudence heralds a significant change in the attitudes of jurists towards the epistemological status of *uṣūl al-fiqh*. Such an infiltration represents a natural (though not logically necessary) state of development the origins of which may be traced down to the history of the concept of *ʿilm* (knowledge). The interest of *uṣūlists* in the notion of *ʿilm* as the point of departure in the study of their field made its first appearance in the second/eighth century. But it was not until the third/ninth and the beginning of the fourth/tenth century that the concept was developed in the arenas of *kalām* to encompass a variety of categories and methods which soon became part and parcel of the *kalām* oriented *uṣūl al-fiqh*. To the *uṣūlists, ʿilm* meant the knowledge of the law and the methods and procedures which lead to this end. It could not have, therefore, been more fitting than to introduce logic and its sophisticated tools for the enhancement of the existing knowledge about knowledge. It would seem that what logic—as understood, for instance by Ghazālī—had to offer stood in total consonance with the established doctrine of *ʿilm*. Logic was seen as instrumental in grounding legal theory within a larger system of knowledge, a system which was already recognized in the equally authoritative discipline of *kalām*.

Thus in the theories of a number of influential jurists of all schools, logic and its formal arguments served not only as the general epistemological framework of legal theory but also as the guiding methodology of the highest order in reasoning about individual positive legal cases. The theories of the acquisition of knowledge, definition and syllogistics were viewed as universal organons of control through which the precarious position of legal certitude can be strengthened. By means of logic legal argument could be constructed in the most formalized form possible. The

---

[61] Ibn ʿAbd al-Shakūr (with Anṣārī), *Sharḥ*, I, 18-23.

details of legal analogy, one of the most prevalent forms of legal argument, had to fit indirectly in this scheme of formal logic. Insofar as *logical* construction is concerned, analogy was deemed as a consequent or secondary to formal arguments. In the final analysis, analogy, in order to be formally valid, had to conform to the laws of logic. This is perhaps the pivotal point in the process which Ghazālī had started when he affirmed time and again that analogy must ultimately revert to first figure syllogism.

Part II. Formalization of Arguments: Ghazālī on the Modes of Demonstration in Law

Ghazālī regarded legal logic as that part of logic in which legal arguments are subjected to formalization rather than as a logical explication of a peculiar system of arguments. While discarding all Greek philosophical formulations, he tenaciously clinged to formal Aristotelian logic and made it the methodological foundation of all enquiries. His conception of formal logic as an indispensable instrument for all areas of knowledge is evidenced in the fact that the examples which he provides in his logical works extend over a wide spectrum of religious sciences. But in these same works, law and legal examples are often no more than an «illustration» of how a demonstrative argument must be constructed and validated; for, after all, as Ghazālī tells us, «reasoning about legal matters does not differ from reasoning about rational matters ... except in what concerns the premises.»[62] Although for Ghazālī the forms of legal and rational arguments are identical, one looks in vain in his logical works—as well as in the logical-legal treatise *al-Mustaṣfā*—for an analysis of legal arguments from the standpoint of logic. A noteworthy exception, however, is found in his otherwise traditional legal work *Shifāʾ al-Ghalīl*, where in one chapter[63] he analyzes, mostly in terms of syllogistics, three major legal arguments commonly subsumed under juridical *qiyās*; namely, causal demonstration, non-causal (indicative) demonstration and *reductio ad absurdum.*

The central question with which Ghazālī had to grapple was the validity of the essentially inductive character of legal argument. The underlying issue in his discussion of the above mentioned causal and non-causal demonstrations was the cause (*ʿilla*), the

[62] Ghazālī, *Miʿyār*, p. 60, ll. 15-16.
[63] Ghazālī, *Shifāʾ*, pp. 435-45.

term common to the minor and the major premises. In analogical inference, the fundamental problem lies in the obscurity or uncertainty of the distinction between essential and nonesssential elements with regard to two similar matters (or cases). Viewed from the standpoint of formal logic, analogical inference does not rest on logical necessity; that is, the similarity between the two cases is not a fundamental logical relation. A typical analogical argument precludes the syllogistic procedure:

All A is (has the characteristic) C
All B is (has the characteristic) C

Therefore, all B is (must have the characteristic) A

Rather, the similarity in analogical inferences does not necessarily entail the conclusion. As Ghazālī points out repeatedly, the argument for a particular similarity may well be controversial because the typical form of analogical inference is as follows:

All A is (has the characteristic) C
All B is (has the characteristic) D

Therefore, all B is (must have the characteristic) A

In this argument it is assumed that A is similar to B in all essential respects. With this assumption the argument is rendered valid, for if we assume that C and D are sufficiently similar to justify our treating them as one, say C-D, the argument reverts to its strict syllogistic form:

All A is (has the characteristic) C-D
All B is (has the characteristic) C-D

Therefore, All B is (must have the characteristic) A

It is in this light that one must view Ghazālī's insistent claim that in order to be valid analogy must adopt the form of categorical syllogism. But to do so, it is of utmost importance to establish, as Ghazālī repeatedly attempts to do, that the 'characteristic' (*khāṣṣiyya*) common to both premises (cases) is an essential characteristic in all respects. The crux of the problem of formalizing inductive legal arguments thus lies in the circle of similarity and the extent to which it can be proven to logically entail a conclusion.

Ghazālī's concern about the formal validity of legal argument was not wholly shared by his successors. As far as I know, no later *uṣūlist* attempted a formal reconstruction of inductive legal arguments. Ghazālī's real legacy, however, appears most clearly in the attempt of later *uṣūlists* at grounding legal theory in a formal conception of knowledge.[64] This attempt manifested itself in emulating Ghazālī's *Mustaṣfā*, in which the introduction to the fundamentally formal Aristotelian logic set the grounds for legal theory, but had little effect on the practical construction of legal argument.

TRANSLATION[65]

//435// *Concerning The Explication Of The Modes of Analytical Demonstration Used in Legal Matters*[66]

The aim [of this chapter] is the exposition of the methods [of demonstration] used in cases which jurists consider to be inferential rather than revelational.[67] These demonstrations (*barāhīn*) are

[64] Although Ibn Ḥazm preceded Ghazālī in this attempt, and indeed went further in this direction, it is highly improbable that the later Sunnī *uṣūlists* whom we discussed in Part I were influenced by Ibn Ḥazm's ideas. This is simply due to the qualitative differences in the approaches of Ibn Ḥazm and Ghazālī. The former reserved no place in his legal and analytical system for anything that was not demonstrative, thus excluding all inductive and nonformal arguments from the domain of reasoning. Ghazālī and the later jurists rejected such an approach altogether.

[65] In this translation I have found it necessary to diverge from the editor's division of paragraphs. Occasionally I have split or joined paragraphs without, however, pointing that out in the footnotes. I have also found it preferable on a few occasions to use the alternative manuscript reading provided in the footnotes to the Arabic text. When I did so, I pointed this out in the footnotes to the translation. Numbers appearing in the translation between double slant lines, e.g., //436//, represent the beginning of pages in the Arabic text.

[66] «*Analytical Demonstration*» (*al-Barāhīn al-Naẓariyya*) in the title must be understood in the context of the division of knowledge (*ʿilm*) into immediate (*ḍarūrī*) and mediate or acquired (*naẓarī*). Immediate knowledge is that which the mind cannot help but assimilate; it compels itself on the intellect without any inference. The knowledge of an object in motion or of pain resulting from hammering your finger is immediate. Acquired or mediate knowledge is that which obtains in the mind through the medium of inference. Thus, «Analytical Demonstration» is here used by Ghazālī in contradistinction to the immediate knowledge of Scripture. See Ghazālī, *Mankhūl*, pp. 52-58; Bāqillānī, *al-Tamhīd*, pp. 7-9. Further on textual immediate knowledge see the next footnote as well as my article «Non-Analogical Arguments in Sunnī Juridical *Qiyās*.»

[67] The distinction being made here is between *qiyāsī* and *naqlī* arguments, that is, between what belongs to the domain of inferential reasoning on the one hand

three: Causal (*iʿtilāl*) demonstration, indicative (*istidlāl*) demonstration[68] and *reductio ad absurdum* (*khulf*) demonstration.[69]

---

and self-evident textual premises on the other. Muslim jurists conceive of the texts of the primary sources as linguistically consisting of two basic categories, one is self-evident and the other ambiguous, capable of varying interpretations. Texts in the first category yield necessary knowledge and thus reasoning about them becomes superfluous. It is only in cases where God did not clearly stipulate the ruling of a case that *qiyās* is allowed. In the beginning of *Shifāʾ al-Ghalīl*, Ghazālī asserts that in any case where there is no *ʿilla* (cause) *qiyās* cannot be undertaken. This, of course, precludes from *qiyās* all textual statements which are so clear as to yield in the mind necessary knowledge of the case, including its species. Thus, in Quran V:3 «Forbidden to you are carrion, blood, pork (*laḥm al-khinzīr*) ...» the jurist takes the term *khinzīr* to cover all types of swine meat, including that of wild boars (*khinzīr barrī*). Though reasoning in this case can be reduced to a syllogistic inference, jurists, including Ghazālī, insisted that reaching the conclusion 'The meat of wild boars is forbidden' needs no inference since it is understood from the language of revelation (*naqlan*, or as otherwise stated *min jihati al-lafẓ*). Ibn Rushd, *Bidāyat al-Mujtahid wa Nihāyat al-Muqtaṣid*, I, 3; Tahānawī, *Kashshāf*, s.v. «*mafhūm*», II, 1153-1154.

68 In his *Miʿyār al-ʿIlm*, pp. 243-245, Ghazālī dwells on the distinction between *qiyās al-ʿilla* and *qiyās al-dalāla* in a chapter entitled «On the Supplements to *Qiyās*». The subtitle, «On Matters the Knowledge of which Complements the Knowledge of Demonstration,» is quite telling. Here, he establishes the terminological connection between the juridical *qiyāses* of *ʿilla* and *dalāla* and the equivalent philosophical types of demonstration *burhān al-limā* and *burhān al-li'anna*. As we have previously mentioned, when the middle term of a syllogism is an efficient cause, the inference is called by jurists *qiyās al-ʿilla* and by logicians *burhān al-limā*. But when the middle term constitutes non-causal evidence in the relationship between the major and minor premises, jurists call this inference *qiyās al-dalāla* and logicians *burhān al-li'anna*. An example of causal demonstration in the realm of sense perception is 'This piece of wood was burnt because it was subjected to fire.' In the inference 'This man is satiated because he has just eaten,' the major and minor premises are 'All men who eat become satiated,' and 'This man has eaten', with the conclusion 'This man is satiated.' However, in the example 'This man is satiated; therefore, he has just eaten,' the effect (*natīja*) points out the so-called cause (*muntij*). The effect in the *qiyās al-dalāla* (*burhān al-liʾanna*) demonstrates the existence rather than the efficiency of the cause. Non-causality in this inference comes through clearly in the syllogism 'All those who write poetry are learned,' 'This man writes poetry'; therefore, 'This man is learned.' Learnedness here is not a cause, but the customary co-existence of learnedness and the ability to write poetry enables us to infer that this man is learned. See also Ibn Taymiyya, *Radd*, p. 90, ll. 15-20. This distinction between causal and non-causal demonstration seems to have originally been made by Aristotle who termed these types of inferences demonstrative and dialectical syllogisms, respectively. The latter is an argument from signs (quite synonymous to the Arabic *dalālāt*) rather than causes, for it yields no understanding of the logical connection between the two premises. Further on the Aristotelian conception see H. W. B. Joseph, *An Introduction to Logic*, Oxford, 1906, pp. 398-399.

69 In the *Miʿyār*, pp. 159-160, Ghazālī intimates that *qiyās al-ḫulf* is used in scholarly disputations (*munāẓarāt*). «You take the claim of the opponent and make it a premise [in a syllogism]. Then you add to it another premise whose

Causal demonstration (*burhān iʿtilāl*) is bringing together the assimilated case (*farʿ*) and the original case (*aṣl*) through a cause (*ʿilla*), as it has been mentioned in the [discussion about] *qiyās*. The form of this demonstration reverts to two premises and a conclusion. You illustrate this by saying: 'A usurped object must be restituted'—this is a premise—and 'The property is usurped'—this is a second premise—and their conclusion is 'The property must be restituted'. You also argue: 'The usurped must be restituted,' and 'The son of a usurped woman is usurped'; therefore, 'He must be restituted'. You also argue: 'Property is restitutable if destroyed,' and 'Fructuous assets are property,'; therefore, 'Fructuous assets are restitutable if destroyed'. You also argue: 'The thief's hand must be amputated,' and 'The body-snatcher is a thief'; therefore, 'The body-snatcher must be amputated'. You also argue: 'Foodstuffs are usurious,' and 'Quince is a foodstuff,' therefore, 'Quince is usurious.'[70]

To begin with, all this reverts to the principle of subsuming a particular under a given general.[71] If you will you may argue:

---

truthfulness cannot be doubted. The conclusion of the inference will be clearly false, and it will thus become clear that that is due to a false premise [i.e., the premise of the opponent]. Ghazālī explains that assigning the term *ḫulf* to this type of demonstration may be due to the fact that the conclusion is established in order to refute one of the premises, thus *returning* after reaching a conclusion to an earlier premise (*liʾannaka tarjiʿu min al-natījati ilā l-ḫalf*). Another possible reason for this nomenclature is the inclusion of a false premise (*muqaddima kāḏiba*) in the syllogism (*ḫulf* also means falseness or lying).

[70] All these are syllogisms of the first figure where the middle term is the subject in the major premise and predicate in the minor. Further on this, see Ghazālī, *Miʿyār*, pp. 134 ff.

[71] The subsumption of a particular under a general stands out as one of the most fundamental characteristics of any categorical syllogism. It is one of the chief characteristics which distinguishes deductive from inductive (and analogical) reasoning. Unlike deduction which entails a necessary relationship between the premises and the conclusion, analogy involves a probable judgment about a particular when it resembles another particular in a *relevant* respect. In this and the following lines, Ghazālī is attempting to show that analogical arguments can be converted to deductive inferences by means of establishing the *ʿilla* (middle term) as a conclusive term. Once this is done, the legal premise, which is ordinarily particular, will be rendered universal; e.g., if it is conclusively established that the cause of the prohibition of usury in wheat is edibility, it can then be categorically stated that all edible things are usurious. On the basis of this categorical proposition, one can conclude that because apples are edible, they are usurious. Further on the differences between inductive and deductive arguments see Ghazālī, *Miʿyār*, 131-177; Khaḍr b. Muḥammad b. ʿAlī l-Rāzī, *Sharḥ al-Ghurra fī l-Manṭiq*, ed. A. Naṣrī Nādir, Beirut, 1983, pp. 81 ff. Also the *Sharḥ* of ʿIsā b. Muḥammad al-Ṣafawī on the same treatise, *ibid.*, pp. 195 ff.

'Edibility is the cause of usury,' and 'Edibility is found in quince'; therefore, '[Quince] is usurious'. Likewise, 'Usurpation is the cause of restitution,' and 'Usurpation is found in real estate';[72] therefore, 'Restitution [in usurped real estate] is obligatory'. The jurists' reasoning in this category is that quince is edible just like wheat, or that analogous to wheat it is usurious. Or that immovable property is capable of being usurped and therefore it is restitutable like movable property.

All this reverts to the principle of subsuming a particular under a universal. In rational demonstration it takes the form of two premises and a conclusion, as it was previously mentioned.

//436// Disagreement may be assumed to arise concerning the first premise, while the second premise is agreed upon. The adversary may argue: «I agree that quince is edible but I do not agree that edibility is the cause of [prohibiting] usury, or that edible objects are usurious. Rather, some edible objects are usurious but not due to their being edible.»[73] The adversary may agree upon the first premise but may disagree on the second. He may argue: «I agree that usurpation is the cause of restitution, but do not agree that [restitution in] usurpation applies to real estate, to the son of a usurped woman, or to fructuous assets. Likewise, I agree that theft is the cause of amputation, but do not agree that the body-snatcher is a thief.»

If there is disagreement concerning the first premise, it cannot be settled except through legal evidence, for what is being argued, namely, edibility being the cause, is legal.[74] This cause may be established by the revealed, unambiguous texts, by textual allusions (*īmāʾ*),[75] by the setting of the case,[76] by the occurance [of the effect]

---

[72] That is, unlike air, for instance, real estate is capable of being usurped.

[73] The opponent here aims in fact at destroying the basis on which analogy was converted to a deductive argument through the universalization of the major premise. The second objection concerning the minor premise does not pertain to logical analysis; rather, the issue at stake is the determination of the property in the minor premise (*farʿ*) *relevant* to the *ratio* of the major premise.

[74] By first premise Ghazālī means the *aṣl*, the textual context of the case. Irrespective of the form of argument used in *qiyās*, the cause of the ruling in the text must always be determined by revelational (*sharʿī*) evidence. See Muḥammad b. ʿAlī l-Shawkānī, *Irshād al-Fuḥūl ilā Taḥqīq al-Ḥaqq min ʿIlm al-Uṣūl*, Cairo, 1909, p. 205, ll. 8-9.

[75] *Īmāʾ* is an allusion concurrently stipulated with the judgment in the text and functioning as a means leading to the cause. For instance, from the textual statement 'The judge shall note decide in a case while he is upset', it is inferred that

with the occurance of the property, or by effectiveness (*taʾthīr*). The latter, as has been previously mentioned, is establishing the effect of the cause in the essence of the judgment in another case through a text, consensus, relevance (*munāsaba*), or coextensiveness and coexclusiveness.[77] Or through consensus reached on the indispensability of a sign (*ʿalāma*), or, subsequently, through investigation (*sabr*). This is in order to negate all signs aside from that which has been stipulated—as we have mentioned concerning the premises of *argumentum a simile*. [The stipulated sign] is also termed a cause (*ʿilla*) according to the majority of legal theoreticians. Shāfiʿī also pointed to this cause when speaking of edibility and cash.

If there is disagreement concerning the second premise—that is, concerning the existence of the cause in the assimilated case subsequent to admiting that the [existing] property is the cause—the cause may be identified either through sensory perception if the property is sensory, or through custom or language. It may also be identified through seeking definition (*ḥadd*) and conceptualizing (*taṣawwur*) the inner reality of the thing, or through revealed scriptural evidence.

An example of the sensory is the large body of water which is spoiled by an impurity. //437// If dust falls into this water, the water is not spoiled because dust does not render water impure, just like wind when it blows [carrying with it, e.g., tree leaves] or when water is stand-still for a lengthy period of time. The form of the argument is: 'That which does not spoil water [by changing its characteristics] does not render it impure,' and 'Dust does not [change water]'; therefore, 'Dust does not render water impure.' The adversary may argue: «I agree that what does not spoil [water] does not render it impure, but I do not agree that dust does not change [the characteristics of water]. Rather, dust conceals the characteristics of water, just like saffron and musk.»[78] This can be known through natural sensory perception.

'the state of being upset' is the *ʿilla* of impermissibility. Jurists disagree on whether *īmāʾ* is the type of evidence inclusive of both the judgment and cause, or of only one to the exclusion of the other. See Tahānawī, *Kashshāf*, II, 1433-1435, s.v. «*Tanbīh*». Ghazālī seems to use *īmāʾ* as inclusive of causal and non-causal statements. See his *Mankhūl*, pp. 338 ff., 343 ff.

[76] I take this to mean the circumstantial and contextual evidence pertaining to the case in the texts.

[77] See note 96 below.

[78] The discussion here revolves around the cause of impurity in water used for

An example of the customary is our argument: «Since the sale entailing risk is prohibited, and since the sale of a non-existent commodity is a sale entailing risk, the sale of a non-existent commodity is null and void.» The adversary may argue: «I agree on the first premise, but disagree that the sale of non-existent commodities is a sale entailing risk.» He may be answered that this is known through custom (*ʿāda*) in which practice (*ʿurf*) decides.[79]

An example of the linguistic is our argument: «Since manumission (*ʿatāq*) is carried into effect by equivocal, probable declaration,[80] and since divorce may be effected by manumission, divorce may be brought about by equivocal, probable declaration.[81] The adversary may agree on the first premise, but disagree on the second; that is, that divorce may be effected by manumission. Then he seeks [to prove his claim] by means of metonymies, figuratives and metaphors.

[An example of] what is established by revealed texts is proving the body-snatcher to be a thief by [citing] ʿĀʾisha's statement, may God be pleased with her: «The robber of the dead is just like the robber of the living.» Likewise, we prove //438// that real estate is subject to usurpation by citing the Prophet, peace be upon him: «He who usurps a span of land ...» We also prove the homosexual to be an adulterer, by citing the Prophet's statement: «If a man had a sexual intercourse [with another man] then both men are adulterers.» The mode of reasoning in this case is: 'Adultery must be punished,' and 'He who is involved in homosexuality is an

---

ritual ablution. The fundamental assumption is that any body of water which has come in contact with other corrupting elements is rendered ritually impure. The reason for impurity is that any change affecting the characteristics of water will nullify its ritual purity. But a body of water which has come in contact with ritually pure substances, such as potash, saffron or musk, remains pure. See Ghazālī, *al-Wajīz*, 2 vols., Cairo, 1317 H., I, 5 ff.; ʿAlī b. Abī Bakr al-Marghīnānī, *Hidāya: Sharḥ Bidāyat al-Mubtadī*, 4 vols., Cairo, 1980, I, 18 ff.

[79] Ghazālī apparently conceives *ʿurf* as a component of *ʿāda*, which I take here to be the 'custom' of God in running the world. The normative behaviour and practices of Muslims constitute a *ʿurf* that is part of God's design. On the concept of *ʿāda* in Ghazālī's doctrine see H. Wolfson, *The Philosophy of the Kalam*, Cambridge, 1976, pp. 544-551.

[80] Manumission may be effected by unequivocal declaration (*ṣarīḥ*) or by indirect expression (*kināya*), e.g., 'you are not in my possession'. The latter, however, often falls short of constituting a decisive and irrevocable commitment. See Marghīnānī, *Hidāya*, II, 50 ff.; Ghazālī, *Wajīz*, II, 273-274.

[81] Such as expressions which do not have the term 'divorce' in them; e.g., 'go to your family,' or 'leave the house.' See Ghazālī, *Wajīz*, II, 54.

adulterer'; therefore, 'He who is involved in homosexuality must be punished.'

An example of that which is known through conceptualizing[82] the innateness of the thing and through seeking a comprehensive but exclusive (*jāmiᶜ māniᶜ*)[83] definition is our argument: The son of the usurped person is usurped because the definition of usurpation is: «The hostile seizure of a property in a manner which prevents the owner from a [free] disposal of the property.» And that took place. The adversary may dispute the definition as well as its validity, or he may approve of it but may deny its applicability to the son of the usurped. He may argue that it is not a hostile seizure because there was no resistence on the part of the owner, or that the owner is not //439// unfree to dispose of the property, or that he did not oppose seizure. However, [usurpation is established] by proving that the usurper hindered the free hand of the owner. He may cite the case of the young of hunted animals. He may prove that [the owner] has no free disposal [of his property] by proving that the usurper is in control [of it], and that the absence of [the owner's] free disposal is legally due to the [usurper's] control. The absence of free disposal has the effect of dispossession.

If the basis of definition is disputed, and if it is argued that usurpation means «taking hold [of a property] in a manner which forces out the owner; but the owner is in possession of neither the offspring nor the usufruct so that he can be forced out,» then 'forcing out' which he included in the definition of usurpation must be omitted. He then ought to show that the name of usurpation or its judgment exists without forcing out the owner, e.g., the custodian (*mūdaᶜ*) who refuses to return the entrusted object (*wadīᶜa*) does not force out the owner though he is considered a usurper. Such is the reasoning concerning definitions.

Discourse on this category may be connected with the editing of the locus of judgment (*tanqīḥ manāṭ al-ḥukm*).[84] We agree, for

[82] On concept, *conceptio*, or conceptualization (*taṣdīq*) see Part I, section ii, above.

[83] One of the most authoritative definitions of 'definition' (*ḥadd al-ḥadd*) is that which encompasses the totality of the characteristics of the object defined while excluding all non-essential qualities from it. See Robert Brunschvig, «Ǧāmiᶜ Māniᶜ,» in *Études d'islamologie*, ed. Abdel Magid Turki, 2 vols., Paris, 1976, II, 355-357.

[84] *Tanqīḥ al-Manāṭ* ranks as the second in a triad of methods by which the cause in the original text is verified. By this method, the cause, or its constituent properties, is isolated from those properties which have been mixed with it in the text

instance, that the name of 'usurpation' is not applicable, but the underlying reason for restitution in usurpation is the occurence of hostile seizure. We also agree that the name of 'theft' (*sariqa*) is not applicable to the body-snatcher (*nabbāsh*), but the underlying reason for amputating the hand in theft is the taking of legally owned and guarded property. We also agree that the homosexual is not an adulterer, but the underlying reason for punishment in adultery is wasting [a potential] offspring by satisfying a person's sexual desire with another person. Accordingly, the form of inference changes and the dispute reverts to //440// the first premise; for, in line with this, we do not argue that adultery necessitates [punishment], nor that the homosexual is an adulterer, nor that the body-snatcher is a thief. Rather, we argue that the wasting of offspring in order to satisfy one's desire with another person necessitates [punishment], and that the homosexual possesses the same characteristic. Likewise, the taking of legally owned and guarded property necessitates [punishment]. This characteristic is found in the body-snatcher. The adversary may dispute the first premise and may say: «I do not agree that what necessitates punishment is what you have specified; rather, what necessitates punishment are the acts of adultery and theft.»

He who seeks the truth must distinguish between the two methods, for through them[85] the dispute shifts from one premise to another.

Our aim is to show that all causal demonstrations revert to two premises and a conclusion, all of which [in turn] revert to the cause of the ruling,[86] its existence in the text disputed, and to grounding the ruling in it.[87]

---

of revelation and which have no relevance or causal relationship with the judgment. An example of this is the original case of an Arab who was told by the Prophet to free a slave as penance for having had a sexual intercourse with his wife in the month of Ramaḍān. The fact that the man was an Arab must not be taken as part of the cause. The ruling must equally apply to all Muslims violating the law, regardless of ethnic origin. See Ibn Qudāma, *Rawḍa*, pp. 249-250.

[85] Read the alternative «*bihādhā l-ṭarīq*» instead of «*fa-hādhā huwa l-ṭarīq*». See footnote 3, p. 440 in the Arabic text.

[86] Read «*ilā ʿillati l-ḥukm*» instead of «*ilā daʿwā ʿilla li-ḥukm*». Preference is given to the alternative version appearing in notes 4 and 5, p. 440 in the Arabic text.

[87] In this passage Ghazālī establishes the most fundamental issues involved in the logical exposition of *qiyās al-ʿilla*. These issues are logical and legal at one and the same time. The argument is unmistakably formal, and the material premises are undeniably legal. The validity of constructing a syllogistic argument depends heavily here upon the truthfulness of the middle term which is not always evident

An example of this from rational demonstration is: 'Knowledge is the cause of the self to be knowing,' and 'Knowledge exists in God,' may He be exalted; therefore, 'God is knowing.' An example of sensory perception is as follows: 'Animality is the cause of feeding,' and 'Man is an animal'; therefore, 'Man feeds.' Its syllogistic mode is: 'Every animal feeds,' and 'Every man is an animal'; therefore, 'Every man feeds.' It is inconceivable //441// to dispute the conclusion once the two premises are accepted [as true]. If, however, the two premises are disputed, they can be proven in some way. In such matters rational demonstration does not differ from legal demonstration, to the exception, however, of the methods which we specified[88] concerning the two premises, and which are suitable for legal but not rational demonstration.[89]

The second demonstration is indicative demonstration (*burhān istidlāl*). It is the inference of a matter from another which is not its necessary cause. The cause is established in a rational manner. There ought to be no objection to calling causal demonstration indicative demonstration, for the cause which brings about the effect also *indicates* that effect. [In indicative demonstration, however,] the effect may indicate the cause but does not necessarily effect it.[90]

---

or well-defined. The logical relation between the minor and major premises, and the conclusion which they entail, is thus entirely dependent on the validity of the *ʿilla*.

[88] Read the alternative «*sharaṭnāh*» in Mss *d* and *z*, instead of «*yuthīr ẓannanā*». The latter makes no sense whatsoever.

[89] Ghazālī constantly distinguishes between certain or truthful premises and probable premises. Pure rational propositions (*yaqīniyyāt*), such as the premise that two is a number bigger than one, are truthful and therefore suitable for rational demonstration. They are, of course, also suitable for lesser forms of argumentation; i.e. legal, dialectical, sophistical, rhetorical, etc. But those propositions belonging to the latter types are not suitable for rational demonstration, for they fall short of being conclusively certain. However, immediately after rational propositions rank legal propositions which are subsequently divided into three levels of probability: the *maẓnūnāt* being highly uncertain, the *maqbūlāt* being less uncertain, and finally, the lowest on the ladder of probability, the *mashhūrāt*. Anything below the ranks of legal and rational demonstration is considered by Ghazālī as a premise appropriate only for mere sophistry. See his *Miʿyār*, pp. 182 ff., 193-198.

[90] In other words, all causal demonstrations belong to the category of indicative demonstration since the cause necessarily 'indicates' the conclusion. The *ʿilla* in indicative demonstration, on the other hand, may point out the conclusion but does not necessarily induce it. Further on *qiyās al-ʿilla* see Āmidī, *Iḥkām*, III, 96; Ibn Qudāma, *Rawḍa*, pp. 280-281.

This type of non-efficient causal inference is divided into three [kinds]:

[1] An inference with regard to a matter on the basis of its characteristic, or on the basis of its effect. The existence of the characteristic indicates the existence of that which possesses the characteristic. And the absence of the characteristic indicates the absence of that which possesses the characteristic. Likewise, the existence of the effect indicates the existence of that which produces the effect, and the absence of the effect indicates the absence of that which produces the effect.

An inference concerning a matter from a similar or equivalent matter.[91] What is established as [a property] of a matter is, by necessity, established as the property of its equivalent or that of a similar matter.

An example of inference on the basis of a characteristic is the argument that the recommended additional prayer (*watr*) is like the voluntary prayer (*nafal*) because both can be performed while on a journey. Performing prayer on a journey is coexistent with voluntary prayer and coexclusive to [the minimal] obligatory prayer (*farāʾiḍ*). This is so //442// because performing prayer while journeying is characteristic of voluntary prayer; an obligatory prayer (*farīḍa*) should by no means be performed on a journey.[92] If the characteristic of a thing exists, it indicates the existence of that thing. The indication [of coexistence] becomes obvious once the characteristic is accepted [as valid]. The significance of the characteristic is its coexistence with the essence of the thing in a

---

[91] The inference presented in this paragraph is the third kind of indicative demonstration. Ghazālī reverts to it later when he has completed the detailed exposition of the first and second types. In the next paragraph he resumes the discussion about the first kind.

[92] Ranging from one to eleven prostrations, the *watr* is a recommended prayer according to the Shāfiʿīs. More recommended, but not obligatory, is the *nawāfil* prayer which must, according to Shāfiʿī, consist of at least ten prostrations. See Ghazālī, *Wajīz*, I, 53-54. On the 'old' and 'new' doctrines of Shāfiʿī and for a comparative account of these laws among the various schools of law inclusive of the *Shīʿa*, see Shaykh al-Ṭāʾifa Abū Jaʿfar Muḥammad b. al-Ḥasan al-Ṭūṣī, *al-Khilāf fī l-Fiqh*, 2 vols., Tehran, 1377 H., I, 198 ff. The inherent characteristic or distinguishing property of *watr* is that it is allowed to be performed while on a journey. *Nawāfil* share the characteristic found in *watr* in that it is a prayer performed while on a journey. The ordinary, obligatory prayer (*farīḍa* or *farāʾiḍ*) lacks this characteristic, viz. it may not be performed on a journey. From this it is concluded that *watr* is of the genus of *nawāfil*. To ensure the validity of the conclusion, the characteristic common to both premises must be of the essence, not contingent.

manner which makes them inseparable: The existence of the thing indicates the existence of that which accompanies it, and is inseparable from it.

The adversary may argue: «I do not agree that the permissibility of performing prayer while on a journey is characteristic of voluntary prayer, because the recommended additional prayer is not like the voluntary prayer, yet voluntary prayer is performed while journeying.» Such an objection is unwarranted because if we first assume that the ruling of recommended additional prayer, which is to be derived through revelatory indications, cannot be established by revelation one way or the other, we will find that recommended additional prayer is drawn towards voluntary prayer due to a characteristic unessential to obligatory minimal prayer. Therefore, in all probability it is [like] voluntary prayer.

We think it conceivable that the adversary may find textual evidence to the effect that recommended additional prayer is like the obligatory minimal prayer. The evidence may thus invalidate this characteristic.[93] Otherwise, in the absence of textual evidence, the characteristic remains valid, and through it the ruling about recommended additional prayer can be known. If, however, there exists specific textual evidence, the claim for the similarity of characteristics is dropped. But the adversary must produce evidence if he has it.

The adversary may well argue: «The permissibility of performing prayer while journeying is characteristic of non-obligatory prayer; therefore, obligatory prayer must not be performed while journeying. I do agree that recommended additional prayer is not like obligatory minimal prayer (*farḍ*), //443// but it is still incumbent (*wājib*) [upon the individual]. Thus, I do take into consideration the necessary [common] characteristic.» Though this objection is actual, the adversary is required to demonstrate the difference between the obligatory and the incumbent. According to our [Shāfiʿī] school, there is no difference between them; thus, we find that their argument is invalid, and the inference on [the basis of] characteristic maintains its validity.[94]

---

[93] Identifying the *watr* as an ordinary, obligatory prayer necessarily entails the nullification of what was presumed to be the intrinsic characteristic (*khāṣṣiyya*) common to *watr* and *nawāfil*.

[94] According to the Shāfiʿīs and the majority of the Ḥanbalīs and Mālikīs the terms *wājib* and *farḍ* are synonymous. The Ḥanafīs, however, hold that an act

Also of the same type is our argument that the manumission of slaves by contract (*mukātab*) is unlike manumission of penance (*kaffāra*)[95] because manumission by contract takes effect contractually. We know this from the slave's quest for acquiring livelihood and offspring, which is characteristic of contractual manumission, and which indicates the continued validity of manumission. This clear evidence continues to assert itself until the adversary demonstrates that //444// what is owed for the master is the owned portion of the slave and the rest is the freed portion, until slavery is terminated when all installments are payed—and so on until the adversary completes his argument concerning this issue.

What we are driving at is that this is not an inference through a necessary cause; the performance of prayer while journeying does not induce nor cause the additional mandatory or voluntary prayers; and the quest for acquiring livelihood and offspring does not induce contractual manumission. Rather, these are qualities which are fixed to the innateness [of the matter], and there being fixed is known through revelation.

We can determine the manner in which these two characteristics are known through coextensiveness, coexclusiveness and similarity.[96] But these [methods] are also used in matters which do

---

which is enjoined through decisive and unequivocal textual evidence is termed *farḍ*, whereas an act enjoined through probable evidence is *wājib*. See Abū l-Walīd al-Bājī, *Ḥudūd fī l-Uṣūl*, ed. Nazīh Ḥammād, Beirut, 1973, pp. 53-55; Ibn Qudāma, *Rawḍa*, pp. 32-37.

[95] A slave may acquire his freedom by buying himself from the master. The procedure of manumission and payment takes the form of a contract. If the master offers freedom for a certain price, and the slave agrees to the conditions, the slave is freed. The only proviso for complete freedom is, of course, a complete payment as agreed. The price may be payed in advance, in installments (*munajjaman*) or at a later date (*muʾakhkharan*). Shāfiʿī, assuming that slaves generally possess very little during their period of slavery, held that immediate full payment is not required for manumission. Payment may be delivered only at a later date and in at least two installments. However, if the slave falls short of completing all payments, the master can claim what remains unpaid in the form of partial slavery. See Marghīnānī, *Hidāya*, III, 253 f.; Ghazālī, *Wajīz*, II, 283 ff.; Ibn Ḥazm, *Muʿjam*, 2 vols., Damascus, 1966, II, 870 ff. A slave may also be freed as an act of penance (*kaffāra*) by his master. One of the acts which require such penance is swearing the name of God in vain. See Marghīnānī, *Hidāya*, II, 74.

[96] Coextensiveness and coexclusiveness, *al-ṭard wa l-ʿaks*, are two complementary methods of enquiry by which the presumed validity of a hypothesis is confirmed or denied. One of the most common uses of these methods concerns the verification of the cause of a judgment. Coextensiveness thus confirms the existence of the judgment when the cause exists, and coexclusiveness, in contradistinction, establishes the absence of the judgment when the cause is absent.

not pertain to what is considered as having a characteristic. That which has a characteristic is more demonstrable than similarity, coextensiveness and coexclusiveness.

[2] The second kind [of indicative demonstration] is the inference from the existence of the conclusion that the cause exists, and from its absence that the cause is absent. Given the [truthfulness of the] conclusion, this demonstration is clear.[97] Thus, knowledgeability is the result of knowledge as well as the existence of knowledge in the self. We say: The Creator, may He be exalted, is knowledgeable, which means that knowledge exists in Him.

The mode of this kind [of inference] derives from coexistence; the effect (*mūjab*) coexists with the cause (*mūjib*)—just as the characteristic coexists [with the thing itself]—the existence of the effect signifies the existence of the cause, because the effect is coexistent. //445// An example of this is our argument: A sale which does not result in ownership, cannot be contractually concluded. Or a marriage which does not legalize sexual intercourse cannot be contractually concluded. Likewise, we argue that if the *commenda* agent becomes the proprietor of the profit, he will also become the proprietor of the profit resulting from the profit. This is so because the profit is its effect; its non-existence signifies the non-existence of proprietorship. We may also argue that if the agent is the proprietor of the entire profit, he would be the proprietor of less than the entire profit. And since the loss [of profit] is incurred by the agent, it indicates that the agent is not the proprietor of the profit.[98]

All this reverts to the inference that from the absence of a thing its effect is [known to be] absent. Given that there is a conclusion, this inference is demonstrable.[99]

The characteristic may also be predicated upon the effect. It may be argued that the quest [of the slave] for acquiring livelihood and offspring is the effect and the result of contractual manumission. Its existence signifies the existence of efficient contractual manumission. Likewise, the prohibition against performing prayer on a

---

See Bājī, *Ḥudūd*, pp. 74-75. Later jurists—perhaps after the fifth/eleventh century—coined the term *dawarān* to include both methods. Tahānawī, *Kashshāf*, s.v. «*dawarān*», I, 469.

[97] The alternative given in note 8, p. 444 (Arabic text) makes better sense: «*wa wajhu dalālatihi, baᶜda taslīmi kawnihi natījatan, wāḍiḥun.*»

[98] See note 112 below.

[99] The Arabic: «*wa-huwa baᶜda taslīmi kawnihi natījatan lā khafāʾa bi-wajhi dalālatihi*».

journey is the effect of mandatory prayer; for if it were made mandatory in its entirety, then it could not be performed partially. So the non-existence of prohibition signifies the non-existence of mandatory prayer. If it were possible to determine the coexistent characteristic, then it would be neither a cause nor an effect, and the two characteristics would be inseparable; thus using one of them to signify the other is acceptable. This inference surpasses the inference based on the effect and the cause.

[3] The third kind [of indicative demonstration] is the inference of a thing from another which resembles it. We may argue that he whose divorce is valid, his temporary separation (*ẓihār*) is also valid.[100] And he who pays tithe and food tax (*fiṭra*) must pay alms tax (*zakāt*). Also, if a small quantity of bodily fluid does not annul ritual ablution (*wuḍūʾ*), a larger quantity of the same fluid can no more annul ritual ablution.[101] Arguments of this type are numerous.

//446// This [argument] can also be constructed on the basis of resemblance or through the method of coextensiveness and coexclusiveness, as it has been previously expounded. But Shāfiʿī, may God be pleased with him, chose the inference of a matter from another similar matter. For his argument is that what is inherent in a matter is inherent in a matter like it.

There is no obscurity concerning this principle. Rather, obscurity lies in the *claim* for similarity.[102] The adversary may not agree that divorce resembles temporary separation, or that tithe resembles alms tax, or that the small quantity of bodily fluid

---

[100] Temporary separation (*ẓihār*) takes effect when the husband says to his wife such phrases as «You are to me like my mother's back.» Such a declaration constitutes a legal impediment against the husband's matrimonial rights, including touching or kissing his wife. *Ẓihār* can never constitute a first step in a divorce procedure. It may be resolved when the husband does penance; e.g., freeing a slave, fasting for sixty consecutive days or feeding sixty needy persons. See Marghīnānī, *Hidāya*, II, 17-19; Ghazālī, *Wajīz*, II, 78 ff.

[101] See Marghīnānī, *Hidāya*, I, 14 f.

[102] In other words, the principle that a property in a given matter is presumed to exist in another matter manifesting a certain *relevant* similarity, constitutes, according to Ghazālī, a valid argument. The issue at stake, however, is not the principle itself but the claim that a certain matter resembles another matter in a *relevant* aspect. The opponent is made to argue that to claim resemblance between two matters the similarity must be of the same genus. Temporary separation and divorce, as two examples of such matters, do not manifest, as the adversary seems to argue, sufficient similarities that can justify the analogy between these two cases.

resembles a larger quantity. He may argue that a similar matter is indeed that which replaces, substitutes and is equal to, another in qualities which are possible, necessary or impossible. And these qualities can by no means be claimed to exist in these cases. However, resemblance and similarity may be conceived in certain respects, just as equating a male and a female is conceivable with regard to manumission and slavery. Thus male and female slaves are alike concerning the effect of manumission and the mitigation of prescribed penalty (*ḥadd*).[103] But this does not preclude differences between male and female slaves with regard to [the requisite of] guardianship in marriage or the right of the master to force the female slave to marry. This also does not preclude differences between men and women in matters of testimony, leading prayer, etc. We can argue for resemblance between males and females only in relation to slavery and manumission.

It may also be argued //447// that the slave is like a freeman who has no means to do penance,[104] and that the concubine is like a [free] married woman in that having sexual intercourse with either of them [when such an act is impermissible] necessitates the doing of penance.[105] These similarities are conceivable provided it is admitted that there are dissimilarities which distinguish marriage from concubinage, although with regard to the nullification of fasting there are no differences. Therefore, it is possible for precepts diverging in characteristics to converge in general issues. We respond that fasting is like prayer as regards intent, and sale is like marriage as regards offer and acceptance. A case is thus inferred from another case on the basis of these properties, and the claim for analogy on the grounds of other matters, which are the characteristics, is precluded.[106]

---

[103] *Ḥudūd* (pl. of *ḥadd*) are punishments for offenses prescribed by the Quran. They are theft, fornication, false accusation of fornication, drinking of intoxicants and highway brigandage. The punishments for fornication is set at one hundred lashes, for false accusation of fornication at eighty lashes, and for consuming intoxicant beverages at forty. In these three offenses male and female slaves receive half the prescribed punishment. See Ghazālī, *Wajīz*, II, 164 ff.; Ibn Ḥazm, *Muʿjam*, I, 300 ff., specially at pp. 306-307, par. 24.

[104] Acts which are performed in the way of penance (*kaffāra*) are listed in note 100 above.

[105] There are a number of circumstances under which sexual intercourse within a legal relationship (i.e., marriage, concubinage) is impermissible; e.g., intercourse with one's wife or concubine during the period of fasting. See, e.g., Marghīnānī, *Hidāya*, I, 122.

[106] The alternative given in note 2, p. 447 (Arabic text), makes better sense.

Once this principle is established, Shāfiʿī would be justified in arguing that temporary separation is like divorce, that is, temporary separation is like divorce in relation to non-belief (*kufr*) and Islam, for both [i.e., divorce and temporary separation] are means of prohibiting matrimonial relations with the wife. The way to prevent non-belief is temporary separation, for according to Abū Ḥanīfa, non-believers are not addressed by the revealed law which stipulates impermissibility. Shāfiʿī argues that being a revealed law, the prohibition of temporary separation is //448// like the prohibition of divorce, and that resemblance is obvious concerning both the Law and the prevention of non-belief. If the prohibition of divorce were not effected, the prohibition of the likes of divorce must not be effected either.

This is the course of reasoning which the adversary seems to fall back upon, and in which divorce is assumed to contradict temporary separation. According to this, if divorce were not obstructed then temporary separation which resembles it in prohibition is also not obstructed in relation to divine speech and the prohibitions of divine speech.

This evidence [remains] clear until the adversary argues that what is established by temporary separation is a prohibition which is removed by doing penance. Unlike divorce, however, penance is not possible for non-believers. Shāfiʿī would answer: «No, penance is possible even though it is agreed that there is no penance. This decisively obstructs prohibition.» And so on concerning the methods of argumentation in this case.[107]

Shāfiʿī, may God be pleased with him, may also argue that if tithe and food tax are obligatory, //449// then all other taxes are obligatory because, being devotional services (*ʿibādāt*), they are both, whether accepted or rejected, equal insofar as childhood is concerned. Thus the claim of similarity is accepted, for the adversary may consider childhood as an obstacle [in the performance of] devotional services [prescribed by] divine speech. Shāfiʿī, may God be pleased with him, then argues: If this is obstructed, then tithe and food tax are also obstructed, for they are, insofar as the child is concerned, uniform devotional services just like alms tax and

[107] «Abū Ḥanīfa and Mālik held that non-believers do not have the right to declare *ẓihār*. Shāfiʿī and Ibn Ḥanbal, on the other hand, held that non-believers have such right, provided that penance is done only by freeing a slave or feeding sixty needy persons.» Editor's note no. 6, p. 448.

other religious financial obligations. The supposition that the child must pay [the taxes], the designation of a guardian for the performance [of these obligations], and the deferring of [the specifications of] divine speech until the child's coming of age, are all equally conceivable. This is an argument for similarity on the basis of [a characteristic]. It may be reduced to the supposition of the adversary that childhood is the motive and that tithe annuls it and the knowledge that in this case alms tax resembles tithe.

Over and above this, the adversary must explain why he holds that tithe is a duty incumbent upon all individuals and that food tax is incumbent [only] upon well-to-do individuals.[108] If this is established then the argument for similarity is annulled. We then argue that tithe and food tax require intent, and that it is lawful to levy land tax from those who do not pay tithe. This will indicate that tithe is not payable by all individuals. However, the reasoner's evidence is *ab initio* probable; he thus gives it up //450// and instead draws the attention to differences. We then proceed by invalidating [these] differences. We also argue that if a small amount of venesected blood does not annul [ablution], then a large amount of the same blood does not annul it either, because a little amount is just like a large amount. The likeness between them is known in relation to the argument of the adversary. His argument is that all loci must follow the accustomed substrata, and in the accustomed substrata small and large amounts are alike. So, if a small amount [of blood which comes out] of veins is unlike that [which is emitted] from the accustomed outlet, then it is also unlike a large amount which is in this context like [the small amount of vein's blood].

If it is asked «What is the reasoning behind the argument of Shāfiʿī—may God be pleased with him—that the act of slaughtering which does not render the meat legal does not render the skin ritually pure either?» we answer that the ritual purity of the skin is the result of rendering the meat lawful, for since the meat to be eaten is from heads, trotters and slaughtered sheep[109] it is deter-

---

[108] The Arabic here is: «*bi-anna l-ʿushra yathbutu ʿalā l-ʿayni wa anna zakāta l-fiṭri maʾūnatun,*» that is, while *zakāt* is a duty incumbent upon all capacitated Muslims who own property for at least one year, food tax (*zakāt al-fiṭr*) is a duty incumbent upon those Muslims whose property is in excess of the basic needs of life—e.g., house, clothing, furniture, horses and slaves. See Ghazālī, *Wajīz*, I, 98-100; Marghīnānī, *Hidāya*, I, 115 ff.

[109] The term used here is *masmūṭ*, literally meaning the slaughtered sheep whose wool is cleaned after having been soaked in boiling water.

mined to be ritually pure and so is the skin on it. If the antecedent (*matbūʿ*) ceases [to yield an effect], the consequent (*tābiʿ*) ceases as well. The ritual purity of skin must be made either a conclusion or a consequent; the coexistence between the antecedent and the consequent is as known as the coexistence between the effect (*natīja*) and the cause (*muntij*).

In this discussion, inference through similarity—as we have mentioned in the cases of temporary separation, divorce, tithe and alms tax—is unlikely.

The third type of demonstration is the *reductio ad absurdum* (*burhān al-khulf*). It is the setting aside of what one intends to prove, and establishing instead the invalidity of its contrary which stands in diametrical opposition to it. If one of the two opposites is proven invalid, then the other opposite would be proven valid. //451// This essentially reverts to [the method of] division and investigation (*taqsīm wa-sabr*), where some of the parts [in the division] are invalidated so the remaining parts would be proven valid. It also involves another method of demonstration, namely, the enumeration of all the parts of a whole and then they are all invalidated so the whole may be established to be invalid.[110]

In the first type of the *reductio ad absurdum* it is argued that «If it were not X it would have been Y; but it is not Y, therefore it is X.»[111] An example of this is the following: If the sale of a non-existing object were valid, the sale would be binding. But the sale is not binding; therefore, the sale is invalid. If the contraction is invalidated, the sale is proven null and void. Another example is: If the *commenda* agent were the proprietor of the profit, then he would be the proprietor of the profit resulting from the profit. But he cannot be the proprietor of the profit because this leads to an

---

[110] Ghazālī, *Miʿyār*, pp. 58 ff. ʿUbaydallāh Ibn Faḍl al-Khabīṣī, *Sharḥ ʿalā Matn Tahdhīb al-Manṭiq* (by Saʿd al-Dīn al-Taftāzānī), Qum, 1965b, pp. 93-94, states that the *reductio ad absurdum* inference reverts either to categorical syllogism or to conditional (hypothetical) syllogism. If we assert, for instance, that 'Every B is A' then it must be true that 'Some A is B.' To prove this last conclusion through reduction, we say that if the first premise were wrong, the opposite of the conclusion must be true, that is, 'No A is B.' And if 'No A is B' were true along with the first premise 'Every B is A,' then the result would be 'No B is B.' But this is absurd because if the falseness of the contrary to what is being proven were established, then the truthfulness of what is being proven is necessarily established.

[111] Literally: «If it were not so it would have been so; but it is not so, therefore it is so.»

imbalance in the agreed upon ratio. Therefore, [the owner's] proprietorship of the profit is invalid.[112]

This [demonstration] concerns itself with invalidation and validation, as we have mentioned. It is evincible and effective because it is employed in rational demonstration. However, if it falls short of both invalidation and validation, it is of no use in rational demonstration //452// but only in probable knowledge. We may argue, for instance, that if edibility were not the cause, then the cause would be either nutritiveness, measurability or value. But all these are invalid; thus edibility is validated. Given that the procedure of establishing the cause is implemented, this cause [e.g. edibility] may be stipulated. This type of reasoning may be questioned on two counts: The first is the claim for inclusiveness and the second is the claim for invalidity.

If division (*taqsīm*) involves both invalidation and validation, doubt concerning the claim for the invalidation of one of the parts is removed. This is why division which involves both invalidation and validation is operative in rational demonstration. We argue: If the world were not created, then it would be eternal; but it is impossible that it is eternal because it would be required to be unchangeable; therefore, it is established that it is created. Examples of this sort are many.

To this demonstration reverts what some scholars call inverted inference (*qiyās al-ʿaks*). To illustrate it they use the following example of Abū Ḥanīfa, may God be pleased with him: «Had fasting been unnecessary in the performance of *iʿtikāf*, it would have also been unnecessary in vowing, just like in prayer.»

Other scholars argued that this is invalid because it is an inference from the opposite (*istidlāl bil-ḍidd*). However, this claim is false //453// because the inference reverts to the demonstration of

[112] The agent in the *commenda* (*muqāraḍa*) contract must return to the investor the principal as well as a previously agreed-upon share of the profits. The agent receives the remaining share of the profits only as a compensation for his effort at investing. It is determined that the agent does not retain all the profit, but is entitled only to a part of it, by reasoning that if he does then he would be entitled to the profit acruing from the profit which had resulted from the invesment of the principal. Since the agent cannot be the proprietor of the profit which results from the investment of the first profit because it creates an imbalance in the agreed-upon proportion, we conclude that the agent cannot exclusively retain the profit in the *muqāraḍa* contract. On this type of contract see Ghazālī, *Wajīz*, I, 221 ff.; Ibn Mawdūd al-Mūṣilī, *al-Ikhtiyār li-Taʿlīl al-Mukhtār*, 5 vols., Cairo, 1951, III, 19 ff.

reductio ad absurdum. The course of this demonstration is: Had fasting not been an obligation, it would not have been an obligation when vowing either. But it is an obligation in vowing; therefore, it is obligatory. This is the demonstration of *reductio ad absurdum*. Its proponent may be asked: Why do you argue that if fasting were not obligatory, then it would not have been obligatory in vowing? And to what extent would vowing be a cause (*sabab*)? So, we argue with him about this impossibility. He may demonstrate its impossibility and argue: «If fasting were necessary in vowing when performing *iʿtikāf*, then prayer would be necessary in vowing.» This reverts to the inference about something from its likeness. He may argue: «Prayer is—insofar as it is rendered obligatory by vowing and relevant in *iʿtikāf*—like fasting. And if prayer is not rendered obligatory in vowing, how would fasting then be rendered obligatory?»[113]

The crux of the argument is that he who vows to fast while performing *iʿtikāf* must fast while performing *iʿtikāf*. This is either because fasting is a prerequisite for *iʿtikāf*, or because of the necessary concomitance (*iltizām*)—though one does not think it to be a prerequisite. It is false, however, to attribute it to necessary concomitance because if concomitance renders it obligatory it would also be obligatory in prayer even though //454// it is not a prerequisite. Prayer is like fasting with regard to vowing. If vowing is nullified in the like of prayer, it would be nullified in fasting as well, and its contrary would be confirmed. We have to show that a difference exists between fasting and prayer, and that fasting is an abstention from the same genus of *iʿtikāf*; it blends with *iʿtikāf*,

---

[113] *Iʿtikāf* is a recommended religious practice of retreat in a mosque. When a Muslim vows to perform *iʿtikāf* for a certain period of time, it is implied that he should fast as well. The practice becomes obligatory and his vow must thus be fulfilled. In this case, fasting is established as a prerequisite for *iʿtikāf*. Conversely, prayer is not a prerequisite because it has not been determined to be a necessary part in the vow for *iʿtikāf*. The original case here is prayer while the assimilated case is fasting. Contrary to fasting, the judgement of the former case does not entail prayer in *iʿtikāf*. The cause (*ʿilla*) for which prayer is not a prerequisite for *iʿtikāf* is that it does not constitute a condition for the validity of *iʿtikāf* when vowing. This cause, however, is not found in fasting which is determined by consensus to be a prerequisite for *iʿtikāf* when the vow is made. Therefore fasting is a prerequisite for *iʿtikāf*. See Ghazālī, *Wajīz*, I, 105 ff., II, 232 ff.; Abū Bakr Aḥmad b. Abī Sahl al-Sarakhsī, *Uṣūl*, 2 vols., Cairo, 1954, I, 47. See also Imām al-Ḥaramayn al-Juwaynī, *Kāfiya fī l-Jadal*, ed. Fawqiyya H. Maḥmūd, Cairo, 1979, pp. 225-226, who rejects the argument on the grounds that the inference is based on negative evidence rather than strict similarity represented by a common *ʿilla*.

and, unlike prayer, is influenced by it when it coexists with it.[114] This is in accordance with what has been written about this question.

In the second type of *reductio ad absurdum* demonstration the parts of a whole are enumerated, and then each part is invalidated until all the whole is invalidated. We argue: If *īlāʾ*[115] were a kind of divorce (*ṭalāq*), it would be pronounced either through an unambiguous declaration (*ṣarīḥ*) or an allusion (*kināya*). Since it is invalid to carry it out through unambiguous declaration or allusion, it is not therefore a divorce. This reverts to two premises and a conclusion, namely, 'No divorce [is effected] except through an unambiguous declaration or an allusion,' but 'There is neither an unambiguous declaration nor an allusion'; therefore, 'there is no divorce.'

All this belongs to the methods of proof, most of which are interconnected. Division (*taqsīm*) and //455// *reductio ad absurdum* demonstration have much to do with all arguments. Most analytical knowledge revolves around them.

This is all we wish to mention about the illustration of the methods by which the causes of the original cases (*uṣūl*) are known.[116] As we have already stated [at the outset of the treatise], this is one of the five principles [which lead to] the knowledge of legal inference (*qiyās*). The four principles remaining to be investigated are the original case, the assimilated case, the judgment and the cause. What we have discussed [in the present chapter] are the methods by which one of the principles—namely, the cause—is identified.

---

[114] In note 6, p. 454 of the Arabic text, the editor remarks that if a Muslim vows to perform *iʿtikāf* while fasting, the validity of *iʿtikāf* rests, according to the consensus of the community, upon his performance of fasting. But if he vows to perform prayer in addition to fasting, the Muslim has the option to abandon one of the two without invalidating his *iʿtikāf*.

[115] *Īlāʾ* represents a form of dissolving a marriage through an oath taken by the husband whereby he abstains from marital intercourse for a period of four months. If the oath is fulfilled, divorce goes into effect. But if the oath is broken before the period comes to an end, divorce does not take place and the husband is under obligation of doing penance. See Ghazālī, *Wajīz*, pp. 72-78; al-Raṣṣāʿ al-Tūnisī, *Sharḥ Ḥudūd Ibn ʿArafa*, Tunis, 1350 H., pp. 202-204.

[116] This and what follows are the concluding remarks to the first part of the book which consists of five parts (*arkān* pl. of *rukn*). The chapter translated here is the closing chapter of part I in which the procedures and methods of establishing the cause (*ʿilla*) are discussed.

IV

On Inductive Corroboration, Probability and Certainty in Sunnī Legal Thought

THE PROBLEM OF INDUCTION

RATIONALITY in drawing inferences means that the conclusion of an argument must follow from the premises and must not go beyond them; it must be true if the premises are true. The rational force of an argument may then be measured by the extent to which the evidence in it entails the conclusion. In valid deductive inferences this rational entailment must constantly hold true. But reasoning cannot be confined exclusively to deductive modes of argument, as the need often arises to draw a general conclusion from a limited body of evidence. Arguments proceeding from a certain number of particulars to a general conclusion do not follow the strict rules of logical entailment and rationality. In other words, they are not analyzable, after the fashion of deductive arguments, into premises and a conclusion; rather, they constitute a perception of relations that are not wholly subject to the rules of rational, deductive validity.

In these nonformal, inductive inferences the evidence does not entail the conclusion but lends it some sort of support or corroboration. Accordingly, the rationality and logical entailment in inductive arguments are a matter of degree and thus do not fit the neat paradigms of formal validity. The conclusion is not entailed by the available evidence but is more or less corroborated by it.[1] Here, there is no demonstrative confirmation unless it can be established beyond any doubt that the total body of evidence needed to prove a generalizing statement has indeed been provided. In such a case there is no problem, for when total evidence becomes available there is no question concerning the certainty of the conclusion if the particulars of the evidence which led to it are true. Instead, the real problem lies in the absence of total evidence, in drawing ampliative inferences by going from the observed to the unobserved with the inevitable result of reaching an uncertain conclusion. At best, therefore, inductive inferences—or inductive leaps, as they are sometimes characterized—establish their conclusions as probable.

This rudimentary conception of induction represents to a varying degree an essential assumption in the logic of Aristotle, of medieval Muslim logicians, as well as of modern Western philosophers.[2] Among the latter, David Hume restated the traditional problem of induction in terms of inferences from past experience to similar future events. If such events establish themselves in a law-like manner as being connected to current or past experiences, then what had applied to a particular case in the past must also apply to it in the future. Clearly, this argument presupposes a necessary causal connection between distinct events which neither Hume nor his posterity could establish.[3] In the absence of such

[1] The term "corroboration" is employed here in the non-demonstrative sense of gradational support. The use of "confirmation," though common among a number of prominent modern philosophers, will be avoided, for, as Salmon observed, this term implies a finalistic force in proving once and for all the validity of a hypothesis. See Wesley C. Salmon, "The Justification of Inductive Rules of Inference," in *The Problem of Inductive Logic*, ed. Imre Lakatos, (Amsterdam: North Holland Publ. Co., 1968), p. 28. Further on corroboration, see Georg Henrik Von Wright, *The Logical Problem of Induction* (Oxford: Blackwell, 1957), p. 117 ff.; A. J. Ayer *Probability and Evidence* (London: Macmillan, 1972), p. 63 f.

[2] William Kneale, *Probability and Induction* (Oxford: Clarendon, 1949), p. 24 ff., 53–56; H. W. B. Joseph, *An Introduction to Logic* (Oxford, 1906), p. 395; Ibn Rushd, *Talkhīṣ manṭiq Arisṭū*, ed. Gerard Jehamy, 3 vols. (Beirut: al-Maktabah al-Sharqīyah, 1982), 1:352, 353, 2:513–514; Salmon, "Justification," especially p. 25 ff.; L. S. Stebbing, *A Modern Introduction to Logic*, 7th ed. (London: Methuen, 1950), pp. 243–349, 402 ff.; Joseph Horovitz, *Law and Logic: A Critical Account of Legal Argument* (Vienna: Springer-Verlag, 1972), p. 4 ff.

[3] Von Wright, *The Logical Problem*, pp. 13–39; Nelson Goodman, *Fact, Fiction, and Forecast* (London: Athlone Press, 1954), pp. 63–65.

causal connection, Hume resorted to the next guiding principle in extending our present knowledge of things to yet unobserved instances, namely, the principle of the "uniformity of nature," which affirms that what held good in the past will hold good in the future.[4] But should this principle be grounded in an assumption that cannot be logically justified, then we have no good reason to trust any inference of this kind. Hume therefore concluded that inductive inferences cannot yield conclusive assurances but are at best highly probable.[5] To rephrase this argument and to eliminate the concern with future events—which is of no interest to us here—Hume's proposition comes down to the question of whether or not we are able to reach, on the basis of incomplete but highly corroborative evidence, a conclusion or a generalization which can be deemed conclusive. The answer, of course, is that we are not. Corroboration strengthens a generalization but does not render it certain; it enhances its credibility to the extent of the corroborative evidence.

While multiple pieces of corroborative evidence cannot establish the certainty of a proposition, it takes only a single negative instance to falsify that proposition. Like Greek and modern Western philosophers, medieval Muslim logicians acknowledged the validity of this principle. The oft-quoted and long-lived example of the crocodile was frequently introduced to illustrate this point. An investigation into the eating habits of animals, such as humans, horses, rabbits, birds, and so on, leads to the conclusion that "All animals move their lower jaw when they chew." This statement, however, is falsified when we examine crocodiles, which move their upper jaw, and which we failed to investigate before we formed our conclusion.[6] This example teaches that whatever the level of corroboration may be, there will always

[4] Frederick L. Will, "Will the Future be Like the Past?" in *Logic and Language*, ed. Anthony Flew (New York: Doubleday, 1965), p. 248 ff.

[5] For a lucid analysis of Hume's ideas on this issue see A. J. Ayer, *Probability and Evidence*, pp. 3–26; idem, *The Central Questions of Philosophy* (Middlesex: Penguin, 1976), p. 137 ff., 174 ff.; For a statement and critique of the same see Goodman, *Fact, Fiction*, chapter 3, especially p. 63 ff., 81 ff.

[6] Abū Ḥāmid al-Ghazālī, *Maqāṣid al-falāsifah*, ed. Sulaymān Dunyā (Cairo: Dār al-Ma'ārif, 1961), p. 89; Taqī al-Dīn Ibn Taymīyah, *Jahd al-qarīḥah fī tajrīd al-naṣīḥah* (being an abridgement by Suyūṭī of *Al-Radd 'alā al-manṭiqīyīn*), ed. 'Alī Sāmī al-Nashshār (Cairo: Maṭba'at al-Sa'ādah, 1947), p. 296 ff.

exist the possibility of falsifying the conclusion because of counter evidence. This problem of induction, whether in its basic Aristotelian and medieval Muslim form or in its highly articulated reformulation by Hume, Mill, Carnap, Keynes, and others, cannot be solved except in terms of probabilistic, nondemonstrative logic.[7]

MUSLIM USE OF INDUCTION IN LEGAL THOUGHT

In light of these fundamental problems of induction, I propose to investigate a number of central issues in Sunnī legal thought. My concern centers on the use which Muslim theoreticians of law made of the theory of induction, and the extent to which they diverged in their juridical formulations from the precepts of this theory. It must be immediately stated, however, that Muslim jurists were acutely conscious of the precarious logical status of induction, and had no illusions concerning its probabilistic nature. The oft-quoted ruling about *watr*, a type of prayer whose performance is recommended rather than obligatory, is particularly illustrative. On the basis of an inductive survey, it was found that, unlike *watr*, no obligatory prayers examined could be performed while on a journey. The ruling that the performance of *watr* is only recommended and not obligatory was deemed probable (*ẓannī*) rather than certain (*qaṭ'ī*) precisely because the inductive survey of prayers was admittedly incomplete, since *watr* was not included in the survey.[8] The judgment that the performance of obligatory prayers while on a journey was impermissible was reached on the basis of an examination of a number of individual types of prayer. In other words, there was a need for a reasonable number of prayers in order to establish this ruling as being highly probable. Reaching a ruling on the basis of examining a single prayer would have resulted in a ruling of a considerably

[7] Ayer, *Probability*, pp. 54–88; Max Black, "Induction," in *Encyclopedia of Philosophy*, 8 vols. (New York & London: Macmillan, 1972), 4:169–181.

[8] Fakhr al-Dīn al-Rāzī, *Al-Maḥṣūl fī 'ilm uṣūl al-fiqh*, ed. Ṭāhā J. 'Ulwānī, 2 vols., 6 parts (Riyadh: Lajnat al-Buḥūth wa-al-Ta'līf wa-al-Tarjamah wa-al-Nashr, 1979-1981), 2.3:217–218; Abū Ḥāmid al-Ghazālī, *Al-Mustaṣfā min 'ilm al-uṣūl*, 2 vols. (Cairo: al-Maṭba'ah al-Amīrīyah, 1324 A.H.), 1:51; Shihāb al-Dīn al-Qarāfī, *Sharḥ tanqīḥ al-fuṣūl*, ed. T. Sa'd (Cairo: Maktabat al-Kullīyah al-Azharīyah wa-Dār al-Nashr, 1973), p. 445.

lower degree of probability. Therefore, increasing the number of cases relevant to a certain issue constitutes added corroboration that raises the level of probability.

INDUCTIVE CORROBORATION AND THE NUMBER OF WITNESSES

The notion of inductive corroboration has indeed played a major role in the elaboration of a number of central concepts in Islamic legal theory. On the most basic level, this notion appears clearly in the discussions concerning the rationale behind the number of witnesses. Although the number of witnesses in a court of law was considered a divine prescription subject to no human stipulation, jurists argued for a rational explanation of the divine command.[9] As stated in the case of the *watr* prayer, reasoning on the basis of a single case would yield a conclusion with a rather low degree of probability. This principle was used to justify the unacceptability of one witness whose testimony without any corroboration is nearly as good as none (*testis unus, testis nullus*).[10] At least one other corroborating witness was thought to constitute a reasonably sufficient basis for deciding a case. While one witness's testimony would yield doubtful knowledge, the testimony of two trustworthy witnesses would enhance the credibility of testimonial evidence enough to render it highly probable. In the words of Sarakhsī, this highly probable knowledge assures our hearts and minds (*ṭuma'nīnat al-qalb*) that the probability of an error is quite slim.[11] To phrase it according to modern legal jargon, the testimonies of two genuine witnesses bring up the level of probability near enough to certainty for the verdict to be "beyond reasonable doubt."

In what may be termed an extraordinary legal case, where the Qur'ān stipulates punishments for committing adultery (*ḥudūd al-zinā*), four witnesses are required to satisfy the criteria

[9] Abū Ya'lā al-Farrā' al-Baghdādī, *Al-'Uddah fī uṣūl al-fiqh*, ed. A. Mubārakī, 3 vols. (Beirut: Mu'assasat al-Risālah, 1980), 3:856. For a contrary view see Shams al-Dīn Ibn Sahl al-Sarakhsī, *Uṣūl*, ed. Abū al-Wafā al-Afghānī, 2 vols. (Cairo: Dār al-Kitāb al-'Arabī, 1372 A.H.), 1:332.

[10] Muwaffaq al-Dīn Ibn Qudāmah, *Rawḍat al-nāẓir wa-junnat al-munāẓir*, ed. Sayf al-Dīn al-Kātib (Beirut: Dār al-Kitāb al-'Arabī, 1981), p. 91, ll. 7–8.

[11] Sarakhsī, *Uṣūl*, 1:290, 331, l. 10. For the definition of *qalb*, see Farrā', *'Uddah*, 1:89, ll. 3–6.

of evidence.[12] The importance attached to this particular case makes further corroboration necessary. The more serious the litigated issue is, the more witnesses the court requires. Although two trustworthy witnesses are normally sufficient in ordinary cases, and four in cases of adultery, the judge has the prerogative of requiring additional witnesses if he sees fit to do so. According to one prominent jurist, seeking testimonial corroboration beyond the required standard evidence is permitted by the Sharīʻah.[13]

Corroboration, however, does not depend merely on the number of witnesses required in a case. Rather, it must have as a prerequisite the condition of independence. What this means is that all testimonial statements relevant to a particular case must be given by independent witnesses. There must exist an intact means of transmission between the primal event and the subsequent utterance of the testimony. If one witness is told by another witness what to say, or is influenced by the testimony of another witness, or is involved in any kind of collusion with him, then the validity of his testimony becomes highly questionable, if not altogether worthless. For example, in a case where a man had a quarrel with the inhabitants of a village regarding a certain matter, the testimonial statements of the villagers in favor of each other were

[12] Insofar as procedural evidence and testimonial corroboration are concerned, a fully capacitated witness is a male witness. In "ordinary" cases the testimony of either two male witnesses or one male and two female witnesses is admissible. In adultery cases, on the other hand, only the testimony of four men may be accepted. The Ẓāhirī school seems to stand alone in recognizing the validity of women's testimony in adultery cases. Accordingly, Ibn Ḥazm accepts the testimony of eight women when four men are not available. See *Muʻjam Fiqh Ibn Ḥazm al-Ẓāhirī* (Damascus: Maṭbaʻat Jāmiʻat Dimashq, 1966), 2:535, par. 17.

[13] Imām al-Ḥaramayn al-Juwaynī, *Al-Burhān fī uṣūl al-fiqh*, 2 vols., ed. ʻAbd al-ʻAẓīm al-Dīb (Cairo: Dār al-Anṣār, 1400 A.H.), 1:573. Cf. Joseph Schacht, *Introduction to Islamic Law* (Oxford: Clarendon, 1964), pp. 193, 195, who argues that a greater number of witnesses does not lend additional value to their testimony. Articles 1698 and 1699 of the essentially Ḥanafī text *Al-Majallah* (English trans. as the *Mejelle* by C. R. Tyser, et al., Lahore: All Pakistan Legal Decisions, 1967) not only deem a *tawātur* number of evidential testimonies valid, but also irrevocably conclusive. It must, however, be added that Article 1732 states that: "By reason of one of two parties having more witnesses than the other party, it is not necessary that it should be preferred, unless the number of witnesses amounts to the degree of tevatur," in which case (Articles 1698, 1733) any contrary evidence must be dismissed.

rejected on the grounds that they were made in collusion.[14] On the same grounds, the testimony of a father in favor of his son is deemed unacceptable in a court of law.[15] Thus, to yield a genuine corroboration, the testimonial statements must correspond with each other on points of fact and must be given independently of one another. They must not be adulterated by extrinsic factors. In fact, the quality of rectitude (*'adālah*) required of every Muslim witness may be said to have been intended as a safeguard against hampering the independent character of the testimonial evidence.[16] In due course, we shall observe the importance of the role which the principle of independence, as a validating condition of inductive corroboration, played in Islamic legal theory.

MUTAWĀTIR REPORTS

The *raison d'être* of witnesses in a court of law is obviously the creation of a connecting link between the judge and the facts or actual events of the case. Through true testimony our knowledge is extended to things beyond our individual experience, such as our knowledge of the existence of remote cities which we have never visited or, as in a criminal law suit, of events which took place sometime in the past. In a religion such as Islam, where the Prophetic past constitutes a fundamental source of religious belief and behavior, testimonial evidence of this sort is deemed indispensable. The theory of *akhbār* (Prophetic reports) and the various modes of their transmission draws heavily upon the very principles by which testimonial evidence is established. Not only cases of positive and substantive law, but also the methods and procedures through which these cases were established, found their

[14] The case, cited in Herbert J. Liebesny, *The Law of the Near and Middle East* (Albany: SUNY Press, 1975), p. 41, was decided by the renowned Ottoman Shaykh al-Islām Abū al-Su'ūd.

[15] Abū al-Barakāt al-Nasafī, *Kashf al-asrār sharḥ al-manār fī uṣūl al-fiqh*, 2 vols. (Cairo: Maṭba'at Būlāq, 1316 A.H.), 2:22, ll. 22-24. In the same vein, Article 1702 of the *Majallah* stipulates that "there must not be enmity as regards temporal things between the witnesses and the person against whom evidence is given." But Article 1701 accepts as valid the testimony of a person in favor of his friend, provided that the two cannot, by operation of the law, dispose of the property of each other.

[16] For the constitutive characteristics of *'adālah*, see Muḥammad Ḍiyā' al-Dīn Ibn al-Ukhūwah, *Ma'ālim al-qurbah fī aḥkām al-ḥisbah*, ed. and trans. R. Levy (London: Luzac, 1937-1938), p. 211 ff. (Arabic text).

source and rationale in these reports. The strength of a legal ruling or a method of interpretation (*ṭuruq al-ijtihād*) depended to a significant extent on the degree of authenticity of these Prophetic reports. The determination therefore of the status of reports was in matters of law of utmost importance for the purpose of assessing the epistemic value of legal premises. How then was the conclusiveness of the report determined with regard to the authenticity of the "testimony" it intends to convey? Let us begin with the *mutawātir* (recurrent) report.

The *mutawātir* report, whose authenticity is absolutely certain, reaches us through channels of transmission sufficiently numerous to preclude any possibility of collaboration on a forgery. Moreover, the persons witnessing the Prophet saying or doing a particular thing must be sure of what they saw or heard, and their knowledge of what they witnessed must be based on sensory perception (*maḥsūs*).[17] All of the above conditions must be met at each stage of the transmission if the status of *tawātur* is to be maintained.[18]

Epistemologically, this report yields necessary or immediate knowledge (*'ilm ḍarūrī*) in the mind of the hearer, a knowledge that is not inferred but directly imposed on the intellect.[19] In contradistinction to mediate knowledge (*'ilm muktasab* or *naẓarī*), where by definition inference is the means of its acquisition, necessary knowledge does not allow for any reflection; it simply occurs in the intellect without the awareness of the process—if any—through which knowledge is obtained. Now, when a person hears a report narrated by only one witness, he is presumed to have gained only probable knowledge concerning the authenticity of that report. To reach the stage of conclusive knowledge, the report must recur (*yajibu an yatawātara*) in the presence of the hearer a sufficient number of times, and each time it must be transmitted by a different witness. In the view of the great majority of scholars

[17] Qarāfī, *Sharḥ*, p. 349, ll. 9–10, 15–17.

[18] Muḥammad al-Izmīrī, *Mir'āt al-uṣūl fī sharḥ mirqāt al-wuṣūl*, 2 vols. (Istanbul, 1884), 2:199; Qarāfī, *Sharḥ*, pp. 349–350; al-Muḥaqqiq al-Ḥillī, *Ma'ārij al-uṣūl*, ed. M. Riḍwī (Qum: al-Maṭba'ah al-'Ilmīyah, 1403 A.H.), p. 139. On Ghazālī's theory of *tawātur*, see B. Weiss, "Knowledge of the Past: The Theory of *Tawātur* According to Ghazālī," *Studia Islamica* 61 (1985): 81–105, especially at 88–89.

[19] Farrā', *'Uddah*, 3:847, 848.

the report of two or four witnesses falls short of meeting the criteria of *tawātur*. Their argument for rejecting such reports takes its premises from the procedural law of testimony. Since, they assert, the *mutawātir* yields necessary knowledge, there must not be any intermediary stage of reflection between the actual reporting and the occurrence of knowledge in the intellect. Even when there exist as many as four witnesses, the judge must first establish their rectitude before accepting their testimony. The procedure of establishing rectitude is viewed by jurists as a prelude to the admission of their testimony, a prelude which *ipso facto* precludes the testimony of four witnesses from leading to immediate knowledge. As argued by the renowned theologian and jurist Bāqillānī, the testimony of four witnesses does not yield certain knowledge, much less immediate knowledge, because had it not been so, God would not have commanded us to investigate the character of as many as four witnesses before accepting their testimony as valid.[20]

While some scholars fixed the minimal number of witnesses in *tawātur* at five, other groups, basing themselves on some Qur'ānic verses or religious accounts, set the number variably at 12, 20, 40, 70, or 313.[21] It seems, however, that sometime during the fourth/tenth or early fifth/eleventh century there emerged a dominant view that the smallest number of transmissions constituting *tawātur* is known only to God.[22] In other words, to try to determine the number at which immediate knowledge obtains would be in vain. The impossibility of pointing to a particular number stems from the fundamental assumption that what leads to certainty in the case of one person may not lead to certainty in the case of another; the reason being that each instance of transmitting a report is surrounded by circumstantial evidence (*qarā'in al-aḥwāl*) which may be known to one hearer but unknown to the

[20] Abū Bakr al-Bāqillānī, *Tamhīd*, ed. R. J. McCarthy (Beirut: Librarie Orientale, 1957), pp. 384, 385. See also Qarāfī, *Sharḥ*, p. 352; Farrā', *'Uddah*, 3:856; Sayf al-Dīn al-Āmidī, *Al-Iḥkām fī uṣūl al-aḥkām*, 3 vols. (Cairo: Maṭba'at 'Alī Ṣubayḥ, 1968), 1:230.

[21] Āmidī, *Iḥkām*, 1:229; Juwaynī, *Burhān*, 1:569–570; Farrā', *'Uddah*, 3:856–857; Ḥillī, *Ma'ārij*, p. 139. The choice of 70, for instance, is based on the alleged number of the followers of Moses, and 313 on the number of Muslim fighters in the battle of Badr.

[22] Āmidī, *Iḥkām*, 1:229, ll. 7–19.

other. Knowledge of such evidence lends special corroboration to the number of reports so far heard, and consequently brings to one person a conclusive knowledge that has not yet been obtained by another person who has been exposed to the same number of reports but who has no special familiarity with the relevant *qarā'in al-aḥwāl*. A number of instances of transmission may yield equally conclusive knowledge in the minds of two persons at the same time only when the number of reporters are in excess of four and the circumstantial evidence relative to all instances of transmission are either absent or equally comprehended by the two persons.[23] This clearly implies that *mutawātir* knowledge is subjective in character; that is, that different people perceive it differently.

Another source of difficulty involving the determination of the minimal number of *tawātur* transmissions relates to the premise that the knowledge imparted by this type of report is immediate. A person simply does not know how and when he reaches such knowledge. Ibn Qudāmah gives as an illustration an example of the knowledge about the existence of Mecca gained by people who have never paid a visit to it. They can never determine the exact instance at which they became absolutely certain of its existence. Likewise, if a man were killed in the marketplace, and we were told by the first passing person that such a murder had taken place, we would think only that this event has probably happened. But when a second person informs us of the same news, and then we hear it from a third, fourth, fifth, and sixth person, the probability in our minds is increasingly strengthened until we become totally convinced that such an event has indeed taken place. We do not, however, know the precise moment or by which individual report we reached such a conclusive knowledge.[24] The precise degree of corroboration which draws the line between probable and certain knowledge is as impossible to determine as the exact day a person ceases to be a minor and becomes an adult, or the exact instant at which night ends and the light of day begins.[25]

[23] Ibid., 1:230, 232, ll. 6–18; Bāqillānī, *Tamhīd*, pp. 384, 385; Farrā', *'Uddah*, 3:856, ll. 2 ff.

[24] Ibn Qudāmah, *Rawḍah*, p. 88, ll. 18–22; Āmidī, *Iḥkām*, 1:229.

[25] Ibn Qudāmah, *Rawḍah*, p. 89, ll. 3–5.

The obvious impossibility of determining the minimal number of *mutawātir* reports leads us to resort ultimately to the intellect of the hearer as the point of reference for measuring qualitatively as well as quantitatively the reports leading to conclusive knowledge. It is the moment at which a person realizes that he is completely certain of a reported matter which determines the number of reports, not the other way around; the number may be decided only when conclusive knowledge is reached.[26]

The knowledge of the *qarā'in* surrounding an individual report and of its chains of transmission varies, as we have intimated, from one person to another. It is the number of instances of reporting plus the *qarā'in al-aḥwāl* that make up the body of knowledge in the mind. A report recurring a few times, say five, may lead, with the help of many *qarā'in*, to conclusive knowledge, while another report, recurring seven or eight times but without *qarā'in*, may fail to yield such knowledge. The corroboration through *qarā'in* may best be illustrated by the example of a suckling child. When we observe a mother nursing her child, we do not in fact see the milk reaching the stomach of the child. However, when we see the child sucking the breast of his mother, the movement of its throat, and its thorough satisfaction, and when we further know that it had not been fed for sometime and that its mother is in the nursing period, we come to the conclusive knowledge that the milk is indeed reaching the stomach of the child.[27] Although we have not seen the milk itself, the accompanying evidence conclusively proves that the child has taken it in.

Circumstantial evidence may be strong enough to take the place of what would have been additional instances of transmission. In throwing its weight behind the report, this evidence yields, together with the instances of transmission it accompanies, conclusive knowledge.[28] This means that when the number of instances

[26] Qarāfī, *Sharḥ*, p. 352, ll. 12–13; Farrā', *'Uddah*, 3:855, ll. 10–11; Ibn Qudāmah, *Rawḍah*, p. 89, ll. 10–11; Fakhr al-Dīn al-Rāzī, *Lubāb al-ishārāt* (Cairo: Maṭba'at al-Sa'āda, 1355 A.H.), p. 27.

[27] Ibn Qudāmah, *Rawḍah*, p. 87 f.; Wael B. Hallaq, "Notes on the Term *Qarīna* in Islamic Legal Discourse," *JAOS* 108 (1989), 3:478f.

[28] Āmidī, *Iḥkām*, 1:232, 238; Ibn Qudāmah, *Rawḍah*, p. 87; "li-anna al-qarā'ina qad tūrithu al-'ilma wa-in lam yakun fīhi ikhbār, falā yab'udu an tanḍamma al-qarā'inu ilā al-akhbāri fayaqūmu ba'ḍu al-qarā'ini maqāma ba'ḍi al-'adadi min al-mukhbirīna."

of transmission is above four but still incapable of leading to conclusive knowledge, the quality of the circumstantial evidence may be such that it complements the instances of transmission with the result that conclusive knowledge is attained.[29] Conclusive knowledge is not attained when the number is less than five and the circumstantial evidence is not sufficiently persuasive.

DOES *TAWĀTUR* YIELD MEDIATE OR IMMEDIATE KNOWLEDGE?

The significance and weight of circumstantial evidence in this theory are given equal weight to the number of *tawātur* reports.[30] A few jurists went so far as to argue that when circumstantial evidence surrounds even a solitary report (*khabar wāḥid*), which necessarily falls short of fulfilling the conditions of *tawātur* and therefore leads by itself to probable knowledge only,[31] it sometimes renders the knowledge gained from that report conclusive.[32] Since circumstantial evidence is resorted to when the channels of transmission are less than the *tawātur* number, the knowledge

---

However, Ibn Taymīyah was among a smaller group of jurists who rejected the view that *qarā'in* in isolation of *ḥadīth* can yield certainty. See his *Raf' al-malām 'an al-a'immah al-a'lām*, in *Majmū' rasā'il* (Cairo: al-Maṭba'ah al-Ḥusaynīyah, 1323 A.H.), p. 67.

[29] Ghazālī, *Mustaṣfā*, 1:135, ll. 4ff., 138; Ibn Qudāmah, *Rawḍah*, p. 87–88. It should be noted that a number of jurists argued that immediate knowledge may obtain when the number is four provided that the instances of reporting are accompanied by strong *qarā'in al-aḥwāl*. See, e.g., Qarāfī, *Sharḥ*, p. 352, par. 2.

[30] The great majority of jurists accepted this view of *qarā'in al-aḥwāl*. Abū Bakr al-Bāqillānī seems to have been in the minority in rejecting the role of *qarā'in* in the theory of *tawātur*. See Ghazālī, *Mustaṣfā*, 1:135.

[31] Ibn Qudāmah, *Rawḍah*, p. 91. Āmidī, *Iḥkām*, 1:234, remarks that the majority of jurists (*al-jumhūr*) espoused the view that solitary reports can under no condition or circumstance yield certainty.

[32] Kamāl al-Dīn Ibn al-Humām, *Al-Taḥrīr fī uṣūl al-fiqh* (Cairo: Muṣṭafā al-Bābī al-Ḥalabī, 1351 A.H.), p. 331; Juwaynī, *Burhān*, 1:576-577; Ḥillī, *Ma'ārij*, p. 141, 148; Ibn Qudāmah, *Rawḍah*, p. 91, 92; Ibn 'Abd al-Barr, *Jāmi' bayān al-'ilm*, 2 vols. (Cairo: al-Maktabah al-Salafīyah, 1968), 2:41–42. For the views of Ibrāhīm al-Naẓẓām, who is reputed to have been the first to propound this doctrine, and for their refutation see Sarakhsī, *Uṣūl*, 1:330 (also 2:321). Qarāfī, *Sharḥ*, p. 349, ll. 12–14, 357, considers this type of report as belonging to an independent technical category which is neither *āḥād* nor *tawātur*, because the report has not been transmitted through a sufficient number of channels and yet it yields certainty. According to Kamāl al-Dīn al-Anbārī (*Luma' al-adillah fī uṣūl al-naḥw*, ed. Attiya Amer [Stockholm: Almqvist & Wiksell, 1963], p. 34), the majority of jurists do not deem such a report conclusive.

that such a report imparts is necessarily mediate rather than immediate, for to ascertain the sufficient degree of persuasiveness of the circumstantial evidence involved, and to verify the uninterrupted chain of transmission of the solitary report—or reports—throughout generations of Muslims entails a good deal of contemplation and thought.

It may well be argued that even in cases of *tawātur* transmission the mind comes to a conscious realization of the instances of corroboration, whether they be instances of transmission or *qarā'in al-aḥwāl*.[33] In such cases, the knowledge obtaining in the intellect may be deemed inferential and thus mediate. The process by which this knowledge occurs is clearly cumulative and corroborative. The aggregation of statements made by trustworthy informants will increase the level of probability until certainty is achieved; and this is precisely the moment when we realize that what we heard is a *mutawātir* report.[34] But the problem that quickly unfolds here is the incompatibility of the assumed immediacy (*ḍarūrah*) of knowledge, on the one hand, and the intellect's awareness of the gradual process of corroboration that yields an increase in the level of probability, on the other, for any degree of such awareness naturally precludes knowledge from being immediate.

The solution to what seems to be an epistemological dilemma is claimed by jurists and theologians to be found in an inner psychological ability given to people by God, an ability to reach a level of certainty without consciously perceiving the gradation of evidential corroboration imposed on the mind.[35] In other words, the Almighty creates in us the power to attain conclusive knowledge through a *mutawātir* report without a conscious cognizance of the means and data through which that knowledge is attained. This argument may be explained only in terms of an unconscious method of inference in which the conscious intellect is totally oblivious to the hidden, ongoing cumulative process of constructing knowledge.

[33] Rāzī, *Lubāb*, p. 27; Ḥillī, *Ma'ārij*, p. 138.
[34] Ghazālī, *Mustaṣfā*, 1:44, ll. 3–8, 46, l. 12.
[35] In the exact words of Bāqillānī, *Tamhīd*, p. 10, this ability is "ḍarūratun tukhtara'u fī al-nafsi ibtidā'an"; Sarakhsī, *Uṣūl*, 1:331.

While the conscious intellect remains heedless of the inner process of acquiring *tawātur* knowledge, this process itself operates on the basis of a set of assumptions which are thought to justify the occurrence of immediate knowledge. Although God creates in us such knowledge,[36] there still exist outside the intellect certain conditions that must be fulfilled in order for that intellect to reach a state of immediate knowledge. As we have intimated earlier, in the fulfillment of these conditions the number of instances of transmission ranks supreme. A *mutawātir* number precludes any possibility of conspiring on a forgery or a lie. Lying within the framework of a *tawātur* number is impossible, the reasoning being that the *tawātur* transmitters cannot all have a single reason to lie, and therefore it is inconceivable that they should conspire to tell the same lie.[37] The differences between individuals, their multifarious ambitions and interests, make it impossible for them to agree on the same lie, since this cannot conceivably serve their divergent purposes and goals.[38] And even if they attempt to conspire on a lie, their great number will eventually bring their conspiracy into the open; it is simply impossible to preserve a secret among such a large group of people.[39] Thus, when they all transmit one and the same report, we know that the report is absolutely true.

Admittedly, the credibility of the thesis that a large number of people cannot succeed in conspiring on a lie cannot be justified on sheer objective grounds, for it is conceivable under given circumstances that such a thing might happen. But the nature of man and the world as created by God does not allow for a conspiracy under the conditions of *tawātur*. We know from God's habitual way (*'ādah*) of running things in this world that a *mutawātir* number of people simply cannot agree on a lie.[40] Abū Ya'lā al-Farrā' goes so far as to say that God directly creates in us such knowledge as soon as we hear a *mutawātir* number of people transmitting a Prophetic report, although He could also posit the same knowledge in us even without our actually hearing

[36] Farrā', *'Uddah*, 3:850, ll. 2-3.
[37] Rāzī, *Maḥṣūl*, 2.1:335-337; Farrā', *'Uddah*, 3:844.
[38] Nasafī, *Kashf*, 2:5.
[39] Bāqillānī, *Tamhid*, p. 382.
[40] Ibid., p. 382; Qarāfī, *Sharḥ*, pp. 349–350.

the report. This is precisely analogous, he asserts, to the birth of a child subsequent to sexual intercourse, although God has the power to create the same child without any such intercourse.[41]

Although it would seem that this theory of *tawātur* is on the verge of losing itself in a highly subjective justification devoid of any conception of causality, the attempt to argue for its credibility stems from the need to have a rational basis for believing the evidence of witnesses. Since individual instances of transmission (*āḥād*) cannot by themselves yield certainty, a large number of transmissions becomes indispensable as a guarantee for conclusiveness. As *tawātur* numbers cannot lead to anything but certainty, it is therefore assumed that the continued recurrence of transmissions will eventually yield immediate knowledge. The realization of having reached certainty with no reflection upon the means by which we attained that state of knowledge tells us that the number of transmissions involved is *mutawātir*, and therefore we *must* assume that the conditions which preclude the possibility of a conspiracy have been met. This theory then comes down to the fundamental requirement of number, since increasingly large numbers will preclude the possibility of a conspiracy and inevitably lead to immediate knowledge.

Here, indeed, lies the solution to the problem concerning the hearer's awareness of the very process by which immediate knowledge is attained. At a particular time, the hearer, after having reached a state of immediate knowledge, looks back and realizes that the report was transmitted a sufficient number of times. He does not, on the other hand, know for certain (nor is he expected to know) that the transmitters of the report did not lie. All he knows is that he heard the report a number of times sufficient to yield immediate knowledge in his mind. Presumably, he does not count the times of transmission, but realizes that they were sufficient to engender this knowledge in him. This is precisely analogous to the process of memorizing a lesson; you continue to repeat the lesson until you memorize it. You do not have to count the number of times you have read it, but you know that they were sufficient and that *now* you know the lesson by heart.[42] Furthermore, the

[41] Farrā', *'Uddah*, 3:850, ll. 3–6.

[42] Ibid., 3:843.

hearer does not attempt to establish the relationships among the transmitters of the report, but he assumes, *post eventum*, that those who relayed the report to him could not have met or conspired. This is certainly in consonance with the established theory. First, immediate knowledge occurs, and subsequently the hearer comes to the realization that the number of transmissions was a *tawātur* number, for if it were not, he would not have attained this knowledge. Second, once the number of transmissions involved is established as a *tawātur* number, we know that what the transmitters relayed is true, because God, in his *'ādah*, cannot allow for a falsehood to circulate among a *tawātur* group.

Each instance of transmission in a *mutawātir* report may be taken to constitute a member of a class of things—a class which is the *mutawātir* report in its entirety. According to the theories of inductive logic set forth in the first passages of this article, no conclusive knowledge can be attained with regard to a class until there is an exhaustive account of all the members of that class. The need for a full enumeration of members stems from the absence of any necessary relationship between the observed members of a class and its unobserved members. It is precisely here where the Muslim *juristic* conception of logic drastically differs from its Aristotelian and Western post-Aristotelian counterpart. A full account of all the instances of transmission, that is, all members of the class, is not deemed in the *tawātur* theory to be indispensable for conclusive knowledge. A relatively large number, but not necessarily the whole, suffices for attaining certainty. A person may therefore reach certain knowledge without having been exposed to all the instances of transmission in existence.[43]

[43] This is perhaps the most significant difference between logical induction and the *tawātur* theory. Nonetheless, it must be asserted that in principle *tawātur* operates within the framework of the general rules of induction. B. Weiss, "Knowledge of the Past," pp. 103–104, points out, and rightly so, two similarities between induction and *tawātur*, but a few lines later he says that there is, as implied by Ghazālī, an important difference between the two: that is, inductive knowledge is a generalization from particular experiences, whereas *tawātur* knowledge is not (p. 104). Weiss does not cite the place where Ghazālī implied this difference. Our sources, however, do not allow us to reach the same conclusion. Like inductive knowledge, *tawātur* knowledge is based on experience. This is why the validity of *tawātur* presupposes, among other things, that the knowledge of the report's contents must be grounded in sense-perception (*maḥsūsāt*) (see note 18 above, and pp. 88, 91 of Weiss's 1985

TAWĀTUR MAʿNAWĪ

To stress the crucial importance of multiple transmission must not imply that individual instances of reporting are of no significance. Indeed, there is a fundamental epistemological value in solitary reports. Aside from the circumstantial evidence that may surround them and may thus lend them further support, the *āḥād*, merely by virtue of their having an uninterrupted chain of transmission from the time of the Prophet, boast a degree of probability in excess of 0.5.[44] And when two *āḥād* reports relayed by

---

article). The immediate knowledge which the *tawātur* engenders in the intellect eliminates, as we have already seen, any possibility of inference, thus connecting the original *maḥsūs* with the comprehension and sense-perception of the hearer. Therefore, when one hears a *mutawātir* number of identical reports transmitted, the knowledge that accumulates therefrom carries with it the actual original experience, almost as if it were the direct experience of the hearer himself. In *tawātur*, knowledge of past events stands on the same footing with particular sensory experiences, such as seeing a bird fly or experiencing pain when your finger touches fire. See Abū Isḥāq al-Shīrāzī, *Al-Tabṣirah fī uṣūl al-fiqh*, ed. M. H. Haytu (Damascus: Dār al-Fikr, 1980), pp. 291, ll. 4-6, 293, l. 6. The difference between empirical experiences and hearing a report may perhaps lie in the designation of certain senses as means of assimilating *tawātur* knowledge (e.g., hearing), while assigning to other senses the function of attaining *tajrībī* knowledge (e.g., smell). Fakhr al-Dīn al-Rāzī, *Maḥṣūl*, 1.1:100–101, observes that knowledge obtaining through rational faculties along with the sense of hearing is *tawātur*, but that which occurs through rational faculties along with other means of sense-perception is inductive (*tajrībī*). Ḥasan ibn Zayn al-Dīn al-Shahīd al-Thānī, *Maʿālim al-uṣūl*, ed. Mahdī Muḥaqqiq (Tehran: Shirkat-i Intishārāt-i ʿIlmī va-Farhangī, 1985), p. 210, ll. 4-5. As we shall see later (pp. 24–29), Shāṭibī considers *tawātur* to be squarely based on inductive principles. It is also interesting to note that the Aristotelian theory of induction, which undoubtedly formed the main source of the Islamic theory of induction, insisted that knowledge of particulars, the backbone of any inductive inference, is possible only through sense-perception. See Von Wright, *Logical Problem*, p. 8. The connection between inductive and *tawātur* knowledge is discussed in clearer terms in works of logic. See, for instance, Ibn Taymīyah, *Jahd al-qarīḥah*, p. 316, who equates *tajrībīyāt* with *mutawātirāt*; also Quṭb al-Dīn al-Rāzī, *Taḥrīr al-qawāʿid al-manṭiqīyah fī sharḥ al-risālah al-shamsīyah* [of Kātibī], (Cairo: Muṣṭafā al-Bābī al-Ḥalabī, 1948), pp. 207–208.

44 Sunnī jurists are unanimous with regard to the *ẓannī* status of *āḥād* reports. The statistical probability of *ẓann* is certainly above half. According to Ghazālī, *ẓann* occurs when the soul is inclined to believe something but senses the existence of its opposite ("wa-yakūnu lil-nafsi sukūnun ilā al-shay'i wa-al-taṣdīqu bihi wa-hiya tashʿuru binaqīḍihi ... wa-hādha yusammā ẓannan"). See his *Mustaṣfā*, 1:44, ll. 3-4. Therefore, the lowest degree of probability in *ẓann* is greater than 0.5. A degree of probability equal to 0.5 is termed *shakk*. Jurists also recognized degrees of probability higher than 0.5 but lower than 1.0, which they called according to an ascending order

different transmitters support a particular point or issue, their probability together increases to a significant degree. That is, if we assume that two solitary reports possess in common a given theme, and the probability that each report being true is, say, 0.51, the aggregate probability of their being true is increased to a degree significantly higher than 0.51 but lower than 1.0. When a greater number of *āḥād* reports, all having independent channels of transmission, possess in common one theme, the knowledge of this theme becomes conclusive as well as immediate. While the previous type of *tawātur* is known as *lafẓī* on the grounds that the wording of the report in all instances of transmission is identical, this type of *tawātur* is recognized as *ma'nawī*, that is, although the transmissions differ from one another in wording, they all share the same meaning (*ma'nā*).[45]

Although the justification of *al-tawātur al-ma'nawī* ultimately reverts to the same principles which underly *al-tawātur al-lafẓī*, those Muslim jurists who admitted the authoritative character of the former (and they were the great majority) seem to have stressed the element of inductive support as the cornerstone of its validity. The emphasis here is placed on the differences among the reports insofar as the chains of transmission and the verbal contents are concerned. Given the common theme that they convey, these reports cannot but enhance the argument that this common theme is unquestionably true. The degree of probability attached to them individually is immediately eliminated once they are grouped together as one aggregate.[46] In other words, the possibility that these reports are separately false is soon dismissed when, taken all together, they testify uniformly to a particular issue. An argument in favor of the certainty yielded by such corroborative evidence is the reputed generosity of Ḥātim, about whom there is no single *mutawātir* report. The multitude of the solitary reports which testify to his generosity,

---

of strength *ghalabat al-ẓann*, *al-ẓann al-qawī*, and *al-ẓann al-mutākhim lil-yaqīn*. See Abū al-Walīd Ibn Khalaf al-Bājī, *Al-Ḥudūd fī al-uṣūl*, ed. N. Ḥammād (Beirut, 1973), p. 30; idem, *Al-Minhāj fī tartīb al-ḥijāj*, ed. A. M. Turki (Paris: Maisonneuve et Larose, 1978), p. 11, ll. 4-5; Farrā', *'Uddah*, 1:83, ll. 3–4.

[45] Āmidī, *Iḥkām*, 1:232–233; Bājī, *Al-Minhāj*, p. 76; Ḥillī, *Ma'ārij*, p. 140; Ibn Taymīyah, *Raf' al-malām*, p. 67.

[46] Ghazālī, *Mustaṣfā*, 1:48.

however, collectively engender in us an immediate, conclusive knowledge.[47]

The process by which knowledge obtains in the mind through *al-tawātur al-ma'nawī* is similar to that which obtains through *al-tawātur al-lafẓī*. Without being aware of the actual process of reporting, the intellect accumulates knowledge until the point when it becomes entirely certain of the information reported. The process is purely corroborative and cumulative. It is likened by jurists to drops of water or small pieces of bread; individually they are insufficient, but when they are continuously consumed they will eventually quench the thirst and fill the stomach.[48] An outstanding example of the conclusive corroboration and complete confirmation that *al-tawātur al-ma'nawī* lends to what may first appear as a probable issue is the authoritative basis of Sunnī consensus. As there existed no clear Qur'ānic verse or *mutawātir lafẓī* report to the effect that the consensus of the community, represented by its scholars, is infallible, Sunnī jurists sought another means by which they could prove the infallible character of this central institution. What they found was a large number of *āḥād* reports all sharing the theme that God will not allow his community as a whole to fall into error. The individual reports, which were deemed to yield only probable knowledge, are now as a whole taken to yield certain as well as immediate knowledge. And to confirm even this conclusive knowledge, other corroborative pieces of evidence derived from the other "sources of Sharī'ah" were taken into consideration.[49]

TAWĀTUR AND CONSENSUS

The central role that the corroboration of multiple transmissions plays in bringing about certainty is obvious in the theory of

[47] Muwaffaq al-Dīn Ibn Qudāmah, *Taḥrīm al-naẓar fī kutub ahl al-kalām*, ed. and trans. George Makdisi (London: Luzac, 1962), p. 39, par. 68 (English trans. pp. 26–27); Āmidī, *Iḥkām*, 1:164, 232–233, 237–238. See another example given in my article "On the Authoritativeness of Sunni Consensus," *International Journal of Middle East Studies* 18 (1986): 445.

[48] Qarāfī, *Sharḥ*, p. 350; Sarakhsī, *Uṣūl*, 1:295.

[49] For a detailed analysis of this problem see my "On the Authoritativeness of Sunni Consensus," pp. 427–454, especially pp. 441–450. Also see Ibn Qudāmah, *Rawḍah*, pp. 118–119; Qarāfī, *Sharḥ*, pp. 338–339.

the *mashhūr* report, a report which originated as *āḥādī* but acquired the status of *tawātur* subsequent to the demise of the Companions and the Followers.[50] This report yields certain, though mediate knowledge. The assumption that the Companions and the Followers could not, by virtue of having lived in so early and pristine a phase of Islam, have lied or conspired on a forgery, precludes the possibility that this *āḥādī* report is probable. And once it becomes highly circulated after the Followers, the great number of instances of transmission will certainly secure its conclusiveness. The verification of the *mashhūr*'s early stages of transmission, however, presupposes an amount of conscious thinking, a fact which renders the knowledge obtained from it mediate rather than necessary.[51]

Despite their full awareness of the probabilistic nature of the early stages of the *mashhūr*'s transmission, the jurists who upheld this theory insisted on the impossibility of error or forgery when a sufficient—*mutawātir*—number of people were involved in its later stages. The mere fulfillment of the condition of *tawātur* number could, one is compelled to conclude, ensure infallibility and, consequently, certitude. *Tawātur* number as such can therefore be used interchangeably with consensus. Indeed, commenting on the *mashhūr* report, 'Alā' al-Dīn al-Samarqandī observes that "the *mashhūr* tradition is that which the scholars [of the age] have favorably received, so that there exists a consensus of the people

[50] For what seems to have been the beginnings of the notion of *mashhūr*, and for a highly interesting but unrepresentative view of *tawātur*, see the early treatise of Ḥasan ibn Sahl ibn Ghālib, *Al-Taṣdīq*, with a French translation by Marie Bernand-Baladi, "Des critères de la certitude: un opuscule de Ḥasan Ibn Sahl sur la crédibilité du dire transmis par un grand nombre," *Journal Asiatique* 257 (1969): 102–138. The translator's remarks in the introduction (pp. 98–100) to the text concerning the circularity of *ḥadīth* and consensus should be read with great caution.

[51] Sarakhsī, *Uṣūl*, 1:291–292; Nasafī, *Kashf al-asrār*, 2:6–7. While the majority of the jurists who recognized the category of *mashhūr* held that the knowledge resulting from this report is certain though mediate, a minority, such as 'Īsa ibn Abān, argued that such report can yield only a high degree of probable knowledge (*ṭuma'nīnah*). Against this last claim, Sarakhsī, *Uṣūl*, 2:292, cites *mashhūr* reports concerning the prohibition of usury and the prohibition of concluding a marriage with the maternal or paternal aunt of one's wife. Such reports, he asserts, are so certain that they may be used to abrogate verses from the Qur'ān. "Nothing can abrogate the verses of the Book unless it yields conclusive knowledge [*'ilm al-yaqīn*]."

of the age to accept it. Its status is thus that of consensus, and since the latter imposes certain knowledge, so does the former."[52]

In explaining the rationale behind the certitude of consensus, Sarakhsī insists on the significance of the number of people involved. Attaining certainty on the level of the community is tantamount to a combination of a great number of degrees of probability. Identical instances which are probable will conjoin to create certainty. In the section dealing with consensus he asserts that "what is established in sensory and legal matters by an aggregate of things (*ijtimā'*) cannot be established by individual things severally (*infirād*). Individuals cannot separately carry a heavy log; but if they group together they will be able to do so.... [This principle] we have already expounded when we dealt with the *mutawātir*."[53] The very principle of *tawātur* then constitutes the rationale for the certitude of consensus.[54] The association of consensus with *tawātur* comes out quite clearly in the debate about the number of qualified jurists (*mujtahids*) who make up consensus. While such legists as 'Abd al-Wahhāb al-Subkī refuse to accept as consensus any agreement from which even a less than *mutawātir* number of *mujtahids* are absent, some Mālikīs and early Mu'tazilīs accept any consensus as valid as long as the number of *mujtahids* who do not partake in it is less than *mutawātir*.[55] In either case, a

[52] Cited in A. Zysow, "The Economy of Certainty: An Introduction to the Typology of Islamic Legal Theory" (Ph.D. diss., Harvard University, 1984), p. 26. See also the discussion, pp. 24–29, concerning the Ḥanafī arguments against and for the *mashhūr*'s certitude.

[53] Sarakhsī, *Uṣūl*, 1:295–296. See also Sa'd al-Dīn al-Taftāzānī, *Sharḥ al-'aqā'id al-nasafīyah*, ed. Claude Salāmah (Damascus: Wizārat al-Thaqāfah wa-al-Irshād al-Qawmī, 1974), p. 17, ll. 12-15.

[54] See Ibn 'Abd al-Barr, *Jāmi' bayān al-'ilm*, 2:41–42, who associates consensus with *tawātur* in the following words: "The Sunnah [of the Prophet] may be divided into two parts, one of which is a consensus transmitted through a sufficient number of people, generation after generation. This constitutes a conclusive proof if there existed no disagreement [concerning its transmission]. He who rejects this consensus would, in effect, be rejecting a divine text. The second part of the Sunnah is the solitary [*āḥād*] report...." It should be cautioned, however, that the association of consensus with *tawātur* should not imply that the argument for the authoritativeness of consensus involves a *petitio principii*, because whereas consensus rests on the notion of *tawātur*, *tawātur*, whatever its form, does not derive its authoritativeness from consensus.

[55] Qarāfī, *Sharḥ*, p. 336.

mutawātir number of *mujtahid*s opposing consensus will certainly nullify that consensus.

If consensus grounded in *tawātur* acquires legitimacy, then a consensus in which all the scholars of the community partake will, *a fortiori*, lead to certitude. In such a consensus the enumeration of probable instances goes beyond the already conclusive *mutawātir* to encompass each and every instance, thereby reaching a conclusion squarely based upon summative induction. Each confirming instance, represented by a legal opinion of an independent *mujtahid*, is a member of a class. The *mujtahid* upholds an opinion which is admittedly probable. But in reaching this opinion, he, as an acknowledged authority on the Law, establishes himself as a self-contained agent; that is, he himself must reach the opinion through a direct analysis of the authoritative legal sources, and thus his opinion represents the ruling which was *probably* decreed by God. If all the other *mujtahid*s who reached their opinions through similar, independent means agree on the same point of law, then they will be corroborating each other as well as conclusively demonstrating that the ruling of that particular case is certain. Here we attain a full enumeration of all the members of the class. The certitude resulting from this enumeration hardly needs any justification, especially in a system which is endowed with divine providence against error once *tawātur* obtains.

ABŪ ISḤĀQ AL-SHĀṬIBĪ

Partly grounded in what may be described as a subjective theological transcendentalism and partly in rational-cum-empirical justification, this theory of inductive corroboration stood as the underlying logical-methodological foundation for a number of material and theoretical legal principles, ranging from the various types of Prophetic reports to consensus. The theoretical elaboration and development of this inductive doctrine as part of legal theory came about after the introduction of Greek logic into *kalām* and *uṣūl al-fiqh*. Whether or not there existed a necessary connection between the introduction of Greek logic into the domain of law and the development of a theory of inductive corroboration, it remains true that it is only during the fifth/eleventh century and thereafter that this theory began to surface in the works of the jurists. In fact, it was not until the seventh/thirteenth century that logic, whether formal or inductive, made itself an integral part of an important segment of *uṣūl al-fiqh* works, and affected in one way or another the construction of theoretical legal precepts.[56] While the majority of *uṣūl*ists confined the use of the theory of inductive corroboration to problems such as those discussed above, we find that some others have utilized this theory even more extensively. In his *Al-Muwāfaqāt fī uṣūl al-aḥkām*,[57] for instance, Abū Isḥāq al-Shāṭibī (d. 790/1388) went so far as to anchor his entire theory of *uṣūl al-fiqh* in inductive principles.

Shāṭibī begins with the fundamental premise that general theoretical legal principles and the sources of law are firmly grounded in certitude and that they derive their authoritativeness from God, for should there be any degree of probability concerning these principles and sources, there might follow the ominous conclusion that such probability (*ẓann*) may well decline to a degree of doubt (*shakk*),[58] thereby rendering the Sharīʿah, the decree of God, mutable. The certitude surrounding the general principles and sources of the law must then be derived either from conclusive pieces of textual evidence (*adillah*) which, Shāṭibī admits, are rare if they exist at all, or through an inductive survey of the multitude of probable pieces of evidence supporting these principles.[59] Shāṭibī argues that the aggregation of such pieces of evidence is perhaps the main source of certainty in law. The *tawātur*, whether *lafẓī* or *maʿnawī*, derives its certainty from this principle. Each individual chain of transmission is undeniably probable, but when a sufficient number of transmitted reports are heard, certainty of the contents of the report obtains. He asserts that both the conclusive certainty concerning the Five Pillars of Islam and the indubitable authoritativeness of consensus and *qiyās* are established in this manner. Likewise, such fundamental juridical principles as the

[56] On the infiltration and assimilation of Greek logic in Sunnī legal theory, see part 1 of my article "Logic, Formal Arguments and Formalization of Arguments in Sunni Legal Theory," *Arabica*, forthcoming.

[57] Ed. M. M. ʿAbd al-Ḥamīd, 4 vols. (Cairo: Maṭbaʿat al-Madanī, 1969-1970).

[58] Shāṭibī, *Muwāfaqāt*, 1:10–12. For the distinction between *ẓann* and *shakk* see note 44 above.

[59] Shāṭibī, *Muwāfaqāt*, 1:13.

natural right to have a religion, to own property, to procreate, and so on, are advocated by the Sharī'ah in no uncertain terms, terms that are individually probable, but in their multitude they corroborate and affirm the validity of these principles beyond any doubt.[60]

The evidence that may be utilized in proving the certainty of legal principles may not be confined to the formal verbal expression contained in the Prophetic reports and the Qur'ān. Rather, these principles derive from the meaning which may be found, by means of induction, to permeate the entirety of *shar'ī* material sources. Induction in Shāṭibī's theory is not merely an exhaustive account of the reports that pertain in their totality to a particular issue, but rather a thematic induction (*istiqrā' ma'nawī*) of the spirit and the letter of the Sharī'ah. The evidence may not be especially decreed for a particular case, or may not even directly touch upon the issue in question, but its indirect relatedness to, and subsidiary support of, the issue yields certainty in the event of obtaining a sufficient number of corroborative instances.[61]

In other words, the certainty of the general legal principles results from the cumulative corroboration of statements and indications found in passages and contexts that are not as a whole necessarily relevant to these principles. Corroborative pieces of evidence may appear in passing, or as minor points in a larger body of evidence.[62] The conclusive knowledge of Ḥātim's generosity, for instance, obtains upon hearing countless anecdotes in all of which there exists, irrespective of the differing nature and contents of these anecdotes, a common theme to the effect of his generosity.[63] It is therefore the recurrence of a meaning or a theme in a Prophetic report, Qur'ānic verse, or any circumstantial evidence, which will inevitably lead to certainty in the mind of the hearer. Shāṭibī plainly states that widespread and constantly recurrent themes or statements ("mā ḥaṣala fīhi

[60] Ibid., 1:13–14, also pp. 15–16 (on the authoritativeness of *al-istidlāl al-mursal* and *istiḥsān*).

[61] Ibid., 2:35–36.

[62] Ibid., 1:15.

[63] Ibid., 3:189. See also Qarāfī, *Sharḥ*, p. 239.

al-takrār wa-al-ta'kīd wa-al-intishār") rank equally with decisive and conclusive texts.[64] In Shāṭibī's theory then, all *mutawātir* and *mashhūr* reports have a force equivalent to that of summative induction.[65] But what are the logical properties and logical justification of this induction?

In contradistinction to the particularistic nature of positive legal rulings (*furū'*), legal theory entails the construction of general principles and universal truths (*kullīyāt*). The great majority, if not the entirety, of these *kullīyāt* are based, as Shāṭibī has already intimated, on a multitude of probable instances or particular statements (*juz'īyāt*) which corroborate each other to the degree of certainty.

Shāṭibī is acutely conscious of the basic rule of induction which premises that to attain certainty with regard to a matter all the particulars or species subsumed under that matter must be enumerated and found to be mutually corroborative. If, on the other hand, one succeeds in reaching a *kullīyah* on the basis of enumerating the great majority of instances, then there should be no instance which will contradict the *kullīyah*. This curious assertion may be explained in light of his assumption that if a particular instance is proven to be in contradiction with the rest of the instances constituting a given *kullīyah* then one of the two, the instance or the *kullīyah* is invalid. But our author remains insistent upon the claim that once a *kullīyah* is reached on the basis of the great majority of relevant, corroborative instances, then such *kullīyah* cannot be invalidated by what appears to be a non-conforming or non-corroborative instance. Indeed, upon examining such an instance one would find that its essence (*dhāt*) differs from the essences of the other corroborative instances, a difference which justifies its unsubsumability under that *kullīyah*. The essences of the particulars under a *kullīyah* must be identical, and must not be subject to external influences (*umūr khārijah*). Take, for instance, the essence of humanity, namely, acting with intent and premeditation. You survey a great number of humans who will indeed corroborate and ultimately confirm this assumption. You may, however, come across

[64] *Muwāfaqāt*, 3:192, 194, ll. 17–18.
[65] Ibid., 1:13, ll. 1 ff.; 3:189, ll. 4-9.

an individual who does not act with premeditation because he is afflicted with a certain severe disease. This particular individual will not invalidate the *kullīyah* which premises that humans act with premeditation, for illness has effected a change in his essence. Likewise, the general principles of contractual law will not be rescinded just because the contract of *'arāyā* conforms to a different set of contractual legal assumptions.[66] Similarly, *tayammum* (ritual cleanliness with sand or soil) cannot abrogate the prescribed *kullīyah* of ritual purity (*ṭahārah*) which God intended as a means of cleanliness.[67] These non-conforming instances each have an essence, designed by divine wisdom (*ḥikmah*), which is not identical to the essences of the instances subsumed under that particular *kullīyah*.

That a particular species is proven to be unlike other species forming a genus and thus is rightly excluded from enumeration, creates no difficulty in Shāṭibī's theory. When a species is shown to have no common denominator with a number of other species, there would be, to begin with, no sense in utilizing it as a corroborative instance. But the logically problematic issue in Shāṭibī's theory is that he accepts as conclusive a *kullīyah* even though there has not been a complete survey of all the relevant instances. "In the Sharī'ah," he says, "the great majority of particulars [constituting a *kullīyah*] are considered as tantamount to a conclusive general, since the instances diverging from a *kullīyah* cannot constitute another *kullīyah* which can then compete with the first established *kullīyah*."[68] Put differently, a truly authoritative as well as conclusive *kullīyah* will not allow for a significant number of diverging instances to constitute another equally authoritative *kullīyah*. Therefore, Shāṭibī argues, an already established *kullīyah* will not be undermined because a single instance stands

[66] *'Arāyā* is a type of contract in which unripe dates on the palm tree are bartered against their value calculated in terms of edible dried dates. Although Islamic law does not allow the element of risk in contracts, the *'arāyā* contract was recognized despite the risk and uncertainty it involves. Taqī al-Dīn al-Subkī, *Takmilat al-Majmū'*, 12 vols. (Cairo: Maṭba'at al-Taḍāmun, 1344 A.H.), 11:2 ff.

[67] Shāṭibī, *Muwāfaqāt*, 2:36–37, 43–44, 3:7–8.

[68] Ibid., 2:37, ll. 6–7.

in opposition to it.[69] Only a significant number of competing particulars can weaken or undermine a *kullīyah*.[70]

In support of this thesis, Shāṭibī introduces the example of the solitary reports which are generally considered authoritative for practice (*'amal*) although some of them are dubious. In comparison with those sound reports, the few doubtful ones pale into insignificance. Similarly, in rational sciences a mistake remains isolated and unaccounted for, but once scholars continue to reiterate the same mistake, it becomes the rule rather than the exception. When exceptions are numerous in legal matters no general principle can be derived. It is only when the number of exceptions is insignificant that a *kullīyah* may be reached. Shāṭibī's awareness of his unconventional stance towards inductive logic seems to have compelled him to justify his thesis on the grounds that it is the only conceivable means by which general principles of law can be formulated.[71]

CONCLUSION

Although Shāṭibī's theory represents a novel approach to Sunnī legal theory, it can by no means be maintained that it was unique in its reliance on principles of inductive logic. The strictly logical presentation of the theory of induction in the context of legal studies appeared first in the works of Ghazālī, but it could not gain a foothold as an integral part of legal theory until the seventh/thirteenth or eighth/fourteenth century, with the emergence of such powerful writings as those of Taqī al-Dīn Ibn Taymīyah. But none of these scholars could, like Shāṭibī, build a full-fledged theory of law grounded solely in inductive logic. His is a consummate theory representing the most advanced stage in a prolonged

[69] Ibid., 1:119 ("waqad 'ulima anna al-kullīyata idhā 'āraḍahā al-juz'īyu falā athara lil-juz'īyi"); 2:36 ("al-kullīyatu ... la yarfa'uhā takhallufu āḥādi al-juz'īyāt"); 3:7 ("al-kullīyu lā yankharimu bi-juz'īyin"). It is significant that Ibn Rushd, *Talkhīs manṭiq Arisṭū*, 1:352–353, distinguishes between demonstrative induction (*istiqrā' burhānī*) and dialectical induction (*istiqrā' jadalī*). The former must, in order to be valid, encompass all the particulars in existence, but the latter need only include those particulars which are deemed to have gained credence (*mashhūrāt*) on account of their acceptance by people in general.

[70] *Muwāfaqāt*, 3:5, l. 11 ("fa-al-i'rāḍu 'an al-juz'īyi jumlatan yu'addī ilā al-shakki fī al-kullī").

[71] Ibid., 1:84, 85.

process of theoretical development. The embryonic beginnings of this process first appeared in the fourth/tenth and fifth/eleventh centuries in connection with *al-tawātur al-ma'nawī* of *āḥād* reports. As one traces down the sources there emerges a clear pattern of attempts to lay down a general theory of *tawātur* in terms of the *tawātur ma'nawī*. In this theory, the traditional theory which came to be known as *al-tawātur al-lafẓī* played an important, but partial role. The central concept in this general theory was inductive corroboration, not necessarily of reports transmitted in a verbally identical fashion but of reports having in common the same meaning. Shāṭibī's concept of thematic induction (*al-istiqrā' al-ma'nawī*) represents an extension of *al-tawātur al-ma'nawī*; instead of restricting the application of the principle to Prophetic reports, Shāṭibī utilized it in extracting from the entirety of the *shar'ī* sources a set of principles of universal validity.

While Shāṭibī went beyond his predecessors in developing a legal theory of induction, he remained faithful to the logical assumptions underlying the already established theory of *tawātur*, which, as we have indicated, formed the basis for his general theory. The adoption of these assumptions, along with their logical properties, resulted in an inductive theory of law constructed of these same properties. *Tawātur*, which in practical terms is a state of immediate knowledge obtaining in the mind, is subjectively determined by the hearer and does not need, once reached, to exhaust the entirety of the instances of transmission in existence. The same degree of conclusive certainty is claimed to be reached in Shāṭibī's inductive theory, although the enumeration of all the members of a particular class may not be totally exhausted.

The intellectual world of Shāṭibī and his co-religionists was anchored in the premise that what makes things the way they are in this world is none other than the Almighty. The unshaken belief and faith in the words of the Prophet existed in the factual world of certainty, and that had to be explained in terms of divine intent and volition. Thus knowledge and the lack of it were the works of God; if we "know," it is because our knowledge has been granted and guaranteed by God. Had Hume been a Muslim jurist, he would certainly have found his otherwise aborted theory of necessary causal connection between events guaranteed to him by his Creator. And if this were not the case, he would have encountered no problem in constructing a world view based on the principle of the uniformity of nature; for, after all, Muslims were indeed the recipients of divine providence, expressed in the *'ādah* of their Lord.

V

WAS THE GATE OF IJTIHAD CLOSED?

INTRODUCTION

As conceived by classical Muslim jurists, *ijtihād* is the exertion of mental energy in the search for a legal opinion to the extent that the faculties of the jurist become incapable of further effort. In other words, ijtihad is the maximum effort expended by the jurist to master and apply the principles and rules of *uṣūl al-fiqh* (legal theory) for the purpose of discovering God's law.[1] The activity of ijtihad is assumed by many a modern scholar to have ceased about the end of the third/ninth century, with the consent of the Muslim jurists themselves. This process, known as 'closing the gate of ijtihad' (in Arabic: '*insidād bāb al-ijtihād*'), was described by Joseph Schacht as follows:

> By the beginning of the fourth century of the hijra (about A.D. 900), however, the point had been reached when the scholars of all schools felt that all essential questions had been thoroughly discussed and finally settled, and a consensus gradually established itself to the effect that from that time onwards no one might be deemed to have the necessary qualifications for independent reasoning in law, and that all future activity would have to be confined to the explanation, application, and, at the most, interpretation of the doctrine as it had been laid down once and for all. This 'closing of the door of *ijtihād*', as it was called, amounted to the demand for *taḳlīd*, a term which had originally denoted the kind of reference to Companions of the Prophet that had been customary in the ancient schools of law, and which now came to mean the unquestioning acceptance of the doctrines of established schools and authorities. A person entitled to *ijtihād* is called *mujtahid*, and a person bound to practice *taḳlīd*, *muḳallid*.[2]

J. N. D. Anderson remarked, as did many others, that about the end of the third/ninth century it was commonly accepted that the gate of ijtihad had become closed.[3] And to confirm that this closure was a *fait accompli*, H. A. R. Gibb asserted that the early Muslim scholars held that the gate "was closed, never again to be reopened."[4] W. M. Watt seems to be aware of some inaccuracies in the standard account about this subject but has not formulated an alternative view.[5] Depending on the particular subject of their discussion, many scholars would have us believe that the closure of the gate had an impact on, or was influenced by, this or that element in Islamic history. Some use it to explain the immunity of the Shari^{c}a against the interference of government, and others to illustrate the problem of decadence in Islamic institutions and culture.[6] Some date the closure at the beginning of the fourth Islamic century and others advance it to the seventh,[7] depending on the facts and analyses involved in each study. Thus, on the basis of this alleged closure, aspects of Islamic history were reconstructed and interpreted time after time.

A systematic and chronological study of the original legal sources reveals that these views on the history of ijtihad after the second/eighth century are entirely baseless and inaccurate. In the following pages, I shall try to show that the gate of ijtihad was not closed in theory nor in practice. To do so, I shall first demonstrate that ijtihad was indispensable in legal theory because it constituted the only means by which jurists were able to reach the judicial judgements decreed by God. In order to regulate the practice of ijtihad a set of conditions were required to be met by any jurist who wished to embark on such activity. An exposition of these conditions will prove that, unlike the often-held view, the demands of legal theory were relatively easy to meet and they facilitated rather than hindered the activity of ijtihad. Further, it will enhance our thesis to examine the relationship between this theory, in which ijtihad was deemed a perennial duty, and the actual practice of Muslim jurists. Such an inquiry will disclose that ijtihad was not only exercised in reality, but that all groups and individuals who opposed it were finally excluded from Sunnism.

By chronologically analyzing the relevant literature on the subject from the fourth/tenth century onwards, it will become clear that (1) jurists who were capable of ijtihad existed at nearly all times; (2) ijtihad was used in developing positive law after the formation of the schools; (3) up to *ca.* 500 A.H. there was no mention whatsoever of the phrase 'insidad bab al-ijtihad' or of any expression that may have alluded to the notion of the closure; (4) the controversy about the closure of the gate and the extinction of mujtahids prevented jurists from reaching a consensus to that effect.

Let us now turn to examine ijtihad in legal theory and the conditions that this theory required for its practice.

IJTIHAD IN LEGAL THEORY (*uṣūl al-fiqh*)

In Islamic legal theory, discovering the law of God was of crucial significance, for it was the law that informed man of the conduct acceptable to Allah. It is exactly for the purpose of finding the rulings decreed by God that the methodology of usul al-fiqh was established.

The Quran and the Sunna of the Prophet do not, as a rule, specify the law as it might be stated in specialized law manuals, but only contain some rulings (*aḥkām*; pl. of *ḥukm*) and indications (*dalālāt* or *amārāt*) that lead to the causes (*ᶜilal*; pl. of *ᶜilla*) of these rulings. On the basis of these indications and causes the mujtahid may attempt, by employing the procedure of *qiyās* (analogy) to discover the judgement (*ḥukm*) of an unprecedented case (*farᶜ*; pl. of *furūᶜ*). But before embarking on this original task, he must first search for the judgement in the works of renowned jurists. If he fails to find a precedent in these works he may look for a similar case in which legal acts are different but legal facts are the same. Failing this he must turn to the Quran, the Sunna, or *ijmaᶜ* (consensus) for a precedent that has a ᶜilla identical to that of the farᶜ. When this is reached he is to apply the principles of *qiyās* (analogy) in order to reach the ruling of the case in question. This ruling may be one of the following: the obligatory (*wājib*), the forbidden (*maḥẓūr*), the recommended (*mandūb*), the permissible (*mubāḥ*), or the disapproved (*makrūh*).[8]

The primary objective of legal theory, therefore, was to lay down a coherent system of principles through which a qualified jurist could extract rulings for novel cases. From the third/ninth century onwards this was universally recognized by jurists to be the sacred purpose of usul al-fiqh.[9]

Legal theory in all its parts is sanctioned by divine authority, that is, it derives its authority (*ḥujjiyya*) from revealed sources. It is partly for this reason and partly for the reason of man's duty to worship his Creator in accordance with divine law that the practice of ijtihad was declared to be a religious duty (*farḍ kifāya*) incumbent upon all qualified jurists whenever a new case should appear.[10] Until ijtihad is performed by at least one mujtahid, the Muslim community remains under the spell of this unfulfilled duty.

In theory at least there is certainly nothing to indicate that ijtihad was put out of practice or abrogated. In due course it will become clear that legal theory played a rather significant role in favor of ijtihad. Thus, if the practice of ijtihad was the primary objective of the methodology and theory of usul al-fiqh throughout Islamic history, the question that may be asked is in what way was the gate of ijtihad thought to have been closed? It has been assumed, among other things, that the practice of ijtihad was abandoned because the qualifications required for its practice "were made so immaculate and rigorous and were set so high that they were humanly impossible of fulfillment."[11] This supposition can be refuted through an examination of the writings of jurists on the subject.

The earliest complete published account[12] of usul al-fiqh in which the qualifications of mujtahids are stated is Abu Husayn al-Basri's (d. 436/1044) *al-Muᶜtamad fī Uṣūl al-Fiqh.*[13] Basri's first requirement for ijtihad entails a knowledge of the Quran, the Sunna of the Prophet and the principles of inference (*istidlāl*), and qiyas. The investigation of the ways of *ḥadīth* transmission and the trustworthiness of transmitters is necessary for verifying the credibility of *akhbār* (prophetic reports). The overall emphasis of Basri falls especially on qiyas as an indispensible tool in any undertaking of ijtihad, which in turn involves the practical knowledge of all rules related to ᶜilla, *aṣl* (the legal part in the texts), farᶜ, and hukm. In the process of deducing the ᶜilla from the aṣl, the text, with its inner contradictions and linguistic-legal complications, has to be analyzed. To solve these contradictions and to understand intricate exegetical matters the jurist must have a thorough knowledge of the principles of *majāz* (metaphors), particularization, and abrogation. Familiarity with the Arabic language, particularly with the *khāṣṣ* (particular) and the *ᶜāmm* (general), is a prerequisite. Curiously, Basri regards familiarity with customary law (*ᶜurf*) as a qualification required for ijtihad, for it is essential, he argues, to determine God's law in the light of the exigencies of human life. Much the same, the jurist must acquaint himself with God's attributes, which are the only guarantee for arriving at a correct understanding of His intentions as expressed in scripture. Equally important is the doctrine of the infallibility of the Muslim community to which the Prophet had attested. Although Basri makes no demands on the mujtahid to know the positive rulings (*furūᶜ*) that had been subject to ijmaᶜ, he asserts that no jurist is allowed to reinvestigate a case the ruling of which has already been derived. This implies that whoever intends to practice ijtihad to solve a specific case must first be certain that it was not treated before, and this consequently requires of him to know the furuᶜ of at least his school.[14]

Finally, Basri mitigates the rigorousness of these requirements in the law of inheritance. Whenever a jurist is capable of practicing ijtihad in a single case of inheritance and has no access to the above-mentioned skills, he may still be allowed to do so. According to Basri, this is justified on the grounds that methodical principles and textual subject-matter related to inheritance are independent of, and unconnected with, other parts of the law. Otherwise, the jurist must not attempt ijtihad in any other area of law until he is well equipped with the necessary tools.[15]

Shirazi (d. 467/1083) limits the knowledge of the Quran and the Sunna to those provisions that have a direct relevance to Shariᶜa, thus omitting irrelevant parts such as proverbs, tales, etc.[16] Principles of the Arabic language, points of agreement and disagreement among previous generations, and qiyas are all necessary usul rudiments. The jurist must know the texts from which he can extract the ᶜilla and must possess the methods to do so. Given the fact that more then one ᶜilla may be deduced in a single case, he must be able to distinguish between a variety of ᶜilal and to determine which deserves to be advanced over the others.

When discussing the requirements of ijtihad, Ghazali (d. 505/1111) maintained that in order to reach the rank of mujtahid the jurist must:[17]

1. Know the 500 verses needed in law; committing them to memory is not a prerequisite.
2. Know the way to relevant hadith literature; he needs only to maintain a reliable copy of Abu Dawud's or Bayhaqi's collections rather than memorize their contents.
3. Know the substance of furuᶜ works and the points subject to ijmaᶜ, so that he does not deviate from the established laws. If he cannot meet this requirement he must ensure that the legal opinion he has arrived at does not contradict any opinion of a renowned jurist.
4. Know the methods by which legal evidence is derived from the texts.
5. Know the Arabic language; complete mastery of its principles is not a prerequisite.
6. Know the rules governing the doctrine of abrogation. However, the jurist need not be thoroughly familiar with the details of this doctrine; it suffices to show that the verse or the hadith in question had not been repealed.
7. Investigate the authenticity of hadith. If the hadith has been accepted by Muslims as reliable, it may not be questioned. If a transmitter was known for probity, all hadiths related through him are to be accepted. Full knowledge of the science of *al-taᶜdīl wal-tajrīḥ* (hadith criticism) is not required.

These qualifications, Ghazali remarks, are required from jurists who intend to embark on ijtihad in all areas of substantive law. Those who want to practice ijtihad in one area, e.g., family law, or only in a single case, say a case of divorce, need not fulfill all the conditions but are instead required to know the methodological principles and the textual material needed to solve that particular problem.[18] Accordingly, a jurist may practice ijtihad in the area of liquor drinking (*muskirāt*) though his knowledge of hadith is limited. He must, however, be proficient in the procedure of qiyas and in the Quran, because muskirat cases depend heavily on the Quran and qiyas.

Apart from a slight emphasis on a few matters of religion and belief with which the mujtahid must be acquainted, and apart from the additional prerequisite of familiarity with the circumstances under which the Quran was revealed (*asbāb al-nuzūl*), Amidi (d. 632/1234) adds nothing to what others had previously said.[19] Noteworthy only is his emphasis that a less qualified mujtahid is allowed to solve a case without meeting the requirements set forth by Basri, Shirazi, Ghazali, and himself. All that he needs to know are the immediate tools to solve the issue in question.[20]

Only space here prevents us from discussing later jurists' writings on this issue, but to be sure, the successors of Ghazali and Amidi, such as Baydawi (d. 685/1286), Subki (d. 771/1369), Isnawi (d. 772/1370), Ibn al-Humam (d. 861/1456), Ibn Amir al-Hajj (d. 879/1474), Ansari (d. 1119/1707) and Ibn ᶜAbd al-Shakur (d. 1225/1810),[21] did not depart significantly from the established Sunni legal doctrine propounded by Ghazali. Some of these authors, such as Baydawi, demanded encompassing knowledge of the Quran and some others like Ibn al-Humam and Ibn Amir al-Hajj reduced the number of hadiths required to 1,200.[22] The more important point is that the divisibility (*tajziᵓa*) of ijtihad was recognized to be lawful in Sunni law and thus a limited knowledge of usul was sufficient to allow a jurist to practice ijtihad in an individual case.[23] Basri and Shirazi are nearly alone in not specifying that the divisibility of ijtihad is permissible in all areas of law.

It would therefore be implausible to maintain that the qualifications for ijtihad as set forth in Muslim legal writings made it impossible for jurists to practice ijtihad. The total knowledge required on the part of lawyers enabled many, as we shall see later, to undertake this practice in one area of law or another. The practice of ijtihad was further facilitated by removing the charge of sin from the mujtahid who commits an error and even made him entitled to one reward in heaven. In the case of a mujtahid whose ijtihad was sound, it was determined that he be doubly rewarded.[24] This being so, one can state with a fair amount of confidence that legal theory, including the qualifications required for the practice of ijtihad, can hardly be held responsible for narrowing the scope of ijtihad's activity, much less closing its gate. Further discussion of the role of ijtihad and mujtahids in Islamic legal history after the second/eighth century will show that ijtihad remained an integral part of the Sunni legal doctrine and that those who opposed it were finally excluded from Sunnism.

ANTI-IJTIHAD TRENDS AND THEIR EXCLUSION FROM SUNNISM

Throughout the third, fourth, and fifth Islamic centuries, ijtihad, the only channel of legal development, was rejected by various elements. Among these were extreme legal and theopolitical groups (or sects) that called for taqlid or condemned the principle of qiyas—a principle that constituted the backbone of ijtihad. These groups came mainly from the lines of the 'people of hadith', or

Traditionalists,[25] who were primarily concerned with the study of transmitted sources and their literal interpretation, while denying human reason any right to be exercised in ijtihad or in the process of legal reasoning. It is necessary to distinguish between types of hadith upholders, since within this vast heterogeneous body of Traditionalists there existed diverse groups ranging from those moderate scholars who were somewhat willing to co-exist with the 'people of *raʾy*' (who employed qiyas), to those extremists who rejected the strict procedure of qiyas even when based solely on scripture. To this last category belonged Dawud al-Zahiri (d. 270/883) and his school, the Hashwis, and other independent hadith scholars.[26]

Because of their inimical attitude towards ijtihad, these groups found no place inside the pale of Sunnism. Immediately after Dawud's death, a wave of writings in favor of qiyas was generated in response to Dawud's treatise which had attacked this analogical method. Qashani, himself one of the deserters of the Zahiri school, and the Jariri Nahrawani composed refutations against Dawud's treatise *Kitāb fī Ibṭāl al-Qiyās.*[27] More than two centuries later, when all legal schisms became well defined, the Shafiᶜi jurist Mawardi (d. 450/1058) described the status of this extreme Traditionalist party vis-à-vis Sunnism as follows:

> There are two kinds of people who reject analogy. Some reject it, follow the text literally and are guided by the sayings of their ancestors if there is no contradiction to the text in question. They reject completely the independent *ijtihād* and turn away from individual contemplation and free investigation. No judgeships may be entrusted to such persons since they apply the methods of jurisprudence insufficiently. The other category of people does reject analogy, but still uses independent judgement in legal deduction through reliance on the meaning (spirit) of the words and the sense of the address. The *ahl al-Ẓāhir* belong to the latter. Al-Shafiᶜi's followers are divided as to whether or not such theologians may be entrusted with a judgeship.[28]

Still later there seems to have prevailed a common idea that the Zahiri school must not be taken into consideraion whenever there is a discussion on legal matters in the Sunni community. This was clear in one of Ibn al-Salah's (d. 643/1245) influential *fatāwā* (legal opinions), which represented, to a great extent, the Sunni view on the illegitimacy of the school. Ibn al-Salah's main objection was to the attitude that the Zahiri school had adopted towards qiyas as a principle.[29]

Although Dawud disapproved of taqlid and claimed that one need not follow a human authority if he can use the legal sources,[30] his ijtihad was rejected by the Sunnis since he avoided the procedure of qiyas. Nevertheless, until the first half of the fourth century, Dawud's school remained as Sunni as any other major school. But when the legal theory was finally established and promulgated as the only Sunni doctrine, the Zahiri school gradually slipped outside the orb of Sunnism. This was manifest in the career of one of the most fervent advocates of Zahirism, the Andalusian Ibn Hazm, who was forced to flee his country because of his unorthodox beliefs.[31]

The fifth/eleventh century scholar Ghazali, when enumerating the Sunni schools of his time, counts only the schools of Abu Hanifa, Ibn Hanbal, Malik, Shafiᶜi, and Sufyan al-Thawri.[32] The fourth- and fifth-century *ikhtilāf* works, which dealt with differences in legal matters, excluded as a matter of principle the tenets of the Zahiris from consideration in determining the consensus.[33] In the eighth/fourteenth century, Ibn Khaldun remarked that "the Zahirite school has become extinct today as the result of the extinction of their religious leaders and disapproval of their adherents by the great mass of Muslims."[34] Thus it is clear that there was no school or a wing of a school inside the Sunni Muslim community that could have opposed ijtihad as a principle.[35]

This contention may invite some controversy, for it may be argued that the Hashwiyya, which is assumed to be an extreme Hanbali faction, rejected ijtihad in favor of taqlid.[36] Laoust considered the Hashwiyya a part of the Hanbali school.[37] In fact, the Hashwiyya was an ill-defined objectionable nickname indiscriminately applied against various groups who were thought to have possessed a weak apparatus of reasoning and have heavily relied on scripture.[38] The pieces of evidence that can be deduced from the fifth/eleventh century legal literature and thereafter indicate that the Hashwis were a radical non-Hanbali group of Traditionalists that possessed an incomplete legal doctrine. Their chief interest was theology (*uṣūl al-dīn*) rather than law;[39] they touched upon legal matters only when these had immediate relevance to theology. Sunni sources do not associate the Hashwiyya with any school of law. Ghazali condescendingly remarked that the Hashwis "believe that they are bound to a blind and routine submission to the criterion of human authority and to the literal meaning of the revealed books,"[40] and Subki clearly stated that they were a fanatic hadith group.[41] Such groups were impugned even by conservative Hanbalis like the historian-traditionalist Ibn al-Jawzi.[42] Moreover, the Hanbali Ibn ᶜAqil practically excluded the Hashwiyya from Sunnism when he declared that one of its main tenets was the rejection of human reason. "They believed," he remarked, "that there is something in human reason that contradicts the Shariᶜa."[43]

That the Hashwiyya could not have been a Hanbali faction is evident in the attitude of Hanbalism and Hashwism towards the issue of the necessity of ijtihad. While there is ample evidence to show that the Hanbali school had a consolidated posture towards the perpetual necessity for ijtihad and the existence of mujtahids,[44] the Hashwis persistently denied the Muslim jurists the right to practice ijtihad or any sort of human reasoning.

Although Halkin found the theological and political beliefs of the Hashwis and the Hanbalis to be identical,[45] it is certain that these theological similarities existed only in the third/ninth century. In that period the Hashwiyya may have been allied with the Hanbali Traditionalists. But since then Hanbalism, which was characterized by rigid views on legal theory, particularly on matters of qiyas, took a different road and pulled apart from the Hashwiyya as well as from other fanatic hadith groups. Until the end of the third/beginning of the tenth century, Hanbalism, generally speaking, was not credited with the status of a law school but was merely recognized as a hadith-theological faction. Tabari is known to have started a prolonged quarrel with the Hanbalis when he impugned Ibn Hanbal's juristic qualifications.[46] Thus, it was natural that in his *Ikhtilāf al-Fuqahā*ᵓ Tabari did not consider the views of Ibn Hanbal. Many other scholars did not view Hanbalis as law experts.

From the very end of the third/beginning of the tenth century onwards, Hanbalism had started a process of acquiring a comprehensive juristic character alongside its theological one. The upsurge of Hanbalism as a law school coincided with, and was influenced by, the recently established legal theory of Sunnism, whose spearheads and representatives were mainly the Shafiᶜis and the Hanafis. Hanbalism placed itself under the aegis of this theory, which obviously proved to be the theory most favored by the main body of Sunnism after long struggles between the 'people of raᵓy' and Traditionalists. As a consequence, Hanbalism had to adopt the main features of the legal theory which entailed the acceptance of qiyas as a source of law, almost equal in power to the Quran, the Sunna, and the ijmaᶜ. It is worth remembering that Ibn Hanbal established no legal system of his own, but in his answers to his pupils' questions he made pronouncements on certain points of law. Ibn Hanbal made concessions to human reasoning only under pressure of sheer necessity and where possible derived every law from scripture.[47] Three centuries later, Ibn ᶜAqil accepted qiyas as readily as any Hanafi or Shafiᶜi jurist, and the illustrious Hanbali Ibn Taymiyya not only endorsed qiyas but also defended sound *istiḥsān*.[48] In order to survive within Sunnism, Hanbalism had to go through a process of moderation and change from an extremist theological group to a peculiarly moderate law school while still maintaining certain theological inclinations. On the other hand, the Hashwiyya maintained its rigid attitude, which finally led to its exclusion from the Sunni community.[49]

That these groups failed to impair to the least degree the foundations of ijtihad was due mainly to the institutionalization of the science of usul al-fiqh, of which ijtihad was an indispensable ingredient. It is difficult to assume that at the time the theory of usul was finalized—about the beginning of the fourth/tenth century—Muslims had decided to 'close the gate of ijtihad'. In fact, an examination of the writings of jurists after the third/ninth century will demonstrate that ijtihad was exercised with no interruption.

IJTIHAD IN PRACTICE

Mujtahids in the Fourth/Tenth Century

During the third/ninth and fourth/tenth centuries mujtahids, whether independent or affiliated with legal schools, have expressed highly original views on law. Ibn Surayj (d. 306/918), Tabari (d. 310/922), Ibn Khuzayma (d. 311/923), and Ibn Mundhir (d. 316/928) are perfect examples of the independent type.[50] In the admission of the eighth/fourteenth-century lawyer Subki, these four mujtahids, though originally Shafiᶜis, have diverged from the rulings of Shafiᶜi,[51] and as is known, Tabari went further to establish his own school of law.[52] The scanty literature from the fourth/tenth century is insufficient to determine precisely what had occurred during this period, but it can be inferred from later sources that the scholars' activity, however creative, had to be contained in a certain school's doctrine, and in essence all teachings had to be attributed to one eponym or another. Like Abu Yusuf (d. 182/798), Shaybani (d. 189/804), and Muzani

(d. 264/877), creative scholars of the fourth/tenth century attributed their own doctrines to a great master. By so doing, they could avoid attacks that were the automatic reaction against fissiparous tendencies and could certainly earn immediate recognition once their opinions were put under the aegis of a great jurist such as Shafiᶜi. The Hanbali experience is a perfect example of this trend. As previously mentioned, Ibn Hanbal established no legal system. Nevertheless, by the end of the fourth/tenth century an elaborate Hanbali doctrine could be discerned. It is therefore evident that the positive law of the Hanbali school was constructed after the death of Ibn Hanbal by later great men like Khallal, Khiraqi, and others who attributed their doctrines to him.

Yet, although joining a law school and attributing new ideas to older authorities became the prevailing norm, a number of scholars openly disagreed with the established doctrines of the schools. Consider the following:

1. Ibn Hasan al-Tanukhi (d. 318/930): A famous Hanafi jurist who diverged to a certain extent from the teachings of Abu Hanifa, Abu Yusuf, and Shaybani.[53]
2. ᶜAli b. al-Husayn Ibn Harbawayh (d. 319/931): A famous Shafiᶜi jurist who, in a number of cases, disagreed with Shafiᶜi.[54]
3. Abu Saᶜid al-Istakhri (d. 328/939): A Shafiᶜi jurist who elaborated a number of furuᶜ cases that were at variance not only with Shafiᶜi's doctrine but also with the entire doctrines of the other schools.[55]
4. Abu ᶜAli b. Abi Hurayra (d. 345/956): "One of the greatest Shafiᶜis"[56] who formulated his own legal decisions concerning issues related to divorce, penal law, prayer, slavery, etc.
5. Ibn Haddad al-Misri (d. 345/956): Considered a prominent Shafiᶜi mujtahid, Ibn Haddad had his own independent opinions as regards matters related to marriage, *liᶜān* (imprecation), *riḍāᶜ* (fosterage), etc.[57]
6. Abu Hasan al-Dariki (d. 375/985): Nawawi relates[58] that al-Dariki displayed the largest degree of independence from the Shafiᶜi school. When asked for an opinion, "he would ponder at length, and would often make a decision not only contrary to Abu Hanifa's teachings but also to that of al-Shafiᶜi. When called to account for this he would reply: Here is the tradition A on the authority of B on the authority of C . . . down to the Prophet; it is better to follow this tradition than to act according to what Abu Hanifa or Shafiᶜi taught."[59]

It can be stated with certainty that from Tabari's time onwards an ijmaᶜ on the validity of the existing Sunni schools had begun to be finalized (except the Zahiri school which was gradually excluded from the Sunni legal system) and it seems that in the last three or four decades of the fourth/tenth century a comprehensive but implicit agreement on the illegality of establishing new schools and of any 'separatist' tendencies was reached. Thus, we find that all jurists from the fifth/eleventh century onwards officially follow one school or another, and in no single case did any jurist attempt to establish his own school although the activity of deriving solutions for new problems continued indefinitely. It must be noted, however, that until the modern period Muslim jurists, generally speaking, did not try to explain the fact that new schools had not been established after the year 300/912; neither did they try to rationalize the implicit consensus on prohibiting the establishing of such schools. The one case known to me where this phenomenon is explained can be found in Ibn Amir's *al-Taqrīr wal-Taḥbīr* and later in Ibn ᶜAbidin's *Rasāʾil.* Ibn Amir, quoting a certain Ibn al-Munir, remarked that the existence of a new legal system, i.e., a system of usul and furuᶜ, within the general context of Muslim religion is hard to perceive because early scholars, by exhausting all methodological means and deriving all possible solutions, have left no room for an additional school of law.[60] It is rather significant that neither Ibn Amir nor Ibn ᶜAbidin claimed the existence of ijmaᶜ on prohibiting the founding of new schools. Equally significant is the fact that they did not use the closing of the gate of ijtihad to explain this phenomenon.

Ijtihad in Law and Government in the Fifth/Eleventh Century

The jurists of the fifth/eleventh century seem to have followed their predecessors in taking ijtihad for granted. This is quite evident in the writings of all lawyers of the period. ᶜAbd al-Jabbar (d. 415/1024) and his disciple, Abu Husayn al-Basri, deemed ijtihad to be an indispensable ingredient in law. They further viewed qiyas, which is in itself only a method of ijtihad, as an element without which law would be incapable of growth. For them taqlid is to be used only by the commoner (*ᶜāmmiyy*) and by those for whom the exercise of ijtihad is impossible.[61] The views of ᶜAbd al-Jabbar and Basri on ijtihad and taqlid, although essentially Muᶜtazili, express the standard doctrine of Sunni Islam. Ibn ᶜAbd al-Barr (d. 463/1070) devoted a whole chapter in refutation of taqlid. He maintained that on the basis of many Quranic verses an agreement among scholars has been reached on the nullity of taqlid.[62] Al-Khatib al-Baghdadi (d. 463/1070) and al-Mawardi (d. 450/1058) expressed similar views.[63] The works of these scholars reflect the conviction of Muslim lawyers with regard to matters of religious and legal practices. Ibn ᶜAbd al-Barr, for example, is well aware of the fact that furuᶜ and new cases are endless and the only way for a jurist to encompass all branches of law, including the cases which may or may not have been previously solved, is to master the science of usul.[64] It is significant that he mentions that Islamic law must and can deal with new issues. It is through qiyas and ijtihad, he argues, that Shariᶜa can cope with the needs of Muslim society.

The importance of ijtihad exceeded the domain of law to penetrate the political thought of medieval Islam. A discussion of the changing politics in relation to ijtihad in the fifth/eleventh century will show the extent to which ijtihad was indispensable to the political institution in which the ulama played a prominent role. Such a discussion will also demonstrate that whereas political theory (which was, in the final analysis, the product of juristic thought) recognized the failure of Caliphs to meet the requirements of Shariᶜa by their incompetence to practice ijtihad, it asserted the ulama's important function as law interpreters in default of a sovereign who is ideally supposed to be in charge of Shariᶜa. It is relevant to assert here that although political theory was an extension of the basic principles of Islamic law, it was not in reality speculative, but rather pragmatic: It is the depiction of the past in a normative form and its adaptation to the present conditions with the purpose of illustrating a system of morals, the applications of which will maintain the unity and integrity of the Muslim community. Political theory then had to be practical, because its genesis and development were motivated by the ambition to restore the golden age of the Muslim Empire.[65]

In his discussion of the qualifications of the Imam, Baghdadi (d. 429/1037) considers the ability to practice ijtihad as one of the four conditions that the Imam (or Caliph) must satisfy in order to rule efficiently.[66] The same condition is required by Mawardi, who explains that ijtihad must be one of the Imam's skills because knowledge of law and of the means by which new problems (*nawāzil*) must be solved are an essential part of his duties.[67] The Imam is not the only individual who may practice ijtihad within the political institution; officials who are delegated by the head of the state may also practice it. The entire body of state officials is classified, according to Mawardi, into two categories; namely, executive (*ᶜummāl al-tanfīdh*) and delegative (*ᶜummāl al-tafwīḍ*). The latter are authorized to use their own reasoning—based on the principles of Shariᶜa—to tackle any problem that may arise while at governmental service. Mawardi insists that delegated officials must apply the results of their own ijtihad even though it may disaccord with that of the Imam.[68] Using the overriding usulist principles in his century as a base, Mawardi demands that the mufti as well as the judge (*qāḍī*) must fulfill the requirements of ijtihad.[69] With this last demand Mawardi does not but describe what had prevailed in the golden age and what ought to prevail in the present and the future. He had in mind all the official judges that were mujtahids from the time of *qāḍī al-quḍāt* Abu Yusuf through his own time, including himself. Mawardi, who was considered a mujtahid, was appointed by the Caliph as qadi and was granted the title of *aqḍā al-qudāt* (the most qualified of qadis).[70] His political doctrine unfolds the conviction that the jurists and scholars of the time can fulfill the requirements of the theory. But Mawardi's insistence that the Caliph must be capable of ijtihad proves that he (as well as Baghdadi) still hoped to restore the strength of the institution of the Caliphate which had been in constant decline since the fourth/tenth century.

Motivated by the same ambition of prominent jurists to maintain the solidarity of the Caliphate, Juwayni (d. 478/1085) composed a treatise on political-legal conduct addressed to the vizier Nizam al-Mulk; most likely during the reign of Muqtadi.[71] Following Baghdadi and Mawardi, Juwayni deems the quality of ijtihad to be a prerequisite for the ideal imam and for the well-being of the community. Should the Imam be a muqallid, Juwayni contends, it would impell him to consult other eminent jurists, a course of action that would impair his power of decision making and expose him to contradictory opinions. The Imam's practice of taqlid therefore, does not befit his status as the head of the community. Nevertheless, Juwayni was realistic enough to realize the impotency of the Caliphate at the time and its need for support by a broad class of professionals, chief among whom were the jurists. Juwayni's suggested solution to the problem where the Imam cannot fulfill the requirements of ijtihad is that he must, although ideally inadvisable, consult the ulama because "they are the real sovereigns" and "the leaders and masters of the community."[72] "If the sovereign (*sulṭān*) does not reach the degree of ijtihad, then the jurists are to be followed and the sultan will provide them with help, power, and protection."[73] Thus, it is clear that while trying to derive theory from the actual experience of the distant and near past, Juwayni puts the entire responsibility on the backs of the jurists.

But what if the Muslim jurists or Shari^{c}a become extinct? In trying to answer this question Juwayni mentions some facts that are of great significance to our inquiry. The following is indicative of the state of affairs prevalent at the second half of the fifth/eleventh century: "If an age becomes devoid of muftis who are mujtahids but is not devoid of transmitters of sound doctrines of the bygone eponyms—a description that almost fits this age and its people . . . "[74] But it does not quite fit. Elsewhere in the book when the author hypothetically assumes the extinction of muftis (who, in his definition, must be qualified mujtahids) and jurists, he bids his readers to try to envisage this *unreal* situation.[75] Needless to say, Juwayni, whose word in this case is definitely reliable, believed that mujtahids were extant at his time. This becomes wholly certain when we realize that Juwayni himself was not only a great theologian and poet but also a distinguished mujtahid.[76]

In the process of his discussion, Juwayni attempts to find solutions to a further hypothetical situation of decay. On the possible extinction of mujtahids he remarks:

> I have imagined the dissolution of Shari^{c}a, the extinction of those in charge of it and the disinterest of people in it . . . I have also seen that the great eponyms of the legal schools once defunct are not replaced and those who seek knowledge are satisfied with superficialities . . . Therefore, I know that should this state of affairs persist, the ulama of Shari^{c}a will soon become extinct and there will remain nothing after them but their books.[77]

The ulama, Juwayni contends, are in charge of affairs, especially when the Imam has no way to ijtihad, and their opinion is final and must be accepted even though it may contradict an opinion of a school's eponym. When speaking of past and present mujtahids, Juwayni argues that it is difficult to imagine that the ijtihad of later mujtahids must always correspond to that of the head of the school, because the ways of ijtihad and the methods of reasoning are numerous and thus the results of such ijtihad may differ.[78]

Ghazali, himself a student of Juwayni, argued (and his argument seems a natural sequence to Juwayni's thought and a further step towards accepting the political impotency of the institution of Caliphate) that ijtihad is not a requirement to be necessarily fulfilled by the Imam himself. It is a pure legal qualification required neither by Shar^{c} nor by public interest (*maṣlaḥa*).[79] If the purpose of the Caliphate is to comply with Shar^{c}, Ghazali contended, what difference does it make if the Imam reaches a legal opinion through his own interpretation or through the interpretation of a mujtahid? In order to justify this, Ghazali draws a parallel between the legal and the political situation. Thus, since the Caliph's political and military authority that is 'delegated' to the Sultan (*ṣāḥib al-shawka*) was accepted *de facto* as *de jure*, a legal authority that is also 'delegated' to the best qualified mujtahid must be equally justified.[80] That the mujtahid must be the best of jurists and the "most extensively learned" is an essential requirement of which one cannot dispose. Ghazali, trying to show that the reliance on mujtahids is always possible, states that Baghdad is rarely devoid of a jurist whose knowledge of law is very advanced.[81] Although Ghazali does not mention here the term *mujtahid*, it can be safely stated, from the context and theme of his discussion, that he was speaking of one, for it is the issue of ijtihad which was after all the subject of the entire discussion.

The weakening of the Caliphate, which found its expression, *inter alia*, in the legal impotency of the Caliph, constituted for the ulama an urgent problem that was seriously treated, although ineffectively, in a mass of writings. The insistence of jurists on the requirement of ijtihad, whether fulfilled by the Caliph himself or by others, furthermore enhances the fact that inasmuch as ijtihad was indispensable in legal matters it was equally indispensable in political matters. Had the idea of ijtihad been slightly less important, Ghazali would have done away with it as a requirement to be met by the Caliph or his functionaries. This would have been gladly done in order to justify the long-established fact that Caliphs were not mujtahids. The political theory of Juwayni and Ghazali, let alone that of Mawardi, Baghdadi and others, leads to the conclusion that ijtihad was considered an essential element both in the political and the legal life of Islam up to at least the end of the fifth/eleventh century. And, as we shall see later, ijtihad remained so long afterwards.

Indeed, there is no reason to believe that the jurists could have avoided dealing with the problem of the closure of the gate of ijtihad or the question of the extinction of mujtahids when they had already dealt with a similar but less crucial problem, namely, the legal impotency of the Caliphate. That they did deal with the problem of the gate of ijtihad at a later period further affirms our conclusion that by the time of Ghazali this problem had not yet risen. For, if the discussion about the gate was not censored, and there is no evidence to show that it was, why should it not be discussed at the time when it supposedly appeared?

The Ijtihad of Juwayni, Ghazali, and Ibn ᶜAqil

The highly developed juristic thought of the fifth/eleventh century was the product of the legal activity of mujtahids. An examination of the careers of Juwayni, Ghazali, and Ibn ᶜAqil will show that these jurists, like many of their contemporaries, not only opposed taqlid in favor of ijtihad, but also presented themselves as qualified mujtahids and were accepted by others as such.

Juwayni must be credited with an extensive knowledge in several fields, particularly law, theology, and belles-lettres. His education under the guidance of his father and other eminent scholars seems to have given him the courage to express radical views in Shafiᶜi law and Ashᶜari *kalām*; the schools to which he adhered. In his usul work *al-Burhān*, he seems to have deviated from Shafiᶜi's usul doctrine and incorporated new ideas that stirred some opposition in later centuries.[82] Subki, one of the most thorough biographers, consistently elevates Juwayni to the rank of *mujtahid fī al-madhhab*, (mujtahid within the boundaries of the school) and advances him over his predecessors in the mastery of usul and furuᶜ.[83] Subki points out the special difficulty of *al-Burhān* and its uniqueness as a book the theory of which, unlike others in the field, was not dictated by the doctrines of previous authorities.[84] Ibn Khallikan ascribes to his furu^c work, *al-Nihāya*, the same features, indicating that it is unprecedented in Islam.[85] Subki openly admits that in *al-Burhān* Juwayni is not guided by the principles of Shafi^{c}i's doctrine but by his own reasoning and ijtihad.[86] This last makes Juwayni an independent mujtahid (*mujtahid muṭlaq*) since he had set up an independent system that seems to differ from Shafi^{c}i's school at least as much as Tabari's system does. Therefore, Subki's statements that Juwayni was a highly original jurist and that he reached the degree of mujtahid fi al-madhhab contradict themselves, because Muslim jurists have always argued that the mujtahid fi al-madhhab must not exceed the limits of the school's teachings. In this light the views of Abu al-Fida (d. 732/1331) and al-Dhahabi (d. 748/1348) must be considered as a counterbalance to Subki's account of Juwayni. Abu al-Fida remarked that Juwayni claimed for himself the rank of independent mujtahid because he fulfilled the conditions required, but added that he, Juwayni, finally decided to abandon this position and follow Shafi^{c}i.[87] This is in accord with Subki's remark that in his youth Juwayni refused to follow the doctrine of the Shafi^{c}i school embodied in the teachings of his father and his father's contemporaries. It also accords with the fact that the principles of Shafi^{c}i's usul have not served as a guide for Juwayni. Subki's teacher, al-Dhahabi, who was a fervent anti-kalam Traditionalist, also hinted that in his *al-Burhān* Juwayni deviated from the right path of the forefathers (salaf). Abu al-Fida and Dhahabi represented a trend which Subki covertly opposed in his biographical notice of Juwayni. He consistently upheld the orthodoxy of Juwayni and asserted that he persistently followed the path of the salaf[88] and remained a follower of Shafi^{c}i throughout his life despite the fact that he had developed a set of nonconformist views. This in itself, namely, being nonconformist and a salaf follower, is again an obvious contradiction of which Subki could not rid himself.

That Juwayni was a mujtahid is unquestionable, but what kind of a mujtahid was he? Although Juwayni did not venture to establish a new school, he seemed to have claimed ijtihad mutlaq, at least for a period of time, as Abu al-Fida argued. Subki denied this in order to defend Ash^{c}arism and Ash^{c}aris against the Traditionalist attacks which aimed at placing Ash^{c}arism outside the domain of Sunnism.[89] It follows that Subki's insistence that Juwayni was a mujtahid fi al-madhhab is particularly significant in the theological context but hardly so in the legal one. The fact remains that by the admission of every scholar, Juwayni was a remarkably creative jurist and a mujtahid of the highest caliber. It is only fair to say that part of Ghazali's much-lauded creativity may be attributed to his eminent teacher: It may well be true that a thorough study of Juwayni's legal and political works, when all these are published, will uncover certain aspects of his creativity that have been hitherto ascribed to Ghazali. This is certainly true, at least, of Ghazali's early legal theory found in *al-Mankhūl* and his political writings which seem to have been influenced by ideas expressed in Juwayni's *Ghiyāth* and in other works.

This need not necessarily imply that Ghazali's intellectual contribution to religious sciences was in any way less significant. Although biographical dictionaries do not emphasize Ghazali's quality of ijtihad, as is the case with Juwayni, it is quite obvious that Ghazali reached the rank of mujtahid fi al-madhhab. Apart from his argument that he is a mujtahid who had abandoned the practice of taqlid,[90] he is the first scholar known to have claimed that he was chosen by God to revive the religion of Islam.[91] And because he lived during the first five years of the sixth Islamic century, jurists of the Shafiᶜi school as well as others looked upon him as the renovator (*mujaddid*) of the sixth/twelfth century. The fact that renovators had to be qualified mujtahids implies that even those biographers who made no explicit mention that Ghazali was a mujtahid nevertheless implicitly admitted that he was one. Ibn al-Najjar maintained that a universal consensus had taken place concerning the fact that Ghazali was the mujtahid of his time.[92] In a convincing manner, Subki also presented Ghazali as the renovator of the sixth/twelfth century who had perfected the science of legal theory, 'renewed' the fiqh (positive law) of the Shafiᶜi school, and molded the science of *khilāf* (legal differences).[93]

There was no doubt in Ghazali's mind that ijtihad is attainable through diligent study, intellectual exercise, and immersion in scholarly disputations (*munāẓarāt*).[94] He admitted the extinction of independent mujtahids who were able to establish their own school of law, but he certainly did not imply the same for those jurists who could lead the community and revive the Shariᶜa when this need arose.[95] Therefore, it is entirely inaccurate to say, as some later jurists did,[96] that Ghazali thought all mujtahids to be extinct; such a claim not only has no basis in Ghazali's writings but also sharply contradicts the several statements he made throughout his books.

To Ghazali, only two kinds of mujtahids were known, the independent (*muṭlaq*) and the limited (*muqayyad*).[97] The latter's activity remains within the limits of his school. Because Ghazali admitted the fact that the eponyms of the schools are defunct and irreplaceable, and because the task of *tajdīd* (renovation) requires a jurist of high caliber who does not practice taqlid, it can be safely said that Ghazali recognized the existence of mujtahids fi al-madhhab, especially that he himself was a mujtahid in the Shafiᶜi school.

Ghazali was not bold enough to attribute to himself and to his fellow scholars the supremacy of ijtihad over his predecessors. Unlike Ibn ᶜAqil, he was satisfied with a rank lower than that of Shafiᶜi. Ibn ᶜAqil refused to accept for himself and for his colleagues such a relatively modest role; he strongly argued that earlier lawyers have no superiority over their successors and that many later jurists surpassed in legal knowledge their older teachers.[98] He attacked and ridiculed the taqlid by his contemporaries of their forefathers and asserted that Ibn Hanbal himself went out against the blind following of earlier jurists and called for reasoning on the basis of the scripture. For this reason, Ibn ᶜAqil openly declared that any legal opinion must be guided by a textual *dalīl* (evidence) rather than by what Ibn Hanbal had said.[99] Given this, it is of no surprise that Ibn ᶜAqil, with his deep knowledge of usul and furuᶜ, had reinterpreted the doctrine of his school and that he came up with new opinions for many new and old problems. More than twenty of his unique legal opinions are recorded in Ibn Rajab's biographical work.[100] Many more of these singular problems appear in *al-Funūn*, his *magnum opus*, where he demonstrates not only his remarkable originality, but also his preference for the ijtihad of contemporaries over that of the ancestors. In fact, the purpose of Ibn ᶜAqil in writing his *Kitāb al-Funūn*, which is replete with contemporary opinions and problems, seems to stem from his desire to prove the commensurability, if not the superiority, of later mujtahids to their predecessors.[101]

The desire of Juwayni, Ghazali, Ibn ᶜAqil, and other jurists to assert themselves vis-à-vis their precursors and their unceasing constructive criticism of their contemporaries was perhaps partially motivated by the general mood of the age; a mood which was to persist as a psychological factor in the attitude of Muslims for centuries afterwards. This mood was expressed in the general conviction that Muslims were experiencing bad times and that the more distant they were from the Golden Age of the Prophet and his Companions the worse the state of decline would be.[102] A keen search throughout the legal literature for the causes of such conviction yielded very little to show that the legal state of affairs was responsible for it. It is highly likely that the disintegration of the political institution was the main element that brought about the growth of this conviction.[103] The Shariᶜa had not been at the center of criticism as had been the political and socioeconomic situation as a whole. Ghazali's revivalism, for instance, was not addressed specifically to law. The 'weaknesses' of religion, Ghazali argued, were caused by the internal theopolitical conflicts and by religious malpractices. This is his main theme in his *Iḥyāᵓ* and *Munqidh*. In the latter he also criticizes several institutions and groups such as the philosophers and the Shiᶜi Imamiyya, but nothing, except for a few passing remarks, was devoted to legal sciences or jurists. In fact, in Ghazali's doctrine jurists are instrumental in any attempt at religious revival.[104]

The Role of Ijtihād in Developing Positive Law

As far as the potential and ability of the legal system to provide solutions to all newly arising problems is concerned, it need not be reiterated that up to Ibn ᶜAqil's time, and for a long time afterwards, jurists had performed their task most appropriately. Therefore, the dissatisfaction of Muslims with the status quo could not have been the result of the impotency of lawyers to supply the required answers. Legal activity, whether in theory or practice, continued unceasingly. The vast bulk of *fatwās* (legal opinions) that appeared and continued to grow rapidly from the fourth/tenth century onwards is a telling example of the importance of fatwas as legal decisions and precedents. It is in this large body of material that one may look for positive legal developments. But the current state of scholarly research does not enable us to undertake the investigation of this important subject. When a record of consecutive collections of fatwas throughout a given period of time is made available, the growth of legal materials and of unprecedented decisions, which may be coupled with developments of technical legal thought, can be followed step by step. This does not mean that developments and new ideas cannot be found elsewhere. Subjects of interest and of vital importance were discussed in a variety of works such as, for example, the *Kitāb al-Funūn* of Ibn ᶜAqil and the *Iḥyāᵓ* of Ghazali. These include numerous cases that were either raised to be decided for the first time or older problems that were reinterpreted through fresh legal reasoning.[105] Subki also recorded in his *Ṭabaqāt* hundreds of new and unconventional legal opinions, the great majority of which belong to the fourth century and thereafter.

Although later positive developments were not usually incorporated in furuᶜ works, a clear development had taken place within this branch of legal literature. And although the main features of this development were manifest chiefly in the field of technical legal thought, it is nonetheless a development that at least signifies the extent to which jurists of later centuries were free to express views that diverged from the doctrines of their predecessors.

It is our common, but rather inaccurate, belief that during the first three centuries of Islam, the highest and final stage of legal thought had been reached. It may be astonishing, therefore, to realize that the sophistication of technical legal thought was in fact achieved after these centuries, particularly during the fifth/eleventh and sixth/twelfth centuries. The elaboration of the Hanbali positive doctrine, for instance, could not have possibly started before the end of the third/beginning of the tenth century and it could reach its utmost refinement only in the beginning of the seventh/thirteenth century—in Ibn Qudama's voluminous work, *al-Mughnī*.[106] Even much older systems, such as the Hanafi school, were, during the fifth/eleventh and sixth/twelfth centuries, subject to extensive refinement that did not exist before. We need not restate the detailed study of the late Chafik Chehata supplemented by that of Meron concerning the developments in the Hanafi legal texts.[107] It suffices to say that the furuᶜ works of Quduri (d. 428/1036) and Sarakhsi (d. 490/1096), let alone those of ᶜAlaᵓ al-Din al-Samarqandi (d. 539/1144) and Kasani (d. 587/1191), represented a great advance over earlier works of the school.[108] *

Early Hanafi law, embodied in works such as those of Shaybani (d. 189/804), Tahawi (d. 321/933), and Abu al-Layth al-Samarqandi (d. 375/985),[109] does not present us with a sufficiently developed system of legal thought. The disorderly arrangement of subjects and the negligence to set forth the process of reasoning of each decision are sufficient indicators of the unclarity and the incomprehensiveness that characterized the writings of the early jurists.[110] Although Tahawi and Abu al-Layth al-Samarqandi wrote more than a century after Shaybani, they seem to have contributed very little to what had already been achieved by their older master.[111] It was only in the fifth/eleventh century that there was a significant change in the arrangement of material, terminology, and technical legal thought. Precise definition of terms, distinction between legal acts and legal facts, and reformulation of earlier doctrines are characteristic features in the works of Quduri and Sarakhsi; even more so in the works of the sixth/twelfth century ᶜAlaᵓ al-Din al-Samarqandi and Kasani.[112] Quduri is clearly superior to his predecessors in the arrangement of his legal data; his work "presents us with an effort at systematization which constitutes a foreward step in the history of fiqh."[113] Sarakhsi significantly improved on older Hanafi authorities; his concepts and notions of pure law are much more crystalized and well defined than those of Shaybani and Tahawi.[114] Thus, it would be implausible to say that "from the tenth century (i.e., the fourth Islamic century) onwards the role of jurists was that of commentators upon the works of the past masters," and that the authors of commentaries, such as Quduri, Sarakhsi, ʿAlaʾ al-Din al-Samarqandi, and Kasani "betrayed a slavish adherence, not only to the substance but also the form and arrangement of the doctrine as recorded in the earlier writings."[115] The aforementioned studies of Chehata and Meron prove, once and for all, the invalidity of such statements.

From all this it becomes clear that in practice and in theory the activity of ijtihad during the period under discussion was uninterrupted. Furthermore, mujtahids proved to have existed at all times, a fact which finds full support in the ample material available from the period itself. It is no surprise then that in the fourth/tenth- and fifth/eleventh-century sources utilized in this study (except Ibn ʿAqil's *Funūn* which will be discussed later) there is no mention of the phrase 'insidad bab al-ijtihad' or of any expression that may allude to the notion of the closure.[116]

* * *

In the light of our preceding conclusion that during the first five Islamic centuries the activity of ijtihad remained uninterrupted on both the practical and theoretical levels and that the idea of the closure has not even occurred to Muslims, we shall now proceed to investigate the subsequent history of ijtihad in order to show that the notion of the closure had appeared for the first time as late as the end of the fifth/eleventh century (and more likely the beginning of the sixth/twelfth) and that disagreements on the closure and on the availability of mujtahids prevented Muslims from reaching a consensus to that effect. It will further become clear that ijtihad was exercised up to the premodern era and that claims for the right of ijtihad and its superiority over taqlid were voiced incessantly.

THE APPEARANCE OF THE EXPRESSION '*insidād bāb al-ijtihād*' AND ITS MEANING

As often used in legal discussions, the term '*bāb*' means 'way.' Thus, *saddu bābi al-ṭalāqi* may be rendered as 'closing the way of divorce' or 'making divorce infeasible'.[117] Similarly, *insadda bābu al-qiyāsi* may be translated 'the way of qiyas was closed' or 'the procedure of qiyas was suspended'. The seventh Arabic *maṣdar* form, *insidād*, and the verb form *insadda* do not denote the agent. Hence, *insadda bābu al-ijtihādi* conveys no idea as to who had actually closed the gate. This notion of the closure is in complete accord with the Islamic belief which asserts that no one at any time has demanded that the practice of ijtihad be suspended.[118] In theory, should this practice decline or stop permanently, the methodology of ijtihad is not to be blamed because this deficiency can only stem from fallible elements, namely, the mujtahids. Ijtihad may cease only when mujtahids either decline to perform it or when they become extinct. Since, as previously mentioned, ijtihad was considered a fard kifaya and thus incumbent upon mujtahids, the possibility of extinction remains as the only alternative. The dying out or the lack of well-learned jurists then can be the only reason for the closure of the gate of ijtihad. This was precisely how Muslims thought of this issue. They believed that the disappearance of scholarship does not come about through its demise, but rather coincides with the dying out of the scholars. To maintain this posture, a prophetic report was adduced over and over again: "God does not remove knowledge suddenly from mankind (while alive) but removes it when scholars pass away. And when all scholars perish, there will remain only ignorant leaders, who when asked to decide cases, will give judgments without having (the necessary) knowledge, thereby falling in error and leading others astray."[119]

Thus, whether the gate has always been open or had at one point of time been closed is virtually determined by two elements that complete each other: (1) the existence or extinction of mujtahids, and (2) the jurist's consensus that the gate of ijtihad, for the reason of extinction, was, or was not, closed. In usul works, only the question of whether or not mujtahids can, by reason or by sharᶜ, become extinct was discussed and there had hardly been a direct reference to the concept of 'the gate of ijtihad'. This is perhaps due to the fact that the usulists, being the guardians of law, felt responsible for the continuity of ijtihad and saw in the whole idea of the gate a negation of the very *raison d'etre* of the divine methodology of usul al-fiqh.

We may assume that discussions concerning the existence of mujtahids had their origin in the Saljuk period, more specifically towards the very end of the fifth/eleventh century or the beginning of the sixth/twelfth. A thorough search in the fifth/eleventh century legal literature including the usul works of ᶜAbd al-Jabbar, Abu Husayn al-Basri, Baghdadi, Shirazi, Juwayni, Sarakhsi, Pazdawi, and Ghazali did not lead to any information, related directly or indirectly to this subject. The author in whose works this discussion appears for the first time in Islamic history is the illustrious Hanbali jurist and theologian Ibn ᶜAqil. His notebook *al-Funūn* and the excerpts from *al-Wāḍiḥ fī Uṣūl al-Fiqh*, cited in the *Musawwada* of the Taymiyya family, afford us with a fairly satisfactory account of the beginning of this issue.

The discussion of the existence of mujtahids seems to have been first motivated by practical necessity rather than by mere intellectual curiosity. In order to ensure the continual functioning of law, usulists of the fifth/eleventh century, including Ibn ᶜAqil, maintained that at least one mujtahid at each age must 'sit' for *iftāʾ* (giving legal opinions) and be the guide for less qualified muftis. It was primarily for this reason that Ibn ᶜAqil insisted that a mujtahid must be in existence at all times to look after the interests and needs of the Muslim community and to solve its newly arising day to day problems.[120] This information, derived from his usul theory, fully corresponds to the details of a controversy that occurred between him and a Hanafi jurist in Baghdad.

The jurist that adhered to the school of Abu Hanifa said: "Where are the mujtahids? This issue closes the gate of judgeship" (*bāb al-qaḍāʾ*).

The Hanbali (Ibn ᶜAqil) swiftly responded with two decisive answers. First, he argued that "if the gate of judgeship is closed because it is required that the judge be a mujtahid, then the gate is (also) closed because you claim that the ruling (hukm) of the non-mujtahid judge is not valid until certified by a mujtahid. If you claim that mujtahids are not extant and if you need a mujtahid to guide judges and if you do not hold rulings to be nowadays invalid . . . then the mujtahid whom you need to validate the ruling of the non-mujtahid disproves your claim concerning the inexistence of the mujtahid . . . "

"This claim of the Hanafi jurist is groundless for another reason. If you are asked: Can ijma^c be suspended at a certain age? If you say yes, you would be nullifying one of Shari^ca's sources and would be contending that God had removed an infallible source from amongst the sources of shar^c . . . On the other hand, if you say that ijma^c is (always) valid, it would then be asked: Can the ijma^c of the mujtahids be concluded in an age where there are no mujtahids? Therefore, your argument is null and void."[121]

Elsewhere, Ibn ^cAqil made the following statement: "It is not possible for an age to be devoid of a mujtahid. This is contrary to the claim of some muhaddiths who argue that there remained no mujtahids at our age."[122]

Obviously, Ibn ^cAqil uses in his arguments pure human reasoning and makes no reference whatsoever to the scripture. Compared with the more elaborate arguments that were developed in later works, it appears that Ibn ^cAqil's disputation with his interlocutors was only the beginning of what was later to become an established usulist controversy. The characteristics of his responses indicate that the entire issue was not of great importance at that time, although it might have been so for Ibn ^cAqil himself.

THE CONTROVERSY ABOUT THE EXISTENCE OF MUJTAHIDS

Amidi (d. 632/1234) was the first usulist known to us to have devoted a special section to the treatment of the issue of the existence of mujtahids.[123] The polemical character of his account, which contains arguments and counter-arguments, is a clear indication of the established controversy that had left its mark on the form of the discussion. It is highly probable that the entire debate on the existence of mujtahids had been inspired or perhaps provoked by the Hanbali insistence, which was initiated by Ibn ^cAqil, that a mujtahid must exist at all times. This is why Amidi's account is more of a counter-attack, or rather an antithesis, than an ordinary discussion. This attitude became a common heritage for the majority of Hanafis, Malikis, and some Shafi^cis, who together opposed the primarily Hanbali tendency. Amidi's account clearly sums up the entire controversy.[124] First, Amidi sets forth the postulations as advocated by the Hanbalis and a number of Shafi^cis who maintained that mujtahids must exist at all times, and then goes on to refute them one by one. Hanbalis and others, Amidi remarked, presented two arguments to support their position; one is *shar^cī* (related to divine texts) and the other *^caqlī* (related to human reason). In the shar^ci argument, they adduced three prophetic reports, the theme and contents of which validate the view that at all times learned men will lead the community of Muhammad and that knowledge and sound judgement will accompany Muslims throughout all ages until the Day of Judgement. The ^caqli argument begins with the premise that the practice of ijtihad and the study of law are fard kifaya, i.e., a religious duty incumbent upon qualified jurists. Therefore, should this activity be abandoned, the Muslim community would inevitably be in error, something which cannot possibly happen. Moreover, the community would fall into anarchy and the edifice of Shari^ca would be demolished should ijtihad cease to exist, because ijtihad is the only means by which the believers can pursue the true path of God whenever a new case comes up.

In countering this argument, Amidi approaches the problem from the same angle. First, he introduces five different prophetic reports (the number of reports is important because five outnumber the three adduced by Hanbalis) which enhance the view that in the course of time the Shari^ca will deteriorate and lawyers will become extinct. Against the ^caqli argument presented by Hanbalis, Amidi argues that ijtihad is not a fard kifaya when it is possible to rely on the laws of ancestors which have accumulated throughout centuries and which can be attained through the medium of an uninterrupted transmission. Amidi's position then is to recognize the possibility of the extinction of mujtahids at a certain period of time. The Hanbalis and a group of Shafi^ci scholars were the only ones who denied even the theoretical possibility of the mujtahids' extinction. In a briefer manner Ibn al-Hajib (d. 646/1248) repeats Amidi's argument without addition.[125]

The Hanbali dialogue quoted by Amidi differs entirely from that adduced by Ibn ^cAqil a century before. As noted above, Ibn ^cAqil uses no textual evidence to prove his point, neither does he use the rational argument produced by later Hanbalis. Had he known of any further argument he would have undoubtedly incorporated it into his controversy with his Hanafi adversary. The absence of hadith from Ibn ^cAqil's response, coupled with the nature of his reasoning, is indicative of the embryonic character of this controversial issue at that time. Because this issue had just recently been raised, the time had not yet come to give it full attention or full elaboration, which, in part, means support by the Sunna and/or the Quran. Considering all this and considering the fact that besides Ibn ^cAqil no fifth/eleventh century jurist made any mention of the phrase 'insidad bab al-ijtihad' or of the matter of the mujtahids' extinction, which became later a part of usul works, it must be concluded that the origin of this controversy lies at the very end of the fifth/eleventh century, and more likely at the very beginning of the sixth/twelfth. Nonetheless, this issue does not seem to have acquired immense importance even during the sixth/twelfth century. This is confirmed by Ibn Qudama's disinterest in this important matter. Had it been customary to discuss it in usul works in the fifth/eleventh and sixth/twelfth centuries, the Hanbali Ibn Qudama undoubtedly would not have missed such an occasion to deal with this subject (and he certainly would be inclined to do so because of the uniqueness of the Hanbali attitude towards it).

Over a century after the death of Amidi, the polemic as to whether or not an age can be devoid of mujtahids began to acquire wider dimensions, so much so that Amidi's basic premise and exposition became only the nucleus of a considerably complicated argument. Of particular interest to this study are those aspects of the argument that contribute to our understanding of the problem as hitherto outlined. Subki (d. 771/1369) has nothing original to say but confirms the postulations of Amidi and Ibn al-Hajib and asserts that though the extinction of mujtahids is possible its actual occurrence has not been proven.[126] While Isnawi (d. 772/1370) essentially accepts Amidi's theses, he disapproves of Baydawi's (d. 685/1286) statement that "at this time mujtahids do not exist." Isnawi argues that since ijma^c is concluded only by mujtahids, and since it would be impossible to live without ijma^c's force, mujtahids must be extant at the present time at least.[127] Taftazani (d. 790/1388), a younger contemporary of Isnawi, contributes to the counter-argument of Amidi against the Hanbali proposition that ijtihad is an obligation imposed on the totality of Muslim scholars. He argues that ijtihad becomes a compelling obligation if there are qualified scholars still alive, but Muslims are absolved from this obligation once it is determined that scholars are defunct. Therefore, the Muslim community would not fall into error despite its inability to produce scholars who are potentially capable of ijtihad.[128]

Ibn Amir al-Hajj (d. 879/1474) adopts the argument of Amidi and Taftazani and goes further to suggest that one of the three hadiths adduced by the Hanbalis to enhance their position is dubious. Moreover, he dismisses Subki's statement that the nonexistence of mujtahids in an age has not actually been proven, by contending that al-Qaffal al-Shashi and Ghazali maintained that independent mujtahids are extinct.[129] It is worthwhile noting that Subki has not specified what rank of mujtahids he was contemplating, but it seems certain that he used the term 'ijtihad' generically to denote the activity itself, irrespective of whether it is independent or limited. An independent mujtahid, as it is used here, means a master architect of jurisprudence who can set up his own school of law. This is the kind of mujtahid that Qaffal and Ghazali were supposed to believe had become extinct.[130] A limited mujtahid—sometimes called 'mujtahid fi al-madhhab'—is a jurist who is well versed in one school's legal system and can discover the law of any case, of any kind, at any time in all domains of law within the framework of that school. The third rank of jurists may be subdivided into several categories ranging from those who are fairly creative to those who are mere muqallids.[131] We shall return to this later.

Since Ibn Amir was speculating upon the intentions of Subki, he seems to have failed in arguing against the contention that mujtahids were in existence up to the end of the eighth century at least. His calling upon Qaffal and Ghazali to testify on the extinction of mujtahids was equally ineffective because there was little new in maintaining that the phenomena of Abu Hanifa, Shafi^ci, and other eponyms were unique and unreproducible, since this was not the case at issue. In short, Ibn Amir added in substance to Amidi's argument against the Hanbalis, but he was ineffective due to his indiscriminate approach to technical terms. It is significant, however, that elsewhere in his book Ibn Amir says that the gate of ijtihad would have been closed had mujtahids been required to know 500,000 hadiths as part of their qualifications for ijtihad.[132] Also significant, and rather explanatory, is his statement that the practice of ijtihad at his age is "more scarce than the great elixir and the red sulfur."[133]

That Qaffal and Ghazali had only the eponyms of the law schools in mind when they declared the extinction of mujtahids, and that these eponyms are an unreproducible phenomenon once they have vanished are crystal-clear facts in Siddiqi's (d. 971/1563) opinion. While he agrees that in theory mujtahids could disappear, he rejects the claim that they did in reality and his proof of this is shown in the list of jurists who were, beyond any doubt, great mujtahids.[134] Siddiqi's important contention is that although a great variety of opinions had been expressed on this matter, no one has yet argued that mujtahids or ijtihad must cease to exist.[135]

A meticulous argument was presented by Ansari (d. 1119/1707) and his commentator, Ibn ᶜAbd al-Shakur (d. 1225/1810). Ansari is careful not to confuse ranks of mujtahids because any indifference to the type of mujtahids being discussed may lead to an undesirable disputation. Keeping this in mind, Ansari accepts the likelihood of the mujtahids' extinction. He is overwhelmingly convinced that the great jurists of the past, such as the four eponyms, are irreplaceable. If those who contend that mujtahids exist mean mujtahids of the caliber of Abu Hanifa, then mujtahids are nonexistent at present, Ansari and ᶜAbd al-Shakur argued. But if less qualified mujtahids are meant, then their existence is quite possible.[136]

One of the most important elements that largely contributed to the deepening of this controversy is the misuse or the misunderstanding of technical terms. This was due to the absence of a common technical dictionary to which jurists would conform. Although some lawyers tried to define the terms used in describing the ranks of mujtahids, the majority of scholars remained confused. In the course of time, the degree of confusion increased steadily in legal literature. The definition of the term 'mujtahid mutlaq' (absolute mujtahid) in Ghazali's time, for instance, differed from that given to it later. For Ghazali, a mujtahid mutlaq is a jurist who is capable of interpreting all branches of law within a given school, but this mujtahid cannot be the founder of the school.[137] For Majd al-Din Ibn Taymiyya (d. 652/1254) and Ibn al-Salah (d. 643/1245) the terms *muṭlaq* and *mustaqill* (independent) are synonymous. But unlike Ghazali, they give the title 'mujtahid mutlaq' or 'mustaqill' to the eponyms of the schools rather than to less qualified mujtahids. What Ghazali calls 'mutlaq' they call *muntasib* (affiliated).[138] Nawawi (d. 676/1277) follows the arrangement of Ibn Taymiyya and Ibn al-Salah.[139] Suyuti (d. 911/1505) uses 'mutlaq' for men like Shafiᶜi and Malik, and 'mustaqill' for mujtahids within the school, such as Ibn Surayj and himself.[140] By so doing, Suyuti differs from Ibn al-Salah and Ibn Taymiyya who, in turn, differ from Ghazali. Like Ibn al-Salah, Siddiqi means by 'mustaqill' the rank of a school founder.[141] He observes that some jurists consider muntasib a rank higher than mutlaq.[142] And Laknawi (d. 1304/1886) conferred the compound title 'mujtahid mutlaq-muntasib' upon a jurist who performs ijtihad within a school.[143] It is of no surprise then that a good deal of the disputation over the subject of mujtahids and ijtihad had been caused by such misunderstanding.[144]

It is now relevant to examine the controversy about the existence of mujtahids while paying special attention to the question of whether or not an ijmaᶜ had taken place on the closure of the gate. Without such an ijmaᶜ, the closure and its credibility cannot be ascertained. It must be remembered that, in theory, ijmaᶜ comes about when all mujtahids of an age agree, in one way or another, upon a certain matter. In reality, however, ijmaᶜ takes place when Muslim jurists look backward to the generations that preceded them and find that a certain doctrine or opinion had gained acceptance. The criterion for acceptance was decided by the absence of a dissenting voice among the scholars regarding that doctrine or that opinion. But whatever the case may be, any expressed objection especially when supported by major scholars, will remove that opinion from the domain of ijma^c to the domain of ikhtilaf. This means that this opinion is usually incorporated in the ikhtilaf literature (dealing with differences in legal matters). But in order to be established as an ikhtilaf matter, another tacit consensus is required. Otherwise, it becomes a matter having what may be termed 'unsettled status'.[145]

At the turn of the seventh/thirteenth century, the Shafi^ci jurist al-Rafi^ci (d. 623/1226) observed that "Muslims seem to agree that at present there are no mujtahids."[146] What he exactly meant by 'mujtahids' cannot be determined from the scanty information which reached us from him, but it is highly likely that he meant independent mujtahids who can found schools of law. It would be implausible to assume that Rafi^ci meant limited mujtahids because such an assumption contradicts the reality of his time. During Rafi^ci's lifetime and afterwards, many jurists, including himself, were recognized by their contemporaries and successors as mujtahids within their own schools. Rafi^ci's student, Isfara^ɔini, thought of his master as a mujtahid.[147] Furthermore, Rafi^ci was chosen by a host of scholars to be the mujaddid of the sixth/twelfth century.[148] Razi, Abu Shama, Ibn ^cAbd al-Salam, Ibn Daqiq al-^cId, Ibn al-Imam, and Nasafi, to name but a few, were admittedly renowned mujtahids in their time.[149]

Rafi^ci's aforementioned statement stunned Zarkashi (d. 795/1392), also a Shafi^ci, who wondered how Rafi^ci could maintain that an agreement on the mujtahids' extinction had been reached when it is "well known that this is a controversial (*khilāfī*) issue between us and the Hanbalis who were supported by some of our jurists."[150] Ibn ^cAbd al-Salam, aware or not of Rafi^ci's statement, remarked that Muslims "disagreed as regards the closure of the gate of ijtihad. They expressed different views to the effect of the closure . . . but these views are all void because if a new case comes up and no solution is found in the scripture, or when the case is a subject of khilaf among our forefathers, ijtihad is needed (to determine the ruling of the case)."[151] These statements, coupled with the circumstances under which Rafi^ci wrote (especially the existence of many renowned mujtahids),[152] are enough evidence to prove that he was speaking of limited mujtahids. It is certain, however, that by that time, the absence of independent mujtahids had become a fact subject to universal consensus. It is to this kind of consensus that Rafi^ci referred, but his statement seems to have been misinterpreted.

It must be noted that the great majority of the pronouncements on the issue of the closure did not venture to assume that there was an established consensus on the absence of mujtahids. The phrase that was often used by muqallids and supporters of taqlid was "Muslims seem to agree that mujtahids do not exist nowadays" (*al-nāsu kal-mujmi^cīna* [sometimes *kal-muttafiqīna*] *^calā annahu lā mujtahida al-yawma*). The term "to agree" rarely appears without the preposition *ka* (as; like) which renders the agreement uncertain.[153] This particular usage is significant, since all matters subject to ijma^c were unquestionable, and had the alleged absence of mujtahids been subjected to a definite ijma^c, jurists would see to it that the preposition *ka* did not precede the active participle *mujmi^cūn*. The failure of these jurists to reach an ijma^c on the absence of mujtahids must be ascribed to the fact that a number of them were mujtahids themselves and practiced ijtihad without being in the least criticised.[154]

SUYUTI'S CLAIMS FOR IJTIHAD AND TAJDID

Up to the end of the eighth/fourteenth century, no voice, as far as I know, rose to condemn the claims of mujtahids to practice ijtihad in the context of their schools. But as time lapsed, the doctrine of taqlid was steadily gaining genuine support from the mass of jurists. The amassing of this support had created a powerful movement that was to express itself openly only a century and a half later.

The first incident in which muqallids openly contravened the claims of mujtahids occurred in Egypt, during the lifetime of Suyuti (849/1445–911/1505). The latter had conceitedly claimed for himself the rank of mujtahid. In his polemical work *al-Radd ᶜalā man Akhlada ilā al-Arḍ wa-Jahila anna al-Ijtihād fi kull ᶜAṣr Farḍ* he argues that ijtihad is a fard kifaya to be fulfilled by the Muslim community, and if there were no mujtahids it would mean that the community had agreed upon error, something that is of course impossible. Were all Muslim jurists to become muqallids, ijtihad would cease, and in consequence Shariᶜa would be demolished. Therefore, says Suyuti, ijtihad is the backbone of Shariᶜa and without it no legal decisions can be reached.[155]

The kind of ijtihad that Suyuti claimed to be able to practice is the highest degree within the Shafiᶜi school; a degree that he calls 'mutlaq'.[156] It will be recalled that for Suyuti, 'mustaqill' indicates the highest degree of ijtihad, which is that of the eponyms. But for a great segment of scholars mutlaq is the highest rank of ijtihad.[157] Because of this terminology, Suyuti had put himself in a difficult position and was encumbered in trying to explain that mustaqill is the rank that disappeared while mutlaq is yet attainable.[158] Speaking of himself he said: "God has bestowed on me alone and uniquely the duty of undertaking ijtihad in this age."[159] Suyuti's claim for superiority to his contemporaries was disdainfully resented.[160] To justify these claims he argued that he was striving to fulfill the fard kifaya of ijtihad in order to discharge this duty on behalf of his community. Although he insisted on undertaking the fulfillment of this duty, a number of Suyuti's contemporaries denied him the right of ijtihad.

We must not take the opposition to Suyuti to mean that the Muslim community of the ninth/fifteenth century went out unanimously against ijtihad and the existence of mujtahids. Suyuti's personality must be taken into account in evaluating the antagonistic attitude towards his claim. Opposition was mainly directed against "Suyuti's boastfulness" and against his "immense self-confidence": He was disliked because he praised himself while casually condemning his opponents and calling them "fools, if not worse."[161]

Why did Suyuti want to be a mujtahid? The answer to this question presents us with another matter, intimately related to the issue of the existence of mujtahids. The ultimate ambition of Suyuti was to become the mujaddid of the tenth/sixteenth century. By attaining the rank of ijtihad, which was considered a prerequisite to tajdid, Suyuti had hoped to be qualified for that position.[162]

The idea of tajdid had been predominant since at least the fifth/eleventh century; it was justified on the basis of the prophetic report: "God sends at the turn of each century (*ᶜalā raʾsi kulli māʾa*) a man who renovates for this community the matters of its religion."[163] It has been universally agreed that the first two mujaddids for the second and third Islamic centuries were the Caliph ᶜUmar b. ᶜAbd al-ᶜAziz and Shafiᶜi.[164] For the centuries that followed there was, at one time or another, a difference of opinion as to who the mujaddid was; but there certainly had always been at least one. Ibn Surayj and the theologian Ashᶜari are mentioned for the fourth Islamic century. In this case Subki prefers Ibn Surayj because his death took place closer to the turn of the century than that of Ashᶜari and because he renovated the positive law of Shariᶜa while Ashᶜari was mainly an advocate of usul al-din.[165] For the fifth century a choice was made between Abu Hamid al-Isfaraʾini and Abu Sahl al-Suᶜluki.[166] Ghazali was the mujaddid of the sixth century, and Razi of the seventh. But for the latter century certain jurists designated Rafiᶜi instead of Razi.[167] Ibn Daqiq al-ᶜId was unanimously chosen for the eighth century.[168] In the ninth century, there was a competition between Siraj al-Din al-Bulqini and Nasir al-Din al-Shadhili.[169] Then came Suyuti, who was recognized as such by most later authors,[170] and after him Ahmad al-Sirhindi, who was given the title *mujaddid al-alf al-thānī*, since he appeared at the beginning of the second Islamic millenium.[171] Although after Sirhindi the practice of choosing a mujaddid seems to have lost some importance, it continued up to the past Islamic century, for which al-Maraghi al-Jurjawi was chosen.[172]

By the admission of Muslim scholars, therefore, mujaddids who were, *inter alia*, mujtahids, appeared at least once every century. Sometimes, as we have seen, there was more than one mujaddid for a single century. Now, one may ask, who are the jurists that held the extinction of mujtahids to be an established fact when it was clear that mujaddids were continuously present? At the time of Suyuti these were the Hanafis, the Malikis, and part of the Shafiᶜi school. Most of the leading minds of the Shafiᶜi school, however, rejected the theory of the possible extinction of mujtahids. In fact, almost all of the jurists who were given the task of tajdid were Shafiᶜis.[173] It is evident that those who promoted the idea of mujaddids had also promoted ijtihad and supported mujtahids while denying the possibility of their extinction (some jurists, however, accepted this possibility in theory). Hanafis and Malikis, being consistent in their actions, did not even participate in the race for tajdid.

Even if it is assumed that by the time of Suyuti the extinction of mujtahids had been well established, why cannot Suyuti, or someone else for that matter, provided he is qualified, still become a mujtahid? Is he not only attempting the fulfillment of the fard kifaya which is a perennial duty? And, if for a period of time there were no mujtahids, is the community destined to live without them forever, even if they were to reappear? These questions, to the best of my knowledge, find no answers whatsoever in the legal literature of Medieval Islam.

IJTIHAD AFTER THE TENTH/SIXTEENTH CENTURY

Suyuti's relentless effort to attain the position of tajdid expressed the highest point to which the uninterrupted activity of ijtihad could reach. In other words,

Suyuti can be seen as the last major Sunni mujtahid in a nine-century chain of mujtahids. After his death there was a significant decrease in the number of eminent jurists who had the potential for ijtihad. Those who were known to be mujtahids were very few in number. And from the end of the tenth/sixteenth century, the jurists who claimed the right for ijtihad became even fewer. This fact was reflected clearly in the classification of jurists into ranks or degrees. Although the idea of classifying ijtihad proved to be more deluding in understanding the history of ijtihad than helpful, its external development serves as an indicator of the later Muslim conviction concerning the decline in the number of mujtahids.

Before the fifth/eleventh century no trace could be found of any attempt to classify ijtihad or mujtahids into categories of excellence (*ṭabaqāt*). This does not mean, however, that the concept of tabaqat had not yet been known, but its systematic application to mujtahids occurred only at a later period, perhaps during the fifth/eleventh century.[174] As previously noted, Ghazali distinguished between two ranks of mujtahids; the mutlaq and the muqayyad. It can generally be inferred that Ghazali, representing the fifth/eleventh century scholars, recognized three ranks of jurists, the first of which had become, with his frank admission, extinct. The second was the rank of mujtahids within the school and the third was that of muqallids.[175] About two centuries later the number of ranks reached five, the first of which was assumed to be extinct. The second and the third were ranks of mujtahids who could perform ijtihad on two different levels, the third being more limited in scope.[176] The fourth rank included jurists highly proficient in the doctrines of their school and in the evidence upon which these doctrines were based, although they were not fully qualified to practice ijtihad. The fifth rank consisted of various kinds of muqallids.

By the tenth/sixteenth century, seven ranks of jurists could be discerned.[177] The top three remained as they were on the previous scale of five, that is, they were ranks of mujtahids of various degrees. But the lower four were in reality a redivision of the lower two on the scale of five.[178] In the sixth/twelfth and seventh/thirteenth centuries, for example, the lowest (fifth) rank of jurists included muqallids who 'memorized' the doctrine of the school and understood its details but were incapable of mastering the methodology that their eponym and older teachers applied in order to reach their legal rulings.[179] On the other hand, the tenth/sixteenth century description of the lowest (seventh) rank was entirely different. This rank includes jurists who do not equal any of the jurists from the higher six ranks and who "cannot differentiate between the thin and the fat."[180] The absence of this description from the older five-rank scheme does not suggest that in earlier centuries incompetent jurists did not exist. But the ever-growing conviction that fewer and fewer scholars could perform ijtihad and that most jurists were mere muqallids seems to have had bearing on the increase in the number of ranks; an increase from three to five to seven. This conviction had chiefly contributed to the augmentation of new ranks of muqallids that in theory did not exist before, while maintaining at the same time the old ranks of mujtahids without change.

In a later period, these seven ranks were each applied to a specific group of jurists. The first rank thus was assigned to the fathers of the four schools (to the exclusion of Shaybani and Abu Yusuf, the real founders of the Hanafi school). And although Ibn Hanbal was no jurist he was nevertheless included in this rank.[181] Shaybani, Khassaf, Muzani, and their equals were subsumed under the second rank. To the third, mujtahids like Karkhi, Tahawi, and Shams al-Din al-Sarakhsi belonged.[182] The fourth and fifth are the ranks of non-mujtahids like Marghinani and Razi,[183] while the sixth and seventh were specially designated for pure muqallids. From the end of the sixth/twelfth century onwards jurists are said to belong to the last two ranks.

This classification was promoted by later taqlid advocates who espoused the view that mujtahids had become extinct. This is evident in the seven-rank classification which does not accord with what the upholders of ijtihad maintained. For example, qualified jurists have generally agreed that Razi was a mujtahid as well as a mujaddid. Nevertheless, according to this system of categorization, he was subsumed under the fourth rank which is characterised by taqlid. In addition, the fact that a mujtahid (or, generally speaking, a mujaddid) must appear—and has indeed appeared—at the turn of each century until the Day of Judgement seems to contradict the claim that the jurists of the seventh/thirteenth century and their successors belonged to inferior ranks. This apparent contradiction can be explained by saying that the party which recognized Razi's ijtihad and the indispensable appearance of mujtahids each century was substantially different from the party that elaborated the ranks of jurists and applied them to specific groups. The first party, as is already clear, consisted primarily of Hanbalis and Shafiᶜis while the second was formed mainly of Hanafis who were supported to a greater or lesser extent by Malikis and a number of Shafiᶜis. It is not astonishing, therefore, to find that the Hanafis were the most concerned in classifying jurists into technical ranks, especially in the later period. This is also why the most complete and elaborate accounts of ranks of jurists (and not tabaqat in the biographical sense) are found in Hanafi works.

Convinced that mujtahids were extinct, Hanafis and their supporters not only denied the right of ijtihad to later scholars but also ignored ijtihad itself when this was exercised.[184] A fine expression of this attitude appears in Jabarti's *ᶜAjāʾib al-Āthār*, written in the beginning of the thirteenth/nineteenth century. In the copious number of biographical notes of jurists who died during the twelfth/eighteenth century, Jabarti seems to have been careful not to confer the title of mujtahid on any of them, though he sometimes gives descriptions synonymous to ijtihad. Of Ibn al-Naqib (d. 1183/1769), Jabarti observes that "he used to derive rulings on account of his intelligence and excellent memory."[185] Indeed, what jurists need in order to perform ijtihad is the knowledge of the methods of qiyas, which requires intelligence as well as adept familiarity with the Quran and Sunna, which latter also requires a good memory. Of other jurists like al-ᶜIqdi (d. 1134/1721), al-Manufi (d. 1135/1722), and Ibn ᶜAli al-Bashbishi (d. 1134/1730), Jabarti remarks that they studied diligently, excelled in law, and became proficient jurists. Nonetheless, Jabarti does not see them as mujtahids, although he admits that Bashbishi expressed unconventional views in legal matters.[186] Moreover, Jabarti's father is said to have "abandoned the practice of taqlid" (*irtafaᶜa ᶜan ḥaḍīḍi al-taqlīdi*) and to have excelled, among other things, in legal sciences.[187] His unique scholarship and his capability to derive laws (*kāna yastanbiṭu al-fiqha*) earned him the title of a great scholar. Among his many specialized works is a treatise in which he dealt with the legality of newly invented tools and instruments.[188] Despite all this, Jabarti refrained from calling his father a mujtahid. It is not that all Jabarti's contemporaries were incapable of ijtihad and it is certainly not that he was unfamiliar with the term 'mujtahid', for he employed it to describe the eighth/fourteenth century Zaylaᶜi.[189] More probably, his conviction that mujtahids are not supposed to be extant at all made him hesitant to use the term. In this Jabarti reflects the general positive attitude of the community of jurists towards taqlid, which had become an overriding principle by this time.[190]

The drastic decline in the number of recognized mujtahids did not coincide with a parallel decline in the number and importance of newly arising problems that needed ijtihad in order to be solved. This period, that is, the tenth/sixteenth and eleventh/seventeenth centuries, produced a number of new legal questions that were crucial to economic and social life in the Ottoman Empire. These questions could have been solved only by the ulama. Among the critical issues that drew forceful arguments[191] were the waqf of movables, particularly the waqf of cash, coffee, drugs, tobacco, music, and other matters.[192] In fact, these matters were so important and controversial that Katib Chelebi found it compelling to write an entire treatise setting forth the outlines of these issues.[193]

These issues had been taken up by various jurists who were certainly not known as mujtahids. Moreover, legal reasoning based on scripture and analogical inference was employed by such jurists without the slightest hesitation. In the tenth/sixteenth century Ottoman Empire, an acute controversy broke out as to the validity of the waqf of cash. Since there was not textual evidence in the Quran that indicated its legality or illegality and since sound hadith lacked similar evidence,[194] Ottoman jurists had to seek the guidance of the already established doctrines of the very early jurists. Zufar, a student of Abu Hanifa, seems to have been the only early authority to permit cash waqf. But for reasons that cannot be discussed here, later Hanafi scholars had classified the doctrine of Zufar as less authoritative than those of Abu Yusuf and Shaybani. In consequence, Zufar's doctrine was abandoned and the act of constituting cash waqfs had always been associated with interest (*ribā*) and was therefore prohibited. The need to legitimize the Ottoman practice of this transaction drove Abu al-Saᶜud and Bali Efendi to revive Zufar's long-forgotten doctrine.[195] But to do so it was not sufficient to restate Zufar's argument on its own merits, because, for one, it was universally viewed as weak. The lack of textual evidence and ijmaᶜ on the validity of cash waqf left Abu al-Saᶜud and his partisans with qiyas as the only methodological alternative. And this they used, though somewhat crudely.[196] Abu al-Saᶜud's opponents used the same method, drawing support from the doctrines of Abu Hanifa and Shaybani as well as from hadith material.[197]

Genuine legal reasoning was formulated on many other issues, most conspicuous among which were drugs, coffee, and tobacco.[198] A fine typology of legal problems that needed the treatment of one kind of qiyas or the other can be found, as previously mentioned, in the bulk of fatwa literature. It is not within the scope of our research to indulge in a study of these fatwas, for the aforementioned examples suffice to prove our point; that is, newly arising problems were inevitable even in a slowly developing society, and ijtihad (aside from the Ottoman Qanun) constituted the only method through which such problems were solved.

In practice, therefore, the methodology of ijtihad continued to be employed but mostly without being recognized under its proper name. Many jurists admitted that it was indispensable, and so it was, but they were convinced that no contemporary jurist possessed the qualification to practice it. Many others held the view that undertaking ijtihad in their age was heretical and that it was an art that was perfected only by the forefathers.[199] These views, however, provoked the advocates of ijtihad in the twelfth/eighteenth and thirteenth/nineteenth centuries to respond with a mass of writings in which the main subjects treated were taqlid, the evils that resulted therefrom, and ijtihad as a divinely prescribed legal principle. The authors of anti-taqlid works had increasingly mounted fierce attacks not only against those who claimed that mujtahids were extinct and that the gate of ijtihad was closed but also against the very essence of taqlid, the implementation of which had become a firmly rooted practice among the populace * (including the great majority of its intellectuals). The most prominent of these authors were Shah Wali Allah (d. 1176/1762), San^{c}ani (d. 1182/1768), Ibn ^{c}Abd al-Wahhab (d. 1202/1787), Ibn Mu^{c}ammar (d. 1225/1810), Shawkani (d. 1255/1839), and Ibn ^{c}Ali al-Sanusi (d. 1313/1895).

It suffices for the purpose of this article to deal only with Shawkani, whose writings seem to represent not only the classical Sunni trend in favor of ijtihad but also the highest stage to which the controversy between the advocates of ijtihad and taqlid had reached. While accepting the kind of taqlid that usul al-fiqh permitted to the laity, Shawkani abhors the taqlid of the ulama, a taqlid which necessitates the unquestionable acceptance of a given doctrine, without inquiring into the evidence which forms the basis of that doctrine. In all cases, the jurist who is asking the legal opinion of another must also ask, even though he may not be a mujtahid, about the textual evidence that lies in the asl.[200] Shawkani laments the common practice of taqlid which, according to him, became the prevailing norm that was not to be violated. In consequence, any attempt to claim the right of ijtihad was inevitably met with resistance, condemnation, and even public defamation. This is why, Shawkani contends, mujtahids might appear to have vanished; it is not because they have really vanished that their voices are not heard, but because their existence will be significantly endangered should they insist on claiming the right of ijtihad for themselves.[201] The alleged closure of the gate of ijtihad, Shawkani argues, is but one indication of the insipience of these blind muqallids who claimed that after the sixth/twelfth or seventh/thirteenth century, mujtahids ceased to exist.[202] In order to prove the contrary, Shawkani compiled a two-volume biographical work entitled *al-Badr al-Ṭāli^{c} bi-Maḥāsin man ba^{c}d al-Qarn al-Sābi^{c}* in which he was able to show that after the seventh Islamic century, mujtahids continued to exist. He further argued that ijtihad at later times was facilitated by the skillfully compiled manuals that make available to the jurist details and materials that were otherwise unattainable to jurists of earlier centuries. In fact, this was a counter-argument against the muqallids, who justified their taqlid on the grounds that it was extremely difficult and complex to undertake ijtihad which, of course, entails the study and analysis of the texts and the application of the methodological principles of usul.[203] Against the muqallids' view that ijma^c^ was reached on the closure of the gate and on the nonexistence of mujtahids, Shawkani explains that in ijma^c^ only the opinions of mujtahids count, and since it is clear that those who maintained the existence of ijma^c^ on the gate's closure consider themselves muqallids, it would seem absurd to claim that mujtahids reached an ijma^c^ on the nonexistence of mujtahids.

CONCLUSION

This study has shown that in Islamic legal theory ijtihad was reckoned indispensable in legal matters because it was the only means by which Muslims could determine to what degree their acts were acceptable to God. To facilitate the practice of ijtihad, minimal legal knowledge was required, and each mujtahid who exerted himself to formulate legal decisions was entitled to a heavenly reward irrespective of whether the result of his ijtihad was right or wrong.

The idea of closing the gate of ijtihad or the notion of the extinction of mujtahids did not appear during the first five Islamic centuries. This is entirely in consonance with the fact that the practical and theoretical importance of ijtihad had not declined throughout this period: Ijtihad and mujtahids were employed in the domain of law and were required in the higher ranks of government. That ijtihad constituted the backbone of the Sunni legal doctrine was manifest in the exclusion from Sunnism of all groups that spurned this legal principle.

It has also been shown that the controversy about ijtihad and the existence of mujtahids started, in its primitive form, only in the beginning of the sixth/twelfth century. Throughout the following centuries, differences among jurists, encouraged by ambiguities in legal terminology, made any consensus on the nonexistence of mujtahids and on the closure of the gate of ijtihad impossible to reach. Consensus was thwarted by three additional principal factors: First, and most important, is the continual existence of renowned mujtahids up to the tenth/sixteenth century. Though the number of mujtahids drastically diminished after this period, the call for ijtihad was vigorously resumed by premodern reformists. Second is the Muslim practice of choosing a mujaddid at the turn of each century. Though this practice may not have had the full support of the entire community of jurists, it proved that at least one mujtahid was in existence each century. Third, the opposition of the Hanbali school which was supported by influential Shafi^c^i jurists who, by their support, not only added substantial weight to the Hanbali claim that mujtahids existed at all times but also weakened the coalition in which Hanafis and Malikis took part.

The conclusion that the gate of ijtihad was not closed entails a re-evaluation of what we have thus far considered to be the legal history of Islam. The continuity of ijtihad throughout Islamic history suggests that developments in positive law, legal theory, and the judiciary have indeed taken place, and only through a chronological study of the jurists' writings is it possible to trace these developments and to reconstruct a more accurate picture of the legal history of Islam.

NOTES

Author's note: I wish to thank Professors Farhat Ziadeh and Nicholas Heer for their valuable comments on the manuscript.

[1]ᶜAli b. Abi ᶜAli al-Amidi, *al-Iḥkām fī Uṣūl al-Aḥkām*, 3 vols. (Cairo, 1968), III, 204; Taj al-Din al-Subki, *Jamᶜ al-Jawāmiᶜ*, with the commentary of Jalal al-Din al-Maḥallı, 2 vols. (Bombay, 1970), II, 379–381; Muḥammad b. ᶜAli al-Shawkani, *Irshād al-Fuḥūl ilā Taḥqīq al-Ḥaqq min ᶜIlm al-Uṣūl* (Cairo, 1909), pp. 232–233. On the meaning of 'ijtihad', see M. M. Bravman, *The Spiritual Background of Early Islam* (Leiden, 1972), p. 189.

[2]J. Schacht, *An Introduction to Islamic Law* (Oxford, 1964), pp. 70–71.

[3]J. N. D. Anderson, *Law Reform in the Muslim World* (London, 1976), p. 7. Such statements on the closure of the gate can be easily multiplied. See, e.g., M. Khadduri, "From Religious to National Law," in J. H. Thompson and R. D. Reischauer, eds., *Modernization of the Arab World* (Toronto, 1966), p. 41; F. Rahman, *Islam* (Chicago, 1966), pp. 77–78; H. A. R. Gibb, *Mohammedanism* (New York, 1962), p. 104; A. S. Tritton, *Materials on Muslim Education in the Middle Ages* (London, 1957), p. 163; N. J. Coulson, *A History of Islamic Law* (Edinburgh, 1964), p. 81. See also the introduction of G. L. Lewis to Katib Chelebi's *The Balance of Truth* (London, 1957), pp. 18–19. For additional citations on this, see notes 6 and 7 below.

[4]H. A. R. Gibb, *Modern Trends in Islam* (Chicago, 1947), p. 13; idem., *Mohammedanism*, p. 98.

[5]See W. M. Watt, "The Closing of the Door of Igtihad," *Orientalia Hispanica*, I (Leiden, 1974), 675–678.

[6]W. M. Watt, *Islam and the Integration of Society* (Evanston, 1961), pp. 206–207, 242–243; H. Liebesny, "Stability and Change in Islamic Law," *Middle East Journal*, 21 (1967), 19; Coulson, *History*, pp. 80–81; Schacht, *Introduction*, p. 75; Rahman, *Islam*, pp. 77–78.

[7]Cf. C. L. Ostrorog, *The Angora Reform* (London, 1927), p. 31; Anderson, *Law Reform*, p. 7; C. Pellat, "Les étapes de la decadence culturelle dans les pays Arabes d'Orient," in R. Brunschvig and G. von Grunebaum, eds., *Classicisme et declin culturel dans l'histoire de l'Islam* (Paris, 1957), p. 85.

[8]On the procedure of ijtihad, see Abu Ishaq al-Shirazi, *al-Lumaᶜ fī Uṣūl al-Fiqh* (Cairo, 1908), pp. 83–84; Shawkani, *Irshād*, p. 420; Ibn Habib al-Mawardi, *Adab al-Qāḍī*, ed. M. Sarhan, 2 vols. (Baghdad, 1971), I, 535–555; B. Weis, "Interpretation in Islamic Law: The Theory of Ijtihad," *The American Journal of Comparative Law*, 26, 2 (Spring, 1978), 209–210.

[9]See, e.g., Shirazi, *Lumaᶜ*, p. 4; Amidi, *Iḥkām*, I, 6; Abu Hamid al-Ghazali, *al-Mustaṣfā min ᶜIlm al-Uṣūl*, 2 vols. (Cairo, 1907), I, 5; Shawkani, *Irshād*, p. 3.

[10]Amidi, *Iḥkām*, III, 222; Saᶜd al-Din al-Taftazani, *Hāshiya ᶜalā Mukhtaṣar al-Muntahā*, 2 vols. (Cairo, 1974), II, 308; Ibn al-Humam, *al-Taḥrīr fī ᶜIlm al-Uṣūl*, with the commentary *al-Taqrīr wal-Taḥbīr* by Ibn Amir al-Hajj, 3 vols. (Cairo, 1898–1899), III, 292.

[11]Rahman, *Islam*, p. 78.

[12]Unfortunately, Volume 17 of ᶜAbd al-Jabbar's *al-Mughnī fī Abwāb al-Tawḥīd wal-ᶜAdl*, 20 vols. (Cairo, 1962–), which deals with usul al-fiqh has many lacunae, especially in the chapter on ijtihad.

[13]See Muhammad b. ᶜAli al-Basri, *al-Muᶜtamad fī Uṣūl al-Fiqh*, ed. M. Hamidullah, et al., 2 vols. (Damascus, 1964), II, 929–931.

[14]Ibid., II, 930, line 2 and 931, lines 9–10.

[15]Ibid., II, 932.

[16]Shirazi, *Lumaᶜ*, pp. 85–86.

[17]Ghazali, *Mustaṣfā*, II, 350–354; H. Laoust, *La politique de Gazali* (Paris, 1970), pp. 179–180.

[18]Ghazali, *Mustaṣfā*, II, 353–354.

[19]Amidi, *Iḥkām*, III, 204–205.

[20]Ibid., III, 205–206.

[21]For the requirements of Baydawi and Isnawi, see *Nihāyat al-Sūl fī Sharḥ Minhāj al-Wuṣūl*, 3 vols. (Cairo, 1899), III, 307–313. On Subki see *Jam*ᶜ, II, 382–386, especially p. 383. For the requirements of Ibn al-Humam and Ibn al-Amir, see *Taqrīr*, III, 292–294. For those of Ansari and Ibn ᶜAbd al-Shakur, see *Sharḥ Musallam al-Thubūt fī Uṣūl al-Fiqh*, 2 vols. (Cairo, 1907), I, 363–364.

[22]Isnawi, *Nihāyat al-Sūl*, III, 308; Ibn al-Amir, *Taqrīr*, III, 292.

[23]The divisibility of ijtihad was recognized by the great majority of jurists. See Shawkani, *Irshād*, p. 237.

[24]Mawardi, *Adab*, I, 533 f.; Amidi, *Iḥkām*, III, 218.

[25]Shaᶜrani defined 'ahl al-hadith' as follows: "By *ahl al-hadīth* is meant that which comprises the traditionalist (ahl al-Sunna) among the juristconsults, even though they may not be tradition experts." Cited in G. Makdisi, "The Significance of the Schools of Law in Islamic Religious History," *The International Journal of Middle Eastern Studies*, 10 (1979), 4.

[26]I. Goldziher, *The Zahiris: Their Doctrine and their History*, trans. W. Behn (Leiden, 1971), pp. 34–36. On the Hashwiyya see *Shorter Encyclopaedia of Islam*, s.v. "Hashwiya."

[27]Ibn al-Nadim, *al-Fihrist*, ed. G. Flügel (Beirut, 1964), pp. 213, 236; Goldziher, *Zahiris*, p. 35.

[28]Quoted in Goldziher, *Zahiris*, p. 35.

[29]ᶜAbd al-Rahman Ibn al-Salah, *Fatāwā* (Beirut, 1970), pp. 32–33. Relating from Abu Ishaq al-Isfaraᵓini, Ibn al-Salah remarked that "the great majority of scholars believe that the adversaries of qiyas are not qualified to perform ijtihad and may not be entrusted with judgeship; thus, Dawud cannot take part in any ijmaᶜ." See also other similar opinions on the Zahiris recorded in this *Fatāwā*.

[30]Goldziher, *Zahiris*, p. 30.

[31]Ibid., pp. 156–157.

[32]Abu Hamid al-Ghazali, *Iḥyāᵓ ᶜUlūm al-Dīn*, 5 vols. (Cairo, 1967), I, 38.

[33]Goldziher, *Zahiris*, p. 36.

[34]Ibn Khaldun, *al-Muqaddima* (Beirut, n.d.), pp. 446–447 (F. Rosenthal's trans. III, 5–6).

[35]Yusuf Ibn ᶜAbd al-Barr, *Jāmiᶜ Bayān al-ᶜIlm* (Cairo, 1975), p. 323.

[36]On the fact that they rejected ijtihad, see Ghazali, *Mustaṣfā*, II, 387.

[37]Laoust, *La politique de Gazali*, p. 180.

[38]Al-Khatib al-Baghdadi, *al-Faqīh wal-Mutafaqqih*, 2 vols. (Beirut, 1975), II, 72, 76–77.

[39]See Maturidi, *Kitāb al-Tawḥīd*, ed. K. Fathallah (Beirut, 1970), pp. 10–11, 12, 14, 318, 331, 378, passim.

[40]Cited in A. S. Halkin, "The Hashwiyya," *Journal of the American Oriental Society*, 54, 1 (1934), 12.

[41]Ghazali, *Iḥyāᵓ*, I, 133; Taj al-Din al-Subki, *Ṭabaqāt al-Shāfiᶜiyya al-Kubrā*, 6 vols. (Cairo, 1906), II, 287.

[42]Ibn ᶜAli Ibn al-Jawzi, *al-Muntaẓam fī Tārīkh al-Mulūk wal-Umam*, 9 vols. (?) (Haidarabad, 1940), VIII, 268.

[43]Abu al-Wafaᵓ Ibn ᶜAqil, *Kitāb al-Funūn*, ed. G. Makdisi, 2 vols. (Beirut, 1970–1971), II, 510. See also a similar opinion expressed by Muhammad b. Ahmad Ibn Rushd, *Faṣl al-Maqāl*, ed. G. F. Hourani (Leiden, 1959), p. 8.

[44]Amidi, *Iḥkām*, III, 253–254.

[45]Halkin, "Hashwiyya," pp. 3–20. See the views of Hashwiyya and ahl al-hadith, including Ibn Hanbal, on matters of government in ᶜAbd Allah b. Muhammad al-Nashiᵓ al-Akbar, *Masāᵓil al-Imāma wa-Muqtaṭafāt min al-Kitāb al-Awsaṭ fī al-Maqālāt*, ed. J. van Ess (Beirut-Wiesbaden, 1971), pp. 65–67.

[46]Makdisi, "The Significance of the Sunni Schools of Law," p. 6.

[47]*Shorter Encyclopaedia of Islam*, s.v. "Aḥmad Ibn Ḥanbal," by I. Goldziher.

[48]Sound istihsan is the analogical inference of rulings based on sound usul methodology. See Ibn Taymiyya, "Masᵓalat al-Istihsan" in G. Makdisi, ed., *Arabic and Islamic Studies in Honor of Hamilton A. R. Gibb* (Massachusetts, 1965), pp. 454–479.

[49]See Subki, *Ṭabaqāt*, V, 34; Halkin, "Hashwiyya," p. 27.

[50]See Subki, *Ṭabaqāt*, I, 105, 244; II, 89, 96, 126, 131. See also Goldziher, *Zahiris*, p. 31.

[51]Subki, *Ṭabaqāt*, II, 126. Of Ibn al-Mundhir, Subki remarks that "he was a mujtahid that followed no one" (*wakāna mujahidan lā yuqallidu aḥadan*). Subki also considered Ibn Surayj as the

renovator of the fourth/tenth century, see ibid., I, p. 244. Undoubtedly, for later Shafiᶜis, Ibn Surayj was the first great representative of the Shafiᶜi school. He seems to have been the first to reproduce the totality of the Shafiᶜi law, while synthesizing the internal difference of doctrines, e.g., the differences between Shafiᶜi and Muzani. In fact, he composed a work entitled *Kitāb al-Taqrīb bayna al-Muzanī wal-Shāfiᶜī* (see Ibn al-Nadim, *Fihrist*, p. 213).

[52]See Ibn al-Nadim, who allots a separate section in his book for the Jariris; *Fihrist*, p. 234 ff.

[53]Ibn Abi al-Wafaᵓ al-Qarashi, *al-Jawāhir al-Muḍīᵓa fī Ṭabaqāt al-Ḥanafiyya*, 2 vols. (Cairo, 1978), I, 137–138.

[54]Subki, *Ṭabaqāt*, II, 303–307. See some of his views in pp. 306 f.

[55]Ibid., II, 193–205; for his views see especially pp. 195 ff.

[56]Ibid., II, 206–210.

[57]Ibid., II, 112–125. See especially pp. 115 f., 118 f. Subki remarked: "As to his deep knowledge of precise concepts and his excellent ability to extract positive law, Muslims agreed that he was unique in (doing) this. No one from the following generations could equal him in his knowledge . . . He was remembered as a man of good reputation and ijtihad."

[58]See Goldziher, *Zahiris*, p. 26.

[59]Cited in ibid., p. 26. For a different version of this account see Subki, *Ṭabaqāt*, II, 240.

[60]Ibn Amir, *al-Taqrīr*, III, 345; Ibn ᶜAbidin, *al-Rasāᵓil*, 2 vols. (Lahore, 1976), I, 30.

[61]See Basri, *Muᶜtamad*, II, 934 ff.

[62]Ibn ᶜAbd al-Barr, *Jāmiᶜ*, pp. 384, 397.

[63]Baghdadi, *al-Faqīh*, II, 66–70; Mawardi, *Adab*, I, 269–273.

[64]Ibn ᶜAbd al-Barr, *Jāmiᶜ*, pp. 467–468.

[65]On the relationship between political theory and political practice in medieval Islam, see I. J. Rosenthal, "The Role of the State in Islam: Theory and Medieval Practice," *Der Islam*, 50, 1 (1973), 1–28.

[66]ᶜAbd al-Qahir al-Baghdadi, *Uṣūl al-Dīn* (Istanbul, 1928), p. 277. This Baghdadi is not to be confused with al-Khatib al-Baghdadi who died in 463/1070.

[67]ᶜAli b. Muhammad al-Mawardi, *al-Aḥkām al-Sulṭāniyya* (Cairo, 1960), p. 6. See also E. I. J. Rosenthal, *Political Thought in Medieval Islam* (Cambridge, 1958), p. 29.

[68]Mawardi, *Aḥkām*, p. 116.

* [69]Ibid., p. 66. Cf. my article "Considerations on the Function and Character of Islamic Legal Theory," (forthcoming).

[70]Subki, *Ṭabaqāt*, III, 303–305; H. A. R. Gibb, "Al-Mawardi's Theory of the Caliphate," in B. Shaw and W. Polk, eds., *Studies on the Civilization of Islam* (Boston, 1962), pp. 152, 164 n. 6, 165 n. 10.

[71]Muhammad al-Juwayni, *Ghiyāth al-Umam* (Iskandariyya, 1979).

[72]Ibid., p. 274.

[73]Ibid., p. 275; this idea is reiterated throughout the book. See, e.g., pp. 271, 282, 283 passim.

[74]Ibid., p. 300. Although the last phrase reads: "*watakādu hādhihi al-ṣūratu tuwāfiqu hādha lizamānin waᵓahlihi*," the last three words ought to be read as "*hādha al-zamāna waᵓahlahu*."

[75]Ibid., p. 309.

[76]See, e.g., the extensive account of Subki, *Ṭabaqāt*, III, 249–282. See also Abu al-Fida, *Tārīkh*, 4 vols. (Qustantiniyah, 1870), II, 206; Ibn al-Salah, *Fatāwā*, pp. 31–31; *Shorter Encyclopaedia of Islam*, s.v. "Taḳlīd," by J. Schacht.

[77]Juwayni, *Ghiyāth*, p. 376.

[78]Ibid., pp. 397–398.

[79]Ghazali, *Faḍāᵓiḥ al-Bāṭiniyya*, in I. Goldziher, ed., *Streitschrift des Gazali gegen die Batinijja-Sekte* (Leiden, 1956), p. 76.

[80]Ibid., p. 76.

[81]Ibid., p. 78.

[82]Subki, *Ṭabaqāt*, III, 264.

[83]Ibid., III, 251, 256.

[84]Ibid., III, 264; IV, 124.

[85]Ibn Khallikan, *Wafayāt al-Aᶜyān*, ed. Ihsan ᶜAbbas, 8 vols. (Beirut, 1968–1972), III, 168.

[86]Subki, *Ṭabaqāt*, III, 264.

[87]Abu al-Fida, *Tārīkh*, II, 206.

[88]Subki, *Ṭabaqāt*, III, 261–263. Before his death Juwayni is said to have remarked: "(I call upon you) to attest that I abandon any piece of writing that is inconsistent with the (doctrine of the) forefathers." Ibid., III, 263.

[89]On the purposes of Subki in writing his *Ṭabaqāt*, particularly his defense of Ashᶜarism, see G. Makdisi, "Ashᶜari and Ashᶜarites in Islamic Religious History," *Studia Islamica*, 17 (1962), 56–80.

[90]Ghazali, *al-Munqidh min al-Ḍalāl*, printed with ᶜAbd al-Halim Mahmud's *Abḥāth fī al-Taṣawwuf* ᶜan al-Imām al-Ghazālī (Cairo, 1965), p. 68. In several places throughout his books Ghazali conspicuously speaks as a mujtahid. See for instance his *Mustaṣfā*, II, 353, 372; idem, *Munqidh*, pp. 68, 71, 77, 141–142.

[91]Ghazali, *Munqidh*, pp. 141–142; *Iḥyā*ᵓ, I, 110–111.

[92]Subki, *Ṭabaqāt*, IV, 112.

[93]Ibid., IV, 107.

[94]Ghazali, *Mustaṣfā*, II, 372.

[95]Ghazali, *Iḥyā*ᵓ, I, 63; idem, *Munqidh*, p. 142.

[96]For these opinions see Shawkani, *Irshād*, p. 235.

[97]H. Laoust, "La pédagogie d'al-Gazali dans le Mustasfa," *Revue des Études Islamique*, 44 (1976), 77–78.

[98]Ibn ᶜAqil, *Funūn*, II, 649–650.

[99]Ibid., II, 606; ᶜAbd al-Rahman b. Shihab Ibn Rajab, *al-Dhayl ᶜalā Ṭabaqāt al-Ḥanābila*, ed. H. Laoust and S. Dahhan (Damascus, 1951), pp. 189–190.

[100]Ibn Rajab, *Dhayl*, pp. 190–194.

[101]Ibn ᶜAqil, *Funūn*, II, 602–607, 645–647, 649–650. See also the introduction of G. Makdisi to this book in Vol. I, xlix–l.

[102]This conviction is expressed in a prophetic report. See Abu al-Fida Ibn Kathir, *Nihāyat al-Bidāya wal-Nihāya*, 2 vols. (Riyad, 1968), I, 18.

[103]J. Schacht, "Classicisme, traditionalisme et ankylose dans la loi religieuse de l'Islam," in R. Brunschvig and G. vonGrunebaum, eds., *Classicisme et declin culturel dans l'histoire de l'Islam* (Paris, 1957), p. 148.

[104]Ghazali, *Iḥyā*ᵓ, I, 44, 111.

[105]See, e.g., Ibn ᶜAqil, *Funūn*, I, 126–129, 349–350; II, 504, 524–525, 529 n. 463, 641–645, 745–747 passim.

[106]Published in 9 vols. (Cairo, 1968?).

[107]See his penetrating research in *Études de droit Musulman* (Paris, 1971). Chehata's results were supplemented and confirmed by Y. Meron's "The Development of Legal thought in Hanafi Texts," *Studia Islamica*, 30 (1969). The early sources that were used by Chehata and Meron are mentioned in the next two notes.

[108]Abu al-Hasan al-Quduri, *al-Mukhtaṣar*, printed with Ghunaymi's *al-Lubāb fī Sharḥ al-Kitāb* (Cairo, 1961–63); Shams al-Din al-Sarakhsi, *al-Mabsūṭ*, 30 vols. (Beirut, 197-); ᶜAlaᵓ al-Din al-Samarqandi, *Tuḥfat al-Fuqahā*ᵓ, 3 vols. (Damascus, 1964); Abu Bakr al-Kasani, *Badāᵓiᶜ al-Ṣanāᵓiᶜ*, 7 vols. (Beirut, 1974).

[109]Muhammad b. Hasan al-Shaybani, *al-Aṣl*, 4 vols. (Haidarabad, 1966–1973); Ahmad b. Muhammad al-Tahawi, *al-Mukhtaṣar* (Cairo, 1954); Abu al-Layth al-Samarqandi, *Khizānat al-Fiqh*, ed. S. D. Nahi (Baghdad, 1965).

[110]See Chehata, *Études*, pp. 21–22. For a detailed discussion of the developments in the area of legal capacity, see ibid., pp. 93–106: For developments in the area of the wife's maintenance, see Meron, "Development of Legal Thought," pp. 74, 78–84.

[111]Meron, "The Development of Legal Thought," p. 74.

[112]Chehata, *Études*, pp. 98, 100, 105, 166–167; Meron, "The Development of Legal Thought," pp. 78–84.

[113]Chehata, *Études*, p. 166.

[114]Ibid., pp. 105, 170.

[115]Coulson, *A History of Islamic Law*, pp. 81, 84.

[116]Professor G. Makdisi remarked in his *The Rise of Colleges* (Edinburgh, 1981), p. 290, that he

has "not come across any statement to this effect (i.e., the closure) in any document of the Middle Ages . . . " If this remark was intended to apply to the period up to the end of the fifth/eleventh century, it does not but support our forementioned conclusion. Professor Nicholas Heer has also noted to me that he has not found in classical literature any piece of evidence contrary to my conclusion.

[117]This phrase appeared in a discussion in Muhyi al-Din al-Nawawi, *al-Majmū*ᶜ*: Sharḥ al-Muhadhdhab*, 8 vols. (Cairo, 1966–71), I, 76. For similar usages see Ghazali, *Mustaṣfā*, II, 315–316; Subki, *Ṭabaqāt*, III, 276–277; Ibn ᶜAqil, *Funūn*, I, 92.

[118]Muhammad Bakri al-Siddiqi, *al-Iqtiṣād fī Bayān Marātib al-Ijtihād* (MS) Princeton, Garrett Collection, Yahuda section 253, fol. 98b.

[119]Ibn Kathir, *Nihāya*, I, 30. Another version of the same hadith was translated by Goldziher, "On al-Suyuti," p. 85.

[120]See Majd al-Din, Shihab al-Din, and Taqi al-Din Ibn Taymiyya, *al-Musawwada fī Uṣūl al-Fiqh* (Cairo, 1964), pp. 472, 545.

[121]Ibn ᶜAqil, *Funūn*, I, 92–93.

[122]Ibn Taymiyya, *Musawwada*, pp. 472, 545.

[123]In fact, Razi (d. 606/1209) is said to have dealt with this problem. But the paucity of information about his views makes any evaluation of his doctrine impossible. See Shawkani, *Irshād*, p. 235.

[124]Amidi, *Iḥkām*, III, 253–254.

[125]Ibn al-Hajib, *Mukhtaṣar al-Muntahā* (Cairo, 1908), pp. 233–234.

[126]Subki, *Jam*ᶜ *al-Jawāmi*ᶜ, II, 398–399.

[127]Isnawi, *Nihāya*, III, 331, 349.

[128]Taftazani, *Ḥāshiya*, II, 307.

[129]Ibn al-Amir, *Taqrīr*, III, 339–340.

[130]Ghazali, *Iḥyā*ᵓ, I, 63.

[131]On the ranks of mujtahids and degrees of ijtihad see Mirza Kazim Beg, "Notice sur la march et les progrès de la jurisprudence," *Journal Asiatique* 15, ser. 4 (January 1850), 181–192, 204–214; Siddiqi, *Iqtiṣād*, fols. 98a–98b.

[132]Ibn al-Amir, *Taqrīr*, III, 293.

[133]Ibid., III, 346.

[134]Siddiqi's list includes Qaffal, Ghazali, Ibn ᶜAbd al-Salam, Ibn Daqiq al-ᶜId, Taqi al-Din al-Subki, Taj al-Din al-Subki, and Jalal al-Din al-Suyyuti; see *Iqtiṣād*, fols. 99a–99b.

[135]Ibid., fol. 98b.

[136]Ibn ᶜAbd al-Shakur, *Sharḥ*, II, 399–400.

[137]Laoust, "La Pédagogie," p. 77.

[138]Ibn Taymiyya, *Musawwada*, p. 546.

[139]Nawawi, *Majmū*ᶜ, I, 71.

[140]E. M. Sartain, *Jalal al-Din al-Suyuti* (Cambridge, 1975), p. 65.

[141]Siddiqi, *Iqtiṣād*, fol. 97b.

[142]Ibid., fol. 97b.

[143]ᶜAbd al-Hayy al-Laknawi, *al-Fawā*ᵓ*id al-Bahiyya fī Tarājim al-Ḥanafiyya* (Benares, 1967), p. 89.

[144]These misunderstandings can further be illustrated by an anecdote that took place at the time of Ibn ᶜAbd al-Salam. When the latter claimed the right of ijtihad for himself, the Sultan Musa b. Ayyub wrote to him: "If you claim to be a mujtahid you must prove it (in a convincing manner) that befits such a serious claim, in order that you become a head of a fifth school." Ibn ᶜAbd al-Salam replied: "As to what has been mentioned about ijtihad and the fifth school, (I say that) the usul of religion are not subject to differences (meaning that there is no place for a fifth school) . . . Differences are only in (matters of) furuᶜ." See Subki, *Ṭabaqāt*, V, 93, 95.

[145]Mawardi, *Adab*, I, 463. See examples in Ibn al-Amir, *Taqrīr*, III, 351 and Ghazali, *Mustaṣfā*, II, 384.

[146]Ibn al-Amir, *Taqrīr*, III, 340. Rafiᶜi remarked: "*wal-khalqu kal-muttafiqīna* ᶜ*alā annahu lā mujtahida al-yawma.*"

[147]Subki, *Ṭabaqāt*, V, 120.

[148]Ibid., I, 106. It must be noted that a mujaddid had to qualify as a mujtahid.

[149]Ibn Kathir, *al-Bidāya wal-Nihāya*, 14 vols. (Cairo, 1932), XIII, 250; Ibn al-Amir, *Taqrīr*, III,

340; Subki, *Ṭabaqāt*, V, 18; S. Rizwan Ali, *Izz al-Dīn al-Sulamī* (Islamabad, 1978?), p. 22; Ibn ᶜAbd al-Shakur, *Sharḥ*, II, 399; Suyyuti, *Ḥusn al-Muḥāḍara fī Akhbār Miṣr wal-Qāhira*, 2 vols. (Cairo, 1904), I, 141–147.

[150]Cited in Shawkani, *Irshād*, pp. 235–236.

[151]Cited in Zarqa, "Dawr al-Ijtihād wa-Majāl al-Tashrīᶜ fī al-Islām," *International Islamic Colloquium Papers* (London, 1960), p. 107.

[152]See n. 154 below.

[153]See, e.g., ᶜAbd Allah al-Samhudi, *al-ᶜIqd al-Farīd fī Aḥkām al-Taqlīd* (MS) Princeton, Garrett Collection, Yahuda Section 5183, fols. 177a, 177b; Ibn al-Amir, *Taqrīr*, III, 340; Shawkani, *Irshād*, pp. 235–236.

[154]Consider the following mujtahids: Subki maintained that the Muslim community had agreed that Ibn Daqiq al-ᶜId was a mujtahid as well as a mujaddid. Ibn Daqiq "was a mujtahid mutlaq with complete knowledge of legal sciences" (*Ṭabaqāt*, VI, 2, 3, 6). Ibn al-Rifᶜa, like Subki, professed that an ijmaᶜ had been reached concerning "Ibn Daqiq al-ᶜId and Ibn ᶜAbd al-Salam who reached the rank of ijtihad" (see Siddiqi, *Iqtiṣād*, fol. 99a). Yaᶜmuri described Ibn Daqiq as follows: "He was excellent in deriving rulings from the Sunna and the Quran" (Subki, *Ṭabaqāt*, VI, 2–3; Suyuti, *Ḥusn*, I, 143). Dhahabi and Ibn Nubata considered al-Qadi al-Zamalkani a mujtahid: For Dhahabi, Zamalkani was one of the remaining mujtahids and for Ibn Nubata he was a "mujtahid on whose opinion doubt must not be cast" (Subki, *Ṭabaqāt*, V, 251, 252; Suyuti, *Ḥusn*, I, 145). Subki maintained that Razi was chosen by his successors as the mujtahid and the mujaddid of the sixth/twelfth century (*Ṭabaqāt*, I, 106). Abu Shama was acclaimed as a mujtahid within the Shafiᶜi school (Subki, *Ṭabaqāt*, V, 61; Ibn Kathir, *Bidāya*, XIII, 250). Ibn ᶜAbd al-Salam openly declared himself a mujtahid within the Shafiᶜi school and his claim for the position did not provoke disavowal (Subki, *Ṭabaqāt*, V, 93, 95; see also n. 144 above). Although belonging to the Hanbali school, Ibn Taymiyya did not comply entirely with the Hanbali doctrine: He considered himself a mujtahid fi al-madhhab. In many legal cases (about twenty are known to us) Ibn Taymiyya has diverged from the doctrines of the four eponyms including Ibn Hanbal. See his *al-Fatāwa al-Kubrā*, 5 vols. (Cairo, 1966), III, 95–96. See also *Shorter Encyclopaedia of Islam*, s.v. "Ibn Taymiyya," by M. Cheneb; Ibn Qayyim al-Jawziyya, *Iᶜlām al-Muwaqqiᶜīn ᶜan Rabb al-ᶜĀlamīn*, 4 vols. (Cairo, 1969), II, 231. Cf. Laoust, "L'influence d'Ibn Taymiyya," pp. 17, 20. Taqi al-Din al-Subki, the father of Taj al-Din (the *Ṭabaqāt*'s author), was universally recognized as a mujtahid. For Taj al-Din he was "the best of mujtahids." In fact, Taj al-Din enumerates dozens of cases in which his father completely diverged from Shafiᶜi or rulings he had chosen to follow although they were disfavored in the Shafiᶜi school (see his *Ṭabaqāt*, VI, 113, 147, 182–196). Safadi and Suyuti also thought of Taqi al-Din al-Subki as a unique mujtahid (see Suyuti, *Ḥusn*, I, 145–146; idem., *al-Taḥadduth bi Niᶜmat Allāh*, ed. E. Sartain [Cambridge, 1975], p. 205). Taj al-Din al-Subki himself is supposed to have said: "Now, I am the mujtahid of the universe; I say this and I need not justify what I say." A century and a half later, Suyuti maintained that the statement of Subki was never contested (Siddiqi, *Iqtiṣād*, fol. 99b; Suyuti, *Ḥusn*, I, 150).

[155]Sartain, *Jalāl al-Dīn*, I, 63.

[156]Suyuti, *Taḥadduth*, p. 205.

[157]The ranks of mujtahids and the confusion about them misled even modern scholars. See, e.g., Snouck Hurgronje, *Selected Works*, ed. G. Bousquet and J. Schacht (Leiden, 1957), p. 282, who thought that Suyuti claimed for himself the highest degree of ijtihad, thus challenging the schools' eponyms.

[158]Sartain, *Jalāl al-Dīn*, I, 64, 65.

[159]Cited in Goldziher, "On al-Suyuti," *Muslim World*, 68, 2 (April 1978), 98.

[160]On this see Suyuti, *Taḥadduth*, pp. 193, 203; Sartain, *Jalāl al-Dīn*, I, 61; Goldziher, "On al-Suyuti," p. 98.

[161]Sartain, *Jalāl al-Dīn*, I, 61; Goldziher, "On al-Suyuti," pp. 98–99.

[162]See the chapter that he devoted to the discussion of this issue in *Taḥadduth*, pp. 215–227.

[163]Ibn Kathir, *Nihāya*, I, 30. Cf. another version of this hadith in Goldziher, "On al-Suyuti," p. 81; Subki, *Ṭabaqāt*, I, 104.

[164]Subki, *Ṭabaqāt*, I, 104; Goldziher, "On al-Suyuti," p. 81.

[165]Subki, *Ṭabaqāt*, I, 105; Goldziher, "On al-Suyuti," p. 82. Ibn ᶜAsakir, however, preferred Ashᶜari; see A. Khuli, *al-Mujaddidūn fī al-Islām*, 2 vols. (Cairo, 1965), I, 13.

[166] Subki, *Ṭabaqāt*, I, 105; Suyuti, *Taḥadduth*, p. 221.

[167] According to the sources that Goldziher used, the Hanbali al-Muqaddisi (d. 600/1203) and the Shafi^{c}i Nawawi (d. 676/1277) were designated; see Goldziher, "On al-Suyuti," pp. 83–84. However, from the Shafi^{c}i viewpoint, Subki chose Razi, favoring him over Rafi^{c}i (see Subki, *Ṭabaqāt*, I, 106).

[168] Subki, *Ṭabaqāt*, I, 106; VI, 3; Suyuti, *Taḥadduth*, p. 220.

[169] Suyuti, *Taḥadduth*, pp. 207, 225; Goldziher, "On al-Suyuti," p. 84.

[170] Shawkani, *Irshād*, p. 236; Goldziher, "On al-Suyuti," p. 82.

[171] *Encyclopaedia of Islam*, 2nd ed., s.v. "Ahmad al-Sirhindi," by Sh. Inayatullah.

[172] Khuli, *al-Mujaddidūn*, p. 1. For further details on mujaddids see pp. 12–29.

[173] Up to the fifth/eleventh century mujaddids were only Shafi^{c}is (see Subki, *Ṭabaqāt*, I, 104–106; Goldziher, "On al-Suyuti," pp. 82–83). The only uncertain exception was Ash^{c}ari who was claimed by Shafi^{c}is as well as Hanafis (see Qarashi, *Jawāhir*, II, 544–545). From the sixth/twelfth century onward Shafi^{c}i mujaddids remained the majority; the Hanbalis produced a few mujaddids and, as far as I know, there were no Hanafi or Maliki candidates for tajdid.

[174] The fifth/eleventh century tabaqat works seem to have been the earliest works that Subki could find as sources for his biographical dictionary; see his *Ṭabaqāt*, I, 114. See also I. Hafsi's bibliographical essay "Recherches sur le genre 'Tabaqat' dans la littérature Arabe," *Arabica*, 23, 3 (1976), 8–12, 17–18, 24.

[175] Laoust, "La pédagogie d'al-Gazali," p. 77.

[176] Kazem Beg, "Notice sur la marche," pp. 181–192, 204 ff.; Ibn Taymiyya, *Musawwada*, pp. 547–548.

[177] Ibn ^{c}Abidin, *Ḥāshiyat Radd al-Muḥtār*, 8 vols. (Cairo, 1966), I, 77; idem, *Rasā$^{\supset}$il*, I, 11–13; M. Suhrawardy, "The Waqf of Moveables" *Asiatic Society of Bangal*, 7 n.s. (1911), pp. 330–331; Laknawi, *Fawā$^{\supset}$id*, pp. 89–90.

[178] Kazem Beg, "Notice sur la marche," pp. 206–214.

[179] Nawawi, *Majmū^{c}*, I, 73–74; Ibn Taymiyya, *Musawwada*, p. 549.

[180] Ibn ^{c}Abidin, *Ḥāshiya*, I, 77.

[181] Ibn ^{c}Abidin, *Rasā$^{\supset}$il*, I, 11.

[182] Suhrawardy, "The Waqf," pp. 330–331.

[183] Ibn ^{c}Abidin, *Rasā$^{\supset}$il*, I, 12.

[184] This attitude seems to have started at an earlier period. When dealing with the four law schools as they have become established by the eighth/fourteenth century, the Maliki scholar Ibn Khaldun (d. 808/1405) observed that the complexity of the schools' legal doctrines had prevented people from attaining ijtihad and for this reason scholars made it an obligation for all Muslims to follow the established schools through the writings of renowned jurists. "Jurisprudence," Ibn Khaldun argues "means this and nothing else. The person who would claim ijtihad nowadays would be frustrated and have no adherents" (Al-Muqaddima, p. 448 [Rosenthal's trans. III, 8–9). Undoubtedly, Ibn Khaldun had independent mujtahids in mind, because it was well known to him, as much as it was well known to all jurists, that a limited mujtahid or a mujtahid within the school, cannot have followers. From the general usages of ijtihad in the *Muqaddima*, it seems to me that, for Ibn Khaldun, ijtihad exclusively meant the kind of major legal activity undertaken during the first three centuries of Islam. Consider what he has to say elsewhere in his *Muqaddima*: "The school doctrine of each eponym became, among his adherents, a scholarly discipline in its own right. They were no longer in a position to apply ijtihad and qiyas. Therefore, they had to make reference to the established principle (*al-uṣūl al-muqarrara*) of their eponyms, in order to be able to solve (new) problems according to (old) similar ones and disentangle them when they got confused (*tanẓīru al-masā$^{\supset}$ili fil-$^{\supset}$ilḥāqi wa tafrīquhā ^{c}inda al-ishtibāhi*). A firmly rooted faculty (of knowledge) was required to enable a person to undertake such (analogy) and disentanglement and to apply the school doctrine of his particular eponym to those (processes) according to the best of his ability. This (practice) of faculty is (what is meant) at this time by the science of jurisprudence" (*Al-Muqaddima*, p. 449). The sentence "*tanẓīru al-masā$^{\supset}$ili . . . ishtibāhi*" was translated by Rosenthal as "to analyze problems in their context and disentangle them when they got confused" (see III, 13). For Ibn Khaldun, therefore, ijtihad is the legal activity that leads to the construction of a new school which will eventually attract adherents. Although the processes of unraveling doctrinal problems and applying analogy to new cases within a school are considered part of the Sunni ijtihad methodology, Ibn Khaldun does not see them a

related to ijtihad. For him qiyas and ijtihad are much more than these processes. But whether he accepts the Sunni usulist terminology or not, this is nonetheless a limited form of ijtihad. One may find it striking that Ibn Khaldun insists on the inability of jurists to practice ijtihad at a time when he is familiar with the reputation and career of contemporary mujtahids such as Subki and Bulqini (d. 805/1403), both universally acknowledged as mujtahids fi al-madhhab. See *al-Muqaddima*, p. 449 (Rosenthal's trans., III, 12); for Subki and Bulqini see Subki, *Ṭabaqāt*, VI, 146–216; Suyuti, *Ḥusn*, I, 168 f.; Goldziher, "On al-Suyuti," p. 84. It is then clear that Ibn Khaldun's conception of this question is an excellent example of the general attitude of muqallids towards the issue of the existence of mujtahids. He knew that the eponyms and their equals were extinct; he also knew that the machine of legal interpretation was constantly at work, but he was still puzzled as to how to square these facts with the ever-growing idea of the extinction of mujtahids. It was, therefore, suitable as well as convenient for him to say that contemporary scholars were incapable of ijtihad, implying the extinction of mujtahids, and that the activity of jurists of his time had nothing to do with ijtihad, despite the fact that it entailed the use of analogy and types of legal interpretation.

[185]ᶜAbd al-Rahman al-Jabarti, *ᶜAjāʾib al-Āthār fī al-Tarājim wal-Akhbār*, 7 vols. (Cairo, 1958–67), III, 41–42.

[186]Ibid., I, 186, 218–219; II, 28.

[187]Ibid., III, 65–103, especially p. 65.

[188]Ibid., III, 88. On *istinbāṭ* see Ibn ᶜAbidin, *Rasāʾil*, I, 31.

[189]Jabarti, *ᶜAjāʾib*, III, 67.

[190]See Shawkani, *al-Qawl al-Mufīd fī Adillat al-Ijtihād wal-Taqlīd* (Cairo, 1974), passim; Muhammad b. Ismaᶜil al-Sanᶜani, *Irshād al-Nuqqād ilā Taysīr al-Ijtihād* (Beirut, 1970), passim; Shah Wali Allah, *ᶜIqd al-Jīd* (Cairo, 1965), passim; G. H. Jalbani, *Life of Shah Waliyullah* (Delhi, 1980), pp. 56–57; Ibn ᶜAbidin, *Rasāʾil*, I, 28.

[191]Chelebi, *Balance*, p. 129; J. E. Mandaville, "Usurious Piety: The Cash of Waqf Controversy in the Ottoman Empire," *International Journal of Middle East Studies* 10 (1979), 295–304.

[192]Husayn b. Iskandar al-Rumi, *Risāla fī al-Dukhān* (MS) Princeton, Garrett Collection, Yahuda Section 3854, fols. 2b–5a; Muhammad b. Mustafa al-Khadimi, *Risāla fī al-Qahwa wal-Dukhān* (MS) Princeton, Garrett Collection, Yahuda Section 3225, fols. 48b–49a. On these subjects see Chelebi, *Balance*, Chapters II, III, V, VII, XII, XX; Mandaville, "Usurious Piety."

[193]*The Balance of Truth.*

[194]J. Schacht, "Early Doctrines on Waqf," in *Mélange Fuad Köprülü* (Istanbul, 1953), 443.

[195]Mandaville, "Usurious Piety," pp. 299–304; Suhrawardy, "The Waqf," 388 ff.

[196]See, e.g., the argument of Bali Effendi in Mandaville, "Usurious Piety," pp. 301–303; Chelebi, *Balance*, p. 129.

[197]Chelebi, *Balance*, p. 129.

[198]See, e.g., the arguments concerning the legality of hashish in F. Rosenthal, *The Herb: Hashish versus Medieval Muslim Society* (Leiden, 1971), pp. 105–130.

[199]See, e.g., Ibn ᶜAbidin, *Rasāʾil*, I, 28; Ibn ᶜAbd al-Shakur, *Sharḥ*, II, 399; Sanᶜani, *Irshād*, pp. 2, 11–12; Samhudi, *al-ᶜIqd al-Farīd*, fol. 177b; Khadimi, *R. fi al-Qahwa*, fol. 48b.

[200]Shawkani, *al-Qawl*, p. 7.

[201]Ibid., pp. 21–24, 31.

[202]Shawkani, *al-Badr*, I, 2.

[203]Shawkani, *Irshād*, p. 236; idem, *al-Badr, I, 3.*

ADDENDA

General remark: since the publication of the article, I have come across a staggering body of evidence, both directly and not so directly related to the issue of *ijtihād*, which clearly supports the thesis advanced in the article. Conversely, I have not, throughout these years, encountered any evidence that may in any way undermine that thesis.

p. 19, n. 108: on the growth and evolution of substantive law, see the more recent work of Baber Johansen, *Islamic Law on Land Tax and Rent* (London: Croom Helm, 1988); id., 'Legal Literature and the Problem of Change: The Case of the Land Rent', in *Islam and Public Law*, ed. Chibli Mallat (London: Graham & Trotman, 1993): 29–47; Wael B. Hallaq, 'From *Fatwās* to *Furū'*: Growth and Change in Islamic Substantive Law', *Islamic Law and Society*, 1, 1 (1994): 29–65; id., 'Murder in Cordoba: *Ijtihād, Iftā'* and the Evolution of Substantive Law in Medieval Islam', *Acta Orientalia*, 55 (1994, forthcoming).

p. 20, n. 115: such statements have been lately challenged by a number of works. See sources cited in the *addendum* to n. 108, above.

p. 32, ll. 19–22: for a useful discussion of the views of Ibn Mu'ammar, Shawkānī, and Sanūsī, see Rudolph Peters, '*Ijtihād* and *Taqlīd* in 18th and 19th Century Islam', *Die Welt des Islams*, 20 (1980): 131–45.

p. 36, n. 69: the article appeared in the *Journal of American Oriental Society*, 104 (1984): 679–89.

ON THE ORIGINS OF THE CONTROVERSY ABOUT THE EXISTENCE OF MUJTAHIDS AND THE GATE OF IJTIHAD

In a recently published article I have tried to show that, contrary to the widespread notion, the 'gate of *ijtihād*' was not closed, and that until the end of the fifth/eleventh century there was no reference in Islamic sources alluding to halting the practice of *ijtihād*. (1) The first item of information directly related to the controversy about the continuity of *ijtihād* appeared around 500 A.H. in the form of scholarly disputation between the Ḥanbali jurist Ibn 'Aqīl (d. 513/1119) and an anonymous scholar belonging to the Ḥanafi school of law. In this disputation Ibn 'Aqīl refuted the argument of his adversary who maintained that the 'gate of judgeship' *(bāb al-qaḍā')* was closed because there no longer were any *mujtahids*. (2) Towards the end of the sixth/twelfth century and the beginning of the seventh/thirteenth all comprehensive works on legal theory, *uṣūl al-fiqh*, included a section devoted to discussing the controversy about whether or not it is possible for an age to be devoid of *mujtahids*. In this controversy the Ḥanbalis and a number of prominent Shāfi'is maintained, while adducing rational and scriptural evidence, that *mujtahids* must exist at all times. On the other hand, the Ḥanafis

(1) W. B. Hallaq, "Was the Gate of Ijtihad Closed?" *International Journal of Middle Eastern Studies*, 16, 1 (1984).

(2) Abū al-Wafā' Muḥammad Ibn 'Aqīl, *Kitāb al-Funūn*, ed. G. Makdisi, 2 vols. (Beirut Dār al-Mashriq, 1970-1971), II, 92.

and the rest of the Shāfiʿis argued that the extinction of *mujtahids* was likely to occur. [3]

This article is concerned with the question of why the issue of the continuity of *ijtihād* and the existence of *mujtahids* arose in Islam? In attempting to answer the question, Joseph Schacht argued that by the beginning of the fourth/tenth century, Islamic law had been elaborated in detail and thus Muslim scholars came to the conclusion that all essential questions had been thoroughly discussed and finally settled. This, Schacht believed, was the reason for raising the question of who was qualified to practice *ijtihād* and who was not and, above all, the reason for the closure of the gate of *ijtihād*. [4] For a number of reasons, this argument, hitherto widely accepted by scholars, [5] must now be revised.

First, long before the fourth century and certainly before the final formation of the positive law of the Sunni law schools, the question of who could or could not practice *ijtihād* came under discussion. In his *Risāla*, Shāfiʿi (d. 204/820) dealt

(3) Sayf al-Dīn al-Āmidi, *al-Iḥkām fi Uṣūl al-Aḥkām*, 3 vols. (Cairo: Muḥammad ʿAli Ṣubayḥ, 1968), III, 253-254. For a later discussion on the possible extinction of *mujtahids* see Ibn Niẓām al-Dīn al-Anṣāri, *Fawātiḥ al-Raḥamūt*, with the commentary of Ibn ʿAbd al-Shakūr, 2 vols. (Cairo: Bulāq, 1324 H.), II, 399f.

(4) J. Schacht, *An Introduction to Islamic Law* (Oxford: The Clarendon Press, 1964), pp. 69-71, especially p. 70 where he states that "during the whole of the formative period of Islamic law, the first two and a half centuries of Islam (or until about the middle of the ninth century A.D.), there was never any question of denying to any scholar or specialist of the sacred Law the right to find his own solutions to legal problems. The sanction which kept ignoramuses at bay was simply general disapproval by the recognized specialists. It was only after the formative period of Islamic Law had come to an end that the question of *ijtihād* and of who was qualified to exercise it was raised." Schacht adds (pp. 70-71) that around 900 A.D. "the point had been reached when the scholars of all schools felt that all essential questions had been thoroughly discussed and finally settled, and a consensus gradually established itself to the effect that from that time onwards no one might be deemed to have the necessary qualifications for independent reasoning in law, and that all future activity would have to be confined to the explanation, application, and, at the most, interpretation of the doctrine as it had been laid down once and for all." See also the statement of Coulson below note 16.

(5) See, e.g., H. J. Liebesny, "Judicial Systems in the Near and Middle East: Evolutionary Development and Islamic Revival," *The Middle East Journal*, 37, 2 (Spring 1983), 202-203: J. L. Esposito, *Women in Muslim Family Law* (Syracuse: Syracuse University Press, 1982), pp. 10-11. For other citations see Hallaq, "Was the Gate of Ijtihad Closed?", p. 34, notes 3, 4 and 6.

with this issue, (6) and by the time of Ash'ari (d. 330/941) it had become an established legal question, to be commented upon and debated. (7)

Second, the argument of modern scholars contradicts a fundamental assumption in medieval Islam. In his excellent work *Knowledge Triumphant*, F. Rosenthal has convincingly demonstrated the centrality of the concept of *'ilm*, knowledge, to Islamic culture. (8) To Sunni Muslim jurists *'ilm* constituted the backbone of Islam itself. *'Ilm* meant knowledge, not primarily of medicine or astronomy, (9) but of the conduct that would please God and bring humans closer to Him. Law in Islam was designated with the term *fiqh* which meant understanting or acquiring knowledge. Jurists often equated *'ilm* with *fiqh*. (10) To Shāfi'i *'ilm* is of two types, one which can readily be found in the Quran and the Sunna of the Prophet and which all Muslims know of, such as the duty to perform prayers, fast in Ramaḍān, shun theft and fornication, etc. The second type is that which the qualified jurist alone can extract from the religious texts. This type of *'ilm* treats of technical and specialized points of law. (11) Elsewhere, Shāfi'i defines *'ilm* as the knowledge of the divine law which can be 'discovered' by means of legal reasoning *(qiyās)*. (12) Shāfi'i's successors also equated *'ilm* with *fiqh* (13) and Juwayni went even further to explicitely state that God has commanded

(6) Ibn Idrīs al-Shāfi'i, *al-Risāla*, ed. M. Kīlāni (Cairo: Muṣṭafa Bābi al-Ḥalabi, 1969), pp. 221-222.

(7) Abu al-Ḥasan al-Ash'ari, *Maqālāt al-Islāmīyīn*, ed. M. M. 'Abd al-Ḥamīd, 2 vols. (Cairo: Maktabat al-Nahḍa, 1969), II, 174.

(8) Franz Rosenthal, *Knowledge Triumphant: The Concept of Knowledge in Medieval Islam* (Leiden: E. J. Brill, 1970).

(9) While such secular fields were included in the definition of *'ilm*, they were reckoned inferior to, and in the periphery of religious science. See Abu Ḥāmid al-Ghazāli, *Iḥyā' 'Ulūm al-Dīn*, 5 vols. (Cairo: Maṭābi' Sijjil al-'Arab, 1967), I, 27.

(10) Abn 'Abd al-Barr, *Jāmi' Bayān al-'Ilm*, ed. A. M. 'Uthmān, 2 vols. (Madīna: al-Maktaba al-Salafiyya, 1968), I, 12-13; al-Khaṭīb al-Baghdādi, *al-Faqīh wal-Mutafaqqih*, 2 vols. (Cairo: Dār Iḥyā' al-Sunna, 1975), I, 10, 11, 22, 35.

(11) Shāfi'i, *al-Risāla*, pp. 154ff. See also p. 25 where he again equates *'ilm* with the knowledge of the Quran, the Prophetic Sunna, consensus and *qiyās*.

(12) Shāfi'i, *al-Risāla*, p. 206, paragraphs 1328-1333. In Shāfi'i's terminology *qiyās* and *ijtihād* are synonymous.

(13) See, e.g., al-Baghdādi, *al-Faqīh wal-Mutafaqqih*, I, 27-29; Ibn 'Abd al-Barr, *Jāmi' Bayān al-'Ilm*, I, 11ff., 38-39; Imām al-Ḥaramayn al-Juwayni, *Ghiyāth al-Umam fī Iltiyāth al-Ẓulam*, ed. F. 'Abd al-Mun'im and M. Ḥilmi (Iskandariyya: Dār al-Da'wa, 1979), p. 377; Ghazāli, *Iḥyā'*, I, 22, 23, 27, 29.

Muslims to use the term *'ilm* to refer to the knowledge of the law. ([14])

Determining what the law is, was not a matter of speculation. Rulings of individual cases had to be arrived at through a highly complex methodology known as *ijtihād*. This methodology, described fully in the works of *uṣūl al-fiqh*, constituted the only means by which the rulings decreed by God, the *'ilm*, could be reached. Therefore, the survival of *'ilm* and in turn, of the Sharī'a, depended on the continual functioning of *ijtihād*. In other words, blocking the gate of *ijtihād* would have meant for Muslims a partial and imperfect mastery of *'ilm* and thus a deficient and incomplete Sharī'a. ([15]) Inability to extend the precepts of Sharī'a to newly arising problems would have also meant that Islam was utterly inadequate.

The modern scholar's argument that the Muslim jurists of the fourth/tenth century raised the question of *ijtihād's* gate and its closure because they felt that all points of law were thoroughly discussed and that a comprehensive legal system was finally erected, in effect amounts to claiming that the Muslims of this period viewed law as quantitatively limited and that the means for solving novel legal problems arising from yet new situations was not provided for in the Sharī'a. ([16]) Ample evidence points to the fact that this argument finds no support whatsoever in the literature, and in fact runs against everything Muslims said and did.

Muslim jurists of the fourth/tenth and fifth/eleventh centuries had no doubts about the infinite number of cases that might appear and that require legal solutions. ([17]) Though there

(14) Imām al-Ḥaramayn al-Juwayni, *al-Kāfiya fi al-Jadal*, ed. F. H. Maḥmūd (Cairo: Bābi al-Ḥalabi Press, 1979), pp. 25-27, especially p. 26 lines 6-9.

(15) Āmidi, *al-Iḥkām*, III, 254.

(16) N. J. Coulson, *A History of Islamic Law* (Edinburgh: Edinburgh University Press, 1964), p. 81 argues that the closure of the gate of *ijtihād* "was probably the result not of external pressures but of internal causes. The point had been reached where the material sources of the divine will—their content now finally determined—*had fully been exploited.*" (italics are mine).

(17) Baghdādi, *al-Faqīh wal-Mutafaqqih*, I, 18-19; 'Ali b. Muḥammad al-Māwardi, *Adab al-Qāḍi*, ed. M. H. Sarḥān, 2 vols. (Baghdad: Maṭba'at al-Irshād, 1971), I, 491; Imām al-Ḥaramayn al-Juwayni, *al-Burhān fi Uṣūl al-Fiqh*, ed. A. Dīb, 2 vols. (Cairo) Dār al-Anṣār, 1400 H.), II, 743, 1332, 1349; idem, *Ghiyāth al-Umam*, p. 291, 305-306, 312; Ibn 'Abd al-'Azīz Ibn Māza, *Sharḥ Adab al-Qāḍi*, ed. M. H. Sarḥān, 4 vols. (Baghdad: Maṭba'at al-Irshād, 1977), I, 126, 128; Muḥammad Ibn Rushd, *Bidāyat al-Mujtahid*, 2 vols. (Cairo: Maktabat al-Kulliyāt, 1970), I, 3.

seems to have existed a tacit consensus on the fact that there was no place for another school of law, Muslims explicitely agreed that for all new cases there were *shar'i* rulings and that finding such rulings was a religious duty incumbent upon the qualified scholars of the community. (18)

The invalidity of the current argument, represented and summarized by Schacht, still leaves us with the following question: *If ijtihād* and *mujtahids* did continue to exist long after the fourth/tenth century, (19) why did Muslim scholars raise the subject of the gate of *ijtihād* and the existence—or nonexistence—of *mujtahids*? Before we attempt any answer, one important point must be clarified. A distinction should be drawn between two intricately related expressions; the first is 'the closure of the gate of *ijtihād*' and the second 'whether it is possible for an age to be devoid of *mujtahids*.' These two fixed expressions with all the significations involved, were not entirely interchangeable, particularly in the early period. In my aforementioned article, I have treated the two expressions interchangeably, thus assuming that the nascent discussions about the existence of *mujtahids* were symptomatic of the emergence of the controversy about the gate. This view needs some modification. Chronologically, the controversial question of the existence of *mujtahids* preceded by at least two centuries the expression 'the closure of the gate of *ijtihād*. And even when the latter emerged it remained for more than three centuries an uncommon expression appearing infrequently in legal literature. (20) While the controversy

In fact, legal theory, which continued to be the concern of scholars until pre-modern times, provided the methodology by which a jurist could derive legal solutions for the *nawāzil*, the unprecedented legal cases. See Abu Isḥāq al-Shīrāzi, *al-Luma' fī Uṣūl al-Fiqh* (Cairo: Maṭba'at al-Sa'āda, 1908), p. 4; Ghazāli, *al-Mustaṣfā min 'Ilm al-Uṣūl*, 2 vols. (Cairo: Bulāq, 1316-1317 H.), I, 5; idem, *al-Mankhūl min Ta'līqāt al-Uṣūl*, ed. M. H. Hītū (Damascus, n,s., 1970), pp. 359, 484-485; Āmidi, *al-Iḥkām*, I, 6; Abu Isḥāq al-Shāṭibi, *al-Muwāfaqāt*, ed. M. 'Abd al-Ḥamīd, 4 vols. (Cairo: al-Madani Press, 1969), I, 17; Muḥammad b. 'Ali al-Shawkāni, *Irshād al-Fuḥūl ilā Taḥqīq al-Ḥaqq min 'Ilm al-Uṣūl* (Beirut: Dār al-Fikr, n.d.), p. 3.

(18) Āmidi, *al-Iḥkām*, III, 222; Sa'd al-Dīn al-Taftazāni, *Ḥāshiya 'ala Mukhtaṣar al-Muntaha*, 2 vols. (Cairo: n.s., 1974), II, 308; Shawkāni, *Irshād al-Fuḥūl*, p. 253. Shāfi'i, *al-Risāla*, pp. 16ff. argues that God enjoined Muslims to practice *ijtihād*. See also Juwayni, *al-Burhān*, II, 743, 805.

(19) On the *mujtahids* who existed in the fourth/tenth century and afterwards see Hallaq, "Was the Gate of Ijtihad Closed?" pp. 10ff.

(20) This is based on extensive reading in legal, semi-legal, biographical and theological sources from the period between ca. 400/1010-1250/1835.

over the existence of *mujtahids* had by 600 A.H. become an integral part of all comprehensive works of legal theory, the expression the 'closure of the gate of *ijtihād*' did not gain currency until well after the tenth/sixteenth century. (21) An inquiry into the reasons that propelled Muslims to deliberate upon the continuity of *ijtihād* must therefore take cognizance of the fact that the discussion started in terms of the existence —or nonexistence— of *mujtahids*: the concept of the gate of *ijtihād* and its closure did not exist in the mind of Muslims in this early period.

Since *ijtihād* persisted in theory and in practice and since *mujtahids* continued to exist in the fifth/eleventh century and long afterwards, (22) the reasons for the emergence of the question concerning the existence of *mujtahids* must be sought outside the boundaries of the legal system. A search for an answer in the fourth/tenth and fifth/eleventh century literature reveals that the origins of the problem lie in the theological doctrine of the end of religion and the comming of the Day of Judgement. The deteriorating political situation in the fourth/tenth and fifth/elenventh centuries, however, was most crucial in reinforcing the belief in this doctrine as well as in rendering the ulama and the *mujtahids* as the only remaining leaders of the community and the sole bearers of *'ilm*.

By the middle of the fifth/eleventh century it had become quite clear that a revival of the institution of caliphate was out of the question. The caliph was no more than a religious symbol whose authority and dominion over the Muslim subjects could hardly reach the peripheries of Baghdad. Instability of political regimes and political and social strife were predominant. In short, these conditions created a great deal of insecurity and threatened the unity of the *umma*. (23) The

(21) The first work in which the controversy over the existence of *mujtahids* had become established is Āmidi, *al-Iḥkām*, III, 253-254. In fact, the expression 'the gate of *ijtihād*' could never establish itself in the works of legal theory and remained outside pure legal formulations.

(22) This has been demonstrated in Hallaq, "Was the Gate of Ijtihad Closed?"

(23) This state of affairs was reflected clearly in political thought. Juwayni and Ghazāli, the most prominent political thinkers of the second half of the fifth century H., were haunted by a fear of civil war *(fitna)*, which would disintegrate the unity of the *umma*. See Juwayni, *Ghiyāth al-Umam*, pp. 15, 125, 126-127, 135ff., 195ff., passim; A. K. S. Lambton, *State and Government in Medieval Islam* (Oxford: Oxford University Press, 1981), pp. 109, 116.

Muslim community in general and the urban communities in particular lacked any sort of all-inclusive political or economic organization. Municipalities or coordinating agencies did not exist, and social cohesiveness was dependent upon a rather different type of institution: this was the religious institution headed by the ulama. In the fourth/tenth and especially in the fifth/eleventh century the ulama emerged as the sole uniting social force in the Muslim community. Their leadership was accepted by virtually all segments of society, and their influence on political and military rulers was often substantial. By the nature of the functions they occupied, they were undoubtedly most instrumental in preserving the social fabric of Islam. They were the legal and religious advisers of rulers, administrators, chief and district judges, emmissaries, *muftis*, prayer-leaders, teachers, merchants, Quran-readers, librarians, preachers, market supervisors, etc. Writings from this period give the unmistakeable impression that the ulama were considered the leading element in the community's religious, social, economic and political life. Books became replete with prophetic reports, the content of which points to their weight and importance. A handful of these reports indicate that the ulama were deemed the heirs of the Prophet and the only trusted leaders of the *umma*. (24)

On the practical level all ulama were given their due weight. But on the theoretical one, which is of more relevance to the case under discussion, the ulama were of only limited importance without the *mujtahids*. While the former were the bearers of the divine law, the latter did not only partake in this responsibility but were also the only qualified persons to inform the community and its military rulers of what was lawful and what was not, particularly when an unprecedented situation arose. Going to war, levying extra-legal taxes, conveying titles on military rulers, and a multitude of other issues required a word of authority—the *fatwa* of the the *mujtahid*. In legal theory *muftis* and judges were required to be *mujtahids*. (25) Sunni

(24) Abu al-Layth al-Samarqandi, *Tanbīh al-Ghāfilīn*, 2 vols. (Jadda: Dār al-Shurūq, 1980), II, 463; Ghazāli, *Iḥyā'*, I, 10, 12-13, 14, 24; Baghdādi, *al-Faqīh wal-Mutafaqqih*, I, 2, 32ff.; Ibn ʿAbd al-Karīm al-Shāhrastāni, *Nihāyat al-Iqdām fi ʿIlm al-Kalām*, ed. A. Guillaume (Baghdad: Maktabat al-Muthanna, 1964), p. 486.

(25) Shīrāzi, *al-Lumaʿ*, pp. 85-86; Māwardi, *Adab al-Qāḍi*, I, 467; Baghdādi,

political theory insisted that the caliph, being in theory the supreme ruler in Islam, must be capable of exercising *ijtihād.* (26). The ulama without *ijtihād* were thought to be mere *muqallids* (immitators) who could hardly be trusted with more than transmitting the doctrines of the forefathers to their contemporaries. The task of bearing the Sharī'a, with all the responsibility that this entailed, was entrusted to the *mujtahids.* (27)

The indispensability of *mujtahids* was equally evident in the institution of government. The monumental political treatises of Juwayni, Ghazāli, Ibn Jamā'a and Ibn Taymiyya demonstrate beyond any doubt that the *mujtahids* were reckoned the partners of the sultan in governing the Muslim community. (28) Juwayni, for example, realizing the weight of jurists, determined that the institution of the caliphate was in effect a combination of power and *'ilm*, represented, respectively, by sultans and *mujtahids.* (29)

Being the trustees of the Muslim community and of its faith, the *mujtahids* of the fourth/tenth and fifth/eleventh centuries were considered the deliverers of Islam, who are alone qualified to carry on the Message after the death of the Prophet and the degeneration of the caliphate. But at the same time, Muslims had begun realizing more clearly that *mujtahids* of the caliber of Abu Ḥanīfa (d. 150/767) and Shāfi'i had ceased to exist and instead only *mujtahids* within the framework of the established schools of law continued to appear. This awareness, coupled with the Muslim belief that the leaders of the *umma*, beginning with the Prophet, his Companions, and later his *khulafā'*, were

al-Faqīh wal-Mutafaqqih, II, 156-158; Āmidi, *al-Iḥkām,* III, 254; Juwayni, *al-Burhān,* II, 1332.

(26) When the caliph was incapable of practicing *ijtihād* they insistad that one of his subordinates must fulfill this function. Juwayni, *al-Burhān,* II, 1333, 1334; idem, *Ghiyāth al-Umam,* p. 275; Ghazāli, *Iḥyā',* I, 61.

(27) Juwayni, *Ghiyāth al-Umam,* pp. 274-275, 282; Baghdādi, *al-Faqīh wal-Mutafaqqih,* I, 2; Ghazāli, *Iḥyā',* I, 10-14.

(28) On this see E. J. Rosenthal, "The Role of the State in Islam: Theory and Medieval Practice," *Islam,* 50, 1 (April 1973), 1-28; W. B. Hallaq, "Caliphs, Jurists and the Saljuqs in the Political Thought of Juwayni," *The Muslim World,* Vol. 74, No. 1 (1984); Lambton, *State and Government,* pp. 115, 119.

(29) Hallaq, "Caliphs, Jurists, and the Saljuqs."

destined to extinction, had led them to contemplate the possibility of the extinction of *mujtahids*. (30)

But this fatalism was preconceived within the context of the larger theological doctrine about the end of Islam and the Hour of resurrection. It is only in view of the Judgement Day doctrine that the whole issue of the extinction of *mujtahids* can be explained. (31) Muslim theologians, who were often concurrently jurists and traditionists, believed that Islam, from its beginning until its end, would last for no more than a millennium. The duration of the world from the Creation until the Day of Judgement was determined to be seven-thousand years, in the last thousand years of which Islam would begin and end. (32) This belief was based upon and justified by several prophetic traditions and Quranic verses. One of the well-known traditions makes the Prophet say: "The world is seven-thousand years and I (came) in the last thousand." (33) Another tradition often adduced to support the view that the Day of Judgement is approaching has the

(30) An excellent example of this trend is Juwayni, who argued that since the Prophet and his companions had perished and since the caliphate had degenerated to a degree of possible extinction, it was quite conceivable that the 'bearers of the Sharī'a', the *mujtahids*, might disappear. In his *Ghiyāth al-Umam*, Juwayni strongly believed that it would be a matter of time before Sharī'a and Islam altogether come to an end. Although he admitted the existence of *mujtahids* at his time, he devoted a whole chapter for the discussion of the possible extinction of not only the *mujtahids* but also the lesser ulama. It is worth noting that he was the first jurist known to me to discourse in detail about this issue. However, his exposition was predominantly theological and it can hardly be reminiscent of the later juristic expositions of Āmidi and his successors. See *Ghiyāth al-Umam*, pp. 11, 18, 82, 281-282, 284, 376-377, 379. For supporting evidence see *al-Burhān*, II, 937, 1346ff.

(31) The doctrine of the Day of Judgement was central in medieval Islam. In the Quran it may be reckoned the greatest after the doctrine of the oneness of God. See W. M. *Watt, Bell's Introduction to the Quran* (Edinburgh: The University Press, 1970), pp. 158ff.

(32) 'Ali b. Muḥammad al-Māwardi, *A'lām al-Nubuwwa*, ed. T. A. Sa'd (Cairo: Maktabat al-Kulliyyāt, 1971), pp. 39-52; I. Goldziher, "On al-Suyuti," *Muslim World*, 68, 2 (April 1978), 84. According to an early prophetic report, the duration of the world is 6 000 years, in the last 500 years of which Islam begins and ends. Needless to say, this report was rejected in the fifth/eleventh century and instead other reports were introduced so as to advance the Day of Judgement another half millennium. See Ibn Khaldūn, *The Muqaddimah*, trans. F. Rosenthal, 3 vols. (Princeton: Princeton Universtiy Press, 1958), II, 204-205.

(33) Māwardi, *A'lām al-Nubuwwa*, p. 39.

Prophet say while joining his middle and index fingers: "My coming (is as close) to the Hour (Judgement Day) as these." [34]

It is noteworthy that the belief in the Day of Judgement was consistent with the popular belief that the age of the Prophet and his Companions represented the Golden Age of Islam and that the farther Muslims were from this age the worse the state of degeneration would be. The oft-quoted Prophetic report "the best century is my century and then the one which follows it and then the one which follows..." is expressive of this entrenched conviction. Understandably, Muslims viewed Islam at the time of the Prophet as the purest form of religion and it was thought that subsequent to that Islam was destined to lose its original impulse, particularly when it became evident to later Muslims that the political and social state of affairs as well as the moral and pietistic standards of their times were incompatible with those standards assumed to have prevailed at the age of the Prophet. And since the Day of Judgement was considered to be an inevitable event, it was only reasonable that Islam, the last in a series of religions, would have to degenerate sufficiently as to justify the happening of the expected Day.

In the fifth/eleventh century, it was believed that the coming of the Hour would fall sometime within the next five centuries. [35] The signs of the approaching of this Day were untirely reiterated by Muslims and, to be sure, a number of *ḥadīths* enumerating these signs were repeatedly cited. [36] One of these signs was the disappearance of religious knowledge, *ʿilm*. [37] But *ʿilm* could disappear only with the demise of

(34) *Ibid.*, p. 39. The Arabic: "*buʿithtu wal-sāʿatu kahātayni.*"

(35) Juwayni, *al-Burhān*, II, 1348; Māwardi, *Aʿlām al-Nubuwwa*, p. 50.

(36) In an extensive treatise, ʿAbd al-ʿAzīz al-Maqdisi (seventh/thirteenth century?) collected all relevant *ḥadīths* and accounts about the coming of the Mahdi and the signs which will precede his coming. He drew heavily upon fourth/tenth and fifth/eleventh century sources. See his *ʿIqd al-Durar fi Akhbār al-Muntaẓar*, ed. A. M. Ḥilu (Cairo: Maktabat ʿĀlam al-Fikr, 1979), especially pp. 3-10, 43ff., 245-326. See also A. Raḥbāwi, *al-Yawm al-Ākhir*, ed. S. Saqqa (Ḥalab: Dār al-Balāgha, 1973), pp. 57-75.

(37) Ibn ʿAbd al-Barr, *Jāmiʿ Bayān al-ʿIlm*, I, 180; Baghdādi, *al-Faqīh wal-Mutafaqqih*, I, 37; Juwayni, *Ghiyāth al-Umam*, p. 377; Muḥammad b. Ibrāhim al-Thaʿlabi, *Qiṣaṣ al-Anbiyāʾ* (Cairo: Būlāq, 1869), p. 8. Cf. the Quranic signs of the Hour, Watt, *Bell's Introduction*, p. 159. The illustrious Ibn Rashīq (d. 456 or 463/1063-4 or 1070-1) remarked that "... sciences and tools (of knowledge) have

the scholars: "God does not remove knowledge suddenly from mankind (while alive) but removes it when scholars pass away. And when all scholars perish, there will remain only ignorant leaders, who when asked to decide cases, will give judgements without having the necessary knowledge, thereby falling in error and leading others astray." (38) Thus, the extinction of *mujtahids*, the bearers of *'ilm*, was one of the signs of the Hour. This is why Juwayni, for example, discusses the possibility of the extinction of scholars in the context of the fading out of the Shari'a. (39)

The connection between the possibility of the *mujtahids'* extinction and the Judgement Day was still relevant, though to a lesser degree, to the juristic argumentations in the works of legal theory. The above quoted *ḥadīth* about the removal of knowledge constituted at a later time a major scriptual citation in justification and support of the Ḥanafi-Shāfi'i argument which aimed at proving the likelihood of the extinction of *mujtahids.* (40) The theological influence on this controversy becomes all the more evident when it is observed that to counter this view, the Ḥanbalis, the staunch advocates of the permanent existence of *mujtahids*, introduced other *ḥadīths* to the effect that *mujtahids* will continue to exist until the appearance of the Anti-Christ, who would signal the coming of the Judgement. (41)

It is relevant to emphasize here that the *mujtahids* did not have to disappear to make their existence a subject of discussion. The possibility of their extinction was debated in the context

become weak. No one denies that with the lapse of each day, time becomes shorter and that the world is approaching its end. There remains from knowledge only its last breath, hanging (by a thread dependent on divine) omnipotence and held by He who holds the heavens" *(inna al-'ulūma wal-ālāli ḍa'ufat walaysa yadfa'u aḥadun anna al-zamāna kulla yawmin fī naqṣin wa'anna al-dunyā 'alā akhirihā walam yabqa mina l-'ilmi illa ramaquhu mu'allaqan bil-qudrati mā yamsikuhu illā alladhī yamsiku al-samā'a).* See Ibn Rashīq, *al-'Umda fi Maḥāsin al-Shi'r,* ed. M. 'Abd al-Ḥamīd, 2 vols. (Cairo: Maṭba'at al-Sa'āda, 1964). II, 238.

(38) See, e.g. Samarqandi, *Tanbīh al-Ghāfilīn*, II, 467 Ghazāli, *Iḥyā'*, I, 20; Baghdādi, *al-Faqīh wal-Mutafaqqih*, I, 37, 42-43; Ibn 'Abd al-Barr, *Jāmi' Bayān al-'Ilm*, I, 180-181.

(39) Juwayni, *al-Burhān*, II, 1348.

(40) Āmidi, *al-Iḥkām*, III, 254; Kamāl Ibn al-Humām, *al-Taḥrīr fi Uṣūl al-Fiqh*, 3 vols. (Cairo: Būlāq, 1317 H.), III, 339-340.

(41) Āmidi, *al-Iḥkām*, III, 253; Ibn al-Humām, *al-Taḥrīr*, III, 339-340; * Shawkāni, *Irshād*, p. 253.

of the Day of Judgement and the signs which will indicate the comming of this Day. Such a speculative exposition was not unprecedented in Islam. The question of whether or not it was possible that caliphs become extinct [42] is a perfect example of a theoretical argument that has no factual foundation in reality. It must be remembered that by the very beginning of the fourth/tenth century, when this argument became an established Muslim controversy, caliphs did not only exist but the institution of the caliphate was still relatively strong and the discussion about the possibility of their extinction was no more than mere theological speculation. This was precisely the case with the elaborations on the extinction of *mujtahids*.

Now, why should a theological matter of this nature find a way to legal theory? The answer may be found in the developmental history of *uṣūl al-fiqh*; a theory which encompassed a system of thought expanding over several fields. The subject matter of this theory had grown primarily as a result of the development of positive law. But a portion of its infra-structure was also derived from theological issues pertinent to jurisprudence, for, after all, it was theology which lent law, in both of its theoretical and positive forms, the logical foundation necessary for its epistemological validity.

The belief in the ultimate extinction of *mujtahids*, though initially a theological concern, was most relevant to legal theory, for *mujtahids* were considered the vehicle of the legal system. Legal theory was not concerned with the pure theological arguments relative to the controversy about the extinction of *mujtahids*. Nor was it interested in the forms and substance of these arguments. Since *ijtihād* and the qualifications required for its practice were a basic ingredient in this theory, *uṣūl al-fiqh* borrowed only the question of the possible extinction of *mujtahids*, in isolation of its thelogical backgound, and proceeded on its own to construct argumentations and answers relevant to its own mold.

The fact that the origins of the legal controversy about the existence of *mujtahids* and the continuity of *ijtihād* lie in theology rather than in law is quite significant. While on

(42) Ash'ari, *Maqālāt*, II, 150.

the one hand it demonstrates the extent to which theological doctrines can influence and enrich legal theory, on the other it proves all the more that the gate of *ijtihād* could not have been closed. That the gate was discussed in terms of existence or non-existence of *mujtahids* confirms the theoretical nature of the problem, which was raised in isolation of the realities of medieval positive law.

ADDENDUM

p. 139, n. 41: the theological origins of the controversy are explicitly stated by Ibn Amīr al-Ḥājj who notes that the question of whether or not it is conceivable for an age to be devoid of a *mujtahid* is one of the strictly *kalām* issues which have infiltrated legal theory (*'mabāḥith al-ḥusn wal-qubḥ … wasīla ilā mā huwa min al-'aqā'id al-dīniyya fa-talḥaqu bihā fī kawnihā min masā'il al-kalām … ka-mas'alat al-mujtahid yukhṭi' wa-yuṣīb wa-mas'alat yajūz khuluww al-zamān 'an mujtahid'*). See his *al-Taqrīr wal-Taḥbīr*, 3 vols. (Būlāq: al-Maṭba'a al-Kubrā al-Amīriyya, 1316/1898), I, 39, ll. 26–9. See also article III, p. 334, n. 57.

VII

WAS AL-SHAFIᶜI THE MASTER ARCHITECT OF ISLAMIC JURISPRUDENCE?

I

During the last three or four decades, modern scholarship has increasingly come to recognize Muhammad Ibn Idris al-Shafiᶜi (d. 820) as having played a most central role in the early development of Islamic jurisprudence. It was Joseph Schacht who, more than anyone else, demonstrated Shafiᶜi's remarkable success in anchoring the entire edifice of the law not only in the Qurᵓan, which by his time was taken for granted, but mainly, and more importantly, in the traditions of the Prophet.[1] Shafiᶜi's prominent status has been further bolstered by the fact that he was the first Muslim jurist ever to articulate his legal theory in writing, in what has commonly become known as *al-Risāla*.[2]

Schacht's portentous findings, coupled with the high esteem in which Shafiᶜi is held in medieval and modern Islam, have led Islamicists to believe that Shafiᶜi was the "father of Muslim jurisprudence" and the founder of the science of legal theory, properly called *uṣūl al-fiqh*.[3] His *Risāla* is thought to have become "a model for both jurists and theologians who wrote on the subject."[4] And although it is acknowledged that later theory further elaborated the themes of Shafiᶜi's treatise and sometimes even modified them, the origination of legal theory nonetheless remains his achievement. The medieval dictum that "Shafiᶜi is to *uṣūl al-fiqh* what Aristotle was to logic" is still as valid as when it first appeared.[5] *

This being the state of our knowledge, there appears to be little reason to question the purported fact that since its inception in the work of Shafiᶜi, *uṣūl al-fiqh*, as we now know it, became, in an unwavering continuity, the standard legal methodology of Sunni Islam. There is even less reason to question the 9th century, chronologically so close to Shafiᶜi, as an era that was dominated by the influential Shafiᶜites who were zealously safeguarding the teachings of their master. True, there were some tendencies in legal thought—such as the Zahiriyya—that diverged from the mainstream jurisprudence as expressed in the legacy of Shafiᶜi, but these soon dropped altogether out of the scene and, consequently, they are thought to be rather marginal. Thus, the continuity between Shafiᶜi's theory and classical *uṣūl al-fiqh* would seem to represent a natural development, especially in that it tallies with our

Wael B. Hallaq teaches at the Institute of Islamic Studies, McGill University, 3485 McTavish Street, Morrice Hall, Montreal, Quebec H3A 1Y1, Canada.

perception of Shafiᶜi, not only as the "master architect" of Islamic jurisprudence,[6] but as the jurist-victor who brought the 8th-century unbridled law down to the knees of revelation.

The assumption of this continuity, and of Shafiᶜi as the master architect of legal theory, turns out, upon a close examination of the sources, to be seriously flawed. Historical evidence in the early and medieval sources is not only discordant with this assumption but, in its aggregate effect, also seems to contradict it. In the following pages I shall attempt to show that we have no good reason to believe that such a continuity ever existed; that Shafiᶜi's *Risāla* and the theory that it embodied had very little, if any, effect during most of the 9th century; and that the image of Shafiᶜi as the founder of *uṣūl al-fiqh* was a later creation.

II

The most striking fact about the 9th century is that it yields no single work on *uṣūl al-fiqh*. By that we mean a work whose primary task is to lay down a systematic, comprehensive, and organically structured legal methodology whose purpose in turn is to derive legal rulings from the material sources—as was clearly the case in the 10th century and thereafter.

That we possess no complete work on the subject from that century initially becomes clear from reading the later *uṣūl* authors who mention from this period no work that can be identified as a treatise on *uṣūl al-fiqh* proper. Nor do these authors mention any authority from this period with whom we can associate a complete exposition of legal theory. We do, however, notice occasional references to such thinkers as Nazzam (d. after 835), Dawud al-Zahiri (d. 884), ᶜIsa ibn Aban (d. 835), and their like, but they, as we shall see, did not write works on *uṣūl al-fiqh*, and are nearly always cited as proponents of erroneous and even heretical doctrines that are to be refuted.

When biographical and bio-bibliographical dictionaries are consulted, the absence of such works from the 9th century becomes even more evident. But in searching for titles that refer to treatises on legal theory one must be cautious, for the term *uṣūl* had a wide range of applications. Ibn al-Nadim reports, for instance, that the Hanafite Abu Yusuf (d. 798) was the author of works on *uṣūl* (*lahu min al-kutub fī al-uṣūl . . .*). It immediately turns out that these books dealt with such subjects as prayer, fasting, sales, and so forth,[7] subjects clearly belonging to positive law (*furūᶜ*). Similarly, Abu Yusuf's younger contemporary, Shaybani (d. 805), is also reported as having written "books on *uṣūl*" regarding such subjects as prayer, alms tax, and so on.[8] Thus, when we read that Muᶜalla ibn Mansur al-Razi (d. 826) and Ibn Samaᶜa (d. 847) have transmitted the *uṣūl* of Abu Yusuf and Shaybani, respectively,[9] it is beyond doubt that what they have transmitted are positive-law works of the two Hanafite masters.

Ibn al-Nadim also informs us that al-Rabiᶜ ibn Sulayman al-Muradi (d. 884) has "transmitted Shafiᶜi's works on *uṣūl*, and what he transmitted was entitled *al-Mabsūṭ*."[10] The latter, Taj al-Din al-Subki explicitly tells us, is a work on positive law, dealing with such issues as rituals, prayer, family law, and, we expect, the entire subject matter of *furūᶜ*.[11] It is significant that the application of the term *uṣūl* to a wide range of writings, not necessarily confined to *uṣūl al-fiqh*, was predominant not only during the lifetime of Ibn al-Nadim, but even as late as the time of Subki (d. 1370). Having read Ibn al-ᶜIfris's (d. ca. 1010) *Jamᶜ al-jawāmiᶜ fī nuṣūṣ al-Shāfiᶜī*—a work clearly treating positive law[12]—Subki, impressed with it, remarks that it is "one of the earliest *uṣūl* (*min al-uṣūl al-qadīma*) . . . and has become one of the *uṣūl* of the [Shafiᶜite] school of law."[13]

Although it is often possible to establish whether or not the term refers to works on legal theory, there are instances where the term could be misleading. An excellent example is Abu Yahya al-Saji's (d. 920) treatise entitled, interestingly enough, *Uṣūl al-fiqh*. This work, in fact, has nothing to do with legal theory. Its main subjects are positive law and *khilāfiyyāt*, disagreements on positive legal doctrine, particularly, in this treatise, among Abu Hanifa, his two students, Malik, Shafiᶜi, Ibn Abi Layla, Ibn Shubruma, Abu Thawr and others.[14] Likewise, one would have no reason whatsoever to doubt that Ibn Maryam al-Aswani's *Jumal al-uṣūl al-dālla ᶜalā al-furūᶜ fī al-fiqh*, written presumably in the very beginning of the 10th century, is a work that treats legal theory, but the fact is that it does not. Subki, to whom a copy of the work was available in the *waqfiyya* of Dar al-Hadith in Damascus, felt compelled to explain to us that "what is meant by *uṣūl* [in the title] are the doctrines (*nuṣūṣ*) of Shafiᶜi. . . . The author mentions that the work represents an abridgment of the doctrines. . . . In it, the author would occasionally object to these doctrines, *as he did in the chapter on bequests*" (italics mine).[15]

Now, if we take into account the ambiguities involved in the use of the term *uṣūl*, the 9th century produces no work whatsoever that has the complete characteristics of *uṣūl al-fiqh*.[16] In the hundreds of titles and bio-bibliographical notices belonging to the 9th century, there is no allusion to such works. And in his refutation of the *uṣūl* principles of Sunni juristic thought, al-Qadi al-Nuᶜman, writing around the middle of the 10th century, confirms the data provided by the bio-bibliographical sources.[17] All that is to be found in the sources are individual treatises, mainly polemical, bearing such titles as *Fī ithbāt al-qiyās*, *Naqḍ ithbāt al-qiyās*, *Ijtihād al-raʾy*, *Khabar al-wāḥid*, *al-Ijmāᶜ*, and *al-Khuṣūṣ wa-al-ᶜumūm*. ᶜIsa ibn Aban, for instance, wrote on qiyas and *ijtihād al-raʾy*.[18] Qasim ibn Sayyar (d. 889) also wrote two treatises, one on solitary traditions and the other in refutation of *muqallids*.[19] The authors associated with such specialized tracts are known to have been involved in the polemics that so much pervaded the 9th century. The purpose of these treatises, as attested in their titles, seems to have been the defense of one juridical—and perhaps theologically related—position or another, but not to lay down, consciously and deliberately, an organically structured legal methodology whose explicit raison d'être, as was declared later, is to discover God's law. In any case, it is significant that no jurist is reported to have written—whether in one or several treatises—on all of these issues, much less on all the issues subsumed under *uṣūl*. Dawud ibn Khalaf al-Zahiri, somewhat of an exception, composed a number of works in refutation of a variety of doctrines held by other jurists. But these works, as Goldziher rightly noted, are "pamphlets against Hanafite works . . . put into circulation in order to dismiss the theological scruples of the reaction inclined towards traditions."[20] Interestingly, among the works attributed to Dawud is a tract entitled *al-Uṣūl*. Ibn al-Nadim, however, lists the work in the midst of titles on positive law.[21] That the work did not treat *uṣūl al-fiqh* may also be gleaned from the fact that a student of Dawud, Abu Saᶜid al-Raqqi, wrote a work, also titled *al-Uṣūl*, "on the model of Dawud's work" that consists of a hundred chapters (*kutub*). Having already enumerated these *kutub*—clearly treating positive law—in the bio-bibliographical notice of the master, Ibn al-Nadim remarks that "we need not mention them here."[22]

The proposition that the 9th century was devoid of works on *uṣūl al-fiqh* finds further attestation in the manner in which the biographers cover this in comparison with their treatment of later centuries. The biographers never employ nomenclatures indicative of specialized knowledge of legal theory to characterize authors of the 9th century. Such descriptions as "*uṣūlī*," "he wrote on *uṣūl*," "he excelled in *uṣūl*," "he was most knowledgeable in *uṣūl*," were, with one partial exception,[23] absent from discourse on the 9th century. It is striking that once the biographers move to the 10th-century authors, such descriptions become not only frequent but indeed the norm. Moreover, on the pedagogical plane, while such statements as "he studied *uṣūl* under so and so" are countless in the biographies of the 10th century and onwards, they are markedly absent in those belonging to the 9th century.

To add to all this, the *Risāla* of Shafiᶜi is mentioned rarely in the context of the 9th century, and when it is alluded to, it is usually in passing. In the immense literature relative to the legal movement of the 9th century, there are three prominent references to the treatise in the sources, one of which is quoted frequently. The first appears in Ibn Hanbal's statement in which he allegedly recommends the *Risāla* to Ibn Rahawayh (d. 853).[24] But this recommendation is contradicted frequently by Ibn Hanbal's other statements where he reportedly shuns the work. Having been asked by his student Marwadhi whether the *Risāla* is worth studying, he is said to have replied in the negative, adding that it is religiously dubious.[25] The second instance concerns Abu ᶜAli al-Zaᶜfarani (d. 874), one of Shafiᶜi's most distinguished students, who is reported to have "read the *Risāla*" under his mentor. It is highly likely, however, that he read the old version of the treatise, since he is commonly associated with transmitting Shafiᶜi's old doctrines, doctrines the latter had presumably elaborated in Hijaz and Iraq, before he finally settled in Egypt where he is thought to have written the new *Risāla*.[26] The third, oft-quoted reference is to Muzani's statement, "I have been reading the *Risāla* for fifty years, and each time I read it I learn something that I have not known before."[27] We should, however, hasten to assert that such references to the treatise are relatively few and cannot be culled from the sources with ease.

It is curious, to say the least, that what is assumed to be the *uṣūl* equivalent of Aristotle's *Organon* should be thoroughly ignored in a century that is considered one of the most dynamic phases in Islam's intellectual history. One of the most significant pieces of evidence pointing to the marginal importance of the *Risāla* is the complete absence of any contemporary commentary on, or abridgement of, the treatise. This is at a time, we must emphasize, when commentaries and abridgments have already become commonplace. On the other hand, once the 10th century looms on the horizon, we are suddenly confronted with at least five commentaries on the *Risāla*. But more on this later.

The only so-called *uṣūl* commentary on Shafiᶜi known to us is Muzani's (d. 878) short work, *Kitāb al-amr wa-al-nahy ᶜalā maᶜnā al-Shāfiᶜī*.[28] Interestingly, it is a gloss not on any section of the *Risāla*, but rather on Shafiᶜi's *Kitāb ṣifat nahy Rasūl Allāh*, which constitutes less than two pages of his multivolume *furūᶜ* work *al-Umm*.[29] The greater part of Muzani's work (consisting of a total of ten pages) turns out to be an exposition of his own views on the subject.[30] Fortunately, Muzani's treatise has survived the ravages of time, and we are able to confirm its elementary nature. That Muzani, the most prominent disciple of Shafiᶜi, should comment on a rather slim section of a work on positive law and ignore the *Risāla* altogether is a fact that speaks for itself.

Nor is there to be found a refutation of the *Risāla*—again in a century whose landmark was the intensity with which scholars refuted one another. There were several individuals and groups who must have disagreed with, and even resented, what Shafiᶜi had to say in his treatise. There were the rationalists and the extreme traditionalists,[31] for example, whose beliefs clearly ran counter to the ideas expressed therein. Yet there exists no trace of any attack directed explicitly against the treatise. Again we observe that in the 10th century we do come across such refutations, as shall be seen later.

The fact that the *Risāla* did not elicit any refutation in the first century of its life gains added significance in light of the critiques and refutations directed against Shafiᶜi's system of positive law. The Hanafite Bakkar ibn Qutayba (d. 884), for instance, wrote against Shafiᶜi's critique of Abu Hanifa.[32] And Muhammad ibn ᶜAbd al-Hakam al-Misri (d. 881), who abandoned Shafiᶜi in favor of the Malikite school, criticized his former mentor in a treatise he entitled *al-Radd ᶜalā al-Shāfiᶜī fīmā khālafa fīhi al-Kitāb wal-Sunna*.[33] Judging from the title, the work could be treating only some of Shafiᶜi's positive legal rulings that, Misri apparently thought, found no justification in the Qurᵓan and the Sunna. Since both Misri and Shafiᶜi obviously agree on the fundamental role of the two primary sources of the law and since the controversy about the textual authoritativeness (*ḥujjiyya*) of methodological principles is of a decidedly later origin, we must take it that the treatise dealt with issues of *furūᶜ*.[34] Thus, we need not stress the added significance of the fact that the *Risāla* attracted neither commentary nor criticism when Shafiᶜi's positive law was subject to both.

III

Thus, if we assume the *Risāla* to be the first treatise on legal theory and Shafiᶜi to be the father of the science of *uṣūl al-fiqh*,[35] our assumption would be challenged by evidence from the sources. It would then make perfect sense to question these assumptions, particularly our current perception of the nature of the *Risāla*. It would not be amiss at all to ask whether the treatise truly qualifies as a work of *uṣūl al-fiqh*.

We have earlier intimated that the *Risāla* we now know represents the new or last version of the work, which Shafiᶜi wrote after he settled in Egypt. Although virtually nothing is known about the old *Risāla*, it is thought that it "was written originally as an apologia for the supremacy of the traditions."[36] This is entirely in consonance with what we know of Shafiᶜi's scholarly achievement, namely, that his ultimate goal was to establish the Prophetic traditions, together with the Qurᵓan, as the exclusive material sources of the law. The characterization of the old *Risāla* quoted earlier is apt if we are to judge the old version by the new. The latter is predominantly a hadith work, in the sense that the emphasis on the role of Prophetic traditions in the law represents its overriding and recurrent theme. In the more recent Kilani edition of the work,[37] about 130 pages out of a total of 257 are entirely allotted to various issues of hadith. Significantly, a dozen pages, constituting an independent section, treat Qurᵓanic statements that, Shafiᶜi believes, make it incumbent upon Muslims to follow the Prophet and abide by his Sunna. Even when other issues are discussed, as in the case of *istiḥsān* and qiyas, the permeating theme remains the same: all law and legal reasoning must rest on the Sunna and the Qurᵓan. When issues of language—for example, the general and the particular (*khāṣṣ/ᶜāmm*)—are discussed, it is mainly for the purpose of demonstrating that the Sunna can, and should, particularize and explain the Qurᵓan. Other issues that receive treatment by Shafiᶜi are discussed not so much for their own sake as for the sake of defining their relationship with the Sunna. The exposition of the theory of abrogation, for instance, is intended to delineate the relationship between the Qurᵓan and the Sunna when there is a conflict between the two.

In the final analysis, the *Risāla* appears to offer a number of propositions: (1) law must derive from revealed scripture; (2) the Sunna of the Prophet constitutes a revelation binding in legal matters; (3) there is no contradiction between the Sunna and the Qurᵓan, or among verses or hadiths within each of the two sources; (4) the two sources complement each other hermeneutically; (5) a legal ruling derived from unambiguous and widely transmitted texts is certain and subject to no disagreement, whereas a ruling that is inferred by means of ijtihad and qiyas may be subject to disagreement; and finally, (6) the procedures of qiyas and ijtihad and the sanctioning instrument of consensus are prescribed by the revealed texts.

At best, Shafiᶜi's exposition of these propositions remains rudimentary as well as erratic. Substantively, the *Risāla* has little to offer in the way of systematic methodology. Even the section on legal reasoning (qiyas and ijtihad), which one may argue is the best the *Risāla* has to offer apart from the treatment of the Sunna, is superficial and hardly provides an adequate explanation of how Shafiᶜi arrived at his own legal rulings or, alternatively, how another jurist can learn from Shafiᶜi in reasoning about the law.[38] For after all, *uṣūl al-fiqh*'s whole purpose is universally acknowledged to be the prescription/description of a methodology by means of which legal rulings can be derived from the sources.

On the whole, the *Risāla* not only lacks depth and shirks from a satisfactory, let alone full, treatment of the issues it raises, but it also leaves out altogether a host of fundamental questions considered part of, and indeed indispensable for, *uṣūl al-fiqh*. Questions of legal language, which occupy on average one-fifth to one-fourth of later treatises, are virtually absent from this one. A legion of questions pertaining to consensus, abrogation, legal reasoning, causation, and so forth, receive little, if any, attention. In short, approaching the work without preconceptions and presuppositions, it would not be far off the mark if we characterize it as a work concerned mainly with the Sunna of the Prophet and the utilization of hadith in the elaboration of the law. Indeed, it is not without good reason that the Urdu translation of the treatise bears the title *Kitāb al-risāla yaᶜnī uṣūl-i fiqh va ḥadīs*.[39]

Once the *Risāla* is cut down to size, it is relatively easy to explain the lack of interest in it during the century that followed its author's death. There simply was very little—besides the affirmation that the Sunna and the Qurᵓan must constitute the exclusive foundations of the law—that Shafiᶜi offered in the way of founding principles of *uṣūl al-fiqh*. His achievement, as we now see it, and indeed as medieval Muslims seem to have viewed it, lies rather in his resilient affirmation that God and, more specifically, His Messenger are the ultimate sources of the law. If a similar thesis were advanced with any marked force before Shafiᶜi's time, we would not have thought Shafiᶜi's thesis an achievement. But we do consider it so precisely because, with the benefit of hindsight, we have come to realize that his was an unprecedented synthesis between the rationalists, who were reluctant to accept Prophetic traditions, and the traditionalists who spurned all human reasoning in religious matters. But if it is a synthesis, sensibly reconciling the two camps, why then was it met with such oblivion?

Among the aforestated propositions that Shafiᶜi advanced and brought together in the *Risāla*, propositions 1–4 were addressed to the rationalists and proposition 6 to the traditionalists. Neither side, except Shafiᶜi himself and perhaps a few others (such as Karabisi!),[40] subscribed to a synthesis of the entirety of these propositions. In other words, Shafiᶜi's theory appealed neither to the traditionalists nor to the rationalists, and Shafiᶜi himself does not seem to have allied himself unequivocally with either camp. A careful examination of the sources reveals that he was indeed difficult to classify. In later literature he is made the champion of both orthodoxy and the Sunna of the Prophet (*nāṣir al-Sunna*), which is intended to mean (when it rarely fails to be stated explicitly) that he was an antirationalist. But there are so many references to the contrary, in both early and later sources, that it would be imprudent to ignore them. Even if we set aside the allegation that he was a Shiᶜi,[41] Shafiᶜi was not entirely innocent of Muᶜtazilite association. Not only did he himself admit his intimate knowledge of rationalist kalam, but he studied under Muᶜtazili teachers, notably Ibrahim ibn Abi Yahya al-Madani and Muslim ibn Khalid al-Zanji.[42] Al-Fakhr al-Razi, himself a Shafiᶜite and an anti-Muᶜtazilite, reports that the scholars are unanimous on the fact that the latter had been Shafiᶜi's mentor.[43] Furthermore, the Shafiᶜite al-Abiri (d. 974), in a work entirely dedicated to the virtues and merits (*manāqib*) of Shafiᶜi, asserts that the staunch Muᶜtazilite Bishr al-Marisi was an associate (*ṣāḥib*) of the master.[44] Another of Shafiᶜi's Muᶜtazilite connections is associated with the name of Abu ᶜAbd al-Rahman al-Baghdadi.[45]

All these connections, however, do more to cast a shadow of doubt on Shafiᶜi as a traditionalist than to make him a Muᶜtazilite, which by the most intolerant traditionalist standards he clearly was not. If Shafiᶜi was decidedly a non-Muᶜtazilite and, strictly speaking, a nonrationalist, he certainly was no traditionalist. All indications in the sources point in one direction and one direction only: Shafiᶜi defended the traditions of the Prophet but he was neither a loyal traditionalist nor an outstanding traditionist. As a traditionalist he betrayed his comrades when he insisted on the essential role of qiyas in the law. And as a traditionist his knowledge was flawed. The list of 9th-century critics who disapproved of Shafiᶜi's qualifications as a traditionist includes Yahya ibn Mu^c^in, Ishaq ibn Rahawayh, al-Qasim ibn Sallam, and, reportedly, even Ibn Hanbal.[46] In their standard collections, the prominent Bukhari (d. 870) and Muslim (d. 875) recorded not a single tradition from Shafi^c^i,[47] and they are widely reported to have considered him a weak traditionist (*kāna ḍa^c^īfan fī al-riwāya*).[48] And Ibn Hanbal is said to have told one of his students that the traditionist has no use for Shafi^c^i's books.[49]

Thus, while Shafi^c^i emerges as a non-Mu^c^tazilite, he most certainly did not belong to the camp of the traditionalists[50] (it clearly being understood here that while the traditionists are not interchangeable with the traditionalists, those who criticized Shafi^c^i happened to belong to both groups). The most eloquent testimony for Shafi^c^i's uncertain status in the religious movement of the 9th century is the distinct absence of his name from Ibn Qutayba's (d. 889) two notorious lists of the traditionalists and the rationalists,[51] an absence that can be explained only when Shafi^c^i is situated properly in the ideological configuration prevailing during the century following his death.

It should not come as a surprise, therefore, that Shafi^c^i belonged neither to the camp of the rationalists nor to that of the traditionalists. Muzani, who is universally considered to have been Shafi^c^i's chief follower until the eighth decade of the 9th century, likewise belonged to neither camp. Muzani, true, was an outstanding faqih (*ra^ɔ^san fī al-fiqh*) and dialectician, but as a *muḥaddith* he certainly was considered far from qualified.[52] In addition Muzani had strong leanings towards I^c^tizal. Al-Fakhr al-Razi reports that he studied kalam under the distinguished Mu^c^tazilite ^c^Amr ibn ^c^Ubayd, and that all scholars agree that he had Mu^c^tazilite tendencies.[53] Indeed, it is hard to imagine that the most prominent student of Shafi^c^i could have been as inclined to rationalism as the later enthusiastic Shafi^c^ites reported him to be when his master is supposed to be a paragon of traditionalism. If Muzani could stand in the middle of the road between traditionalism and rationalism, it is because his illustrious mentor had stood there before him.

It is worth considering at this juncture the case of Karabisi, whom we have previously seen[54] to be the only early scholar explicitly associated with *uṣūl al-fiqh*, though no title on the subject has been associated with him. Karabisi has been revealed through the sources as a scholar with an experience similar to Shafi^c^i's: he first followed the doctrines of *ahl al-ra^ɔ^y* but was soon to find the *fiqhī* truth not only in the Qur^ɔ^an but also in the Sunna of the Prophet.[55] Furthermore, he is known widely as a professor or an expert in speculative theology (*ustādhan fī ^c^ilm al-kalām*),[56] and like Shafi^c^i and Muzani, his qualifications as a traditionist were considered suspect by some eminent hadith scholars.[57] That he may have studied or written on *uṣūl al-fiqh*, in the same sense Shafi^c^i and Muzani did, is quite possible. That his writings, if any, represented an advance over Shafi^c^i is improbable, and in any case they failed to make their way to later jurisprudence.

IV

It has already been noted that while the 9th century produced neither works on *uṣūl* nor commentaries on or refutations of the *Risāla*, the 10th century produced a proliferation of literature on the subject. Once the 10th century began, a stunning shift in bio-bibliographical discourse occurs. In what seems to be a rather rapid transformation, scholars are described in new terms quite particular to *uṣūl al-fiqh*; they now appear distinctly and technically as authors of *uṣūl al-fiqh*, as *uṣūlī*s proper, with titles that are indicative of an independent and even prominent science.[58] The following is a list of some of the first jurists who appear, from the sources, to have written or excelled in the field.

1. Abu Naᶜim ibn ᶜAdi al-Astarabadi (d. 935); no title is mentioned.[59]
2. Abu Bakr Ibn al-Ikhshid (d. 938), *al-Maᶜūna fī al-uṣūl*.[60]
3. Abu Bakr Muhammad ibn Ibrahim al-Sayrafi (d. 942), *al-Bayān fī dalāʾil al-aᶜlām ᶜalā uṣūl al-aḥkām*.[61]
4. ᶜUmar Muhammad Abu Faraj al-Maliki (d. 943), *al-Lumaᶜ fī uṣūl al-fiqh*.[62]
5. Abu Mansur al-Maturidi (d. 945), *Maʾākhidh al-sharāʾiᶜ fī uṣūl al-fiqh* and *Kitāb al-jadal fī uṣūl al-fiqh*.[63]
6. Ahmad ibn Abi Muhammad al-Tabari known as Ibn al-Qass (d. 947); no title is mentioned.[64]
7. Abu Bakr Muhammad ibn Ismaᶜil al-Qaffal al-Shashi (d. 948); no title is mentioned.[65]
8. Abu Musa al-Darir (d. during the 940s) has a treatise on *uṣūl al-fiqh* "consisting of eight volumes."[66]
9. Abu Ishaq al-Marwazi (d. 951); title is not mentioned.[67]
10. Muhammad ibn Saᶜid ibn Abi al-Qadi (d. 951), *al-Hidāya*.[68]
11. Abu Bakr Muhammad ibn ᶜAbd Allah al-Bardaᶜi (d. 951), *al-Jāmiᶜ fī uṣūl al-fiqh*.[69]
12. Abu Bakr al-Dabᶜi (d. 953); "he was an outstanding scholar in *uṣūl*."[70]
13. Abu ᶜAli al-Shashi (d. 955), *al-Uṣūl*.[71]
14. Abu ᶜAli al-Tabari (d. 961). *Uṣūl al-fiqh*.[72]
15. Abu Bakr al-Farisi (fl. ca. 960) wrote an extensive treatise on the subject.[73]
16. Abu al-Husayn al-Tawaʾifi al-Baghdadi (d. ca. 960); title is not mentioned.[74]

With the proliferation of *uṣūl* literature, we find a sudden interest in Shafiᶜi's *Risāla* after long neglect. The treatise now succeeds in eliciting at least five commentaries, four of which belong to the 10th century. The commentators are Abu Bakr al-Sayrafi,[75] al-Qaffal al-Shashi,[76] Abu al-Walid al-Nisaburi (d. 960),[77] al-Jawzaqi (d. 989),[78] Abu Muhammad al-Juwayni (d. 1046),[79] and quite possibly ᶜAbd al-Wahhab al-Baghdadi (d. 973).[80] The *Risāla* also manages to attract at least two refutations, one by the Shiᶜi Abu Sahl al-Nawbakhti (d. 940s),[81] and the other by a certain ᶜUbayd Allah ibn Talib al-Katib, who appears to have been a contemporary of Sayrafi.[82] Furthermore, the *Risāla* appears to have become a constitutive part of certain *uṣūl* education. It is reported, for instance, that around the middle of the 10th century Abu al-Fadl al-Nadrawi studied the work in Isfahan under Abu al-Walid ibn Mihran.[83]

The unprecedented and intense interest in the *Risāla* and in *uṣūl al-fiqh* during the first half of the 10th century seems to be associated with certain figures whose intellectual tendencies represent a new formation in the religious history of Islam. One of these figures was Abu al-ᶜAbbas Ibn Surayj (d. 918), without exaggeration the most significant jurist in the Shafiᶜite school after Shafiᶜi himself. Unfortunately, none of Ibn Surayj's works has survived, although if we go by the biographical and doctrinal data provided by early and later sources, he no doubt emerges as the most towering personality in the early history of Shafiᶜism.

Unlike any other Shafiᶜite after Shafiᶜi, Ibn Surayj is universally held to be the unrivaled leader of the school, far superior to all other contemporary and earlier Shafiᶜites, including Muzani. Significantly, unlike Muzani, he is distinguished as Shafiᶜi's loyal and true disciple who single-handedly defended the *madhhab* and rendered it victorious. In his time, he was the most influential professor of Shafiᶜite law, and his students were so numerous that he is credited with "spreading the *madhhab*" to unprecedented dimensions. He also is said to have been the first to teach juridical dialectic and to combine a superior knowledge of hadith and *fiqh*. And like Shafiᶜi, he combined all this with a knowledge of kalam. Small wonder then that he was known as the Little Shafiᶜi, and that he was thought by many as the *mujaddid* (reformer) of the fourth hijri century, Shafiᶜi having been assigned to the third.[84]

Although there is no evidence to indicate that Ibn Surayj wrote a complete work on *uṣūl al-fiqh*, he seems to have assimilated all teachings on the subject from within and without the Shafiᶜite school. He fiercely debated with the Zahirites, both Dawud and his son Muhammad, on matters of legal methodology. He is reported to have written, while mortally ill, a fifteen-folio epistle, addressed to the jurists of Shash and Firghana, in which he expounded, in what must have been an outline, the *uṣūl* principles of the then prominent mujtahids, that is, Shafiᶜi, Malik, Sufyan al-Thawri, Abu Hanifa and his two disciples, and Dawud.[85] But it is indeed telling that even Ibn Surayj, with the intense detail of biographical notices he is accorded, is not reported to have written an *uṣūl* work proper.

Nonetheless, the first and foremost Shafiᶜite authors who did write complete works on *uṣūl* were Ibn Surayj's students. Among these students, who are reported to have made up most of the prominent Shafiᶜites during the first half of the 10th century,[86] are Ibn Haykuwayh (d. 930), Ibrahim al-Marwazi (d. 951), Abu Bakr al-Farisi, Ibn al-Qass, Abu Bakr al-Sayrafi, and al-Qaffal al-Shashi, to mention only a few.[87] Although all of them are associated with the first generation of scholars to have composed works on *uṣūl*, the latter two deserve special attention since in later biographical and *uṣūl* works they emerge as the most significant authors on the subject. Sayrafi, the first commentator on the *Risāla*, is reckoned not only the author of "an unprecedented treatise on *uṣūl*," but also "the most knowledgeable scholar on *uṣūl al-fiqh* after Shafiᶜi."[88] And, as we have seen, Qaffal was the author of both a commentary on the *Risāla* and a treatise on legal theory, as well as the first to have written on juridical dialectic.[89] That both were distinguished *uṣūlī*s, *muḥaddith*s, speculative theologians, and dialecticians betrays their debt to Ibn Surayj who mastered all these sciences and placed them in the service of the law.

The legacy of Ibn Surayj was passed by al-Qaffal to Abu Muhammad al-Juwayni, the last commentator on the *Risāla* we know. Abu Muhammad studied hadith and law under al-Qaffal and is said to have graduated only after he perfected the latter's *ṭarīqa*, the method and treatment of the law peculiar to a jurist.[90] It is therefore far from being a mere historical chance that the rise of *uṣūl al-fiqh*, and consequently the unprecedented interest in the *Risāla*, coincided with the emergence of a community of scholars, belonging to two consecutive generations, who had at their disposal a combination of traditionalist and rationalist sciences—a combination that had no antecedents and that proved to be so crucial.[91]

V

Turning back to the earlier centuries will shed further light on the question of why Shafiʿi's theory, as innovative as it may have been, failed to arouse the interest of his followers for nearly a century and why the flourishing of *uṣūl al-fiqh* came only after a century after the demise of its supposed founder.

We begin with the 8th century, which saw the initial stages of the development of Islamic law and jurisprudence. The studies of Schacht, Goldziher, and others have shown that the 8th century started with an overwhelming movement towards human reasoning, commonly known as *raʾy*. But by the middle of that century, another competing movement stressing the role of traditions was already on the rise. By the time Shafiʿi, as an independent scholar, appeared on the scene, the movement of *ahl al-raʾy* was beginning to decline, and this was due to the rapid increase in the volume of Prophetic traditions that have infiltrated legal doctrines. Shaybani's positive law exhibits, perhaps better than any other, this stage of development, where hadiths constitute an important, but by no means exclusive, element in the law. In Shafiʿi, as we have seen, the ultimate sources of the law become the Qurʾan and the Sunna. *Raʾy* as an expression of rationalist and utilitarian tendencies was to be wholly expunged, hence his vehement opposition to *istiḥsān*. This is precisely where Shafiʿi was his own jurist. While he unconditionally rejected *raʾy* and insisted on the overriding authority of the Qurʾan and Prophetic Sunna, he salvaged certain elements of *raʾy* and molded them into arguments that may be used in the law only insofar as they derive their premises from revelation.

It has been little emphasized since Goldziher's death that the 9th century was as dynamic and as crucial as the 8th in the history of Islamic jurisprudence. And we tend to minimize, perhaps due to our preoccupation with Schacht's findings, the consequential role of the legal movements in the 9th century and their impact on Islamic legal theory and positive law in the centuries that followed. To be sure, Shafiʿi in no way represented the culmination of Islamic law and jurisprudence. If anything, he stood somewhere in the middle of the formative period, half-way between the crude beginnings during the very first decades of the 8th century and the final formation of the legal schools at the beginning of the 10th. For Shafiʿi succeeded neither in ejecting *raʾy* from the domain of legal reasoning nor, in consequence, in rendering the Prophetic Sunna unconditionally admissible. During the decades after his death, most of the Hanafites and no doubt the Muʿtazilites continued to uphold, under different guises, the role of human reason in the law.

A more significant development after Shafiʿi, and by far more influential, is the rise of the anti-*raʾy* movement represented by Ibn Hanbal and Dawud ibn Khalaf al-Zahiri, among others. While both approved of Shafiʿi, they went much further in their emphasis on the centrality of scripture and on the repugnant nature of reasoning. But their positions on reasoning, perhaps the best legal indicator to measure their tendencies, were by no means identical. Ibn Hanbal, as we can glean from his positive law, did not favor the practice of qiyas, unless it was absolutely necessary.[92] Dawud, on the other hand, rejected it categorically.[93]

There emerges here a clear pattern: Shafiʿi's predecessors make recourse to their *raʾy* with, more or less, little attention to the Sunna. Shafiʿi regulates *raʾy* in the form of qiyas and assigns it a role subsidiary to that of the revealed sources although it remains an essential part of his methodology. Ibn Hanbal seldom resorts to qiyas, and he would rather do without it. Dawud completely rejects it in favor of a literal reading of the Qur^{ɔ}an and the Sunna. In both time and doctrine, then, Shafi^{c}i's position is located in the middle between the early *ra^{ɔ}y* libertinism and the later Zahirite conservatism.

Contrary to the pattern according to which traditionalism had evolved in the 9th century, the rationalist movement began to experience a process of decline, particularly, as is well known, after the *miḥna*. From this point on, the rationalists were drawing closer to the traditionalists, but only in one sense: they could no longer afford to ignore the scripture as the exclusive foundation of the law, and they were compelled to submit to the divine decree as the first and last judge of human *shar^{c}ī* affairs.

On the other side, the traditionalist camp also was compelled to make some concessions. Soon the Hanbalites, among others, were to ignore their eponym's dislike for qiyas, and their legal methodology was to become virtually interchangeable with that of the other schools' proponents. It is significant that those who did not make these concessions, such as the ultratraditionalist Hashwiyya and the Zahirites, were ultimately doomed to extinction.[94]

With the death of Shafi^{c}i and for long thereafter, Shafi^{c}i's middle-of-the-road thesis had relatively few supporters. If we go by Subki, the author of the most comprehensive biographical work on the Shafi^{c}ites,[95] we find that the list of Shafi^{c}i's associates (*aṣḥāb*) did not exceed 41, including such jurists as Ibn Hanbal, Abu Thawr (d. 854), ^{c}Abd al-Hakam al-Misri, and Ibn Rahawayh, who did not follow his teachings and who had their own agendas.[96] Many others were merely associated with Shafi^{c}i, and we have no evidence that they studied under him more than some *fiqh* and hadith. His followers who had died by 912 but who did not know him in person, numbered only 31.[97] This is to be contrasted by the number of his followers who died in the fourth hijri century (A.D. 912–1009), which reached the astounding figure of 171.[98]

The rapid growth of the Shafi^{c}ite school coincided with the emergence of the aforementioned compromise between the traditionalists and the rationalists, which resulted in *uṣūl al-fiqh*'s being finally defined, and that must have taken place sometime between the death of Dawud al-Zahiri and the generation of Abu Bakr al-Sayrafi. Being the ultimate synthesis of revelation and systematic human reasoning, *uṣūl al-fiqh* could not have become normative prior to the beginning of the 10th century. Shafi^{c}i's rudimentary thesis was not well supported and none of his students appears to have defended it. Muzani, who was most likely to have carried on Shafi^{c}i's mission, was, as we have seen, tending more to rationality than to hadith, and in any case he was deemed to have diverged from the path of Shafi^{c}i, both in positive law and legal theory.[99] The most important of Shafi^{c}i's immediate disciples turns out, after all, not to have been so faithful to the teachings of the master.[100]

It was not until Ibn Surayj and the generation of his younger contemporaries that the traditionalist–rationalist compromise manifested itself. He, and his disciples, were *muḥaddith*s, faqihs, and speculative theologians, without this entailing a contradiction in terms. And as such, they were to conceptualize legal theory as a synthesis between rationality and the textual tradition. Ibn Surayj's legal theory, we must stress, could have been only the child of its own environment. Aside from the proposition that embodied that synthesis, there is little in Shafi^c^i's theory that survived into the later works. But this synthesis was crucial, and Ibn Surayj as well as his followers accredited it to Shafi^c^i. This is why Ibn Surayj was considered the first true representative and the unequaled champion of the Shafi^c^ite school. And this is why he was, significantly, referred to as the middle-of-the-roader (*sālik sabīl al-inṣāf*).[101] Ibn Surayj, who was an excellent *muḥaddith* and a moderate mutakallim—and who battled the Zahirites to the end of his days—articulated the synthesis and paved the way for his students, the likes of Sayrafi and Qaffal, to discourse on it and elaborate it in greater detail.

When these students found their legal theory to coincide with Shafi^c^i's bare thesis that they began to glorify Shafi^c^i as an *uṣūlī* and as the founder of the discipline. This glorification became increasingly necessary as the other schools, especially the Hanafite, as is well known, to advertise their early masters as the founders of *uṣūl al-fiqh*.[102] But that Shafi^c^i's image as the founder of this discipline began to grow only from the beginning of the 10th century can be illustrated clearly in the development of the *manāqib* genre dedicated to him.

The first work of *manāqib* available to us belonged to Abu Hatim al-Razi (d. 938). In this work Razi allots a number of chapters to demonstrate Shafi^c^i's excellent knowledge of subjects upon which the construction of the law depended. In one chapter, which consists of about 51 lines, the author discusses Shafi^c^i's proficient knowledge of what he calls, significantly, *uṣūl al-^c^ilm*, by which he clearly means *uṣūl al-fiqh*.[103] In these lines, he mentions Shafi^c^i's doctrine of consensus (in one line), and he briefly speaks—in 15 lines—of his theory of qiyas. The rest of the lines deal with a miscellany of subjects including hadith. Nowhere in the entire treatise does Shafi^c^i appear as the founder of *uṣūl al-fiqh*. It is to be noted that Razi's work, in its published form, consists of about 300 pages, each containing an average of 8 lines. It is significant that out of an approximate 2,400 lines, Razi should have devoted only 51 lines to Shafi^c^i's *uṣūl*. Moreover, in this chapter there is no reference whatsoever to the *Risāla*. In fact, in the entire work the *Risāla* is mentioned only twice, and then in passing. In both cases it is referred to, significantly, in the context not of law but rather of *ṭalab al-ḥadīth*.[104]

Over a century later, Bayhaqi (d. 1066) wrote another work on Shafi^c^i's *manāqib*. A comparison between his and Razi's work is most revealing. In Bayhaqi, Shafi^c^i is not only a genius of *uṣūl al-fiqh*, but the founder of the discipline,[105] and the *Risāla*, in its old and new versions, receives a comprehensive treatment, including the reasons for its composition.[106] The new *Risāla* is mentioned at least eighteen times, and the old three times. In addition to a chapter devoted to Shafi^c^i's *uṣūl al-fiqh*, which Bayhaqi uniquely characterizes as "portentous,"[107] there are other chapters describing the master's proficiency in the knowledge of hadith, Qur^ɔ^an, language, positive law, and other issues that are constitutive parts of, or relevant to, *uṣūl al-fiqh*. In contrast to Razi's 51 lines, Bayhaqi allocates a staggering 160 pages (out of a total of 918) to Shafi^c^i as an *uṣūlī*. The image of Shafi^c^i as the founder of the discipline is similarly drawn by al-Fakhr al-Razi (d. 1209) who devotes about 114 pages of his 525-page treatise to the same issues Bayhaqi had already raised.[108]

It would be safe to assume that sometime before Bayhaqi—but certainly after Abu Hatim al-Razi—Shafiᶜi's image as the founder of *uṣūl al-fiqh* had become firmly established. This intervening period between the two *manāqib* authors coincides, we must note, with the career of Abu Muhammad al-Juwayni, the last commentator on the *Risāla*.[109] That Shafiᶜi's treatise failed to attract further commentary in the decades and centuries that followed explains the role that Shafiᶜi, as the founder of the discipline, was required to play in his school. Once this image as the founder was irrevocably established, commentaries on his treatise ceased forever. In a field where commentaries were the norm, the discontinuity of interest in commenting on the *Risāla* also explains the irrelevance of the work's themes to the far more complex and different methodology of *uṣūl al-fiqh*. This irrelevance is attested to eloquently in the relatively infrequent citation of Shafiᶜi's views by later theoreticians.

VI

To conclude, the history of Shafiᶜi's *Risāla* is connected inextricably with the emergence of *uṣūl al-fiqh* as an organically structured and independent science. As a full-fledged methodology, *uṣūl al-fiqh* represents a synthesis of reason and revelation, the former being the means by which the latter is interpreted so that the divinely prescribed law can be known. The constitutive elements of *uṣūl al-fiqh*—epistemology, legal language, the theory of abrogation, transmission of the texts, consensus, qiyas, ijtihad, taqlid, and so forth—are organically interconnected and interdependent, and the absence of any such element would create an incorrigible imbalance in legal methodology. Therefore, *uṣūl al-fiqh* as a legal methodology is larger than the total sum of its constitutive parts. Our sources strongly indicate that this methodology, with all its constitutive parts, did not exist in the 9th century. This conclusion is further bolstered by additional evidence to the effect that in this century the *Risāla* was marginal, attracting neither commentaries nor refutations.

With the advent of the 10th century, *uṣūl al-fiqh* works begin to proliferate, and simultaneously the *Risāla* succeeds in attracting a number of commentaries and at least two refutative dissertations. This simultaneity should by no means be explained away as coincidental, for such an explanation would ignore blatantly the historical sequence of events that led up to the emergence, in the beginning of the 10th century, of *uṣūl al-fiqh* as an organically structured discipline.

Shafiᶜi's *Risāla* as the embodiment of his legal methodology has, in our view, gained the distinction of being the first attempt at synthesizing the disciplined exercise of human reasoning and the complete assimilation of revelation as the basis of the law. Because Islamic law and jurisprudence did finally come to accept this synthesis, we were led to believe that *uṣūl al-fiqh* as we know it began with Shafiᶜi. But Shafiᶜi's synthesis appeared at a time in which only a few were willing to embrace it. It would be rather simplistic to think that once Shafiᶜi laid down his synthesis, which attempted to reconcile the theses of the traditionalists and the rationalists, it was immediately adopted by the two camps. For Shafiᶜi's theory to prevail would have required that the two camps abandon their doctrines once and for all and join Shafiᶜi's ranks. But this did not happen, and evidence in fact points to the contrary: Shafiᶜi's synthesis was, and remained for a long time, a minority view. The traditionalists rejected his qiyas, and the rationalists were reluctant to accept his thesis that revelation is the first and last judge of human affairs. It was only towards the end of the 9th century that the two camps drew closer to each other, and a synthesis of traditionalism and rationalism was accomplished. With the emergence of this synthesis, whose causes and characteristics are yet to be studied, the way to *uṣūl al-fiqh* was finally paved. And once this science bloomed, at the hands of Sayrafi, Qaffal, and their like, the rudimentary synthesis created by Shafiᶜi a century earlier became relevant and thus was rejuvenated in the form of commentaries on the *Risāla* and by attributing the entire ramifications of the synthesis to Shafiᶜi himself. Shafiᶜi thus becomes the founder of *uṣūl al-fiqh.*

Our conclusion presents us with two significant implications. First, Shafiᶜi's achievement must not be carried too far. He advanced or, to put it more accurately, proposed an unprecedented synthesis of rationalism and traditionalism, but his proposal was not to become relevant until a century later, thanks not to him but to such jurists as Ibn Surayj, Sayrafi, and Qaffal whose achievement was the product of a combination of circumstances that arose at the end of the 9th century and the beginning of the 10th. In other words, Shafiᶜi's law and jurisprudence represented not the pivotal point of Islamic law, but rather a middle stage between the crude beginnings at the outset of the 8th century and the true culmination that took place nearly a century after his death. The second implication, which can hardly be overemphasized, is the central importance of the 9th century in the history of Islamic legal theory. This century, no less than the 8th, determined the direction that Islamic jurisprudence was to take in its future course.

NOTES

Author's note: This article represents an expanded version of two lectures delivered at the MESA annual meeting in New Orleans (19–22 November 1985) and at the University of Chicago (5 November 1987).

[1]See Joseph Schacht, *The Origins of Muhammadan Jurisprudence* (Oxford, 1975).

[2]Aḥmad Muḥammad Shākir, ed. (Cairo, 1892). For the original title of the work and the presumed reasons for its composition, see Majid Khadduri, trans., *Al-Imām Muḥammad ibn Idrīs al-Shāfiᶜī's al-Risāla fī Uṣūl al-Fiqh*, 2nd ed. (Cambridge, 1987), 19 ff.; Fakhr al-Dīn Muḥammad ibn ᶜUmar al-Rāzī, *Irshād al-ṭālibīn ilā al-minhāj al-qawīm fī bayān manāqib al-imām al-Shāfiᶜī*, ed. Aḥmad al-Saqqā (Cairo, 1986), 153; George Makdisi, "The Juridical Theology of Shāfiᶜī: Origins and Significance of *Uṣūl al-Fiqh*," *Studia Islamica* 59 (1984): 6, 9.

[3]See, for example, Ignaz Goldziher, *The Ẓāhirīs: Their Doctrine and Their History*, trans. W. Behn (Leiden, 1971), 20–21; N. J. Coulson, *A History of Islamic Law* (Edinburgh, 1964), 56; Joseph Schacht, *An Introduction to Islamic Law* (Oxford, 1979), 48.

[4]See Khadduri's introduction to his translation of the *Risāla*, 42.

[5]See, for example, Rāzī, *Irshād*, 156; Coulson, *History*, 61

[6]Coulson, *History*, 53.

[7]Ibn al-Nadīm, *Fihrist* (Beirut, 1978), 286.

[8]Ibid., 287.

[9]Ibid., 286, 289.

[10]Ibid., 297.

[11]Tāj al-Din al-Subkī, *Ṭabaqāt al-shāfiᶜiyya al-kubrā*, 6 vols., 2nd ed. (repr., Beirut, n.d.), 1:277.

[12]See n. 13 as well as Abū Bakr Hidāyat Allāh al-Ḥusaynī, *Ṭabaqāt al-shāfiᶜiyya*, ed. ᶜĀdil Nuwayhiḍ (Beirut, 1979), 90, where a reference is made to the chapter on ablution, a chapter that has no place in *uṣūl al-fiqh* works.

[13]Subkī, *Ṭabaqāt*, 2:227. The work clearly treats positive law because Subki remarks that he has in his possession an incomplete copy of the work "up to the chapter on bankruptcy (*taflīs*)."

[14]Subkī (ibid., 2:226) characterizes the work as one concerned with "*fiqh* and *khilāfiyyāt*"; see also ᶜAbd Allāh Muṣṭafā al-Marāghī, *al-Fatḥ al-mubīn fī ṭabaqāt al-uṣūliyyīn*, 3 vols. (Cairo, n.d.), 1:177.

* [15]Subkī, *Ṭabaqāt*, 2:108. We ought to mention that the term *uṣūl* is at times used to mean "standard" or "classical" works; see Shams al-Dīn al-Dhahabī, *Siyar aᶜlām al-nubalāʾ*, ed. Shuᶜayb al-Arnāʾūṭ and Akram al-Būshī, 23 vols. (Beirut, 1986), 15:438, who speaks of a certain Abū al-ᶜAbbās al-Miṣrī as having usurped 500 *uṣūl* volumes from the library of a colleague.

[16]It is to be noted here that Shāfiᶜī does not know the designation *uṣūl al-fiqh*, and his use of the term *aṣl* or *uṣūl* does not carry the connotation attached to it later. He seems to have given his treatise the title *al-Kitāb*. Only later did it come to be known as *al-Risāla*, probably going through a period of transition in which it was known as *Kitāb al-risāla*. For evidence of the original title of the work, see Khadduri, trans., *Risāla*, pars, 96, 332, 573, passim.

[17]*Ikhtilāf uṣūl al-madhāhib*, ed. Muṣṭafā Ghālib (Beirut, 1973).

[18]Ibn al-Nadīm, *Fihrist*, 289.

[19]Subkī, *Ṭabaqāt*, 2:78.

[20]Goldziher, *Ẓāhirīs*, 34–35.

[21]Ibn al-Nadīm, *Fihrist*, 303.

[22]Ibid., 306; see also Subkī, *Ṭabaqāt*, 2:46.

[23]The exception is the case of Ḥusayn ibn ᶜAlī al-Karābīsī (d. 859 or 862) who is described by Abū ᶜĀṣim al-ᶜAbbādī in *Ṭabaqāt al-fuqahāʾ al-shāfiᶜiyya* (ed. Gösta Vitestam [Leiden, 1964], 24–25) as "one of the early jurists who was knowledgeable in *uṣūl*" and by Abū Isḥāq al-Shīrāzī in *Ṭabaqāt al-fuqahāʾ* (ed. Iḥsān ᶜAbbās [Beirut, 1970], 102) as having "written many works on *uṣūl al-fiqh* and *furūᶜ*"; see also Dhahabī, *Siyar*, 12:79–81. It is to be noted, however, that later sources report no work written by Karābīsī on the subject. In fact, the most detailed biographical account on Karābīsī provided by Subkī (*Ṭabaqāt*, 1:251–56) does not associate him with *uṣūl al-fiqh*, either as an author or as a scholar.

[24]Muḥammad ibn Abī Ḥātim al-Rāzī, *Ādāb al-Shāfiᶜī wa-manāqibuhu*, ed. ᶜAbd al-Ghanī ᶜAbd al-Khāliq (Cairo, 1953), 61–62.

[25]Muḥammad ibn Abī Yaᶜlā Ibn al-Farrāʾ, *Ṭabaqāt al-ḥanābila*, ed. M. H. Fiqī, 2 vols. (Cairo, 1952), 1:57.

[26]Subkī, *Ṭabaqāt*, 1:250–1.

[27]See, for example, Aḥmad ibn al-Ḥusayn Abū Bakr al-Bayhaqī, *Manāqib al-Shāfiᶜī*, ed. Aḥmad Ṣaqr, 2 vols. (Cairo, 1971), 1:236; Subkī, *Ṭabaqāt*, 1:242.

[28]Muzanī's commentary is edited and translated by Robert Brunschvig in "Le livre de l'ordre et de la défense d'al-Muzani," *Bulletin d'études orientales* 11 (1945–46):145–94; Arabic text, 153–63.

[29]Muḥammad Zahrī Najjār, ed., 8 vols. (Cairo, 1961), 7:291–92.

[30]Only pp. 153–56 (line 4) of *Kitāb al-amr wa-al-nahy* treat the purported meaning (*ᶜalā maᶜnā*) of Shāfiᶜī's doctrine, although it is highly likely that even pp. 153 (line 20)–56 represent Muzanī's own views, not those of Shāfiᶜī.

[31]On the traditionalists (*ahl al-ḥadīth*) and the rationalists (*ahl al-raʾy*), see Goldziher, *Ẓāhirīs*, 6–19; Schacht, *Origins*, 36–81, 253–57, passim.

[32]Zayn al-Dīn Qāsim ibn Quṭlūbughā, *Tāj al-tarājim fī ṭabaqāt al-ḥanafiyya* (Baghdad, 1962), 19–20.

[33]Dhahabī, *Siyar*, 12:500; Subkī, *Ṭabaqāt*, 1:224. Most biographical works attribute al-Miṣrī's critical attitude toward Shāfiᶜī to a personal conflict between the two.

[34]So must we take Abū Zakiriyyāʾ al-Kinānī's (d. 902) *al-Ḥujja fī al-radd ᶜalā al-Shāfiᶜī*; see Fuat Sezgin, *Geschichte des arabischen Schrifttums*, 9 vols. (Leiden, 1967–), 1:475, 485.

[35]It is interesting to note the change in the title of Khadduri's translation of the *Risāla*. When it was first published in 1961, the title read *Islamic Jurisprudence: Shāfiᶜī's Risāla*. In the 1987 edition, however, it was entitled, significantly, *Al-Shāfiᶜī's Risāla fī Uṣūl al-Fiqh: Treatise on the Foundations of Islamic Jurisprudence*.

[36]Khadduri, *al-Risāla*, 41.

[37]Cairo, 1969.

[38]In his *Irshād*, 157, al-Fakhr al-Rāzī apologizes for the defects in Shāfiᶜī's *Risāla*, saying in effect that all pioneering works entail some shortcomings.

[39]Muḥammad Amjad ᶜAlī, trans. (Karachi, 1968).

[40]See n. 23.

[41]Ibn al-Nadīm, *Fihrist*, 295: "al-Shāfiᶜī was a staunch advocate of Shīᶜism" (*wa-kāna al-Shāfiᶜiyyu shadīdan fī al-tashayyuᶜ*).

[42]Rāzī, *Irshād*, 44, 104; on 66, Rāzī speaks of Shāfiᶜī's outstanding knowledge of dialectic, speculation and disputation—qualities that were entirely absent in the camp of the traditionalists. See also Aḥmad ibn Yaḥyā Ibn al-Murtaḍā, *Ṭabaqāt al-muᶜtazila*, ed. S. Diwald-Wilzer (Wiesbaden, 1961), 43.

[43]Rāzī, *Irshād*, 44.

[44]Cited in Subkī, *Ṭabaqāt*, 2:149.

[45]Ibid., 1:222.

[46]Rāzī, *Irshād*, 228–29.

[47]Subkī, *Ṭabaqāt*, 2:4; Rāzī, *Irshād*, 230.

[48]Rāzī, *Irshād*, 230.

[49]Ibn al-Farrāᵓ, *Ṭabaqāt*, 1:38.

[50]On Shāfiᶜī's opposition to the traditionalists, see Schacht, *Origins*, 128–29.

[51]ᶜAbd Allāh Ibn Qutayba, *al-Maᶜārif* (Karachi, 1976), 216–30.

[52]See n. 53.

[53]Rāzī, *Irshād*, 138. Also, Subkī alludes to Muzanī's Muᶜtazilite tendency (*Ṭabaqāt*, 1:241). On his skill as a dialectician and lack of qualifications as a traditionist, see Dhahabī, *Siyar*, 12:492–93; 14:371. That he was not, strictly speaking, a Muᶜtazilite is evidenced by the fact that he is not included in Muᶜtazilite biographical works. See, for example, Ibn al-Murtaḍā, *Ṭabaqāt al-muᶜtazila*.

[54]See n. 23.

[55]Subkī, *Ṭabaqāt*, 1:251–55.

[56]Shīrāzī, *Ṭabaqāt*, 102.

[57]Reported by Subkī on the authority of al-Khaṭīb al-Baghdādī (*Ṭabaqāt*, 1:252).

[58]It is significant that at this time titles carrying the term *furūᶜ* also begin to appear, *furūᶜ* and *uṣūl* being now dichotomous; see, for example, *Kitāb al-furūᶜ* by Ibn al-Ḥaddād al-Miṣrī, who died in 956; Dhahabī, *Siyar*, 15:446.

The evidence in our sources thus indicates that the appearance of the designation *uṣūl al-fiqh* as well as of complete works on the subject belongs to the beginning of the 10th century, not to the end of it, as Makdisi seems to suggest; see his "Juridical Theology of Shāfiᶜī," 5, 13–14.

[59]ᶜAbbādī, *Ṭabaqāt*, 55; Subkī, *Ṭabaqāt*, 2:242–43.

[60]Dhahabī, *Siyar*, 15:217–18; Ibn al-Nadīm (*Fihrist*, 245–46) states that the author did not complete the work.

[61]Ibn al-Nadīm, *Fihrist*, 300; ᶜAbd al-Ḥayy Ibn al-ᶜImād, *Shadharāt al-dhahab fī akhbār man dhahab*, 8 vols. (Cairo, 1931–32), 2:325; ᶜAbbādī, *Ṭabaqāt*, 69; Abū al-ᶜAbbās Aḥmad ibn Muḥammad Ibn Khallikān, *Wafayāt al-aᶜyān wa-anbāᵓ abnāᵓ al-zamān*, ed. Iḥsān ᶜAbbās, 8 vols. (Beirut, 1977), 4:199; Shīrāzī, *Ṭabaqāt*, 111.

[62]Ibn al-Nadīm, *Fihrist*, 283.

[63]Ibn Quṭlūbughā, *Tāj al-tarājim*, 59.

[64]Subkī, *Ṭabaqāt*, 2:103; Shīrāzī, *Ṭabaqāt*, 111.

[65]Shīrāzī, *Ṭabaqāt*, 112; Subkī, *Ṭabaqāt*, 2:176 ff.; Ibn Khallikān, *Wafayāt*, 4:200–201.

[66]Ibn Quṭlūbughā, *Tāj al-tarājim*, 86.

[67]Shīrāzī, *Ṭabaqāt*, 112.

[68]Subkī, *Ṭabaqāt*, 2:159.

[69]Ibn al-Nadīm, *Fihrist*, 330.

[70]Jamāl al-Dīn ᶜAbd al-Raḥīm al-Asnawī, *Ṭabaqāt al-shāfiᶜiyya*, ed. ᶜAbd Allāh al-Jubūrī, 2 vols. (Baghdad, 1970–71), 2:123; Subkī, *Ṭabaqāt*, 2:81–82.

[71]Beirut, 1982.

[72]Shīrāzī, *Ṭabaqāt*, 115; Subkī, *Ṭabaqāt*, 2:217.

[73]Ibn al-Murtaḍā, *Ṭabaqāt*, 102.

[74]Ibid., 109.

[75]ᶜAbbādī, *Ṭabaqāt*, 69.

[76]Shīrāzī, *Ṭabaqāt*, 112.

[77]Asnawī, *Ṭabaqāt*, 2:472; Ḥusaynī, *Ṭabaqāt*, 245–46.

[78]Khadduri, *al-Risāla*, 42.

[79]Subkī, *Ṭabaqāt*, 3:186, 208.

[80]Ibn Khallikān, *Wafayāt*, 3:219 ff.

[81]Dhahabī, *Siyar*, 15:328.

[82]Ṣayrafī not only commented on the *Risāla* but also wrote a rebuttal against al-Kātib's refutation of the work; see Ibn al-Nadīm, *Fihrist*, 300. It was not possible to establish al-Kātib's identity. We must note that the sources report at least three other critiques of Shāfiᶜī by two Mālikites and a Ḥanbalite. The two Mālikites are Bakr ibn Muḥammad al-Qushayrī (d. 955) and Abū Bakr al-Dīnawarī (d. after 940); see Dhahabī, *Siyar*, 4:427, 537. The Ḥanbalite is Ghulām al-Khallāl (d. 947); see Ibn al-Farrāᵓ, *Ṭabaqāt*, 2:119–20. However, it cannot be established whether the object of these critiques was Shāfiᶜī's positive law or legal theory.

[83]Subkī, *Ṭabaqāt*, 2:241.

[84]On Ibn Surayj, see ibid., 2:87–96; Dhahabī, *Siyar*, 14:201–4; Ibn Khallikān, *Wafayāt*, 1:66–67; ᶜAbbādī, *Ṭabaqāt*, 62–63; Ibn al-ᶜImād, *Shadharāt*, 2:247–48.

[85]Reported by Subkī (*Ṭabaqāt*, 2:307) on the authority of the historian ᶜAlī ibn Ḥusayn al-Masᶜūdī. Subkī had in his possession a copy of the epistle.

[86]Shīrāzī, *Ṭabaqāt*, 109.

[87]On Ibn Ḥaykuwayh, see Dhahabī, *Siyar*, 15:379. On al-Marwazī, Ibn al-Qāṣṣ, Ṣayrafī, and Shāshī, see Shīrāzī, *Ṭabaqāt*, 111–12; Ibn al-ᶜImād, *Shadharāt*, 2:339; Ibn Khallikān, *Wafayāt*, 4:199. On Abū Bakr al-Fārisī, see Ibn al-Murtaḍā, *Ṭabaqāt*, 102.

[88]Ibn Khallikān, *Wafayāt*, 4:199; Subkī, *Ṭabaqāt*, 2:170.

[89]Ibn Khallikān, *Wafayāt*, 4:200–201.

[90]Subkī, *Ṭabaqāt*, 3:208; Ibn al-ᶜImād, *Shadharāt*, 3:261–62.

[91]That a jurist of the 10th century combined a proficient knowledge of rationalist and traditionalist disciplines was still considered remarkable even in the 14th century. Subkī, for instance, clearly makes a point of mentioning such a combination; see his *Ṭabaqāt*, 2:79, 81.

[92]Susan Spectorsky, "Aḥmad Ibn Ḥanbal's *Fiqh*," *Journal of the American Oriental Society* 102 (1982): 461–65.

[93]For a brief account of Dawūd's teachings, see Goldziher, *Ẓāhirīs*, 27–39.

[94]See W. B. Hallaq, "Was the Gate of Ijtihad Closed?" *International Journal of Middle East Studies* 16 (1984): 7–10. On the Ḥashwiyya, see A. S. Halkin, "The Ḥashwiyya," *Journal of the American Oriental Society* 54 (1934):12.

[95]Subkī admits (*Ṭabaqāt*, 1:285, 2:18–20) that he includes the biographies of those who are worthy of mention because "there is no sense in mentioning the others, for it would be a waste of ink."

[96]Ibid., 1:186–285. On Ibn al-Ḥakam, Abū Thawr, and Ibn Rāhawayh, see ibid., 1:223–24, 227 ff., 232 ff. For more on Abū Thawr, see Ibn al-Nadīm, *Fihrist*, 297.

[97]Subkī, *Ṭabaqāt*, 1:285–301; 2:2–79.

[98]Ibid., 2:79–322. The rapid increase in the number of Shāfiᶜites during the 10th century must be in good part attributed to Ibn Surayj, under whom, as we have seen (section IV), the major figures of the Shāfiᶜite school have studied. Ibn Surayj's numerous students have in turn become influential and have attracted, in various parts of the Muslim world, a great number of disciples; see sources cited in nn. 86–89.

[99]Ibid., 1:244, 247; Asnawī, *Ṭabaqāt*, 1:34–35.

[100]Muzanī's position vis-à-vis Shāfiᶜī's doctrine is well illustrated in an anecdote that, even if not genuine, also portrays Ibn Surayj's attitude towards Muzanī as Shāfiᶜī's chief student. Ibn Surayj is reported to have said that "on the Day of Judgment Shāfiᶜī will appear [before God] and Muzanī will follow on his heel. Shāfiᶜī will say: O God, this man [Muzanī] has corrupted my sciences (*ᶜulūmī*). Thereupon, I (Ibn Surayj) shall say to him: Go easy on Abū Ibrāhīm [al-Muzanī] for I have mended what he had adulterated." If this anecdote truly illustrates Ibn Surayj's view of Muzanī, it must be taken to refer to Muzanī's rationalist inclination on certain matters of *uṣūl*, not *furūᶜ*, because we know that Ibn Surayj admired his works on positive law and, in fact, wrote in verse to extol them; see Subkī, *Ṭabaqāt*, 2:87, 92–93.

[101]ᶜAbbādī, *Ṭabaqāt*, 62.

[102]See Makdisi, "Juridicial Theology of Shāfiᶜī," 6–7.
[103]Rāzī, *Ādāb al-Shāfiᶜī*, 231–37.
[104]Ibid., 62, 63.
[105]Bayhaqī, *Manāqib*, 1:368–84.
[106]Ibid., 1:230–36.
[107]Ibid., 1:368.
[108]Rāzī, *Irshād*, 153–88, 189–268.
[109]See n. 79.

ADDENDA

General remarks: after the publication of the article, I became aware of Christopher Melchert's doctoral dissertation ('The Formation of the Sunnī Schools of Law, 9th-10th Centuries C.E.', 1991) which he wrote under the direction of Professor George Makdisi at the University of Pennsylvania. Melchert's findings wholly support my thesis that Shāfi'ī was not a thoroughgoing traditionalist; that his legal theory was not taken up seriously until the beginning of the fourth/tenth century; and that Ibn Surayj not only was instrumental in beginning the process of reinvigorating *uṣūl al-fiqh*, but his work 'was crucial to the development of the Shāfi'ī school as we know it from the eleventh century onward' (letter, 17 December 1993). I am greatly indebted to Professor Melchert for bringing his dissertation to my attention, and for readily providing me with parts of it.

In a recent book, Norman Calder approaches the work of Shāfi'ī (mainly his substantive law) from an entirely different angle, but nonetheless reaches conclusions highly supportive of the view that Shāfi'ī exercised little, if any, influence during the third/ninth century. Calder notes that 'the magnificent totality of his (*viz*., Shāfi'ī's) juristic achievement was not recognized by Muslim writers, and had no tangible influence on juristic thought, before perhaps the beginning of the fourth century' (*Studies in Early Muslim Jurisprudence* [Oxford: Clarendon Press, 1993], p. 67). Furthermore, Calder's main conclusion that Shāfi'ī's system of substantive law – represented in what we now know as *al-Umm* – is, in form and content, the product of the later part of the third/ninth century is very plausible, and definitely supports our findings. See chapter 4 and passim.

A note on calenders: when I first wrote the article, the dates were given according to the Hijrī calender. Converting the dates to the Christian calender in conformity with the *IJMES* format proved to be in a few cases cumbersome, and it created certain problems, particularly in references to entire centuries. Thus, the reader is asked to bear in mind that for the purposes of this article, the ninth century A.D. broadly refers to the years falling between 815–905, which roughly correspond to 200–294 H.

p. 587, last line of par. 2: read 'is still considered as valid as when it first appeared'. The desk editor of Cambridge University Press seems to have overlooked my correction in the proofs.

p. 602, n. 15: I am grateful to Muhammad Qasim Zaman for reminding me that the term *uṣūl* may also refer to the main original manuscript, the exemplar, which constitutes the source (hence *aṣl*) from which copies (*furū'* or witnesses) are made. Accordingly, Dhahabī may have used the word *uṣūl* in this sense when he spoke of Abū al-'Abbās al-Miṣrī.

VIII

ON THE AUTHORITATIVENESS OF SUNNI CONSENSUS

I

Sunni Islam recognizes four sources from and through which the laws governing its conduct are derived. These are the Qurʾan, the Sunna of the Prophet, the consensus (*ijmāʿ*) of the community and its scholars,[1] and *qiyās*, the juridico-logical method of inference.[2] The first two sources provide the jurist with the material from which he is to extract through qiyas and *ijtihād* (the disciplined exercise of mental faculty) the law which he believes to the best of his knowledge to be that decreed by God. Except for a relatively limited number of cases where the Qurʾan and the Sunna offer already-formulated legal judgments, the great majority of *furūʿ* cases, which constitute the body of positive and substantive law, are derived by qiyas. Thus, qiyas may be used to "discover" the judgment of a new case provided that this case has not already been solved in the two primary sources. The process of legal reasoning which qiyas involves is charged with innumerable difficulties not the least of which is finding the circle of common similarity, the *ʿilla*, between the original case in the texts and the new case which requires a legal judgment. Since finding the ʿilla entails a certain amount of guesswork (*ẓann*) on the part of the jurist and since it is highly probable that the ʿilla is extracted from a text which is not entirely reliable or a text capable of more than one interpretation, Sunni jurists deemed the results of qiyas to be probable (*ẓannī*). It is only at this point that consensus may enter into play in the legal process. Should Muslims, represented by their jurists, reach an agreement on the validity of a zanni legal judgment, such judgment is automatically transferred from the domain of juristic speculation to that of certainty (*qaṭʿ*, *yaqīn*). Consensus then renders this judgment irrevocable, not to be challenged or reinterpreted by later generations. Furthermore, this judgment, being so irrevocable, acquires a validity tantamount to that of the Qurʾan and the highly reliable traditions embodied in the Sunna of the Prophet. Thus, such a case with its established judgment becomes a precedent according to which another new legal question may be solved. It is only in this sense that consensus functions as a source of law, a source which is infallible.[3]

This theory of consensus was the product of a relatively late period, when legal theory, *uṣūl al-fiqh*, reached maturity. But in first-century Islam, and for that matter in pre-Islamic Arabia, consensus, as we shall see, existed primarily as a social and secular force.[4] With the emerging political struggles and the subsequent growth of the religious movement during the second/eighth century, consensus acquired a religious character and became one of the most remarkable doctrinal features which distinguished *ahl al-sunna wal-jamāᶜa* from other sects and movements. The important role of consensus as a sanctioning instrument and as a source of law of the "middle nation" was bound to generate extensive discussion and criticism from within and without Sunnism.[5] The crucial problem which posed itself was the foundation and validity of consensus as a religious doctrine. In other words, classical Muslim jurists, who undertook the task of developing usul al-fiqh, had to prove that consensus rests on the strength of the two primary sources, the Qurʾan and/or the Sunna. For, according to the fundamental Islamic tenet, nothing can be regarded as valid or binding if it is not somehow grounded in these sources. The implication of accepting consensus as a sanctioning force and, moreover, as a source of law without basing it on the sources was grave. It meant that those jurists who participated in the formulation of consensus were themselves the legislators, the law-givers of the community. But jurists were not vested with an authority to enact law; rather, they and the rest of the community were only the recipients of divine grace, a grace manifest in the very fact of revelation. Consensus as a legal precept had to be thus grounded in this revelation. How the Muslim jurists proved the authoritativeness through the centuries of consensus and the problems which they encountered while doing so will be our concern here.

II

Before we proceed with our discussion of the problem known in Arabic religious sources as *ḥujjiyyat al-ijmāᶜ*, i.e., the authoritativeness of consensus, let us briefly examine the contribution of modern Western scholarship to this question. This will be done with a view to sorting out those opinions and conclusions which this essay attempts to reconsider or complement. The most pertinent are three views expressed by C. Snouck Hurgronje, N. J. Coulson, and George Hourani.[6] Hurgronje maintained, and rightly so, that at a relatively early period, when the doctrine of the infallibility of the community was formulated, "people still dared to give greater convincing force to obvious truths by putting them into the mouth of the Prophet." Thus,

> several traditions, in various forms, make him say that "the whole of his community can never be in error". . . . In the earliest period, people found it sufficient that the Prophet in his last words should have urged the believers most emphatically to "hold fast to the Book." When they [i.e., Muslims] arrived at the conviction that the Muslim way of life was not based on the text of the revelation alone, it was inevitable that the Prophet in his farewell speech should have mentioned his sunna as the second foundation of religious duties; finally, when the infallibility of the community had become an essential dogma, this too had to be supported by his words.[7]

But Hurgronje also argued that when Muslims faced the difficulty of interpreting the texts and distinguishing the authentic traditions from the spurious, the infallible authority of the community was called for. "As a result, not only the laws and institutions which came into being after Muhammad's death, but the whole practice of the Muslim community is based on its own infallibility."[8] Elsewhere, he explicitly argued that

> attempts have been made to demonstrate it [i.e., consensus] by the *Qur᾿an* and the *sunna*, but it is impossible to hide the fact that this is to go round in a vicious circle. Only the infallible community can explain the *sunna* and *Qur᾿an* accurately; it is then completely idle to claim to establish the infallibility of the community by the authority of the *Qur᾿an* and the *sunna.*[9]

In sum, Hurgronje's contention seems to be that in the final analysis consensus was the ultimate authority on interpreting, understanding, and authenticating the Qur᾿an and the Sunna, and that the "foundation of foundations" of Islam was the self-proclaimed infallibility of the community.[10] Hurgronje's conclusion, therefore, was that consensus rested on a *petitio principii.*[11]

This view was also expounded, though less unequivocally, by Coulson who argued that "although the validity of the principle is formally expressed in a Tradition from the Prophet which states: 'My community will never agree upon an error,' it is the *ijmāᶜ* itself which guarantees the validity of the Tradition."[12] A similar view was also held by Joseph Schacht.[13]

George Hourani has studied the question of the authoritativeness of consensus and has reconsidered the statements made by Hurgronje.[14] His findings were published in a lengthy article in 1964. In that article Hourani showed that consensus does not determine the interpretation of the texts on which consensus rests. He also attempted to show that consensus does not rest on a *petitio principii.* On the first point Hourani argued persuasively, but on the second, on the issue of circularity, his answer was brief and did not reflect the centrality and the true weight of this issue in medieval discussions. This inquiry attempts to complement Hourani's contribution. However, it is to be noted that Hourani's assumption—which dictated his approach to and treatment of the sources—that the true religion of Islam is found only in the Qur᾿an and that the traditions of the Prophet are not an essential part of Islam led him to underestimate the role which the traditions played in avoiding a *petitio principii.*[15] In fact this assumption seems to have effected a somewhat extreme conclusion. After sketching the views of some jurists on the subject and stating the results of research about hadith undertaken by Ignaz Goldziher and Joseph Schacht, Hourani finally reached two major conclusions.

> (a) Any sound basis for the authority of an infallible, cumulative consensus, as a definite institution of Islam, must be found in a text of Islamic scripture. On this principle the medieval Muslim scholars were right.
>
> (b) No such basis can be found in the *Qur᾿an*, or in any Tradition that can be regarded with confidence as authentic. This is what modern scholarship leads us to think.

Hourani then went on to say that "Using these two conclusions as premises, we arrive at a third: There is no sound basis for the traditional doctrine of consensus in Islam."[16]

Thus Hourani used the results of modern scholarship to judge whether or not a medieval system of belief had rested on a "sound basis." The question here is not whether we believe the traditions to be authentic, but whether or not Muslims throughout classical and medieval Islam accepted them as such. Insofar as Muslims were concerned, "the entire religion is taken only from God . . . and then from the language of the Prophet."[17] The Sunna was undoubtedly considered as part of the *waḥy*, God's revelation.[18] Believing what the Prophet said was a requisite for *īmān.*[19] The Sunna had the important function of clarifying the ambiguities, and if necessary, abrogating verses, in the Qurʾan.[20] Its rejection was tantamount to heresy. Many jurists and theologians emphasized the fact that the Qurʾan falls short of supplying even a fraction of the rulings of Sharīʿa, and that most rulings are based on the solitary traditions, the *āḥādīs*.[21] Thus, for us now to reject the Sunna as a basis of belief would take us only half way. It would be just as logical to argue that the Qurʾan, like the traditions, is a man-written book. This would necessarily carry us to the objectionable conclusion that Islam as a system of faith is baseless.

Goldziher's and Schacht's results about the spuriousness of hadith literature, though quite illuminating and indispensable for a more accurate understanding of the early developments in Islam, have no bearing whatsoever on whether consensus was authoritative or baseless. Muslims considered (and the majority still do) the Sunna to be a pillar of Islam and as such we must address it in the present inquiry. It must be immediately added that the question of the authoritativeness of consensus must be dealt with as a subject of intellectual history. All propositions designated by the great majority of Muslim scholars as premises to their arguments must be treated as true premises.

III

The question of the authoritativeness of consensus arose only when it became necessary for Muslims to decide once and for all whether they themselves were the ultimate source of authority or whether that authority was God. In the Jāhiliyya, the answer to this question was obvious; the sunna and the consensus of the tribe or the community constituted the law. Consensus, *al-amr al-mujtamaʿ ʿalayh*, created and defined the sunna.[22] With the advent of Islam, the Qurʾan encroached, to the extent dictated by its meagre content of law, on the established secular sunna. Now, with the help of the Qurʾan, God had only begun to partake in determining man's affairs. The spirit and the letter of the Qurʾan and the Prophet's *sīra* had undoubtedly left their mark on that society, but not, strictly speaking, on its law. With the growth of Islam, the ancient notion of sunna came to be associated with a new notion, viz. the Sunna of the Prophet. This is not to say that the Prophetic Sunna existed alongside a non-Prophetic sunna. Rather, the Prophetic Sunna was created by what Schacht termed "the living tradition," the sunna as fixed by the consensus of one particular living generation. Thus the community, by associating its living sunna with the Sunna of the Prophet, granted itself the prerogative of determining the Divine Sunna, which was soon to become the most substantive source of law. In effect this meant that whatever the community decided would prevail. Only with this background can one fully appreciate the later doctrine which prescribed that the

Sunna interprets and, when necessary, abrogates the Qurʾan. In fact, this is a modified version of a second-century dominant view that it is the Sunna which decides upon the Qurʾan and not the reverse.[23] The Prophetic Sunna, the sacrosanctified expression of the "living tradition," along with the Qurʾan, became the ultimate sources of the law. It is only in such an environment that Muḥammad b. Ḥasan al-Shaybānī (d. 189/804) could declare on the authority of the Prophet that "Whatever the Muslims see as good is good in the eyes of God, and whatever they see as bad is bad in the eyes of God."[24]

The process of creating the Sunna of the Prophet out of the "living tradition" began to be interrupted when the Prophetic Sunna was recorded in the form of hadith. Hadith gave permanence to the Sunna, thereby defining and determining its content once and for all. When the literature of hadith exhausted more or less the content of the Sunna, the full authority to determine the law was transferred from the hands of Muslims to those of God and his Messenger. For it was obvious that the process by which the Sunna was vested with divine authority had already come full circle. The transference of this authority was not sudden but gradual. It seems to have ended sometime in the beginning of the third Islamic century (ca. A.D. 830). However, the intellectual justification of the paramount position of revelation in relation to consensus had just begun.[25] The first signs of this process of justification had already appeared in Ibn Idrīs al-Shāfiʿī (d. 204/820), who, to our knowledge, was the first jurist to systematically lay down the jurisprudential principles of substantive law.

Shāfiʿī, whose theory represents the almost complete victory of the authority of God over that of man, elevates the Qurʾan and the Sunna of the Prophet to a supreme position, and relegates consensus to a subsidiary source of law. He distinguishes between two types of consensus. The first is the consensus of the community and the second that of the ulama, the legal specialists. The consensus of the community is again divided into two types. The first is that which is based on the Qurʾan and on a Sunna transmitted "from the generality to the generality," and the second is not based on revelation,[26] and serves as a working consensus (*mufīd lil-ʿamal*, as later jurists would put it) which does not lead to certainty (*iḥāṭa*). The consensus of the ulama stands on an even lower level because it has the force of a solitary tradition, *khabar al-khāṣṣa*, which cannot lead to certain knowledge.[27] Shāfiʿī does not consider this type of consensus authoritative. Only the first type, the consensus which is reached on the basis of the Qurʾan and a Sunna transmitted by the generality of Muslims, can yield certain knowledge of the law decreed by God. Shāfiʿī asserted that "It is impossible that the community should agree on something contrary to the words of the Prophet,"[28] and, *a fortiori*, contrary to the injunctions of the Qurʾan. He went as far as to say that "the generality [of Muslims] cannot agree on . . . an error,"[29] thus anticipating the later Prophetic tradition "My community does not agree on an error." But Shāfiʿī's acceptance of the consensus of the community even when it is not in custody of a text of revelation seems to have required justification, as he himself held that the Qurʾan and the Sunna are the ultimate sources on matters of law.[30] In other words, Shāfiʿī felt bound, in order to be consistent, to base this type of consensus on the two primary sources. This very fact manifests the triumph of revelation in Shāfiᶜī's jurisprudence, where all things must either be based squarely on revelation or derived therefrom.[31]

In addition to Qurᵓan IV:115 (And whoso makes a breach with the Messenger after the guidance had been manifested unto him, and followed other than the believers' way, we appoint for him what unto which he himself had turned, and expose him unto hell), Shāfiᶜī quotes two traditions in justification of consensus, the first of which is: "Three things the heart of the Muslim shall not hate: sincerity of action for the sake of God, good advice for [fellow] Muslims and adherence to their community";[32] the second: "he who wishes to reside in Paradise must hold fast to the community, for Satan comes close to one person but not as close to two."[33] It must be noted that in his discussions of consensus in the *Risāla*, nowhere does Shāfiᶜī adduce the Qurᵓanic verse IV:115. The traditions, on the other hand, appear in the *Risāla* on more than one occasion when consensus is discussed. We are therefore justified in assuming that he did not think of this verse as an important argument.[34]

From the two traditions Shāfiᶜī concludes that the Prophet enjoined Muslims to adhere to the community, because the Muslim community cannot agree on an error. In answer to his interlocutor who inquired about the meaning of the traditions, Shāfiᶜī says that adherence to the community enjoined by the said traditions meant not physical adherence but adherence in belief. The Prophet, he maintained against his opponent, could not have meant that Muslims should physically hold to the body of the community since they reside in far-flung provinces and non-Muslims live amongst them. The Prophet could have only meant that the duty is to hold fast to the doctrines and actions as known and practiced by the community.[35]

Although the meaning of these traditions is sufficiently clear, the argument as a whole gives rise to a serious objection. By the same epistemological standards set forth by Shāfiᶜī himself, it can be maintained that his argument for authoritative consensus is not well knit. Though he does not state that these traditions are solitary (*akhbār al-khāṣṣa*), there is no doubt that he considered them as such. As we have seen, Shāfiᶜī deemed everything that was based on traditions transmitted through channels fewer than those of the "generality to the generality" to lead only to probable knowledge. The consensus of the community on the basis of a text leads, in Shāfiᶜī's opinion, to ihata, a conclusive and irrevocable knowledge. The weakness of his argument thus stems from the fact that he proves the *universal* validity of a principle which leads to certain knowledge by evidence which yields mere probability. It cannot be maintained, however, that Shāfiᶜī fell in the trap of circularity because the authenticity of the traditions adduced is not claimed to be guaranteed by the community, and their meaning is determined by the standard rules of the Arabic language. What Shāfiᶜī needed in order to perfect his theory of consensus was either an unambiguous Qurᵓanic verse guaranteeing the infallibility of the community or an explicit statement from the Prophet transmitted from the generality to the generality to the same effect. Shāfiᶜī would have fallen in the trap of circularity had he held the view that a consensus on a case of law, which is in turn based on a solitary tradition, leads to certainty. Had this been the case, he would have been obliged to justify consensus by the most conclusive and decisive textual evidence, because assigning to consensus the role of transferring rulings from the domain of probability to that of certainty means that consensus is a source of law. To admit, as it were, that consensus can be conclusive only when based on highly reliable texts, absolved consensus of its responsibility as a legislative source, and absolved Shāfiᶜī of the responsibility of proving that it was one. The certainty of consensus is thus a derivative of the certainty of revelation and not one which is self-constituted. This is in perfect consonance with the status which Shāfiᶜī accorded to consensus as a general legal principle.

After the death of Shāfiᶜī, the issue of grounding consensus in revelation became even more problematic. Unlike the theory of Shāfiᶜī, which recognized as infallible only the consensus of the community when based on a reliable text, the great majority of later jurists held that infallible consensus is the consensus of the *mujtahid*s (the qualified jurists who are authorized to discover the law) on any case of law, including a case solved by means of qiyas which may take its premises from ahadi traditions.[36] The authority of consensus to render probable things certain called for serious attempts at proving, on textual grounds, that consensus is a legitimate source of law (*aṣl min uṣūl al-sharᶜ*).

IV

Unfortunately, there are no extant works from the third/ninth century which can shed light on the subject under discussion. The earliest period from which some writings have reached us is around the middle of the fourth/tenth century. From the work of the Ḥanafī jurist Abū Bakr al-Jaṣṣāṣ (d. 370/980)[37] and from that of his Shīᶜī adversary al-Qāḍī al-Nuᶜmān (fl. mid. fourth/tenth century), we can gain insight into how the issue of the authoritativeness of Sunni consensus was treated during the first half of the fourth/tenth century.

By the middle of that century textual evidence in support of consensus had become abundant. Jaṣṣāṣ cites Qurᵓan II:143, "Thus we have appointed you a middle nation, that you may be witnesses against mankind, and that the messenger may be a witness against you." By equating "middle nation" with uprightness and rectitude, he concludes that the community should be described as infallible and as such it is appointed to witness the deeds of other people just as the Prophet witnessed his community's deeds. He also cites IV:115, already quoted by Shāfiᶜī, and argues that the Qurᵓan bids adherence to the call of the Prophet and threatens with punishment those who swerve from the path of Islam. The call for unity behind the Prophet thus gives legitimacy to the agreement of Muslims. IX:16 also supports the same theme: "Or did you suppose you would be left [in peace] when God knows not as yet those of you who strive, choosing for familiar none save God and his messenger and the believers?" From this he infers that opposing the believers is as serious a sin as opposing the Prophet himself. Jaṣṣāṣ produces two more verses which are as inconclusive as the previous ones. They are III:110 "You are the best community that has been raised up for mankind. You enjoin good and forbid evil," and XXXI:15 "And follow the path of him who turns to me." In the first of the two verses Jaṣṣāṣ interprets the praise for the community in terms which indicate that the community cannot agree on an error. In the second verse the reference is, of course, to the Prophet: to follow the Prophet is to save the community from going astray.

Realizing that all these verses have no definite meaning which can establish, once and for all, the authoritativeness of consensus, Jaṣṣāṣ resorts to the Sunna to enhance his argument. In addition to the two traditions which Shāfiᶜī had already introduced, he brings forth five more traditions, all of which are admittedly ahadis.[38]

In his critique of Sunni legal theory, Qāḍī al-Nuᶜmān records the Qurᵓanic verses and traditions used by the Sunni jurists to justify the authoritativeness of consensus. All but three Qurᵓanic verses (VIII:181, XXII:78, LVII:19) are mentioned by Jaṣṣāṣ. The general meaning of these three is identical to that of the aforementioned II:143 and III:110.[39] It is to be observed here that the number of verses and traditions adduced by Jaṣṣāṣ, and obviously by his contemporaries, has increased considerably since the time of Shāfiᶜī. This increase was, as we shall see, of great importance for later legal theorists.

V

One of the earliest writers in whose works we find a comprehensive treatment of this issue is the Muᶜtazilī jurist and theologian ᶜAbd al-Jabbār al-Asadabādī (d. 415/1024). In his definition, consensus is not only the agreement of the qualified jurists but also of the community as a whole.[40] It constitutes an authority whose proof must derive from the revealed sources. Reason is of no use in establishing the authoritativeness of consensus, because there exists no rational evidence which can prove that a group of people or a community is not liable to error.[41] It is scriptural evidence, he states, which is the only acceptable evidence. ᶜAbd al-Jabbār starts by citing Qurᵓan IV:115, already quoted by Jaṣṣāṣ and allegedly by Shāfiᶜī. Using the same polemical style of exposition used by the latter in the *Risāla*, ᶜAbd al-Jabbār undertakes a lengthy explanation of the meaning of this verse. He argues that God's warning with regard to dissenting from the lines of the Prophet and the believers necessarily means that following their lead is the right thing to do. The path which the Muslims tread, he reasons, must be, in accordance with the verse, the most righteous and therefore authoritative. Had such authority not been inherent in them they would not have been endowed with the quality of righteousness.[42] Upon the suggestion of the interlocutor that the warning against breaking away from the path of the Prophet and the believers does not necessarily mean that such path should be followed, ᶜAbd al-Jabbār retorts that the meaning is clear: If dissenting from something is prohibited then it follows that embracing a different thing is also prohibited. From this it also follows that the only choice is to adhere to the path of the Prophet and the believers.

Having conceded to ᶜAbd al-Jabbār this interpretation, the interlocutor then adroitly argues that if the authoritativeness of the community's consensus is contingent upon the condition of following the path of believers, then belief (iman), is the criterion for authoritativeness. This being so, the iman of one person would make him an authority, and therefore, his position on a particular issue becomes authoritative in much the same way that the position of the whole community becomes authoritative. Accordingly, the interlocutor says, the acceptance of consensus on the basis of iman necessitates upholding the decision of an individual Muslim as authoritative. Clearly, the interlocutor is purporting by this *reductio ad absurdum* argument to undermine the interpretation given to the verse by ᶜAbd al-Jabbār. Since the linchpin of this interpretation is the phrase the "believers' path" (or "believers' way"), ᶜAbd al-Jabbār remarks that the "believers' path" is expressed in the deeds, utterances, and creed of Muslims as based on evidence from revelation (or reason!).[43] It cannot be contended, he says, that the path becomes defined only after Muslims reach a consensus on what constitutes iman.

The interlocutor then points to the plural form of the word "*al-muᵓminīn*" (the believers) and argues that the apparent meaning of the verse is that a consensus can be authoritative if three believers reach it—since three is the smallest number in the plural. ᶜAbd al-Jabbār refers his opponent to the chapter in his book entitled "On the General" (*al-ᶜāmm*) where he explains that when the definite article *al-* is prefixed to a noun in the plural, as is the case here, the noun will indicate a class of things, which is in this case all the believers. The opponent then goes on to debate the meaning and definition of the term "believers" and, again, ᶜAbd al-Jabbār does not fail to assert his position. After some discussion, the latter concludes that the believers of the community constitute the consensus-making body, and since God has not specified in the verse a certain time for the validity of consensus, he also concludes that the consensus of each and every generation of Muslims is an authority.[44]

ᶜAbd al-Jabbār dismisses XXXI:15 "And follow the path of him who turns to me"—adduced earlier by Jaṣṣāṣ—on the grounds that the context in which it was revealed makes it evident that the reference is not to any specific group of people, but to mankind in general. Moreover, this injunction, as shown in the lines which open the *āya*, refers to the respect man owes his parents.[45] Similarly, ᶜAbd al-Jabbār dismisses III:103, III:110, IV:59, VII:181, and XI:118, adduced by other scholars in justification of consensus, on grounds that they bear various meanings not necessarily relevant to consensus.[46]

The second verse produced in justification of consensus is II:143 ("Thus we have appointed you a middle nation, that you may be witnesses against mankind, and that the messenger may be a witness against you") which, ᶜAbd al-Jabbār notes, had been adduced earlier by Abū ᶜAlī al-Jubbāᵓī (d. 303/915). Like Jaṣṣāṣ, Jubbāᵓī and ᶜAbd al-Jabbār understand "middle nation" as a metaphor indicating the quality of justice and rectitude inherent in the community of believers. This naturally explains why they were appointed as witnesses against other communities. Had their testimony been dubious in the least, such a responsibility would not have been entrusted to them. God's choice of appointing these witnesses, ᶜAbd al-Jabbār insists, leads us to think that God accepts their word as reliable and truthful. Furthermore, in the second part of the verse, the Prophet is also said to be a witness because he is just and his utterances are authoritative. From all this it is concluded that the collective decision of the community constitutes an authority.[47]

Expectedly, the interlocutor attempts to undermine the relevance of the verse to consensus by pointing out that the apparent meaning of the verse does not correspond to reality. While the community as a whole appears to be described as just, it is obvious that amongst the community there are in reality many dissolute and impious persons. Therefore, he says, one must not use this verse in support of consensus. ᶜAbd al-Jabbār responds "community" means those who qualify as believers and not necessarily all members of the community. In support of his interpretation he cites other Qurᵓanic verses in which collective nouns are used in a restrictive sense. Unsatisfied with this, the interlocutor contends that it is the companions of the Prophet who are addressed in the verse rather than the community at large. The phrase "We appointed you" presupposes an addressee, who can only be the community of the companions. Accordingly, it is the consensus of the companions which is authoritative, and not that of the entire community of believers. ᶜAbd al-Jabbār retorts swiftly and decisively by citing a number of Qurᵓanic verses which make it abundantly clear that those who are appointed witnesses are the Muslims as a whole. Illustrative of these verses is XXIII:78, "And strive for Allah with the endeavor which is his right . . . . He had named you Muslims of old time and in this [Book], that the messenger may be a witness against you, and that you may be witnesses against mankind."[48]

Having discussed the Qurᵓanic evidence, ᶜAbd al-Jabbār goes on to note that Jubbāᵓī based consensus on Prophetic traditions such as "My community shall never agree on an error." The former remarks that traditions with regard to the authority of consensus are plentiful and well known, although some are better known than others. He lists about 10 of these traditions saying that many of them were reported in different versions.[49] The companions of the Prophet knew these traditions and acted upon them. They are so famous, ᶜAbd al-Jabbār says, that we need not trace back the wording of their transmission, just as we find no need to trace down the textual evidence upon which many forms of prayer and rituals are based. They are taken to constitute a proof of the authoritativeness of consensus although the form of their transmission is not a mutawatir. The purpose of scrutinizing the authenticity of these traditions is to reach an understanding of their true meaning, but if their meaning is already known on the basis of their multiple non-mutawatir transmission, then such a scrutiny becomes superfluous. ᶜAbd al-Jabbār, in answer to his opponent, remarks that it is possible that these ahadi traditions may have existed in the mutawatir fashion at the time of the companions and their successors, but that their transmission has been neglected in later generations. Here, the opponent asks why these traditions, if they were indeed the basis of an authoritative consensus, had been so neglected. ᶜAbd al-Jabbār replies that such a happening was possible because all believers acted upon these traditions and their practice of reaching consensus on points of law was so undisputed that the textual basis authorizing such practice was taken for granted. It has been generally known, he says, that some mutawatir traditions have become ahadi due to the neglect of people to transmit them. An excellent case in point is the undisputed *zakāt* which was grounded in traditions from the mutawatir category, traditions which have now become ahadis.[50] It is on these grounds that the ahadi traditions, relative to consensus, are taken to be authoritative.

In all this the interlocutor sees a contradiction (*tanāquḍ*). If the companions were in agreement on accepting the traditions concerning consensus, this would mean, the interlocutor insists, that the companions reached a consensus on the traditions which were in turn used to justify consensus itself. Such a contradiction can indeed undermine ᶜAbd al-Jabbār's argument. ᶜAbd al-Jabbār, however, explains that the validity of the traditions is not determined by consensus but by custom (*al-ᶜāda al-jāriya*). The companions could not have accepted so unanimously these traditions unless they were certain of their authenticity. It was inconceivable that they all would agree on a tradition which was dubious, as each of them was free to exercise his own independent ijtihad. One knows from the custom in evidence (*al-ᶜāda al-ẓāhira*) that when a tradition was not proven authentic, some of the companions would accept it and some would not. Any tradition which is unanimously accepted must, pursuant to the law of custom, be authentic. It is in this order that ᶜAbd al-Jabbār wishes to drive his argument: authenticity leads to unanimity—consensus does not authenticate traditions but is the result of their authenticity.[51]

The authenticity of traditions is thus guaranteed by custom. Custom, a theological concept already known to Ashᶜarī (d. 330/941), is described as the repeated actions of God which seem to us as a continuous course of events. But in contradistinction with nature, which is always continuous, custom may allow a break in its continuum. From custom we know that the sun will rise tomorrow morning and that there is an inevitable change of seasons throughout the year. Knowledge of many things in this world is derived from custom.[52] For instance, if we are able to observe the sun for an extended period of time we know that after every night there is a day and from this we come to a conclusive knowledge that after this night there will be a day, unless, of course, God suddenly decides that He will change his custom of running things in this manner in the world. This change of custom is an irregularity and is known as *kharq al-ᶜāda* or, as ᶜAbd al-Jabbār calls it, *ikhtilāf al-ᶜāda*. The authenticity of a tradition is known by tracing the history of its transmission and finding that there is no *ikhtilāf* in custom. The occurrence of any irregularity in custom will point to the deficiency of the tradition. The most important factor which determines a sound custom is the repeated transmission of the tradition under normal circumstances (*al-takrār maᶜ salāmat al-aḥwāl*).[53] Custom asserts itself every time a transmitter relays the tradition to an audience, and the more the acts of transmission are repeated the more entrenched and certain our knowledge of the authenticity of the tradition under question will be. Continuity guarantees the knowledge of the Prophetic past.[54] Conversely, knowledge of this tradition ceases once its transmission is halted, a course of action which constitutes kharq al-ᶜada.[55]

ᶜAbd al-Jabbār does not set forth the epistemological principles upon which his argument for authoritativeness is based. He is well aware that consensus is conclusively authoritative (*ḥujja qaṭᶜiyya*), but he does not state whether or not the evidence he advances for its justification is equally certain. His argument is based on Qurʾanic verses and traditions which, although admittedly ahadis, he claims them to have been mutawatir at the time of the companions. Although he goes to great lengths to prove that they are mutawatir through the concept of ʿada, ʿAbd al-Jabbār does not take the hadith evidence to be as important or as strong as that of the Qurʾan. He observes that the strongest among all the pieces of evidence is IV:115, the first verse discussed by him.[56] Thus he finds the Qurʾan to be a stronger basis of authority for consensus than the traditions. In light of the principle, which he must have known, that ambiguous Qurʾanic verses do not lead to certainty, he seems to have considered IV:115 as an unambiguous verse which leads to conclusive knowledge. However, by the epistemological standards prevalent at his own times and even afterwards, the Qurʾanic verses which he cites are not unambiguous, as is evident from the different interpretations given to them by ʿAbd al-Jabbār and his adversary. The innumerable objections of the opponent to ʿAbd al-Jabbār's interpretation demonstrate that the verses are each open to more than one interpretation. An unambiguous verse, as defined by Muslim jurists themselves, is a verse the meaning of which is so clear that it would be incapable of another interpretation. Such a verse yields certain knowledge. On the other hand, ʿAbd al-Jabbār makes recourse to the consensus of the companions to prove that the ahadi traditions which support an authoritative consensus were mutawatir in the first Islamic generation. Believing himself to have succeeded in doing so, he uses the allegedly mutawatir traditions with the Qurʾanic verses as the basis of consensus. But if ʿAbd al-Jabbār was totally convinced that he has succeeded in establishing the tawatur of these traditions, why does he insist that IV:115, a verse commonly regarded as ambiguous, is the strongest piece of evidence which can be adduced in justification of consensus? To this question I can find no answer in ʿAbd al-Jabbār's writings.

Nor is it possible to find an answer in Abū Ḥusayn al-Baṣrī's treatise *al-Muʿtamad fī uṣūl al-fiqh*, which is based on ʿAbd al-Jabbār's usul work *al-ʿAhd.*[57] Baṣrī follows ʿAbd al-Jabbār in accepting some Qurʾanic verses (II:143, III:109, IV:115) while rejecting others (III:103, IV:59). He adopts the argument based on ahadi traditions, but without claiming that at the time of the companions they were mutawatir. The fact of their being ahadis is acknowledged, and Baṣrī does not attempt to change their status. He argues, however, that if one is to base consensus on these traditions only, such consensus would not yield absolute certainty, but will merely be authoritative insofar as action (*ʿamal*) is concerned.[58] Commenting on what seems to have been a contemporary argument that although the aforementioned traditions are ahadis their meaning has been transmitted in the mutawatir fashion (*waʾin nuqila bil-āḥādi faʾinna maʿnāhu manqūlun bil-tawātur*), he says that some of these traditions are not genuine, thus their sum total cannot yield absolute certainty.

Rather characteristic of the arguments of ʿAbd al-Jabbār and Baṣrī is the absence of clear-cut epistemological distinctions with regard to the evidence produced in justification of consensus. Such distinctions were always present in the expositions of Baṣrī's younger contemporaries and their successors. The problem that posed itself once these distinctions came to be included in the stated arguments is that consensus was considered conclusively authoritative (*ḥujja qaṭᶜiyya*), but the textual pieces of evidence relative to its authority were, when taken individually, inconclusive. How, in light of this difficulty, later jurists grappled with the problem of authoritativeness will be shown through analyzing, among other things, the writings of Juwaynī (d. 478/1085), Sarakhsī (d. 483/1101), Ghazālī (d. 505/1111), Āmidī (d. 631/1233), and Shāṭibī (d. 790/1388). *

VI

Juwaynī insists that nothing short of conclusive and certain evidence is acceptable in establishing the authoritativeness of consensus, as consensus itself yields the highest degree of certainty. A principle which leads to certainty must be based on equally certain evidence. In the case of consensus, such evidence must be derived from revelation; rational evidence cannot serve in religious matters.[59] Juwaynī quotes Qurᵓan IV:115 and argues that one of the meanings of "makes a breach with the messenger" is secession from Islam altogether. He remarks that the verse is ambiguous and is capable of more than one interpretation. Similarly, he discards the major tradition "My community shall never agree on an error" on the grounds that it is an ahadi and, like the aforementioned verse, may be subject to at least two interpretations. The first of these interpretations is the infallibility of consensus, and the other is apostasy, viz. that the community shall never agree to apostate until the Day of Judgment.[60] By the same token, he dismisses all other traditions thus far introduced.[61] Against the argument that there is a kind of universal agreement on the acceptability of these ahadi traditions, he cautions, and rightly so, that such an argument would be circular. Consensus, he insists, cannot rest on another consensus. The only admissible evidence is either mutawatir traditions (*ḥadīthun maqṭūᶜun bihi naqlan*) or unambiguous, decisive Qurᵓanic verse, and these, he acknowledges, are lacking.[62]

Since consensus could not be justified by arguments based on rational (non-textual) proof, and since there appeared to be no satisfactory textual evidence, how then could consensus, "the foundation (*ᶜimād*) of the Sharīᶜa," be justified? Juwaynī answers that when consensus is reached on a point of law, it takes one of two forms. The consensus of the first form occurs when the qualified scholars in the far-flung Islamic provinces agree on a zanni legal judgment. Such an agreement of opinions could not be reached on the basis of the jurists' rational (non-textual) reasoning because, although theoretically possible, custom (*mustaqarr al-ᶜāda*) has proved the actual occurrence of such an agreement to be impossible. A consensus on a *sharᶜī* matter on which reason cannot decide cannot be reached without a common cause (*sabab jāmiᶜ*) which leads those who partake in the said consensus to hold the same opinion. Therefore, a total agreement is possible only when the original decision is based on a conclusive text, a text which cannot be the subject of disagreement. For this reason, Juwaynī concludes, when a consensus appears to have been reached on a zanni legal judgment, it must be presumed that such consensus is grounded in indubitable texts.[63]

The consensus of the second form, also reached on a zanni judgment, is authoritative, Juwaynī says, on the grounds that

> we have found that past generations and extinct nations (*al-umam al-munqariḍa*) agreed on reproaching those who violate the consensus of the ulama, the ulama of time immemorial. They have charged all those who diverged (from the mainstream) with disloyalty, apostacy and disobedience. Deviation was never considered a trivial matter. [These nations] viewed the disagreement with the ulama an outright heresy (*ḍalāl*). Thus, consensus on this [i.e., reproaching divergence] amounts to certain knowledge based on rational grounds. If such [consensus] were attached to the consensus reached on an uncertain (*maẓnūn*) legal judgment, then the legal judgment is rendered irrevocably certain (*qaṭᶜ*). Therefore, let consensus on reproaching and reprimanding those who diverge be a legal precept which yields certainty (*qaṭᶜ*).[64]

Now, by "past generations and extinct nations" Juwaynī was not referring to the ancient Muslims only but to all "nations" which preceded Islam. And by "ulama" he meant all the sages and scholars who decided in the religious affairs of these nations. But having said this, Juwaynī seems to have immediately realized that basing the infallibility of consensus on another consensus, however ancient and glorified the earlier consensus may be, does not really solve the problem. For as he already stated, consensus must be grounded in conclusive textual evidence. Grounding consensus in a non-textually based consensus leaves his argument assailable on the grounds that it leads to circularity. Juwaynī had just criticized those who use traditions which are authenticated by consensus to justify consensus. In order to avoid this impasse he hastily adds that it is probable that the consensus of the first Muslim generations was based on the aforementioned traditions (which he just discarded), but that such consensus was continually used and taken so much for granted that Muslims neglected to transmit the traditions which once constituted its unshakable basis of authority.[65]

A close look at this argument reveals that for Juwaynī consensus is not universally authoritative. In both forms of consensus which he distinguishes there is obviously no evident textual basis except for that according to which the legal case is solved and which is presumed to have been originally conclusive. By the law of custom, the principles of which ᶜAbd al-Jabbār had already expounded, Juwaynī claims that the consensus on what seems to be a zanni legal judgment must have been reached on the basis of a presumably qatᶜi text. This alone can explain the existence of an agreement on a sharᶜi rule. In the second form, there is an implicit assumption that the zanni textual basis of the case was originally qatᶜi. But since Juwaynī has already advanced this thesis when dealing with the first form, he goes on to prove that it is in the custom of nations and communities to condemn divergent views and fissiparous tendencies, and thus such a universal consensus must confirm any agreement on a sharᶜi rule. Juwaynī admits that he has no textual evidence to prove this (customary) universal consensus, although he allows for the possibility that traditions from the Prophet to this effect were once in existence but are now lost. His ultimate proof for the validity of both forms of consensus is the principle of custom.

Anything else in his argument is merely presumed. Even if one accepts the validity of custom, it follows that in Juwaynī's theory consensus is not authoritative as a universal principle. "The truth," Juwaynī acknowledges, "*is that consensus in itself is not an authority*. It is inconceivable that those who take part in consensus (*mujmiᶜīn*) can decide a rule [of a case] independently. It must be *presumed* that they discovered something which brought about their consensus."[66]

Juwaynī's concept of consensus is limited in scope. His arguments do not reflect the need, apparent in the writings of his predecessors and contemporaries, to establish the infallibility of the community, the universal guarantee for an authoritative consensus. The infallibility of the community as a general principle is not recognized by Juwaynī.[67] Consensus is valid only when the specific case on which it is reached derives from revelation.

In *al-Munkhūl min Taᶜlīqāt al-Uṣūl*, which he wrote while still under the influence of his teacher Juwaynī, Ghazālī reiterates in his own way the argument as presented by Juwaynī. However, he articulates the first part of the argument to make it somewhat more convincing. He says that if the jurists reach a consensus on what seems to be a zanni legal judgment, this judgment becomes certain because the number of those who participate in consensus is at least equal to the number of transmitters required in the mutawatir transmission. If such consensus is doubted, the reliability of mutawatir traditions, which lead to the highest degree of certitude in law and which are universally accepted, must be doubted as well.[68] Although with this point Ghazālī makes his argument easier to digest, the larger problem of authoritativeness has not yet been solved. What Ghazālī succeeds in proving here is that a consensus on a textually based case of law is authoritative only insofar as that particular case is concerned.

In *al-Mustaṣfā*, which he wrote during the last few years of his life, Ghazālī produced a rather thorough statement concerning consensus. His attitude toward textual evidence now differs drastically from that which he adopted when he was under the influence of Juwaynī. While still dismissing the Qurʾanic evidence as unsatisfactory,[69] he now accepts the traditions which were used by his predecessors to justify consensus. He enumerates 11 traditions, among which is the tradition "My community shall never agree on an error." The rest of the traditions, which are all ahadis, were taken to enjoin Muslims to hold fast to the community, to forewarn fissiparous tendencies, and to restate the infallibility of the community.[70]

But Ghazālī is well aware that ahadi traditions do not lead to the certainty required in consensus. He therefore introduces a principle which, though it was known to his immediate predecessors, he did not use earlier in *al-Mankhūl*. Ghazālī maintains that these traditions, though they are not transmitted arithmetically in the mutawatir fashion, lead to *ᶜilm ḍarūrī* (immediate knowledge)[71] because they are mutawatir in meaning (*bil-maᶜnā*). This means that the transmission of these traditions occurs through a multitude of ahadi channels, and all traditions, though different in wording, convey the same meaning. The Prophet, Ghazālī says, has declared the infallibility of this community by a multitude of explicit statements and intimations which make it necessary for the mind to be certain of such knowledge.[72] Certain knowledge of the authoritativeness of consensus immediately occurs in the mind when the mind becomes acquainted with these traditions. Just as the generosity of the reputable Ḥātim is known without any doubt through the transmission of non-mutawatir reports, so is the authoritativeness of consensus. Ghazālī argues that each of these traditions alone can probably be dubious, but the same cannot be said of all of them as an aggregate. The support which each tradition gains from the others makes it improbable that all of them together are doubtful. Thus, like the mutawatir, these traditions as a whole lead to certainty.[73]

Ghazālī then goes on to establish the meaning of the tradition "My community shall never agree on an error." He lists three objections made by the opponent concerning the interpretation of the tradition and then he refutes them. While it is the contention of the opponent that "error" (*ḍalāla*, *khaṭaᵓ*) means disbelief and heresy, thus depleting the tradition by confining the role of consensus to a mere safeguard against heresy, Ghazālī interprets "error" in the general sense of a mistake.[74] He refers to two Qurᵓanic verses in which the term *ḍalāl* was used in this latter sense. From the vast bulk of textual evidence, Ghazālī insists, one necessarily understands (*fuhima ḍarūratan*) that because individual Muslims are fallible, God has bestowed on his community as a whole the quality of infallibility (*ᶜiṣma*), which the Prophet had also enjoyed. Other opponents concede that the meaning of khataᵓ and dalal is a mistake, but they argue that the verse is not universal in meaning and does not guarantee infallibility in all spheres of religious life. What is meant here, they say, is that the community does not err in such matters as testifying on the Day of Judgment and in transmitting the mutawatir traditions. But Ghazālī rejects this interpretation on the grounds that no one in the community has held such exegetical views; the limitation of the meaning of "mistake" is unjustifiable.

The third and final objection concerns the meaning of "community." The opponent claims that by "community" the Prophet meant all the generations of his "nation" from his time until the Day of Judgment. Against this Ghazālī retorts that just as insane people and small children are not counted among the (capacitated) members of the religious community, people who died and who are yet unborn cannot be considered as part of the (present) community. By community, therefore, is meant the living generation of Muslims. In short, Ghazālī, like any other Sunni jurist, accepted the standard meaning of the tradition as guaranteeing the infallibility of the community. It is significant to note here that no comprehensive interpretation of the traditions concerned was attempted by any Sunni jurist. Most of the usulists who dealt with the problem seem to have assumed that the meaning of these traditions is sufficiently clear so as to require no thoroughgoing interpretation. In establishing the meaning of the tradition "My community shall never agree on an error" Ghazālī was chiefly responding to the onslaught of the adversary. It may have been the case that since these traditions differed only slightly in the manner they were expressed it was assumed that the elucidation of the fundamental terms employed in the major tradition commented upon by Ghazālī should suffice to establish the general meaning of the others. In any case, the agreement among scholars upon the meaning of the traditions must not be taken to imply that such agreement constitutes in effect a consensus on the infallibility of consensus. Usulists make it abundantly clear that the meaning of legal propositions is determined by the standard rules of the Arabic language, rules which are normally expounded in the opening chapters of works on usul al-fiqh.

In addition to these arguments Ghazālī goes about proving the authoritativeness of consensus by means of what he calls rational demonstration (*istidlāl*). Referring to the traditions which he quoted, he says that they have been famous since the time of the companions and except for Naẓẓām, whose opinion does not count, no one has cast doubt with regard to using them to prove the authoritativeness of consensus. It is inconceivable that many consecutive generations of Muslims should accept a principle if it has no sound basis, especially that Muslims differed among themselves on many issues, particularly those issues based on ahadi traditions. In other words, what Ghazālī is saying here is that if the principle of consensus were based on less than satisfactory traditions it would have been swept away by the opposition of Muslims. But the fact that consensus was so important a doctrine and that it was met with overwhelming approval is evidence that it must have been based on solid grounds.[75] One knows of the existence of such approval from the lack of contrary evidence; that is, from the absence of opposition. Ghazālī maintains that when Naẓẓām, the first figure in Islam to question and reject the authoritativeness of consensus, voiced his opposition the community immediately knew of it, and that if there had been other voices, especially among those who were qualified enough to be taken into account, they would have been heard. Ghazālī thinks that if Naẓẓām, whom the community did not regard with high esteem, was noticed, other important figures would have been certainly noticed had they cast doubt on the authoritativeness of consensus.

Against the accusation that the authority of consensus is based on traditions which are authenticated by consensus, Ghazālī retorts that the authenticity of traditions is known by the absence of opposition to them, something which is in turn known through ᶜada, custom. As applied to this argument, Ghazālī's concept of custom does not differ from that of ᶜAbd al-Jabbār. Ghazālī insists that through ᶜada one knows, for instance, that the opposition to the Qurᵓan did not succeed and that the report about the Prophet appointing ᶜAlī as caliph is spurious. The course of events would have been different had the opposition to the Qurᵓan succeeded or had the appointment of ᶜAlī been genuine. The acceptability of the traditions in question became, as Ghazālī conceived of it, a "habit" of nature and any break in this "habit" would constitute a break in the ongoing custom (*kharq al-ᶜāda*). This is why he viewed the opposition of Naẓẓām to the textual basis of consensus to be so significant, because had Naẓẓām's opinion been admissible in Sunni Islam, his opposition would have constituted a breach of what Muslims conceived to be a consistent course of events.

Like Juwaynī and particularly ᶜAbd al-Jabbār, Ghazālī utilizes the concept of custom to prove the existence of (presumed) decisive textual evidence in favor of an authoritative consensus in the early period of Islam. He says that when the companions agree on a certain issue, their agreement must be presumed to have been based on a conclusive text, for through the law of custom one knows that such unanimity on a dubious text cannot take place. Thus, the disapproval of the companions and their successors on the matter of divergence from the community must have been based on a revelation which was certain.

The change or development of Ghazālī's views as shown in *al-Mankhūl* and *al-Mustaṣfā* is quite significant. Though his concept of custom and the use made thereof in the latter work are somewhat different from that presented in the former, the fundamental idea remains the same. In fact, the discourse on the notion of custom in ᶜAbd al-Jabbār, Juwaynī, and Ghazālī are variations on the same theme. The more significant point in Ghazālī is his acceptance of the notion of al-tawatur bil-maᶜna, which seems to have become by his time one of the most central arguments advanced in support of an authoritative consensus. The centrality of this notion appears most clearly in the *Uṣūl* of Sarakhsī.

Sharakhsī's argument is based on the Qurᵓan and the Sunna. From the Qurᵓan he cites II:143, III:110, and IV:115. Like ᶜAbd al-Jabbār, he does not point out the weight of the verses in the overall proof for establishing the authoritativeness of consensus. After giving the standard interpretation of the verses he moves on to the Sunna, which, he says, contains abundant and well-known traditions (*mustafīḍa mashhūra*). He lists a number of traditions concerning the infallibility of the community and argues that traditions supporting this point are numerous and mutawatir. The claim for tawatur, he says, derives from the fact that each transmitter heard a tradition to this effect and related it without anyone doubting the truthfulness of the tradition. A multiplicity of traditions transmitted under these conditions must be considered to be on par with the mutawatir (*fadhālika bimanzilati al-tawātur*).[76] Although Sarakhsī does not mention the expression "tawatur bil-maᶜna," it is abundantly clear that he meant this type of tawatur rather than *al-tawātur al-lafẓī*. A rather similar argument is also advanced by al-Khaṭīb al-Baghdādī (d. 463/1070), who explicitly states that *al-tawātur min ṭarīq al-maᶜnā* leads not only to certainty in law in general but also to a conclusively authoritative consensus.[77]

VII

* Toward the end of the sixth/twelfth century or the beginning of the seventh/thirteenth, Sayf al-Dīn al-Āmidī (d. 631/1233), in a rather exhaustive statement on the problem of authoritativeness, elaborated and recapitulated the arguments as they had been developed by Sunni jurists up to his time. In his exposition we find a well-arranged reformulation of the totality of arguments which were presented in the earlier works in a fragmented manner. Āmidī divides his arguments into three types: the first is an argument from the Book, the second from the Sunna, and the third is a rational argument.

In support of the authoritativeness of consensus, Āmidī first cites five Qurᵓanic verses (II:143, III:103, III:110, IV:59, IV:115), all of which have been quoted above. He devotes a dozen pages to the interpretation of these verses and to the refutation of the adversary's claim that the meaning of these verses does not point to the infallibility of the community.[78] But after Āmidī had undertaken the arduous and prolonged task of showing what he believed to be the true meaning of the verses,[79] he remarks that the totality of these verses does not lead to certain knowledge which is required in consensus. But he soon adds that the Sunna is the surest way to prove beyond doubt the conclusive authoritativeness of consensus.[80] He introduces 16 traditions,[81] and although he admits that they are all ahadis, he argues, like Ghazālī, that they lead to certain knowledge because they are mutawatira bil-maᶜna.[82] With an ahadi tradition, certain knowledge occurs when the tradition is supported by *qarāᵓin*, that is, circumstantial evidence including other traditions handed down through various and unconnected channels of transmission or various types of Qurᵓanic verses. Āmidī gives a non-textual example of qaraᵓin: If a man looks often at a beautiful woman we would think (*naẓunn*) that the man is in love with this woman. But if we also know that he stays in her company we gain more, but still inconclusive knowledge (*zāda ẓannunā*) about his love for her. If we know other facts, such as the fact that he buys her many gifts, treats her kindly, and that psychological and behavioral changes occur to him, etc., we conclude that he is certainly in love with her.[83] By the same token, we gain certain and immediate knowledge (*ᶜilm ḍarūrī*), on the basis of a multitude of traditions which are mutually enhanced, that consensus is authoritative.[84] This is despite the fact that each tradition can separately be false (*yataṭarraqu ilayhi al-kadhib*). However, Āmidī adds, the totality of these traditions yields immediate knowledge in the mind of any man of sound reason.

As to the rest of his argument concerning the hadith basis of consensus, Āmidī follows in the footsteps of Ghazālī. He argues that had consensus been based on questionable grounds it would not have been so unanimously approved and supported throughout numerous generations, and had there been any opposition to these traditions or to consensus itself, it would have been immediately known, just as the objections of the infamous Naẓẓām became known. Āmidī also follows the same outlines of Ghazālī's argument with regard to custom as the means by which traditions are authenticated, thus avoiding a circular argument.

What Āmidī designates as a rational argument is essentially an elaboration of Juwaynī's argument which he based on the notion of custom and which Ghazālī subsequently refined. The main point advanced is that when we observe that the scholars of an earlier generation are unanimously agreed on a legal judgment, that judgment must be presumed to have been based on a conclusive textual evidence. This is so because the number of those who agree in the community is equal to, or larger than, the number of transmitters of a mutawatir tradition. From the law of custom, as previously noted, we know that it is impossible for a vast (mutawatir) number to agree on a falsehood or a forgery. However, Āmidī hastens to add that in order to consider such a consensus authoritative, some scholars require the number of those who participate in consensus to be at least equal to that constituting the mutawatir.

The question that may be asked here is why Āmidī introduces this rational argument and, before that, the indecisive Qurᵓanic evidence, if he knows that both arguments are inconclusive? An answer to this question requires reference to the logical principle which he, and Ghazālī before him, brought into play when discussing the question of al-tawatur bil-maᶜna. Though the Qurᵓanic evidence and the rational argument do not conclusively prove the authoritativeness of consensus, they nonetheless function as qaraᵓin, that is, as circumstantial pieces of evidence which, as an aggregate of testimonies, enhance his argument based on traditions. As we are able to gather from later sources (some of which will be discussed below), Āmidī seemingly saw the Qurᵓanic and rational evidence, notwithstanding its weakness, as a supportive proof, just like the kind of proof a single ahadi tradition would offer.

This principle of cumulative or aggregate evidence, still nebulous in the writings of jurists of the fifth/eleventh and sixth/twelfth centuries,[85] was articulated to a large extent by the illustrious Abū Isḥāq al-Shāṭibī (d. 790/1388). In his work *al-Muwāfaqāt fī uṣūl al-aḥkām*, he explicitly states that the "roots" of law, including consensus, are decisive, certain (qatᶜiyya), and infallible (*maᶜṣūma*),[86] because they are founded on conclusive premises (*muqaddimāt qaṭᶜiyya*). The most important source of knowledge which he reckons to be the font of law is that which is based on tawatur, both lafzi and maᶜnawi, as well as induction from the religious texts, *al-istiqrāᵓ fī mawārid al-sharīᶜa*.[87] Shāṭibī argues that induction leads to certainty because in the context of the Shariᶜa one can obtain a complete enumeration of the instances pertaining to a certain issue. In other words, it is possible, Shāṭibī insists, to have a complete induction (*istiqrāᵓ tāmm* or *kullī*), because the subject matter of the Qurᵓan and the Sunna is finite and can thus be exhausted. Because earlier jurists misunderstood this fundamental logical principle, Shāṭibī argues, some jurists thought that consensus itself was zanni. But this is not true, he says, because the cumulative evidence from the two primary sources render consensus certain.[88] Most legal (textual) evidence does not lead to certainty if it is not supported by other pieces of evidence. If the complete aggregation of this evidence is pronounced unacceptable, it would then be impossible to arrive at certainty in law. What Shāṭibī is saying here is that the nature of the Shariᶜa requires a reliance on such inductive principles, for it is the only available means to reach a kind of certainty.[89]

> The recognized evidence here [i.e., in law] is that which is reached through induction from a totality of uncertain (zanni) pieces of evidence which in their multitude support one meaning so much that they result in certainty (qatᶜi); for confluence brings about a strength which disjunction lacks. For this reason the tawatur results in certainty, for it is a variety of induction . . . and this (tawatur) resembles al-tawatur al-maᶜnawi.[90]

The authoritativeness of consensus, Shāṭibī concludes, squarely rests on this principle.

It may be relevant here to note that a century before Shāṭibī, Shihāb al-Dīn al-Qarāfī (d. 684/1285) set forth a number of Qurᵓanic verses and traditions and argued, albeit rather succinctly, that on the basis of the stated textual evidence and through the application of the method of complete induction it is known beyond any doubt that the consensus of the *umma* is authoritative and infallible.[91]

After an examination of the theories of Ghazālī, Āmidī, and Shāṭibī, there remains little doubt that it was primarily the concept of custom and the method of complete induction on the basis of ahadi traditions and equivocal Qur^ↄanic verses (and rational arguments thereof) which were responsible for establishing the authoritativeness of consensus and for saving the Sunni jurists from falling into the trap of circularity. While the great majority of later usulists formulated and presented their arguments each in his own way, the major points which were argued remained essentially the same as those presented by Ghazālī, Āmidī, and Shāṭibī. Of those jurists who dealt with this subject, we need only mention Isnawī (d. 772/1370),[92] Ibn al-Humām (d. 861/1456) and his commentator Ibn Amīr al-Hājj (d. 879/1474),[93] and Anṣārī (d. 1119/1707) and his commentator Ibn ᶜAbd al-Shakūr (d. 1225/1810).[94]

To illustrate how later jurists dealt with the problem of authoritativeness it must suffice here to discuss briefly the arguments of Anṣārī and Ibn ᶜAbd al-Shakūr. They first state that consensus is definitely authoritative and leads to certain knowledge (*al-ᶜilm al-jāzim*). The basis of its authority is the mutawatir texts whose authenticity is known through custom.[95] The law of custom would have made it impossible for all the companions of the Prophet to agree on any matter including the reprehension of those who diverged from their beliefs and practices, unless they knew about a conclusive and unambiguous text (*naṣṣ qāṭiᶜ*) prohibiting dissent and enjoining solidarity. The unqualified acceptance of consensus as a conclusively authoritative principle was brought about by the fact that the number of the companions and the successors (*al-tābiᶜūn*) who must have adopted consensus on textual grounds was at least equal to the number required in the mutawatir category.[96] Such an acceptance was also brought about by concrete mutawatir texts. But before dealing with these texts Anṣārī and Ibn ᶜAbd al-Shakūr cite Qurʾan IV:115 and II:143 and conclude that although these verses can be adduced in justification of consensus, they are indecisive and thus cannot yield certainty. The texts which bring about certainty are the traditions of the Prophet to the effect that the community is infallible (*maᶜṣūma*). These traditions are mutawatir bil-maᶜna; the number and the fashion in which all these traditions were transmitted is identical to that of the mutawatir. The difference, however, is in the text of the traditions. The theme of the infallibility of the community was expressed in each of these traditions in different words, whereas in a mutawatir lafzi tradition the language is the same in all channels of transmission. The question as to how one can know that these traditions lead to a certain knowledge of the infallibility of the community is answered by Ibn ᶜAbd al-Shakūr when he says that the common meaning of their sum total (*al-qadr al-mushtarak*), known by means of an inductive survey of the historical reports and events (*muṭālaᶜat al-akhbār wal-waqāʾiᶜ*) concerning the infallibility of the consensus of the community, leads to such certain knowledge. An inductive survey can yield corroborative evidence, such as the practice of the companions (on the basis of a presumed text) of reprehending those who would diverge from the accepted norm, which further proves the authoritativeness of consensus.[97]

VIII

While formulating their theories the Sunni jurists were acutely aware of the danger of falling into logical contradictions. Most usulists writing after the fourth/tenth century consciously strove to avoid what they called dawr, that is, *petitio principii*. As we have seen in the theories of Āmidī and Ghazālī, and as later emphasized by Ibn al-Humām, Anṣārī, and others, dawr was avoided by arguing that traditions, the major scriptural basis which had been advanced in justification of consensus, were authenticated by ᶜada rather than by consensus. By the same token, they paid careful attention not to fall into a trap when discussing the doctrine of abrogation (*naskh*). Insofar as this doctrine pertained to consensus, it was held by all Sunni jurists that consensus cannot be abrogated by the Qurᵓan and the Sunna nor can it abrogate either of them.[98] The reason for this is that consensus was recognized to be an operative doctrine only after the death of the Prophet when revelation had ceased (*baᶜda inqiṭāᶜi al-waḥy*). During the life of the Prophet consensus was of course unnecessary, because the Prophet was the ultimate source of revelation and he was not in need of the approval of his companions. But after his death, consensus, claimed the jurists, became indispensable because it was the only means through which certainty about any matter could be reached. Thus, consensus could not abrogate the Qurᵓan and the Sunna because it became operative only after the revelation was completed, and any act of abrogation by consensus would have undoubtedly meant that consensus was concluded on a judgment (*ḥukm*) contrary to, or to say the least, different from, that which was decreed in the two divine sources. It is partly for this reason and partly because consensus chronologically occurred after revelation that the Qurᵓan and the Sunna cannot abrogate consensus.[99]

This doctrine of abrogation not only is in consonance with the arguments adduced to establish the authoritativeness of consensus but is also used by such later scholars as Mullā Khusraw (d. 885/1480) and Izmīrī (d. 1166/1752) to further argue, *ex post facto*, on rational grounds in favor of authoritativeness. They maintain that consensus, which rests on mutawatira bil-maᶜna traditions which in turn are authenticated by custom, is infallible and thus irrepealable, whereas even the strongest Qurᵓanic verses or traditions can be subject to abrogation by each other. This universally acknowledged doctrine proves that consensus can take precedence over the two sources in the sense that consensus leads to more certainty and is less susceptible to revocation than these two sources. Because of this fact, they reason, the authoritativeness of consensus must be recognized.[100] It is to be noted that Mullā Khusraw and Izmīrī are aware of the fact that consensus cannot repeal verses from the Qurᵓan or hadiths from the Sunna. Their conclusion that consensus takes precedence over the texts must be understood only in relation to the degree of certitude yielded rather than to the competence to abrogate.

IX

From the foregoing discussion a certain pattern of development in the arguments adduced in justification of consensus can be detected. Shāfiʿī, viewing consensus as a sanctioning instrument rather than a sharʿi source of law, found it sufficient to argue on grounds of a Qurʾanic verse and two Prophetic traditions. Later jurists, however, elevated consensus to the status of a source of law, a source which has the authority of clothing legal rules with the mantle of certainty. This new role of consensus called for a set of arguments which were different from, and perhaps superior to, the arguments adduced by Shāfiʿī. Obviously, it was impossible for jurists to produce mutawatir traditions or decisive Qurʾanic verses to this effect. The problem that posed itself now was related to the type of evidence that must be produced in justification of a principle which leads to certain knowledge.

Muslim jurists utilized three concepts in their endeavor to establish the conclusive authoritativeness of consensus. These were the concept of al-tawatur bil-maʿna, induction, and the originally theological concept of custom. In the early period, the use of one concept did not chronologically coincide with or entail the use of the others. It seems that the notion of custom came to the fore sometime before al-tawatur bil-maʿna, as is clear from the writings of ʿAbd al-Jabbār and Abū Ḥusayn al-Baṣrī. The former knew of al-tawatur bil-maʿna as not an altogether well-defined and important concept; one which he considered to be less important than Qurʾan IV:115. That Baṣrī rejected this type of tawatur and instead relied, as his predecessors did, on the Qurʾan and custom to prove the authoritativeness of consensus is indicative of the fact that al-tawatur bil-maʿna had not yet been established as a concept of central importance. This fact is also confirmed by the absence of this concept in the theory of Juwaynī and the young Ghazālī.

Later, however, Ghazālī argued for authoritativeness on the basis of mutawatir bil-maʿna traditions which are authenticated by custom. This line of argumentation came to be a standard formulation in the expositions of jurists. Two or three centuries after Ghazālī, jurists, such as Shāṭibī and Qarāfī, introduced inductive methods of reasoning, thereby giving the argument for consensus a decisive edge. But in Ghazālī's time the role of induction does not seem to have been fully appreciated. This can be seen in Ghazālī's manner of treating the potential evidence in favor of an authoritative consensus. There is nothing in what he said to indicate that his argument by "rational demonstration" was intended to give inductive support to the argument of al-tawatur bil-maʿna. Nor was the Qurʾanic evidence used for such purposes. Āmidī, on the other hand, was somewhat aware of the importance of the multiplicity of evidence. This is why he expounded virtually every argument and all the pieces of evidence of which he was aware. In this he may be said to have anticipated the articulate theories of Qarāfī and Shāṭibī. The latter maintained that all pieces of evidence, whether traditions, verses, or other types of argument, must be taken into account because each additional piece of evidence enhances, by means of inductive support, the argument for authoritativeness. He argued that through the complete enumeration of such evidence certain knowledge can be reached with regard to consensus as an authoritative doctrine.[101]

With the theory of Shāṭibī, the Sunni argumentation for authoritative consensus seems to have come full circle. Jurists after Shāṭibī seem to have confined themselves to reformulating and rediscussing what their predecessors had said, with, however, one addition. This is an argument (made by Mullā Khusraw and Izmīrī, among others) which proves from the point of view of certitude the superiority of consensus to the Qurʾan and the Sunna. It cannot be contended, however, that this argument leads to a *petitio principii* or that it makes consensus appear absurd for being superior to the sources from which it derives its own authority because this argument is advanced with the knowledge that (1) the authoritativeness of consensus must, as a prerequisite, be established by the texts, and (2) that consensus can by no means abrogate either the Qurʾan or the Sunna.

Given that we accept as true premises whatever the mainstream Muslim scholarship designates as propositions—and we have no right to do otherwise—there is nothing in the theories of jurists after Juwaynī to indicate that their arguments for proving the authoritativeness of consensus were less than convincing, whether we view them from the standpoint of logic, law, or theology.

NOTES

Author's note: This is a revised version of a paper presented at the Eighteenth Annual Meeting of the Middle East Studies Association, San Francisco, November 28–December 1, 1984.

[1]Writers on legal theory (*uṣūl al-fiqh*) disagreed upon the question of who counts in consensus. A commonly held view, however, was that on general issues the community, the *umma*, can reach a consensus, but on technical and specialized points of law only qualified jurists, the *mujtahid*s, count. See Abū Ḥāmid al-Ghazālī, *al-Mustaṣfā min ʿilm al-uṣūl*, 2 vols. (Cairo, 1322 H.), vol. I, p. 181 ff.; al-Khaṭīb al-Baghdādī, *al-Faqīh wal-mutafaqqih*, 2 vols. (Beirut, 1975), vol. I, p. 172.

[2]The definition of qiyas differs from one jurist to another. Thus one may find that in addition to analogy, qiyas encompasses *reductio ad absurdum*, *a fortiori* arguments, deduction, and induction. On the role of deduction in law see Hasan Abdel-Rahman, "La place du syllogisme juridique dans la méthode exégétique chez Gazali," in H. Hubien, ed., *Le raisonnement juridique* (Brussels, 1971), pp. 185–194. On the use of these arguments see my forthcoming articles, "The Logic of Legal Reasoning in Religious and Non-Religious Cultures: The Case of Islamic Law and Common Law," *Cleveland State Law Review*, and "Non-Analogical Arguments in Sunni Juridical *Qiyās*." Also: Abū Ḥāmid al-Ghazālī, *Miʿyār al-ʿilm fī fann al-manṭiq* (Beirut, 1964), pp. 32–33, 113–137, 154, 182 ff.; Abū al-Ḥusayn al-Baṣrī, *Kitāb al-qiyās al-sharʿī*, printed with *al-Muʿtamad fī uṣūl al-fiqh*, ed. Muhammad Hamidullah et al., 2 vols. (Damas, 1964–65), vol. II, p. 1031; Muḥammad b. ʿAlī al-Shawkānī, *Irshād al-fuḥūl ilā taḥqīq al-ḥaqq min ʿilm al-uṣūl* (Cairo, 1909), p. 198.

[3]Abū Isḥāq al-Shīrāzī, *al-Lumaʿ fī uṣūl al-fiqh* (Cairo, 1326 H.), pp. 56–58; Abū al-Walīd Muḥammad Ibn Rushd, *Bidāyat al-mujtahid*, 2 vols. (Cairo, 1974), vol. I, p. 6. The great majority of jurists upheld the infallibility of the community and, consequently, the conclusive certainty of consensus. See Jamāl al-Dīn al-Isnawī, *Nihāyat al-sūl fī sharḥ minhāj al-wuṣūl*, a commentary on Bayḍāwī's *Minhāj al-wuṣūl ilā ʿilm al-uṣūl*, 3 vols. (Cairo, 1316 H.), vol. II, pp. 166–167; Muḥammad b. ʿAlī al-Shawkānī, *Irshād al-fuḥūl*, pp. 78–79.

[4]See, for instance, the argument of M. M. Bravmann, *The Spiritual Background of Early Islam* (Leiden, 1972), pp. 194–198. See further below.

[5]Most noteworthy of the sectarian critics of consensus are the Rāfiḍa (Imāmiya) of the early Shīᶜa, the Ismāᶜiliyya and the Muᶜtazilī scholar Ibrāhīm al-Naẓẓām (d. between 220/835 and 231/845). See Imām al-Ḥaramayn al-Juwaynī, *al-Burhān fī uṣūl al-fiqh*, ed. ᶜAbd al-ᶜAẓīm Dīb, 2 vols. (Cairo, 1979), vol. I, p. 676; Baghdādī, *Faqīh*, vol. I, p. 154; Sayf al-Dīn al-Āmidī, *al-Iḥkām fī uṣūl al-aḥkām*, 3 vols. (Cairo, 1968), vol. I, p. 166. For the criticism of the later Fāṭimī scholar al-Qāḍī al-Nuᶜmān, see his *Ikhtilāf uṣūl al-madhāhib*, ed. S. T. Lokhandwalla (Simla, 1972), pp. 56–115. Cf. Marie Bernand, "L'iğmāᶜ chez ᶜAbd al-Ğabbār et l'objection d'an-Naẓẓām," *Studia Islamica*, 30 (1969), 34 ff. who questions the later accounts attributing to Naẓẓām his position against consensus.

[6]Cf. Camille Mansour, *L'autorité dans la pensée musulmane* (Paris, 1975), pp. 60 ff.

[7]C. Snouck Hurgronje, "The 'Foundations' of Islamic Law," in *Selected Works*, eds. G.-H. Bousquet and J. Schacht (Leiden, 1975), p. 275.

[8]Ibid., p. 276.

[9]Hurgronje, "Sur la nature du 'droit' Musulmane," in *Selected Works*, ibid., p. 227; trans. cited from G. Hourani, "The Basis of Authority of Sunni Consensus," *Studia Islamica*, 21 (1964), 51–52.

[10]Hurgronje, "The 'Foundations'," p. 289.

[11]Idem, "Nature du 'droit'," p. 226.

[12]N. J. Coulson, *A History of Islamic Law* (Edinburgh, 1964), p. 77.

[13]Joseph Schacht, *The Origins of Muhammadan Jurisprudence* (Oxford, 1950), pp. 2, 94, 135.

[14]Hourani, "The Basis of Authority," pp. 13–60, especially pp. 49–54.

[15]Ibid., pp. 14–15: "Thus no assumption is being made at all that consensus is an essential part of Islam, *nor even that Traditions of the Prophet are so*, though they will be considered seriously." (Italics are mine.)

[16]Ibid., p. 59.

[17]Ibn Ḥazm, *al-Iḥkām fī uṣūl al-aḥkām*, 2 vols. (Cairo, 1978), vol. I, p. 12. See also Juwaynī, *Burhān*, vol. II, p. 152.

[18]Ibn Ḥazm, *Iḥkām*, vol. I, pp. 11, 108. On Qurᵓanic verses and hadith asserting that the Sunna is part of revelation see Baghdādī, *Faqīh*, vol. I, pp. 90 ff., 94; Ibn Idrīs al-Shāfiᶜī, *al-Risāla*, ed. M. S. Kīlānī (Cairo, 1969), par. 236–257; Abū ᶜAlī al-Fārisī, *Jawāhir al-uṣūl fī ᶜilm ḥadīth al-rasūl* (Madina, 1973), p. 4.

[19]Ibn Baṭṭa, *Kitāb al-sharḥ wal-ibāna ᶜalā uṣūl al-Sunna wal-diyāna*,ed. and trans. H. Laoust (Damascus, 1958), pp. 56 ff. (Arabic text).

[20]Ibn Ḥazm, *Iḥkām*, vol. I, p. 318.

[21]The *mutawātir* traditions are transmitted by countless persons who hear or see the Prophet say or do a certain thing and, at each stage of transmission, the tradition is also transmitted by countless persons. The large number of transmitters makes it inconceivable that the witnesses or the transmitters could have agreed on falsifying the report. Because of the authenticity of such a report and the certitude surrounding its transmission, the mutawatir traditions are said to lead to certain knowledge of what they contain. Traditions transmitted by fewer people than those who have witnessed and transmitted the mutawatir traditions are considered ahadi, which do not lead to certain knowledge of the information they convey. Later jurists and theologians distinguished a third type of tradition which they termed *mustafīḍ*. This type stands in the middle between the mutawatir and the ahadi. See Ibn Khalaf al-Bājī, *Kitāb al-ḥudūd fī al-uṣūl*, ed. N. Ḥammād (Beirut, 1973), p. 62; ᶜAbd al-Qāhir al-Baghdādī, *Uṣūl al-dīn* (Beirut, 1928), p. 12.

[22]I. Goldziher, *Muslim Studies*, ed. S. M. Stern, trans. C. R. Barber and S. M. Stern (New York, 1971), vol. II, p. 25; Bravmann, *Spiritual Background*, p. 197; Fazlur Rahman, *Islamic Methodology in History* (Karachi, 1965), pp. 18, 19.

[23]Rahman, *Islamic Methodology*, p. 19.

[24]The Arabic: "*Mā raᵓūhu al-muᵓminūna ḥasanan fahuwa ᶜinda Allāhi ḥasanun wamā raᵓūhu al-muslimūna qabīḥan fahuwa ᶜinda Allāhi qabīḥ*." This is also in line with the statement attributed to Ibn ᶜAbbās: "If you hear from me a saying in the name of the Prophet and you find that it does not agree with the book of God or is not liked by people (*falam tajidūhu ḥasanan ᶜinda al-nāsi*), know that I have reported a lie about the Prophet." Goldziher, *Muslim Studies*, p. 133; Schacht, *Origins*, p. 86.

[25]For the intellectual formulations of the later period (sixth–seventh/twelfth–thirteenth century) see Bernard Weiss, "The Primacy of Revelation in Classical Islamic Legal Theory as Expounded by Sayf al-Din al-Amidi," *Studia Islamica*, 59 (1984), 79–109.

[26]Norman Calder, "Ikhtilaf and Ijmaʿ in Shafiʿi's Risala," *Studia Islamica*, 58 (1984), 76–77.

[27]Ibid., pp. 77–78; Shāfiʿī, *Risāla*, par. 1328–1332, especially 1331.

[28]Cited in Schacht, *Origins*, p. 92, from *Kitāb ikhtilāf Mālik wal-Shāfiʿī.*

[29]Shāfiʿī, *Risāla*, par. 1312.

[30]Ibid., par. 252–257, 266, 1329, passim.

[31]Ibid., par. 266.

[32]Ibid., par. 1102.

[33]Ibid., par. 1315.

[34]Shāfiʿī's reference to this verse is mentioned in the much later works of Aḥmad b. al-Ḥusayn al-Bayhaqī (d. 458/1065), *Aḥkām al-Qurʾān*, 2 vols. (Beirut, 1975), vol. I, p. 39, also p. 32, and the biographical work of Tāj al-Dīn al-Subkī (d. 771/1369), *Ṭabaqāt al-Shāfīʿiyya al-Kubrā*, 6 vols. (Cairo, 1906), vol. II, p. 19. See also I. Goldziher, *Introduction to Islamic Theology and Law*, trans. Andras and Ruth Hamori (Princeton, 1981), p. 51. Schacht, *Origins*, pp. 90, 91, does not seem to have found the verse in any of Shāfiʿī's discussions on the authority of consensus. Further on this point see Abdel-Magid Turki, "L'ijmaʿ Ummat al-muʾminin entre la doctrine et l'histoire," *Studia Islamica*, 59 (1984), 60 (n. 1)–63, 70 (n. 1)–71.

[35]Shāfiʿī, *Risāla*, par. 1319–1320.

[36]Shawkānī, *Irshād*, p. 71 (line 24); "Consensus is the agreement of the mujtahids of the community of Muhammad . . . on a certain matter in a certain age (*Ittifāqu mujtahidī ummati muḥammadin . . . fī ʿaṣrin min al-aʿṣāri ʿalā amrin min al-umūr*)."

[37]Unfortunately, the parts of Jaṣṣāṣ's *Uṣūl al-fiqh* which deal with consensus are still in manuscript and are not available to me. Here I draw on the quotations and discussion found in A. Hasan, *The Doctrine of Ijmaʿ in Islam* (Islamabad, 1976), pp. 40 ff. Hasan used Ms. 229-Usul, Dār al-Kutub al-Miṣriyya, Cairo. My analysis of Jaṣṣāṣ's theory will go as far as the material quoted by Hasan will allow.

[38]These traditions are: (1) "My community shall never agree on an error"; (2) "The hand of God is with the community"; (3) "A section of my community will continue to follow the truth"; (4) "Whoever separates himself from the Muslim community even a span, throws away the tie of Islam from his neck"; (5) Ḥudhayfa is reported to have asked the Prophet: "What can save me from it [schism]?" whereupon he replied: "The community of Muslims and their leader."

[39]Al-Qāḍī al-Nuʿmān, *Ikhtilāf*, pp. 56–58, 77 ff.

[40]ʿAbd al-Jabbār, *Mughnī fī abwāb al-tawḥīd wal-ʿadl*, ed. Amīn al-Khūlī (Cairo, 1963), vol. XVII, p. 212. See also Bernand, "L'ijmaʿ chez ʿAbd al-Ǧabbar," pp. 27 ff.

[41]ʿAbd al-Jabbār, vol. XVII, pp. 199, 206.

[42]Ibid., p. 160; "*liʾannahum law lam yakūnū ḥujjatan lam yajib dhālika fīhim.*"

[43]Ibid., p. 164 (line 2). It is rather difficult to square "rational evidence" in this context, as this runs in diametrical opposition to ʿAbd al-Jabbār's argument as it has thus far been outlined.

[44]Ibid., pp. 165–167.

[45]Ibid., p. 170.

[46]Ibid., pp. 196–203.

[47]Ibid., pp. 171 ff., 178.

[48]Ibid., pp. 172–175.

[49]Ibid., pp. 180–181. Samples of these versions have already been given by Shāfiʿī and Jaṣṣāṣ.

[50]Ibid., pp. 182–185.

[51]Ibid., pp. 186–188, 190. It must be noted in this context that the meaning of certain passages is difficult to make out. Evidently there are gaps in the texts which have not been pointed out by the editor. Confusion can also be detected in the attribution of the arguments to their proponents; i.e., the roles of the interlocutor and ʿAbd al-Jabbar are sometimes switched. See, e.g., p. 186, lines 13, 18.

[52]On the concept of ʿada see H. Wolfson, *The Philosophy of the Kalam* (Cambridge, 1976), pp. 544–551. A highly elaborate treatment of ʿada can be found in volume XV of ʿAbd al-Jabbār's *Mughnī* (*On Prophecies and Miracles*), pp. 335–382, especially pp. 337, 346 ff., 368 ff.

[53]ʿAbd al-Jabbār, *Mughnī*, vol. XV, p. 353.

[54]John Wansbrough, *The Sectarian Milieu* (Oxford, 1978), pp. 81 ff.

[55]ʿAbd al-Jabbār, *Mughnī*, vol. XV, pp. 354–355.

[56]Ibid., vol. XVII, p. 203.

[57]Baṣrī, *Muᶜtamad,* vol. II, pp. 459–478; trans. of the chapter on consensus with critical commentary by M. Bernand, *L'accord unanime de la communauté comme fondement des statuts légaux de l'Islam* (Paris, 1970), pp. 13–35, 128–132.

[58]Baṣrī, *Muᶜtamad,* vol. II, pp. 471–474. Bernand's trans. pp. 26–30.

[59]Juwaynī, *Burhān,* vol. I, p. 679.

[60]Juwaynī, *Ghiyāth al-umam fī iltiyāth al-ẓulam,* ed. F. ᶜAbd al-Munᶜim and M. Ḥilmī (Iskandariyya, 1979), p. 30; idem, *Burhān,* vol. I, p. 678.

[61]Juwaynī, *Ghiyāth,* pp. 34–35; *Burhān,* vol. I, p. 679 at ll. 3–8.

[62]Juwaynī, *Ghiyāth,* p. 34; idem, *Burhān,* vol. I, pp. 677–679, 683. Clearly, Juwaynī was well aware of the then developing concept of al-tawatur bil-maᶜna, which has already been noted but also rejected by Abū al-Ḥusayn al-Baṣrī (see Juwaynī's *al-Kāfiya fī al-jadal,* ed. F. H. Maḥmūd [Cairo, 1979], p. 94). According to this concept—to be discussed in full later—the authoritativeness of consensus rests on a multitude of ahadi traditions which have in common one meaning, i.e., that the community is infallible. Those who espouse this view explain that because these ahadi traditions were transmitted by so many transmitters who could not have known each other they cannot be spurious. Although some of Juwaynī's predecessors rejected al-tawatur bil-maᶜna for epistemological and theological reasons, there is good reason to believe that Juwaynī discarded this concept on political grounds. In his *Ghiyāth al-umām,* a political treatise which aims in part at the advocation and legitimation of the Sunni political regime against the Shīᶜī claims, Juwaynī discusses what he calls the spurious traditions which contain the words of the Prophet appointing ᶜAlī as his successor. He remarks that the Imāmiyya claims the right to the Caliphate on the basis of these widespread traditions (pp. 19–20; *naṣṣun shāʾiᶜun walafẓun mustafīḍ*). These traditions, Juwaynī argues, are merely ahadis, for they are not known to have been transmitted on a wide scale (tawatur) in the community (pp. 22–23). Such ahadi traditions, however they are transmitted, cannot lead to certainty, and thus cannot be used in such serious matters of government as designating a caliph. Juwaynī immediately goes on to say that caliphs are appointed by *ikhtiyār* (election), and the authoritative basis of such election is the infallible consensus of the community (p. 34). Obviously, when Juwaynī proceeded to establish the authoritativeness of consensus he could not use the principle of tawatur bil-maᶜna, since he had just discarded it as incapable of inducing certainty.

[63]Juwaynī, *Burhān,* vol. I, pp. 680–681; idem, *Ghiyāth,* pp. 36, 40–41.

[64]Juwaynī, *Burhān,* vol. I, p. 682.

[65]Ibid.

[66]Juwaynī, *Ghiyāth,* p. 41 at ll. 8–10. In effect, he states the same thing but in a less direct manner in *Burhān,* vol. I, p. 683 at ll. 8–9.

[67]Juwaynī, *Burhān,* vol. I, p. 683 at ll. 8–12.

[68]Ghazālī, *al-Mankhūl min taᶜlīqāt al-uṣūl,* ed. M. Ḥ. Haytū (Damascus, 1970), pp. 305–309, especially p. 307.

[69]Ghazālī, *Mustaṣfā,* vol. I, p. 175 at l. 1.

[70]In addition to the tradition about Satan quoted by Shāfiᶜī and the traditions nos. 1–4 quoted by Jaṣṣāṣ (note 38 above) Ghazālī cites the following: (1) "God would not allow my community to agree on an error"; (2) "I have asked God, exalted may he be, not to allow my community to agree on an error, and He answered my request"; (3) "God does not pay attention to those who diverge"; (4) "They [i.e., the community of Muslims] will not be harmed by the disagreement of those who differ with them"; (5) "If a person leaves the community and dies, he will be considered to have died in the days of Jāhiliyya." See Ghazālī, *Mustaṣfā,* vol. I, p. 175.

[71]Immediate knowledge is that which is forced on the mind through means of sense perception and divine revelation, without inference and reasoning. Such knowledge cannot be doubted. Mediate or discursive knowledge (*ᶜilm naẓarī* or *muktasab*), on the other hand, is that which occurs to the mind by reflection and inference. Bājī, *Ḥudūd,* pp. 25–27; Baghdādī, *Uṣūl al-dīn,* p. 8.

[72]Ghazālī, *Mustaṣfā,* vol. I, p. 177.

[73]See also similar arguments in Shīrāzī, *Lumaᶜ,* p. 47; Ibn Taymiyya, *al-Musawwada fī uṣūl al-fiqh* (Cairo, 1964), p. 319; Ibn Niẓām al-Dīn al-Anṣārī, *Fawātiḥ al-raḥamūt,* printed with Ghazālī's *Mustaṣfā,* 2 vols. (Cairo, 1324 H.), vol. II, pp. 119–120. For the opinions of Shirbīnī, Fanarī and Tāj al-Dīn al-Subkī see *Jamᶜ al-jawāmiᶜ,* 2 vols. (Bombay, 1970), vol. II, p. 130.

[74]Ghazālī, *Mustaṣfā*, vol. I, pp. 177–178.

[75]Ibid., p. 176.

[76]Abū Bakr al-Sarakhsī, *Uṣūl*, ed. Abū al-Wafā al-Afghānī, 2 vols. (Cairo, 1372 H.), vol. I, pp. 296–299.

[77]Al-Khaṭīb al-Baghdādī, *Faqīh*, vol. I, pp. 167–168.

[78]Āmidī, *Iḥkām*, vol. I, pp. 150–162.

[79]For Āmidī's interpretation of the verses see Bernard Weiss, "Al-Amidi on the Basis of Authority of Consensus," in Donald P. Little, *Essays on Islamic Civilization* (Leiden, 1976), pp. 344–351.

[80]It is of interest to note here that a number of later usulists claimed that Āmidī held the authoritativeness of consensus to be zanni rather than qatᶜi, i.e., that consensus, when it is reached on a case of law, does not render the said case conclusive and irrevocable. Fakhr al-Dīn al-Rāzī (d. 606/1209) was said to have held the same view. In *al-Iḥkām* there is nothing to substantiate such claims about Āmidī. However, it is possible that Āmidī held such views in his other works on legal theory or *kalām*. See the commentary of Sh. Muḥammad Ismāᶜīl on *Tahdhīb sharḥ al-isnawī ᶜalā minhāj al-wuṣūl ilā ᶜilm al-uṣūl*, 3 vols. (Cairo, 1976), vol. II, p. 263.

[81]See Weiss, "Al-Amidi," pp. 351 ff. Of the sixteen traditions Āmidī quotes, two have not so far been listed here. These are: (1) "Stay with the great majority"; and (2) The Prophet said: "My people will be divided into more than seventy sects, all of which will go to the fire [of Hell] except one." The Prophet was then asked: "Which sect is it?" and he replied: "My community." Āmidī, *Iḥkām*, vol. I, p. 163.

[82]Āmidī, *Iḥkām*, vol. I, pp. 163, 234.

[83]Ibid., pp. 237–238.

[84]Ibid., pp. 164, 238.

[85]Taqī al-Dīn Ibn Taymiyya (d. 728/1327) also advanced an argument similar to that of Āmidī. See *al-Musawwada*, pp. 317–319; on al-mutawatir bil-maᶜna traditions, pp. 235, 243.

[86]Abū Isḥāq al-Shāṭibī, *al-Muwāfaqāt fī uṣūl al-aḥkām*, ed. M. D. ᶜAbd al-Ḥamīd, 4 vols. (Cairo, 1969), vol. I, p. 10; vol. II, p. 40.

[87]Ibid., vol. I, p. 12.

[88]Ibid., pp. 14, 16–17.

[89]Ibid., p. 15.

[90]Ibid., p. 13.

[91]Shihāb al-Dīn al-Qarāfī, *Sharḥ tanqīḥ al-fuṣūl*, ed. T. Saᶜd (Cairo, 1973), pp. 324–325; on the principle of al-tawatur bil-maᶜna, see pp. 356–357.

[92]Jamāl al-Dīn al-Isnawī, *Nihayāt al-sūl fī sharḥ minhāj al-wuṣūl*, 3 vols. (Cairo, 1317 H.), vol. II, pp. 153–167.

[93]Kamāl al-Dīn Ibn al-Humām, *al-Taḥrīr*, with the commentary *al-Taqrīr wal-Taḥbīr* by Ibn Amīr al-Ḥājj, 3 vols. (Cairo, 1317 H.), vol. III, pp. 83–86.

[94]Anṣārī, *Fawātiḥ*, vol. II, pp. 213–217.

[95]Ibn ᶜAbd al-Shakūr, *Musallam*, vol. II, pp. 119–120, 213.

[96]Ibid., p. 214.

[97]Ibid., p. 216.

[98]Baghdādī, *Faqīh*, vol. I, p. 123; Pazdawī, *Uṣūl*, with the commentary *Kashf al-asrār* by ᶜAlāʾ al-Dīn ᶜAbd al-ᶜAzīz al-Bukhārī, 4 vols. (Beirut, 1308 H.), vol. III, p. 176; Ghazālī, *Mustaṣfā*, vol. I, p. 126; Ibn ᶜAlī al-Fārisī, *Jawāhir*, p. 41; Izmīrī, *Ḥāshiya ᶜalā sharḥ mirqāt al-wuṣūl*, a commentary on *Mirʾāt al-wuṣūl* by Mullā Khusraw, 2 vols. (Istanbul, 1891), vol. II, p. 181; Qarāfī, *Sharḥ*, p. 314; Subkī, *Jamᶜ*, vol. II, p. 76; Anṣārī, *Fawātiḥ*, vol. II, p. 81.

[99]Baghdādī, *Faqīh*, vol. II, p. 181; Qarāfī, *Sharḥ*, p. 314; Subkī, *Jamᶜ*, vol. II, p. 76.

[100]See Izmīrī, *Ḥāshiya*, vol. II, pp. 255–256.

[101]The great majority of modern Arabic authors on usul al-fiqh reproduce the medieval arguments as thus far outlined. See, e.g., Muḥammad al-Khuḍarī, *Uṣūl al-fiqh*, 4th ed. (Cairo, 1962), pp. 314–316. The emphasis on induction as a means of establishing the authoritativeness of consensus also appears in some of these works. See, e.g., ᶜAbd al-Fattāḥ Ḥusaynī, *al-Ijmāᶜ maṣdar thālith min maṣādir al-tashrīᶜ al-Islāmī* (Cairo, 1979), p. 280.

ADDENDA

p. 439, ll. 4–8: since the writing and publication of the article, several works of *uṣūl al-fiqh* have been published, including Abū al-Walīd al-Bājī's *Iḥkām al-Fuṣūl fī Aḥkām al-Uṣūl* (Beirut: Dār al-Gharb al-Islāmī, 1986), 435–80; Abū Isḥāq al-Shīrāzī's *Sharḥ al-Luma'*, ed. 'Abd al-Majīd Turkī, 2 vols. (Beirut: Dār al-Gharb al-Islāmī, 1988), II, 665–89; Aḥmad b. 'Alī Ibn Barhān's *al-Wuṣūl ilā al-Uṣūl*, ed. 'Abd al-Ḥamīd Abū Zunayd, 2 vols. (Riyad: Maktabat al-Ma'ārif, 1984), II, 72–6. Generally, the views of these authors seem to be in agreement with those of the mainstream *uṣūlists* discussed in the article. Fakhr al-Dīn al-Rāzī, however, deviates significantly from them, both in his general view of consensus and in the epistemic status assigned to it as a sanctioning instrument (see his *al-Maḥṣūl fī 'Ilm Uṣūl al-Fiqh*, 2 vols. [Beirut: Dār al-Kutub al-'Ilmiyya, 1988], II, 8–47). In the view of Rāzī, consensus is not knowable because it is impossible to determine that all the *mujtahids* throughout the vast stretches of Muslim territories could agree on a particular issue. The only consensus that can be determined is that of the Companions by virtue of the fact that they were relatively few in number. Being indeterminable, consensus loses its significance in Rāzī's theory. He argues that none of the Quranic verses or Prophetic traditions (severally or collectively) proves its authoritativeness (*ḥujjiyya*) with certainty. And the rational argument does not fare any better. All the available body of textual evidence indicates is that the authoritativeness of consensus is probable (*ẓannī*) and this, he maintains, must be sufficient to make of it an instrument which sanctions practice (*'amal*). In Rāzī, the issue of circularity necessarily does not arise.

In his *Sharḥ Mukhtaṣar al-Rawḍa* (ed. 'Abd Allāh al-Turkī, 3 vols. [Beirut: Mu'assasat al-Risāla, 1989], III, 14–30), Najm al-Dīn al-Ṭūfī also insists that neither the Quran nor the Sunna can be brought to bear upon the conclusive authoritativeness of consensus. Yet, unlike Rāzī, he holds the authoritativeness of consensus to be certain. His argument seems purely rational, based on a *reductio ad absurdum*. He advances two premises from which he derives a conclusion (III, 25–6): (1) that the epistemological superiority of consensus over any conclusive Quranic or Sunnaic text is established by consensus; and (2) that consensus dictates that nothing other than consensus can override such texts. Thus, if the authoritativeness of consensus were less than certain, these two forms of consensus would be contradictory. But Ṭūfī, without explaining why, argues that contradiction here is inconceivable. Again, for an altogether different reason, the issue of circularity does not arise because consensus does not guarantee the very texts by which its own authoritativeness is proven. The argument, however, may be considered circular because the impossibility of contradiction is predicated on the premise that the authoritativeness of consensus is certain, which is the proposition to be proven. Be that as it may, it is noteworthy and significant that Ṭūfī's legitimation of consensus on rational, non-textual grounds amounts to nothing short of sanctioning the collective voice of the community as an independent source of legislation. For the community, on his view, would be seen as having arrogated to itself the power to determine which legal rules are to be accepted as binding and conclusive and which are not.

pp. 444–6: for a detailed account of Āmidī's exposition of the subject based on both of his works *Iḥkām* and *Muntahā*, see Bernard Weiss, *The Search for God's Law: Islamic Jurisprudence in the Writings of Sayf al-Dīn al-Āmidī* (Salt Lake City: University of Utah Press, 1992), pp. 195 ff., 640. See also my critique of Weiss's analysis in the *International Journal of Middle East Studies*, 26, 1 (1994): 152–4.

IX

THE USE AND ABUSE OF EVIDENCE: THE QUESTION OF PROVINCIAL AND ROMAN INFLUENCES ON EARLY ISLAMIC LAW*

In her monograph *Roman, Provincial and Islamic Law*, Patricia Crone argues that provincial legal practice in Syria, the capital of the nascent Islamic state, influenced the Sharî'a no less than did Roman law. She takes as an example of such influence the institution of the patronate (*walâ'*) and attempts to prove that its crucial features derive from provincial and Roman law, rather than from pre-Islamic Arab society. The present article examines the author's assumptions and evidence as well as the methodology she adopts to establish her thesis.

I

ALTHOUGH THE PROBLEM OF foreign influences on Islamic law has engaged the minds of Islamicists for well over a century, it appears that the solution to this problem is no less elusive now than it was when Alfred von Kremer commented on it as early as 1875. The contributors to this issue have ranged over a wide spectrum, from those who affirmed a debt to Mosaic law to those who saw in Roman law the material which the emerging Sharîᶜa was to appropriate. Their estimation of the degree of this debt has also varied from "systematic borrowing" from Jewish and/or Roman law to more modest claims of indebtedness.[1] Dr. Patricia Crone's work, *Roman, Provincial and Islamic Law*, represents the most recent contribution to this problematic issue.

While postulating that Jewish law "manifestly did contribute to the formation of the Sharîᶜa" (p. 2), Crone rejects an unqualified assertion of Roman influence. She argues that if Roman elements had entered the Sharîᶜa they would have done so only through provincial law, which in her definition "refers to the non-Roman law practiced in the provinces of the Roman empire, especially the provinces formerly ruled by Greeks" (p. 1). And since nascent Islamic culture took shape in the Roman Fertile Crescent, the geographical area of influence could have only been Syria and not Iraq as Schacht had argued. Crone criticizes at some length Schacht's thesis that Roman law was transmitted by means of Greek rhetoric in Sassanid Iraq, and shows that not "a single item of Goldziher's and Schacht's list of Roman elements in Islamic law has been proved, and several are demonstrably wrong" (pp. 11, 102–6). The possibility of Roman influences on Islamic law through the Nestorian Syro-Roman lawbook is, after Nallino's findings, rightly dismissed. Having disposed of Schacht, Crone turns to her main point "that the law of the Near Eastern provinces was never wholly Romanised and that numerous peregrine institutions survived under a more or less Roman veneer" (p. 14). But although "provincial practice contributed far more to the Sharîᶜa than did Roman law . . . it would . . . be a mistake to preclude the possibility of Roman influence" (p. 14). Now, the means by which this influence was effected are the early Umayyad caliphs who made Syria their capital, and who "felt at liberty to borrow foreign law."[2] As it was Umayyad law that the jurists took as their starting point, "there may in principle be residues of this component anywhere in the classical [Islamic] system" (p. 16). Obviously, Crone has found at least one of these residues in the form of the institution of the patronate, to which she devotes the rest of her work, with the exception of chapter 2, which provides non-specialists with the basics of Islamic law in order to facilitate their path throughout the book. The third chapter treats the legal effects of the Islamic patronate in its two forms *walâʾ al-ʿitq* (a legal tie arising from manumission) and *walâʾ al-muwâlât* (contractual clientage). Here, Crone declares her intention to prove that pre-Islamic Arabia "supplied the general context of *walâʾ*" but "did not supply the institution itself. The crucial features of *walâʾ* derive from Roman and provincial law" (p. 41). In the fourth chapter, she sets out to prove the first thesis, namely, that *walâʾ* did not originate in pre-Islamic Arabia. The second thesis, i.e., that *walâʾ* and more specifically *kitāba*—which regulated the relationship between manumitter and freedman—came from Roman law (p. 65), is taken up in the fifth chapter. The provincial institution of *paramonê* is claimed to be the progenitor of *kitâba*, and another argument is offered against the latter's pre-Islamic peninsular origins. In the sixth chapter, the author attempts to show that "the legal behaviour of the late Roman patronate coincides with that of pre-Islamic *walâʾ* in certain respects: there was actual continuity in terms of law" (p. 78). Finally, Crone sums up her arguments in the concluding chapter and produces two additional cases (pp. 93–97) concerning wills and divorce to corroborate her conclusion.

Before we proceed to examine Crone's evidence and arguments in support of her thesis, we must address the underlying assumptions of the book, particularly the author's notion of provincial law.

Aside from the definition of provincial law already given, Crone attempts no investigation of what the sources of provincial law may have been, nor does she explore who the people applying this law were. But it seems that in Crone's mind these people are associated with the lofty Hellenic culture, and not with their uncivilized southern neighbors in the Peninsula who were responsible for the "culturally destructive" and "barbarian conquests."[3] Needless to say, the determination of the actual occurrence and the extent of borrowing are intimately related to the manner in which one conceives of the general levels of culture of those who borrow and those who lend. Once a culture is seen as 'sophisticated' it becomes incapable, in the mind of those who see it as such, of borrowing from another, 'primitive' culture; whereas 'desolate' cultures are *a priori* given to appropriating from more developed ones. Crone's pre-Islamic Arabia is "sparsely inhabited and uniformly impoverished," a place where the miserable bedouin goes "to battle for the sake of honour and excitement."[4] This Arabia, which had no history but only primitive events to record, possessed no real culture,[5] and the Islam that it produced makes for no more than a historical mischance. The Muslims—or Arabs for that matter—she declares, "might very well have stayed in their peninsula, and to this extent their conquest was a formidable accident."[6] Crone has reasserted her view more recently when she practically dismissed the socio-economic developments which gave rise to Islam by simply declaring that "Muḥammad had to conquer, his followers liked to conquer, and his deity told him to conquer: do we need any more?"[7]

When the culturally deprived peninsular Arabs conquered Syria, Crone tells us, they found a high culture including a developed provincial legal tradition which was Romanized to some extent. There is scarcely any attempt at revealing the identity of those Syrian provincials, though again we suspect that in Crone's mind they are not Arab, for, after all, they are cultured. Crone's Arabs of *Provincia Arabia* do not fare any better than their southern brothers. They are subservient and disorganized, and when the Yemeni South provided them with a script, all they could do with it was to record the "details of their genealogies and sheep."[8]

Viewing the Arabs thus can only result in assigning them the passive role of recipients of provincial culture and institutions. By insisting on the polarity between the 'primitive' Arabs and cultured provincials, Crone has ignored the findings of an entire field of scholarship without which no study of foreign influences on Islamic law can be conducted. The works of Brünnow and von Domaszewski,[9] Altheim and Stiehl,[10] Nöldeke,[11] Mommsen,[12] Dussaud,[13] Bowersock and a score of others[14] have long been recognized as authoritative sources on the demographic and cultural composition of ethnic groups that existed in Syria and the Syrian desert throughout the millennium before Islam.[15] The best of this massive scholarship has recently been conjoined with the fruits of another scholarly career in the voluminous work of I. Shahîd, the first two tomes of which appeared in 1984.[16] These studies are indispensable for solving numerous problems concerning the rise of Islam and certainly for defining more clearly the contours of legal continuity.

The findings of these works make it clear that the social and cultural map of West Asia during the few centuries preceding Islam cannot be seen in terms of black and white, as Crone seems to envisage it in this book. The massive migrations from the Peninsula to the north, the trade routes between Syria and western Arabia, the Arab *foederati* who constituted a cultural and commercial bridge between Romans and Byzantines on the one hand and the southern Arabs on the other,[17] are among the many factors that clearly created a constant state of flux between North and South, thus making any rigid or well-defined classification of cultural and social institutions suspect, if not impossible. At the same time, and despite the Hellenic imprint that was left on the society of the Fertile Crescent, the distinctive Semitic character of this society was never lost, a fact that constantly impresses itself on the historians of this period.[18] The Arabs of Syria and the Syrian desert preserved their Semitic rites, language, and above all their traditional laws, old tribal structures and ancestral customs.[19] These fundamental facts alone cast grave doubts on any scholarly work which operates on the assumption that geographical units and ethnic and cultural groups were neatly separated one from the other, and that southern Arabs were, to any significant extent, isolated from the ethnic and cultural groups of the Syrian North. In this respect Crone's notion of the international relations existing in West Asia before Islam seems dangerously archaic—at least insofar as it bears upon the question of legal influences.[20]

The fact that Crone failed to take into consideration the significant findings in the fields of *Romano-* and *Byzantino-Arabica* has gravely weakened her thesis, which is based on the erroneous assumption of the non-existence of any meaningful relation between what she sees as the arid South and the flourishing North. Her premise that the Arabs possessed little when they arrived in the Fertile Crescent and that they were forced to borrow virtually everything from the nations they conquered leads her to the most unreasonable of conclusions: even a simple act of charity whereby a slave is freed before he completes his payments for manumission is claimed to have been borrowed by Muslims from the Greeks (pp. 72–73). Thus the backward Muslims needed the example of the Greeks to learn how to be charitable. It is this negative attitude that insists on depriving the (early) Muslims of all 'civilized' values that determines for Crone when a piece of evidence should be admitted, twisted or suppressed. As we shall see, in Crone's work it is the hypothesis that shapes evidence, not the other way around.

II

As we have mentioned, Crone concerns herself with the institution of patronage (a good part of which, as we shall see, was not recognized by three Sunnî legal schools; and for those who did admit it, the institution, juridically speaking, was of little importance).[21] In the third chapter, which begins the real stuff of the book, she opens with a statement to the effect that every society must have a way of incorporating outsiders. All non-Arab newcomers to Islam, she tells us, were affiliated to individual Muslims with whom they were placed in an unequal relationship. This relationship turns out to be *walâʾ*, a general term employed in two types of legal institutions known to Muslim lawyers as *walâʾ al-ʿitq* and *walâʾ al-muwâlât*. We must emphasize from the outset that while the latter may, but does not necessarily, involve converts, the former is a legal institution exclusively related to the manumission of slaves and has nothing to do with the incorporation of outsiders into Muslim society;[22] for it does not, as such, bring slaves into Muslim society. It only changes their legal status; it is an instrument for freeing slaves *within* Islamic society. Be that as it may, our author goes on to enumerate the rights arising from *walâʾ al-ʿitq*. Slavery, needless to say, can hardly constitute a relationship of equals. The manumitter, Crone argues, acquires a right to the freedman's estate, but he does so only as the last agnate (according to the great majority of jurists). The freedman, however, does not possess the same rights to the patron's estate. The manumitter must pay blood-money on behalf of his freedman, but the freedman is not charged with the same obligation toward his former master. This last specification loses importance when the reader is told that a great many jurists do assign such a duty to the freedman (p. 37).

When Crone comes to *walâʾ al-muwâlât*, it is obvious that she has misread the legal texts. These texts specify that *inheritance and blood money are mutual rights and obligations*, provided that *both* parties agree to them. Crone presents these rights in a manner that gives the false impression of the patron possessing rights superior to those of his counterpart. She claims, without any support from the sources, that "[u]sually succession is assumed to be unilateral" (p. 39). One would like to know whose assumption that is, since it is commonly held by the jurists that inheritance is mutual (*wa-yatawârathâni min al-jânibayni*).[23] Although she characterizes *walâʾ al-muwâlât* as "contractual clientage," she fails to bring out clearly the fact that *walâʾ al-muwâlât* rests on contractual obligations and has nothing to do with *walâʾ al-ʿitq*, which arises from slavery. In Crone's account the contractual elements are missing. Any contract in Islamic law must be concluded by two persons of full capacity, persons who are presumed, legally speaking, to be equals. Furthermore, *walâʾ al-muwâlât* (rejected by the Shâfiʿīs, Mâlikîs and Ḥanbalîs) does not necessarily involve conversion, as Crone herself admits in passing (p. 38). In fact, one may convert to Islam "at the hands" of one person and simultaneously enter into a *walâʾ al-muwâlât* contract with another. If *walâʾ al-muwâlât* takes effect simultaneously with conversion, it would be valid but certainly not as a consequence of conversion.[24] Such a contract may be concluded between a *dhimmî* and a Muslim, without conversion being involved.[25] It could even be concluded between two *dhimmî*s.[26] In fact, it does not have to be concluded at all, for it is commonly held to be *jâʾiz* (permissible), not *lâzim* (obligatory).[27] As Crone knows, the only school which insists on *walâʾ al-muwâlât* as the instrument of conversion is that of the Qâsimîs, but they allow this only in *dâr al-ḥarb*, not in Muslim territories. Most important of all is the fact that the *raison d'être* of *walâʾ al-muwâlât* is nothing but *mutual* support between the *two* parties in matters financial and moral. As the jurists put it: *wa-sababu walâʾi al-muwâlâti al-ʿaqdu wal-maṭlûbu minhu al-tanâṣuru.*[28] The term *tanâṣur* (or other derivatives of *n-ṣ-r*, connoting help and mutual support) seems to figure prominently in the language of offer and acceptance in this contract: e.g., *ʿâqadtuka ʿalâ an tanṣuranî wa-anṣuraka.*[29] This contract by itself can hardly be said to create a relationship of dependence. It is important to remember this, for many later arguments in the book rest on Crone's misunderstanding of the exact nature of this contract.

Having discussed what she thinks to be the legal rights and duties in these two (very different) *walâʾ* relationships, Crone concludes that "[a]ll non-Arab newcomers in early Islamic society thus paid for their membership of this society by acceptance of a private relationship of dependence" (p. 40). The reader is left to wonder about the relevance of this statement to the two legal institutions which have in themselves almost nothing to do with incorporating converts into Islamic society.

Crone proceeds to build another argument on what she claims to have demonstrated. She sees a gulf between doctrines of Islamic law concerning *walâʾ* and the social reality of the "homeland of the conquerors," and she sets out to prove the existence of this gulf, aiming ultimately to show that if *walâʾ* was not taken from Arabia, then it must have been appropriated from another source. The gulf, as Crone sees it, is represented by four points (pp. 43–44): (i) "The Islamic patronage is individual. It binds one person to another in a relationship of dependence." In pre-Islamic Arabia such relationships existed between groups, not individuals. (ii) "The Islamic patronage detaches the client from his natal group and incorporates him in that of the patron as a passive member." In pre-Islamic Arabia clients remained in their own groups. (iii) "The Islamic patronate is assimilative. Having been detached from his natal group, the client sooner or later acquires full membership of the new group." "Collective clientage, by contrast, is not necessarily assimilative, and assimilation is effected collectively if it occurs at all." (iv) The Muslim patron must pay "blood-money on his client's behalf in return for a title to his estate. No such rights and duties can be assigned to patrons where clientage is collective, nor can they be documented for pre-Islamic Arabia."

Let us address (ii) and (iii) first. We have seen that *walâʾ al-muwâlât* does not necessarily involve conversion. Nor does conversion, in and by itself, give rise to this *walâʾ*. The client is under no obligation to enter into the contract, and can at any time (as long as the patron has not paid blood-money on his behalf) withdraw without incurring any penalty.[30] The relationship established by the contract is clearly a fictitious kinship which is capable of dissolution. The client, according to many jurists, is not supposed to have a natal group. The doctrines of the jurists give one to understand that the contract of *walâʾ al-muwâlât* is specifically designed to provide for those non-Arabs who have no lineage or relatives. This is the reason why certain jurists insist that for such a contract to be valid the client must have no existing relationship (*wa-kawnuhu majhûla al-nasabi sharṭun li-ṣiḥḥati ʿaqdi al-muwâlâti*).[31] Abû Hanîfa and the

Twelver Shîᶜîs moreover hold this contract to be valid only when *both parties* have no *nasab*.[32] There is nothing in this contract which obliges the client but does not oblige the patron. (Incidentally, the terms "client" and "patron" do not reflect the legal status of the parties in the contract but indicate, respectively, who made the offer and who accepted it.) Rights and duties are mutual between the two parties. At the same time, assimilation does not necessarily follow from these doctrines. How can, for example, a *dhimmî* (let alone a Muslim) entering into such contract with a Muslim or another *dhimmî* be assimilated into Muslim society more than he already is? These considerations certainly confute Crone's point (iii) as well.

Thus, (i) and (iv) remain to be proven. Crone begins by examining modern Arabian society in the nineteenth and what seems to be the first third of the twentieth century. She realizes that what she finds in the modern period "is not of course in itself evidence for pre-Islamic conditions; but in its light the fragmentary pre-Islamic evidence becomes more informative than when it is taken on its own" (p. 44). There is, however, no justification for taking into account situations removed from the main subject of study by more than twelve centuries; the evidential value of such situations is obviously too suspect to be seriously considered. And if it be true that pre-Islamic evidence "becomes more informative" in the light of nineteenth and twentieth century evidence, then the pre-Islamic evidence must be fundamentally problematic.

The first difficulty Crone encounters in establishing (i) and (iv) is that the evidence she needs from the pre-Islamic period is not only meager but also hopelessly confused. As anyone who is familiar with such books as Isbahânî's *Aghânî* and Ṭabarî's *Târîkh* will admit, the term *mawlâ* and its usages are diverse and lack any fixed connotation. When Ṭabarî reports that *x* was the *mawlâ* of *y*, there is simply no way for us to know what the exact social or legal relationship between the two was, unless of course we are provided with detailed information about the persons involved, which is, to be sure, a rare luxury. The other difficulty is Crone's own confusion concerning *walâʾ al-ʿitq* and *walâʾ al-muwâlât*. When she proceeds to try to prove the absence of their equivalents in pre-Islamic Arabia, she insists that they are two items of one and the same set. This, as we have seen, rests on a misunderstanding of the legal texts.

Crone argues that although the pre-Islamic *ḥalîf*, who is an ally or a confederate *mawlâ*, enjoyed full protection and was frequently avenged when killed, he was not incorporated into the host tribe, unless he changed his name to that of the tribe. Such was the case of the *jâr* (protégé) (pp. 51–52). "Some sources claim that the compact between two *ḥalîf*s established, or could establish, mutual succession between the two: whoever died first would leave a sixth of his estate to the other" (p. 53). But this, Crone tells us, is merely later Islamic information (Ṭabarî's *Tafsîr*) which is "typically volunteered in explanation of Sura 4:37." Typically, she quickly dismisses this information as apocryphal, without giving a good reason for doing so. But she finds it a little harder to dismiss other sources on this point, especially the fact that "classical Muslim scholars sometimes identify the contractual client of Islamic law with the pre-Islamic *ḥalîf*, and modern scholars [Nallino, Goldziher and Juda] also tend to seek the origins of *walâʾ* in *ḥilf*. But though *ḥilf* might establish a claim to succession, it does not in fact provide a prototype for *walâʾ* of Islamic law" (pp. 53, 134).

The first reason Crone gives for rejecting the *ḥilf* origin of Islamic *walâʾ* is that *ḥilf* resembles only *walâ*ʾ *al-muwâlât*, not *walâ*ʾ *al-*ʿ*itq*. But we may well ask why it should resemble both? The latter *walâ*ʾ could have scarcely been in question, since it is an entirely different type of relationship from the former; in form and content the two types of *walâ*ʾ possess nothing in common except the first part of their compound names. Neither the pre-Islamic Arabs nor the Muslims could ever have confused the two, but Crone obviously does. The fact that the clients of *walâ*ʾ *al-muwâlât* were not known as *ḥalîf*s (p. 53) is no proof that *walâ*ʾ *al-muwâlât* did not derive from *ḥilf*. What is important is that the legal features of the latter are in many ways identical with the former; *ḥilf*, like *walâ*ʾ *al-muwâlât*, was a compact/contract intended for mutual support, and neither, as we have seen, required any sort of detachment of the parties from their natal groups (assuming they had such groups). Moreover, *mawlâ* and *ḥalîf* were often interchangeable terms, as in the poet's words, *al-mawlâ al-tâbi*ʿ *al-muḥâlif*—quoted by Crone herself in a different context (p. 55). A few lines later Crone quotes another poet who makes a distinction between *mawlâ* by *ḥilf* and *mawlâ* by *kinship* (the latter probably referring to *walâ*ʾ *al-*ʿ*itq*). Had the terms *mawlâ* and *ḥalîf* signified distinctly different meanings, the poet's need to draw the distinction would not have arisen. In yet another context (p. 137, n. 160), Crone tells us that the term *mawlâ* was used to indicate *ḥalîf*. It would thus seem highly likely (at least more likely than Crone's alternative) that *walâ*ʾ *al-muwâlât* represented a modified continuity of *ḥilf al-walâ*ʾ that consisted, as Tyan put it, of the "admission of an individual to a clan, by an agreement *with one* of the members of this clan or by collective assent. This individual, known as *mawlâ*, is generally accorded the same social and juridical position, from the standpoint both of rights and of obligations, *as* *the original members* of the tribe. There is even *established a right of succession between him and the members of the tribe with whom the agreement is made*" (my italics).[33] That the majority of Muslim lawyers rejected *walâʾ al-muwâlât* altogether and that those who accepted it called it *walâʾ al-muwâlât* and not, for example, *walâʾ al-ḥilf* may well have been due to the notion that the Prophet prohibited *ḥilf* in Islam (*lâ ḥilfa fî al-Islâmi*). As testified in an early tradition, however, Muslims still thought of *walâʾ* in terms of *ḥilf*.[34]

Notwithstanding the considerable body of evidence opposing her thesis Crone remains persistent. Contrary evidence in Arabic poetry is rejected on purely inferential grounds (pp. 55–56). This evidence is dismissed also because the *mawâlî* are "almost always mentioned in connection with the theme of mutual help," a theme which does not fit Crone's image of the *mawâlî* as people who must be abused and scorned in order to qualify as *mawâlî* proper. "Thus," Crone concludes, the evidence of poetry is "irrelevant to our concerns" (p. 55). The judgment that this evidence is irrelevant is not surprising in light of Crone's misinterpretation of the legal effects of *walâʾ al-muwâlât*. From this point in the book the reader begins to entertain many doubts about Crone's use and abuse of evidence. Evidence is stricken, not after it has been carefully weighed and compared with other more conclusive evidence, but on the basis of long chains of inference in which the transition from one stage to another can easily be disputed, if not altogether invalidated.

Although the issue of *ḥalîf* is poorly resolved, our author proceeds to prove that the *mawâlî* in pre-Islamic Arabia stood in a collective relationship of dependence with their Arab patrons. Here, she cites the case of those Jewish tribes who were collectively dependent on other tribes (pp. 56–57). We do not dispute this fact, since a mere glance at the chronicles shows its truth. But collective affiliation is not the issue here. What we need is proof that *walâʾ between individuals* did not exist in pre-Islamic Arabia, a proof Crone does not adduce. Again, and to the great frustration of the reader, Crone proceeds to ask the question, "What happened to the slave on manumission?" (p. 58) —without settling, or even attempting to settle, the question of collective dependence. The failure to deal with this matter certainly demolishes Crone's hypothesis number (i), especially since we have no reason to abandon the conclusions of such scholars as W. R. Smith, Goldziher, Tyan and others concerning the existence of individual *walâʾ* and *ḥilf*. In fact a glance at such works as that of Ṭabarî assures us of the existence of *walâʾ* (which kind we do not always know) and *ḥilf* between individuals; we know, for instance, that Marthad b. Abî Marthad al-Ghanawî was the *ḥalîf* of Ḥamza b. ʿAbd al-Muṭṭalib,[35] just as Barrâḍ was the *ḥalîf* of Ḥarb b. Umayya.[36] That *ḥilf* was concluded between two individuals is also obvious from the Constitution of Medina, where it is stated that a believer must not take as his *ḥalîf* the *mawlâ* of another believer to the exclusion of the latter.[37]

In this context we should observe that the pre-Islamic *ḥilf* and *walâʾ*, on both the collective and the individual levels, acquired a parallel in Islamic law. The Ḥanafî and sectarian schools that accepted *walâʾ al-muwâlât* allowed a continuity of the pre-Islamic individual *ḥilf*, whereas the remaining three Sunnî schools endorsed collective *walâʾ* and *ḥilf* in the form of the Islamic dictum *al-walâ lil-Muslimîn*.[38] The admission by the Ḥanafî and the sectarian schools of the individual *walâʾ* should not preclude the likelihood that they also endorsed *al-walâʾ lil-Muslimîn*.

To the aforestated question about what happens to the slave on manumission, Crone's answer is that there is the "implication that freedmen were not incorporated in their manumitter's kin" (p. 60). Here, Crone at least admits that this is only an implication and that "none of the passages" used as evidence "explicitly mentions freedmen" (p. 60). The argument on this point, however, continues for one more paragraph, but is quite thin. The reader is then suddenly confronted with the statement: "Having established this point, we may proceed to an examination of the precise manner in which the freedman's status was regulated" (p. 60)—when, in fact, the point has not been established at all.

And Crone continues: "The two questions of interest to us are, first, who was responsible for the freedman's blood and blood spilt by him? And secondly, who had a claim to his estate?" (p. 61). Her answer to the first, as might be expected, is that the manumitters "might well set out to avenge the freedman, but it would of course be their own honour, not that of the freedman, that they would try to vindicate" (p. 61). It is the freedman's own agnates, Crone tells us, who are responsible for his blood as well as the blood spilt by him. But since the manumitters often avenged the blood of their dead freedman, how do we know that it was always their own honor which they were vindicating? Crone does not explain. Who had a claim to the freedman's estate? "The answer," our author says, "is presumably his agnate . . . not the manumitter." Here Crone concedes that "[t]here is no direct evidence on this point but it is hard to see on what ground the manumitter could have made such claim" (p. 62). To support the entire argument Crone offers three footnotes, none of which in any way constitutes evidence about the pre-Islamic Arabs. They refer exclusively to freedmen in Roman and Jewish law. Nevertheless, Crone concludes the argument as follows: "In short, there is no reason to assume that the manumitter acquired a right to succession by virtue of manumission itself" (p. 62). She follows this by a more general statement concluding the fourth chapter: "It will be admitted that there is little in the evidence to suggest that the legal institution of *walâ*ᵓ came out of pre-Islamic Arabia" (p. 63).

The absence of a reason to establish the existence of *x* is insufficient to prove that *x* is non-existent. If I have little evidence to show that *x* exists in *y*, this does not mean that *x* does not exist in *y*, nor does it imply that *x* exists elsewhere (unless of course 'little evidence' is used rhetorically). Even if we accept Crone's argument and set aside for a moment the fact that it is based on a fallacy, we cannot consider it conclusive. Therefore, it is pointless to proceed to build further arguments on it, something which Crone nevertheless does, and with confidence at that. She opens chapter 5 by asking: "If the personal clientage of Islamic law did not come from Arabia, where could it have come from?" (p. 64).

It is important to note that at this stage in the book *walâ*ᵓ *al-muwâlât* drops out, never to appear again. Not only does Crone fail, as we have seen, to establish its absence in pre-Islamic Arabia, but she does not even make a claim of its having been borrowed. We are left then with the claim that the Islamic institution of personal clientage (*walâ*ᵓ *al-*ᶜ*itq*), and more specifically *kitâba* (manumission contract), has its origins in the Roman Near East. This Near Eastern institution, we are told, is the *paramonê*. It is a service contract by which a slave is manumitted, provided that he render certain services to his patron for a specific period of time during which he "remains" with his master. Crone does find some evidence which shows that "pre-Islamic Arabs were familiar with the institution of *paramonê*, and it may have been known not only to the settled Arabs, but also the bedouin. . . .

But it should be stressed that what they knew was the institution in its ancient Near Eastern form . . . not more sophisticated versions current in the Greco-Roman Near East" (p. 68). The evidence that Crone presents is clearly partial; a few indirect examples are not enough to establish that the institution in Arabia represents an ancient form. Positive evidence is needed to convince the reader that this is the case; without this Crone cannot legitimately proceed to argue that the "evidence relating to paramonar manumission thus confirms that the conquerors were influenced by the legal practice of their subjects" (p. 68).

But she does. In order to prove the influence, she sets out to show that the conquerors were familiar (in the period of pre-classical law) with a wide variety of methods of manumission that existed in the Roman Near East. She cites seven early traditions to the effect that manumission would be granted in return for (i) an obligation to remain; (ii) service for a specified number of years; (iii) payment of alimony; (iv) a share in the freedman's estate; (v) celibacy; (vi) enslavement of the freedman's or the freedwoman's children; and finally (vii) manumission by premature apolysis. Now, (i) clearly existed in pre-Islamic Arabia as testified to in the case (quoted by Crone, p. 67) of Ṣuhayb who made a *ḥilf* with Ibn Judᶜân and stayed with him until he died. The last phrase "until he died," which occurs in at least three other examples quoted by Crone from pre-Islamic Arabia, must be taken to indicate that the duration of the contract was an important factor. Thus, it is highly likely that (ii) did exist in Arabia. As for (vii), it also seems to have existed in pre-Islamic Arabia in one form of *tasyîb* or another (pp. 67, 68). *Tasyîb*, as Crone points out, is manumission without service or payment. What remains then is (iii–vi). While the cases of manumission mentioned in these four traditions have not in any way been proven to have been absent in pre-Islamic Arabia, they have not been admitted to Islamic law because they are of the resolutive type. Manumission of this type is one in which the slave is freed *now* provided he render service *after* his manumission. Islamic law recognizes only suspensive manumission, in which the slave *pays* for his freedom and only after doing so acquires the status of a freedman. Thus, none of these cases proves any borrowing. Even if we assume that they did not originate in pre-Islamic Arabia, their being known to Muslims did not entail their admission into Islamic law.

To be sure, suspensive manumission constitutes only one of many differences between Islamic and Roman provincial law. Before we come to these differences, we should draw attention to the difference in names, which Crone dismisses as a negligible point (p. 74). We recall that one of the reasons for dismissing the institution of *ḥilf* as the progenitor of *walâʾ al-muwâlât* is that the two institutions have different names. The linguistic difference between *kitâba* and *paramonê*, however, is deemed by Crone to be unimportant because this time it obviously serves her purposes to do so.

In a similarly easy and arbitrary way Crone also dismisses the *kitâba* mentioned in the Qurʾân (S. 24:33), holding it to refer to a marriage, not a manumission, contract. The discussion of this crucial point is relegated to a footnote (p. 145, n. 100). Sûra 24:1–35, she explains, "is concerned with sexual morality. . . . It covers subjects such as *zinâ*, *qadhf*, *liʿân*, and female modesty, not manumission." The textual sequence of the Sûra and the general context dictate, Crone insists, that the Qurʾânic expression *fa-kâtibûhum* should be taken as meaning a marriage contract, just like the Jewish matrimonial contract known as *ketubah*. Thus, for Crone, the thematic continuity of the

Sûra is sufficient to preclude the possibility that the Qur'ân meant manumission, although elsewhere she (together with M. Cook) rebukes the Qur'ân for being so "perfunctory in its linking of disparate materials."[39] At one time the Qur'ân is perfunctory, at another coherent, depending on when it is of service to Crone. She does not account for the fact that the Qur'ân never employs terms derived from *k-t-b* for marriage, and that it consistently refers to marriage with words derived from *n-k-ḥ* and *z-w-j*.[40] Indeed, one must be unduly confident, especially on the basis of such extremely poor reasoning, to state that the "exegetes and lawyers alike were unfamiliar with the Qur'ânic use of the word *kitâb*" (p. 145).

Aside from the "crucial difference" of *kitâba* being suspensive and *paramonê* being resolutive, we must look at other differences between Islamic and Roman provincial law, at least those acknowledged by Crone. They are as follows: (i) as a rule, *paramonê* involved service; *kitâba* involved payment; (ii) *kitâba* allows the freedman to leave the residence of his master during the fulfillment of the contract; *paramonê* does not; (iii) *kitâba* for the lifetime of the manumitter is strictly forbidden; *paramonê* allows it. The first difference represents another major difficulty in Crone's thesis, for it opens the door to a yet more serious problem: the *raison d'être* of *kitâba* is manumission; i.e., without manumission there is no *kitâba. Paramonê*, on the other hand, does not necessarily involve manumission, and its *raison d'être* is providing *service.* It is a contract of labor that covers "wide ranges of arrangement from virtual self-hire to hire of services from specific jobs and periods with terms of protection for the worker as well as the employer."[41] In *paramonê* what all the parties to the contract are interested in is labor,[42] not manumission. It should not therefore be surprising that in S. Treggiari's study of Roman contracts for manumission, *paramonê* plays no role whatsoever.[43] It is the reduction, or rather the virtual suppression, of these differences—as well as the overstretching of similarities between provincial and Islamic law—that is characteristic of Crone's mode of argument.

Thus far, Crone has not proven any single influence upon Islamic law from Roman provincial law. She has merely shown that Muslims, like the provincials before them, freed slaves for some kind of compensation. Does the fact that both engaged in the same practice force us to conclude that Muslims borrowed from Roman provincials the idea of freeing slaves for a compensation? Such a conclusion is necessary only if we operate on the assumption that Muslims needed the example of the Greeks to learn how to be charitable.

Crone then discusses five features of manumission reflected in early traditions. Her aim is to "demonstrate" that early Islamic lawyers were familiar with provincial methods of manumission and that "the legal behaviour of the late Roman patronate coincides with that of pre-classical *walâʾ* in certain respects: there was actual continuity in terms of law" (p. 78). We need not go into these features since Crone herself does not make the claim that any of these succeeded in entering Islamic law. Immediately thereafter, however, she introduces four other features that are alleged to constitute similarities between the Roman patronate and pre-classical *walâʾ* (pp. 84–86). They are as follows: (i) both *paramonê* and *walâʾ*, "conferred a title of succession in the absence of certain heirs, not a fixed share." This similarity, however, must not be attributed to provincial influence because the manumitter stands before law as the kin of the *mukâtab* freedman, and therefore he inherits as a relative (*al-walâʾ yajrî majrâ al-nasab*) in accordance with the Islamic rules of inheritance which were regulated to a considerable extent by the Qur᾿ân. The patron could not inherit in any other way. Insisting on provincial borrowing in this case is tantamount to claiming that the Islamic law of inheritance was influenced by, or borrowed from, the Roman provinces—a proposition which has not been proven. Another alleged similarity under this category is "that the patron was entitled to the entire estate of a freedman who died leaving neither relatives nor will." It is only normal that this should be the case. In a slave-master relationship, it stands to reason that in the absence of any relatives on the side of the slave, the master, his original owner, should inherit from him. How could this be otherwise? (ii) "[M]ost of the rights vested in the Roman patronate over freedmen passed to the manumitter's heirs in accordance with the ordinary rules regarding the devolution of property. On the Muslim side succession to the patronate *would likewise seem* to have followed the ordinary rules in pre-classical law" (my italics). But all we have from Crone concerning the Muslim side is speculation, backed by not a shred of evidence. (iii) "Both could be renounced." There is, however, the equally valid possibility that the Islamic renunciation of the patronate could have been an extension or a modified form of the pre-Islamic *tasyîb*, which we have already discussed. At any rate, the evidence Crone adduces with regard to this practice in provincial law is not convincing and cannot be taken seriously. (iv) "Both failed to arise if the freedman had . . . purchased *both* manumission *and* freedom from further obligations." Crone does not in fact establish that this law survived after 212 A.D. The argument here is shaky and is couched in highly speculative terms (e.g., "it stands to reason that . . . ," or "we may thus take it that . . ."). But even if we assume for the sake of argument that the law did survive and that nothing like it developed in pre-Islamic Arabia—a point Crone never settles—we are still left with the fact that it was rejected by all jurists except some Zaydîs, some Ibâḍîs and the Imâmîs (p. 86).

In summing up the last chapter Crone admits that "several aspects of the Roman patronate fail to reappear on the Muslim side." But, she adds, "it should be abundantly clear that the Arab conquerors soon came to be familiar with a cluster of provincial practices in which the predominant element was the *paramonê* of the Hellenized Near East. . . . In both positive and negative terms, the evidence thus points to the conclusion that *walâ*ʾ has its origin in the Roman Near East" (pp. 86–88). These quotations, in fact, are not summaries of the findings of the book but rather are unwarranted leaps from one premise to another. As we have seen, not a single law regulating the institution of *kitâba* was conclusively proven to have infiltrated the Sharîʿa. Furthermore, the differences between the two legal institutions (even to the extent acknowledged by Crone herself) are sufficiently numerous as to cast serious doubts on any alleged borrowing. The fact that Muslims became familiar with the provincial legal tradition *does not in itself constitute evidence of borrowing*, and the value of any evidence based on this familiarity is further diminished, if not eliminated, when one gives full credit to the ingenious processes of legal systematization and cultural synthesis that took place in the first two centuries of Islam. But what is most striking about Crone's book is that while making categorical claims of Islamic indebtedness to Roman provincial (and Jewish) law, it rarely attempts, much less succeeds, in showing influences that *survived* into what has become the Sharîʿa.

The inability to demonstrate conclusively influences is not in the least surprising. It is commonly acknowledged by students of Islamic and comparative law that the Sharîᶜa as a "finished product" resembles none of the legal systems that it came into contact with during the period of its formation. Even if some similarities appear, they are quickly frustrated by serious differences. The ingenious process of assimilation, systematization and Islamicization managed to dissipate all the indigenous features of legal institutions and to recast them in a fashion that is not in the least reminiscent of the older institutions. Systematization in particular had a powerful effect on reshaping and reformulating whatever raw legal material Islam encountered. This systematization was given sharp expression in the profound desire of Muslim scholars for logical coherence, while at the same time they took into full consideration what they deemed to be divinely inspired propositions. The law which Muslims encountered in the conquered territories had, as a rule, to be modified to accord with the laws laid down in the Qurʾân. It is no wonder then that attempts to prove some specific debt of Islamic law to other legal systems in conclusive and clear-cut terms have resulted in failure. Crone's attempt shares this failure, for she obviously does not appreciate the Sharîᶜa's inner logical structure that gives Islam its unique law. The fundamental structural differences between Islamic and ancient Near Eastern legal systems makes the identification of influences on the former by the latter virtually impossible; for though there persists a nagging suspicion of borrowing, this suspicion can never be confirmed, at least not with the present state of documentation. All that we, in fact, have are some vague similarities between indigenous laws and the Sharîᶜa that can never conclusively establish borrowings.

In the concluding chapter of the book, Crone takes an unexpected turn that makes nonsense of the thesis she has tried to defend throughout the book. At this point serious contradictions appear. We recall that a consistent element in Crone's argument was the theme that pre-classical and classical Islamic law could not have been derived in any significant way from pre-Islamic Arabia, and that none of the similarities she was forced to acknowledge could, in her opinion, account for the institution as it appeared in Islam (" . . . if the Arab conquests had not included Roman provinces, there would not have been an Islamic patronate of the type we know" [p. 64]). More specifically we recall that Crone rejected the institution of *ḥilf* as the progenitor of *walâ᾿ al-muwâlât*. However, in the last pages of the book, when speaking about the widespread practice of provincial law in the Near East, Crone acknowledges, in a preliminary manner, that this law was "shared by many or most of the inhabitants of the Near East . . . indeed even, it would seem, by pre-Islamic Arabs themselves to some extent" (p. 92). But then she goes further: "As has been seen, manumission with *paramonê* was known to the pre-Islamic Arabs too, as was the paramonar service contract." "[W]e can see that the *ḥalîf* who arranged for mutual succession between himself and his ally was in fact including a succession pact of the type common in the provinces; and when the Prophet paired off Anṣârîs and Muhâjirûn as brothers in Medina, he was undoubtedly practicing the Near Eastern *adoptio in fratrem*, a special form of the succession pact whereby two men would adopt each others (*sic*) as brothers and institute both common property and mutual succession" (p. 93). Now, if the pre-Islamic Arabs were familiar, even "to some extent," with provincial law, why does one fail to see this fact noted in Crone's work, except in the conclusion and then only in passing? We must ask why she is so adamant, even at the expense of twisting and ignoring evidence, in trying to prove that the Islamic patronate was a provincial and not a peninsular institution. Although the *ḥalîf* provides an excellent possibility of demonstrating legal continuity between pre-Islamic Arabia and Islamic law, she has dismissed it and instead opted for provincial legal precedents. Nonetheless, in her concluding remarks, she concedes that *ḥilf* could have been the source of *walâʾ al-muwâlât*. What are we to make of these contradictions?

In the last few pages of the concluding chapter, it becomes evident that Crone is not, after all, entirely ignorant of the significant extent to which the Islamic patronate finds its origins in pre-Islamic Arabia. However, had she acknowledged the existence and developed nature of the pre-Islamic Arab institution in the beginning of her work, she would have dealt her project a fatal blow, for the entirety of her thesis rests on the assumption that the peninsular Arabs were not in any meaningful way in possession of the institution as it came to be known in Islam. To mention the undeniable influence of the pre-Islamic peninsular institution only toward the end of her work marks a serious defect in the structure of the work, and leaves her thesis in complete disarray.

Confusion increases with yet another concluding remark offered "on the basis of the material reviewed in this book"; namely, that the "tribal legacy of the invaders in conjunction with Jewish concepts provided the Muslims above all with the capacity to reshape, though Jewish law certainly and tribal law possibly contributed raw material too" (p. 99). Assuming that the reader knows what the grammatical object of "to reshape" is, he or she will remain puzzled as to how this statement follows from Crone's work when Jewish law has not even been discussed. But she goes even further. Provincial practice, she says, "contained elements of Roman law in Syria and Egypt, just as it contained elements of Sasanid law in Iraq; and Roman law certainly, and Sasanid law probably, entered the Sharî^ca as a result" (p. 99).

III

We shall not argue against Crone's conclusions, except to say that *none of them* follows from the evidence or the arguments presented in the book. It was precisely this speculative scholarship that Crone severely criticized when she dismissed the writings of Goldziher, Schacht and others on the grounds that they merely *affirm* rather than *demonstrate* what they set out to prove. Her own arguments are far-fetched, her use of evidence is tortuous, and she certainly approaches the subject with a predetermined mind. There is little doubt that Crone writes—here and elsewhere—with the underlying assumption that the Muslim conquerors were culturally impoverished. Like the barbarians who invaded Roman lands (and between whom and the Muslims Crone is fond of drawing analogies), the Muslims could have possessed only little culture, and it follows, therefore, that the civilization or empire they built must have been due to other, 'higher' sources. When she comes to Islamic law, Crone is blinded by her enthusiasm for establishing provincial, Roman, and other influences. Although she knows that the institution of *paramonê* was first attested as early as the second millennium B.C. in Babylonia and that it took until the fourth century B.C. before it surfaced in Greek law, and still another five or six centuries to make an appearance in Roman law (p. 65), Crone never associates this law with the Semitic peoples who were the preponderant inhabitants of the area. If the institution of *paramonê* was present in the Near East long before Greek rule, and if the institution of slavery in the pre-Islamic Near East was characteristically Semitic, as von Kremer rightly asserted,[44] then one must be reluctant, when similarities urge the notion of cultural influences, to claim borrowing from non-Semitic sources.

To sum up, although it is admittedly written in an engaging and stimulating style,[45] Crone's book says nothing of value that has not been said better before. For one, von Kremer's statement on the subject in his *Culturgeschichte*, written over a century ago, remains superior to that of Crone. There is no important argument she adduces which was not stated more succinctly and more *prudently* by von Kremer. Further, his conclusion about the entire legal institution of slavery being of Semitic origin[46] is more in accord with the known facts of the Semitic history of the ancient Near East. Crone's work, in contrast, is confused, methodologically deficient, and definitely a step in the wrong direction. Her thesis does not even meet the minimal requirements of "a working hypothesis," something which she remembers to point out only in the last two sentences of the conclusion. Everyone will acknowledge that history can never aspire to the same degree of certainty as science, and to that extent we have no choice but to live with the problem; but when history is made to mock the most elementary principles of scientific thought, historians should be the first to resist.

* A review of *Roman, Provincial and Islamic Law: The Origins of the Islamic Patronate.* By Patricia Crone, Cambridge: Cambridge University Press, 1987. Pp. 178. Four appendices, bibliography, index. $39.50.

I should like to record my thanks to my colleagues Charles Adams, Donald Little, and Paul Walker for their valuable comments.

[1] Two essays representing the disparate claims for indebtedness are: J. R. Wegner, "Islamic and Talmudic Jurisprudence: The Four Roots of Islamic Law and their Talmudic Counterparts," *The American Journal of Legal History*, 26, 1 (1982): 25–71, and H. J. Liebesny, "Comparative Legal History: Its Role in the Analysis of Islamic and Modern Near Eastern Legal Institutions," *The American Journal of Comparative Law* 20 (1972): 38–52. For other sources see Crone, *Roman*, 1–17, appendices 2–3, and the bibliography.

[2] Crone's thesis concerning the role of provincial law in solving the problem of legal influences was alluded to a century ago by von Kremer and vaguely repeated in 1950 by Schacht himself. See Alfred von Kremer, *Culturgeschichte des Orients unter den Chalifen*, 2 vols. (Wien: Wilhelm Braumüller, 1875–77), 534f.; Joseph Schacht, "Foreign Elements in Ancient Islamic Law," *Journal of Comparative Legislation and International Law* 32 (1950): 10 (ll. 18–19), 11 (l. 36). At the same time, we have no reason to preclude Iraq as a possible source of influence. Crone's almost dogmatic insistence on Syria stems from her reconstruction in *God's Caliph* (with M. Hinds) (Cambridge: Cambridge University Press, 1986). See Norman Calder's useful review of this book in the *Journal of Semitic Studies* 32.2 (1987): 375–78.

[3] Crone, *Slaves on Horses* (Cambridge: Cambridge University Press, 1980), 80, as well as Part I for similar statements; Crone & M. Cook, *Hagarism. The Making of the Islamic World* (Cambridge: Cambridge University Press, 1977), 73.

[4] Crone, *Slaves*, 23.

[5] Ibid., chapter II; Crone, *Meccan Trade and the Rise of Islam* (Princeton: Princeton University Press, 1987), 240.

[6] Crone, *Slaves*, 23, 25, 221 (n. 163).

[7] Crone, *Meccan Trade*, 244. Crone's intense hostility toward her subject has been observed by a number of Islamicists. See, e.g., Fred Donner's review of her *Slaves on Horses* in the *Journal of the American Oriental Society*

102.2 (1982): 367–71; also Richard Bulliet's review of the same work in the *Middle East Studies Association Bulletin* 16.1 (1982): 88–89; Norman Daniel's review of *Hagarism* (by Crone and M. Cook) in the *Journal of Semitic Studies* 24.2 (1979): 296–304; Donald Little's review of *Meccan Trade* in the *Canadian Journal of History* (forthcoming).

[8] Crone, *Slaves*, 24.

[9] R. E. Brünnow and A. von Domaszewski, *Die Provincia Arabia*, 3 vols. (Strassburg: K. J. Trübner, 1904–1909).

[10] Franz Altheim and Ruth Stiehl, *Die Araber in der alten Welt*, 5 vols. (Berlin: Walter de Gruyter & Co., 1964–68), including significant contributions by others.

[11] Th. Nöldeke's important contributions to this field are too numerous to list here. For the most relevant ones see the bibliography of I. Shahîd in *Byzantium and the Arabs in the Fourth Century* (Washington, D.C.: Dumbarton Oaks Research Library and Collection, 1984).

[12] Th. Mommsen, *The History of Rome*, trans. W. P. Dickson, 4 vols. (New York: Charles Scribner's Sons, 1886).

[13] René Dussaud, *La Pénétration des arabes en Syrie avant l'Islam* (Paris: Paul Geuthner, 1955).

[14] See G. Bowersock, *Roman Arabia* (Cambridge, Mass.: Harvard University Press, 1983), including a number of his articles listed in the bibliography. Other important contributions were made by scholars such as A. A. Vasiliev, D. Graf, Franz Cumont, Trimingham and others. See notes below.

[15] But the contributions of Altheim and Stiehl, Bowersock, and Nöldeke do not seem to be totally unknown in such studies as *Meccan Trade* and *Hagarism*.

[16] I. Shahîd, *Rome and the Arabs* (Washington, D.C.: Dumbarton Oaks Research Library and Collection, 1984), and see note 11 above. The other volumes dealing with Arab-Byzantine relations in the fifth and sixth centuries are to appear in the near future.

[17] It is well known that when the southern Arabs deepened their penetration into Syria after the decline of the Seleucids,

there were already other Arabs who had established their own dynasties in the area. When the Romans appeared on the Near Eastern scene, Arab groups existed south of the Taurus, in Antioch, Edessa, Chalcidice, Palmyra, Emesa, and Arethusa. Three of these groups, the Ituraeans, the Nabataeans and the Idumaeans, were in possession of Syria (Shahîd, *Rome*, 4–5; Bowersock, *Roman Arabia*, chs. I–II; Mommsen, *History*, IV:63ff., 162ff., passim). Most of these Arabs had succeeded in maintaining their identity despite the influence of the Greco-Roman culture. Dussaud has shown the impressive extent to which they conserved their character; the Nabataeans, for instance, kept their Semitic rites, Arabic language, as well as their *traditional laws* and *ancestral customs* (see his *La Pénétration des arabes*, 205, passim; see also Shahîd, *Rome*, ch. I, especially p. 10; Bowersock, "A Report on Arabia Provincia," *Journal of Roman Studies* 61 [1971]: 219–42). "[U]nder the native princes," Fr. Cumont asserts, the Arabs "kept their own alphabet, their own religion and traditional laws" (*Cambridge Ancient History* [Cambridge, 1936], XI:616). No less important is the fact that the old tribal organization of the Semites remained very powerful, as is testified to in the case of the Nabataeans (Bowersock, *Roman Arabia*, 154; Cumont, *CAH* XI:622–24). Perhaps the most important factor that contributed to the preservation of the identity of these Arabs was the constant waves of penetrators and immigrants from the Peninsula (Cumont, *CAH* XI:614; J. S. Trimingham, *Christianity among the Arabs in Pre-Islamic Times* [London & New York: Longman, 1979], 3–4). These unceasing incursions must explain both the ongoing cultural replenishment of the northern Arabs and Roman need for the oriental *limes* (Shahîd, *Rome*, 8–12; D. F. Graf, "The Saracens and the Defense of the Arabian Frontier," *Bulletin of the American School of Oriental Research* 229 [1978]: 13). Other external factors also contributed to the preservation of the Semitic character of the Syrians. The Seleucids never attempted the Hellenization of the peoples they ruled, and their administration which took a network of cities as its basis failed to touch Syrian society at large (Trimingham, *Christianity*, 22). Hellenization could reach the municipal middle class only after the Roman conquest, at which time this relatively small class could only supply the provincial administrators. (See G. H. Stevenson, *Roman Provincial Administration* [Oxford: Basil Blackwell, 1939], 85, where he speaks of the absence of a Roman class of civil servants in the provinces.) Again, the Semitic population, which was to survive the Seleucids, the Romans and the Byzantines, was debarred from entering the inner layers of Hellenic culture (Cumont, *CAH* XI:613, 620, 639–41). Syria was no more Hellenic than Mesopotamian Ḥatra was Iranian. On Ḥatra's conservation of its Semitic character under the Persians, see J. Segal, "Arabs in Syriac Literature," *Jerusalem Studies in Arabic and Islam* 4 (1984): 91.

Commercial interests constituted the backbone of Rome's and Byzantium's relations with the Arabs of the Syrian desert and North West Arabia. On the basis of the Rawwâfa inscriptions (and, partly, the *Notitia Dignitatum*), D. Craf has established that in the second and beginning of the third centuries Rome was on good terms with the Thamûd tribal federation, whose elements encompassed up to one hundred tribes extending from al-ᶜUlâ in the south (about 250 km. south of Tabûk) to the Syrian desert in the north (Graf, "Defense," 3, 10–12; see also Bowersock, *Roman Arabia*, 131f. On the Arabs in the *Notitia Dignitatum*, see Shahîd, *Rome*, 51–63). In these inscriptions, Graf argues, "Rome is presented as the major contributor to the erection of the tribal temple of the Thamûdic federation and an esteemed intermediary in their intratribal disputes. This sanctuary and its inscriptions also reveal that such tribal structures were neither primitive nor culturally isolated; for centuries before their encounter with Rome they had been in contact with the major Near Eastern civilizations and involved in the international traffic of the Orient" (Graf, "Defense," 20). The Thamûd tribes were known even before this time to have cultivated land with sophisticated systems of irrigation and to have possessed a boat-building industry on the coast of Midian (Trimingham, *Christianity*, 15–16). On the eve of the Islamic conquests, the Judhâm tribal confederation, which was related to ʿÂmila and Lakhm and which seems to have supplanted Thamûd, was regarded as the guardian of the Syrian *limes*. Their area of control extended from the Dead Sea in the north down to the southern parts of Wâdî al-Qurâ, less than one-hundred miles north of Yathrib (Trimingham, *Christianity*, 120–23). These Arabs, with their *ḥulafâʾ*—the Bahrâʾ, Balî, Wâʾil, Bakr, Ghassân and Tanûkh—were the commercial intermediaries and cultural transmitters between Mecca and Byzantium (Shahîd, *Byzantium*, 15, 18; on the role of Arab *foederati* in Byzantine-Arab relations, see Shahîd, *Rome*, 29–32, 128f., passim; idem, *Byzantium*, passim). Syrian and Mesopotamian Arab merchants operated in Mecca, and the Ghassânids, as the *ḥulafâʾ* of Banû Asad, had an establishment in the neighborhood of the Kaʿba. Representatives of the Syrian (and Mesopotamian) North were to be found in Mecca. The Meccans were constantly in touch with their northern brothers and, as the Qurʾân shows (S. XXX: 1–3), they were fully aware of the wars between Byzantium and Persia (Trimingham, *Christianity*, 258–60, passim). Abû Ṭâlib, Muḥammad's uncle, could not have been the only Meccan to frequent Bostra, and Abû Sufyân himself must have been doing what other Ḥijâzî merchants had done when he purchased a farm near Damascus before Islam (Trimingham, *Christianity*, 258; Shaban, *Islamic History* [Cambridge: Cambridge University Press, 1971], I:43). And of particular interest is what the sources tell us not only about the thriving cities of the Ḥijâz but also about the large slave market at Mecca. It is no coincidence that Zayd b. Ḥârith, the adopted son of Muḥammad, was a Syrian slave. See Trimingham, *Christianity*, 260; E. R. Wolf, "The Social Organization of Mecca and the Origins of Islam," *Southwestern Journal of Anthropology* 7.4 (1951): 334; S. Smith, "Events in Arabia in the 6th Century A.D.," *The Bulletin of the School of Oriental and African Studies* 16 (1954): 467.

Furthermore, when the Muslims occupied Syria, the local Arabs already formed the principal part of the population; many of the Greeks who inhabited the area left when the Muslims arrived. (A. A. Vasiliev, "Notes on Some Episodes Concerning the Relations Between the Arabs and the Byzantine Empire From the Fourth to the Sixth Century," *Dumbarton Oaks Papers* 9–10 [1956]: 309; Shaban, *Islamic History*, 41.) Almost every Arab tribe or sub-tribe was, to a greater or lesser extent, represented in Syria. These tribes had long been established in the area either as half-nomads or as full sedentaries. (See the article of A. Fischer "Ḳais-ᶜAilân," and that of C. Brockelmann "Kalb B. Wabara," in the *Encyclopaedia of Islam*, II:ii, 653, 688–90. Also W. Madelung, "Apocalyptic Prophecies in Ḥimṣ in the Umayyad Age," *Journal of Semitic Studies* 31.2 [1986]: 142.) Indeed, it is these people who undertook the preliminary tasks of building an empire, and it is these people, with the Arab immigrants from the south, who claimed to be the experts on *ḥadîth*; in Ḥimṣ, for instance, a strong school of *ḥadîth* arose, "drawing its inspiration" from the almost five hundred Companions who came to the city. See Madelung, "Apocalyptic," 143.

[18] See note 17 above, and Dussaud, *La Pénétration des arabes*, passim.

[19] See note 17 above.

[20] Although in her *Meccan Trade*, 153, "southern Syria and Ḥîra formed part of Arabia in all respects except one." The exception is unclear, but I take it to be political domination. Further, on Byzantine trade and influence in the Peninsula, see ibid., 115ff., 138–40, 151, 246. Crone's thesis in *Roman, Provincial and Islamic Law* obviously requires the suppression of the facts about Byzantine-Arab relations which she admits in her *Meccan Trade*.

[21] If the space allotted to the treatment of a subject is any indication of its importance, then *walâ*ᵓ stands as one of the least important of legal subjects expounded in the works of

*furû*ᶜ. For example, the space given to the discussion of *walâ*ᵓ *al-muwâlât*, accepted only by the Ḥanafî and sectarian schools, is less than one page in the more than one thousand pages of Marghînânî's *Hidâya*. In *al-Fatâwâ al-Hindiyya* it occupies a page and a half out of about 3200 pages. It is interesting to note that the legal status of hermaphrodites normally takes more than double the space devoted to *walâ*ᵓ *al-muwâlât*.

[22] This is clearly understood from *Al-Fatâwâ al-Hindiyya*, 6 vols., 3rd ed. (Beirut: Dâr Iḥyâᵓ al-Turâth al-ᶜArabî, 1980), V:26, 32; Abû Jaᶜfar Muḥammad b. ᶜAlî al-Ṭûsî, *al-Khilâf fî al-Fiqh*, 2 vols. (Tehran: Maṭbaᶜat Rangîn, 1377–1382 H.), II:648ff.; Burhân al-Dîn al-Marghînânî, *al-Hidâya*, 4 vols. (Cairo: Maṭbaᶜat al-Bâbî al-Ḥalabî, 1980), III:271.

[23] *Al-Fatâwâ al-Hindiyya*, V:32 (ll. 29–30); Ṭûsî, *Khilâf*, II:652; Muḥammad ᶜAlî al-Ṭûrî, *al-Baḥr al-Râᵓiq*, 8 vols. (Cairo: al-Maṭbaᶜat al-ᶜIlmiyya, n.d.), VIII:77 (ll. 26–27).

[24] Shams al-Dîn al-Sarakhsî, *al-Mabsûṭ*, 30 vols. (Cairo: Maṭbaᶜat al-Saᶜâda, 1324–1331 H.), VIII:91 (ll. 13–14), 92, 96 (l. −2).

[25] *Al-Fatâwâ al-Hindiyya*, V:32.

[26] Sarakhsî, *Mabsûṭ*, VIII:96 (l. 12).

[27] *Al-Fatâwâ al-Hindiyya*, V:32 (l. −4).

[28] ᶜAbd Allâh b. Mawdûd al-Mûṣilî, *al-Ikhtiyâr li-Taᶜlîl al-Mukhtâr*, 5 vols. (Cairo: Muṣṭafâ Bâbî al-Ḥalabî, 1951), IV:44 (ll. 17–18); Sarakhsî, *al-Mabsûṭ*, VIII:95 (ll. 9, −4). See also Ṭûsî, *al-Khilâf*, II:652 (*masᵓala* 9).

[29] Ṭûsî, *al-Khilâf*, II:652. The language of offer continues: *wa-tadfaᶜa ᶜannî wa-adfaᶜa ᶜanka wa-taᶜqila ᶜanî wa-aᶜqila ᶜanka wa-tarithanî wa-arithaka* (II:652, l. 4).

[30] *Al-Fatâwâ al-Hindiyya*, V:33; Ṭûsî, *al-Khilâf*, II:652 (ll. 9–10).

[31] *Al-Fatâwâ al-Hindiyya*, V:32 (−9); Ṭûrî, *al-Baḥr al-Râᵓiq*, VIII:77. See also ᶜAlâᵓ al-Dîn al-Samarqandî, *Tuḥfat al-Fuqahâᵓ*, ed. M. Kattânî and W. Zuḥaylî, 3 vols. (Damascus: Dâr al-Fikr, 1964), II:403, who adds the condition that the party making the offer must not have Muslim heirs in existence.

[32] Ṭûsî, *al-Khilâf*, II:652 (ll. 7–9).

[33] E. Tyan, "Ḥilf," *Encyclopaedia of Islam*, 2nd ed., III:388–89; see also the references to his *Institutions de droit public musulman*; W. R. Smith, *Kinship and Marriage in Early Arabia* (Cambridge: Cambridge University Press, 1855), 45ff. who argues much the same.

[34] ᶜAbd al-Razzâq al-Ṣanᶜânî, *al-Muṣannaf*, 11 vols. (Beirut: Dâr al-Qalam, 1970–1972), IX, no. 16,140 (*al-walâʾu bi-manzilati al-ḥilfi* . . .).

[35] Abû Jaᶜfar al-Ṭabarî, *Târîkh al-Umam wal-Mulûk*, 13 vols. (Beirut: Maktabat al-Bayân, n.d.), III:29–30.

[36] Cited by Crone, *Meccan Trade*, 145.

[37] Crone, *Roman*, 32; *The Constitution of Medina*, ed. and trans. M. Hamidullah (Lahore: Ashraf Press, 1968), 57 (12b), and 62 (37b) where *ḥilf* is clearly between individuals.

[38] Abû Isḥâq al-Fazârî, *Kitâb al-Siyar*, ed. F. Ḥamâda (Beirut: Muʾassasat al-Risâla, 1987), 173 (no. 212); Crone,, *Roman*, 87 (ll. 14–15).

[39] Crone & Cook, *Hagarism*, 18.

[40] Cf. under the relevant terms in M. Fuʾâd ᶜAbd al-Bâqî, *al-Muᶜjam al-Mufahras* (Cairo: Dâr al-Kutub al-Miṣriyya, 1945).

[41] J. A. Crook, *Law and Life of Rome* (London: Thames and Hudson, 1967), 192–93.

[42] Ibid., 193; see also pp. 201, 246 for particular services rendered under this contract.

[43] S. Treggiari, *Roman Freedmen* (Oxford: Clarendon Press, 1969), 20–31.

[44] von Kremer, *Culturgeschichte*, I:546–47.

[45] The book is nonetheless marred by a good number of typographical and diacritical errors. Some of these errors have occurred at the following pages: 7 (ll. 6, 36), 11 (l. −6), 19 (l. 15), 20 (l. −14), 35 (l. −7), 37 (l. 3), 40 (l. −19), 43 (ll. 16–17), 45 (l. 3), 46 (l. −14), 53 (l. 17), 56 (l. 26), 59 (ll. 2, 8, 22), 60 (l. 15), 62 (l. 5), 69 (l. 3), 71 (l. 8), 81 (l. 18), 85 (l. 2), 86 (l. 23), 87 (ll. −14, −12, −9), 103 (l. 22), 107 (l. −4), 109 (l. 14), 138 (l. −18).

[46] von Kremer, *Culturgeschichte*, I:546–47; also 524ff.

X

NOTES ON THE TERM *QARĪNA* IN ISLAMIC LEGAL DISCOURSE

The term *qarīna* in Islamic legal discourse represents a central technical concept whose multifarious meanings have not been adequately explicated in the authoritative technical dictionaries. While the *qarīna* plays an important role in the linguistic interpretation of the texts—thus partaking in the very process of defining the language of the law—it is of no less significance in the epistemic evaluation of Prophetic traditions. The various technical connotations of the term *qarīna* in these spheres of legal theory, as well as in positive and substantive law are the main concerns of these notes.

I

An infrequently observed yet characteristic feature of Islamic religious-scientific writings in general and legal literature in particular is the disparity between the variegated and changing technical contents of some terms in actual scholarly expositions and their reduced and simplified meaning in technical dictionaries. This gulf may be substantiated by comparing standard definitions of key terms of legal theory in any unabridged technical dictionary with their diversified uses in treatises on the subject. One such term which may be considered of central importance in juridico-linguistic interpretation and epistemology and which finds little explication in technical lexicons is *qarīna* (pl. *qarāʾin*).

In the *Kashshāf Iṣṭilāḥāt al-Funūn*, one of the most authoritative technical dictionaries, the term *qarīna* is confined to its rudimentary linguistic and logical meaning.[1] Linguistically, the *qarīna* represents a verbal or non-verbal element clarifying a part of speech extraneous to itself. The independence of the *qarīna* from that which it renders unambiguous and, at the same time, the unalterable association which it forms with its subject consign the two to an "associative" relationship. In fact, the notion embodied in such a relationship corresponds to the most basic meaning of the verb *qarana*; namely, to connect, associate, hitch together. The eighth form of the verb likewise means to join or link, and with the preposition *bi* it would mean to be married to, or to be coupled with.[2] These notions also appear in the technical connotation of the logical definition of the term; that is, the necessary connection between the major and the minor premises and the arrangement within these premises of the terms which fashion the moods of the categorical figures in syllogistics.[3]

II

In legal theory the concept of *qarīna* plays an important role in at least two main respects: the linguistic interpretation of the texts, and the knowledge that these texts, especially Prophetic traditions, impart. The differences in the character of *qarīna* in these two separate areas underscore the distinction between two types of *qarāʾin*, one verbal, the very basic notion of which we have already intimated, the other circumstantial. Pertaining to the semantic aspects of words, the first type is known in the Arabic sources as *qarāʾin maqāliyya* or *qarāʾin lafẓiyya*, and the second, being relative to the circumstances of transmitting Prophetic traditions, is accordingly termed *qarāʾin ḥāliyya* (with the more common variation *qarāʾin al-aḥwāl*) or *qarāʾin maʿnawiyya*.[4]

Although they represent two distinct categories, the semantic and circumstantial *qarāʾin* may converge in the same context to determine the precise meaning of a word or a sentence. A primary instance of this occurs in the interpretation of the texts where the scope and content of the divine command constantly call for delimitation. The question, for instance, of whether or not women are also addressed along with men by a divine command commencing with the pronoun "whoever" presents one case in point. As an example of such problematic usage the jurists debated the subsumability of women in a neuter pronominal sentence as that uttered by a master, who, addressing his servant, says: "Whoever enters my house should be respected." Since the servant would be liable to rebuke should he show lack of respect toward any women entering the house, it was argued that the above command, as well as any other command of identical nature, includes both sexes. The problematic issue, however, was whether the universality (*ʿumūm*) of the command derives from the command's language *per se* or from particular extra-linguistic circumstances surrounding the verbal usage that add to the command a meaning which the language itself does not convey. It was argued that the existence of a *qarīnat al-ḥāl* together with the command, namely, the customary Arab practice that guests, whoever they may be, are not to be shown lack of respect without a reason, confirms that the language itself is not independent of reality and that the command acquires an extended meaning through convention. The effect of social norms on the determination of the meaning of the command may be most apparent in the case of a thief entering the master's house for the purpose of robbing it. If the command were universal and bore no relation to the reality of social behavior, the thief should be allowed to enter and practice his profession, for the command was given with no conditions or qualifications.

Against this argument it was maintained that even if the command runs counter to the aforementioned *qarīna*, the universality still persists, as in the command "Whoever enters my house should be insulted." The servant would be rebuked if he were not to insult the guests, although social decorum goes against such behavior. Here, certain jurists insist, there exists no relevant, effective *qarīnat al-ḥāl*, which can change or delimit the meaning of speech. This is precisely equivalent to the command "He who says to you X, say to him Y"; it simply means what it says.[5]

When there exists no *qarīna* the speech must be understood in its literal (*ḥaqīqa*) meaning: a mule is a mule, and a lion is a lion. But in conjunction with a *qarīna*, the word might acquire a new meaning, and a "lion" might cease to refer to a real lion. Conventionally perceived as courageous, the lion is taken to represent that quality in people. Thus, one may metaphorically describe a soldier as "a lion in battle." The *qarīna* surrounding the use of "lion" makes it obvious that the reference is to a person and not to an animal, the clarifying *qarīna* being the battle. The unlikelihood, if not the impossibility, of a real lion participating in a battle between armies forces here the figurative understanding of the word.[6] Thus a word must be accompanied by a *qarīna* for it to be understood metaphorically.[7]

While the absence of a *qarīna* normally precludes the figurative usage of a word and restricts it to a single meaning, a homonym (*lafẓ mushtarak*) stripped of a *qarīna* can never be intelligible, and will thus remain ambiguous (*mujmal*).[8] When you say the word "spring" outside any context, your audience will not be able to determine whether you are referring to a season of the year, an artesian well or to a spiral in your mattress. Only the context, namely, a *qarīna*, can clarify the speaker's intention. An elementary example of such context is furnished in the statement "He drank from this spring," the act of drinking being the *qarīna mukhaṣṣiṣa* which limits "spring" to the meaning of artesian well rather than the particular season in the year or the metal element in the mattress. In homonyms, therefore, *qarāʾin* reduce ambiguity and pinpoint the object intended, whereas in words of *ḥaqīqa* they create additional meanings for the same words. Moreover, weak *qarāʾin* (*adnā al-qarāʾin* or *qarāʾin ḍaʿīfa*) only hint at or clarify the referent in homonyms, but it requires a strong *qarīna* (*qarīna qawiyya*) to make the figurative meaning of a word preponderate over its original, *ḥaqīqa* meaning.[9]

Since the imperative mood in legal language stands at the heart of textual interpretation, a chief task of the jurist is the determination of the precise meaning and scope of the imperative (*al-amr*). Without a *qarīna*, an imperative remains indeterminate on at least two major points. The first is the intended time in which a command must be implemented. In the absence of a *qarīna*, as for example in the decontextualized command "Pray," it is impossible to know whether we should pray now or at a later date. But in the case of a master telling his servant "I am thirsty, bring me some water to drink," or in the Quranic verse (XV: 29) "When I have created him and have breathed into him of My spirit, you shall fall down (*faqaʿū*), prostrating yourselves unto him," the *qarāʾin al-lafẓiyya* of thirst and the use of the sequential *fāʾ* in *faqaʿū* indicate that the implementation of the command was intended to be immediate.[10]

The second problem that the interpretation of an imperative devoid of a *qarīna* poses is whether the command dictates the fulfillment of the obligation once only or repeatedly *ad infinitum*. Apparently, a sizeable majority of jurists held that in the absence of a *qarīna*, the command to perform an act should be implemented only once.[11] The performance of a commanded act becomes an obligation to be continuously repeated only when this is indicated by certain *qarāʾin*. If a master, for instance, orders his servant to buy bread from the marketplace, the latter would be going beyond the instructions of his employer were he to buy bread every day, even though the order of the master may be interpreted to be effective every day. But the absence of a *qarīna māniʿa*, that is, an indication precluding the command from being intended as permanent, necessarily means that once the order is implemented, the task would be considered fully and adequately performed.[12]

With the aid of *qarāʾin* therefore, God's command in the textual sources can be defined precisely. A *qarīna* attached to a command determines whether the performance of that command is obligatory, recommended or left entirely to the discretion of the individual Muslim. Likewise, a command essentially prohibiting the performance of an act (*nahy*) may be interpreted variably, depending on the quality of the *qarīna*, as a strict or "mild" prohibition.[13] *Qarāʾin* may add, reduce, explain, specify, define: *al-qarāʾin al-juzʾiyya* render a statement valid in part, not wholly; *qarāʾin al-takrār* in a command indicate the necessity for infinite repetition of the act commanded; *qarāʾin al-iḥtimāl* make probable the meaning of a statement or the occurrence of an event; *al-qarāʾin al-mukhaṣṣiṣa* or *al-mubayyina* particularize and delimit a general notion.[14]

Ascertaining the import of an ambiguous legal text may prove impossible without a number of *qarāʾin* which must combine in order to make intelligible what seems to the jurist the intended meaning of the text. In other words, the inductive aggregation of *qarāʾin* in support of a meaning is sought by the jurist in order to lend clarity and credibility to his interpretation. Consider, for instance, the problem in the interpretation of a *ḥadīth* with regard to a certain Ghaylān b. Salma who, upon converting to Islam, asked the Prophet what to do with his ten wives, whereupon the Prophet enjoined him to "retain four of them and part with the others." The injunction was taken by later jurists to mean that Ghaylān was to retain four wives without having to remarry them, not, as certain opponents argued, to divorce them all and subsequently marry only four. This interpretation was supported not by a single *qarīna* but by several. First, the Companions, who were presumed to have intimately known the intentions and wishes of the Prophet, understood this statement to mean retaining four wives without remarrying them. Second, the Prophet gave Ghaylān alone the choice to keep four wives; viz., had he wanted him to form another contract of marriage according to the new religion, he, the Prophet, would have mentioned the need to secure the consent of the four wives or that of their marriage guardians. Third, the Prophet began his injunction by uttering the word "retain," which represents a positive command not to part, even momentarily, with the four he decides to keep. Had the Prophet wanted him to divorce all of them first, and only then marry four, he would have said so explicitly. Fourth, if the Prophet intended Ghaylān to enter into a new contract with four wives he would have stipulated the legal conditions and qualifications of marriage under Muslim law, since Ghaylān had just converted to the new religion of Islam, and was thus presumed ignorant of its laws.[15]

Of particular interest in this interpretation is the fourth *qarīna*, which is, in effect, an argument from the negative; it is simply founded on an absent piece of evidence. The absence of a *qarīna* is itself used as a *qarīna*. Apparently, such arguments were not at all infrequent. As one can detect from the legal texts, there lay a claim for the validity and defensibility of the principle that the absence of a certain thing may be taken as a meaningful *qarīna* in support of a given interpretation.[16]

Be that as it may, *qarāʾin* were seen by jurists to constitute an integral part of speech, a part designed by the Creator to yield a certain hermeneutical benefit. God, it was argued, would not have posited *qarāʾin* had there not been a need for them.[17] They are intended not only to facilitate textual interpretation, but also to provide evidence on the basis of which legal rulings are derived. Indeed, the word *qarīna* is often used interchangeably, or in conjunction with the word *dalīl*, the latter defined as that which leads to the knowledge of the unobserved on the basis of the observed.[18] It is not uncommon to unravel and determine the *dalīl* through *qarāʾin*. *Qarāʾin* can then also be instrumental in the *actual* process of law-making.[19]

III

The other category of *qarāʾin*, commonly known as *qarāʾin al-aḥwāl*, was less relevant to the linguistic formulations of legal theory than to the transmission of the second material source of law, the Sunna. Here, *qarāʾin* played a central role in the evaluation of the authenticity of Prophetic traditions. But *qarāʾin* were not deemed merely as epistemic units exclusively relevant to the transmission of the Prophetic past; they occupied a relatively important position in the taxonomy of the construction of knowledge. *Qarāʾin*, that is to say, constituted a source of knowledge about things past and present. Consider, for instance, the facial expressions accompanying anger, the tears shed when crying, the coyness of a shy person, etc. They all are signs instrumental in gaining knowledge about the state of mind or affairs of persons we are curious about. In the same vein, we would believe a person who tells us that Zayd is ill when we see that the latter's face is pale and that he has lost considerable weight.[20] These signifiers or indices of circumstantial evidence ranked high on the jurists' list of the means by which knowledge is obtained (*marātib al-ʿulūm*). Ghazālī, for example, accords *qarāʾin* a fifth place after the knowledge of such things as the law of the excluded middle and the knowledge obtained through sensory perception (*maḥsūsāt*) and recurrent traditions (*tawātur*).[21] Juwaynī, on the other hand, places them as sixth in his classification.[22]

Inasmuch as the considerable loss of weight signifies suffering from illness, the conditions of the transmitters of a Prophetic tradition, their personal integrity, status in society and faithfulness to Islam, the extent of their knowledge of the law and principles of religion, their rank as *mujtahids*, their personal reputation as meticulous and precise, etc., are *qarāʾin* that attest to the authenticity of a Prophetic tradition.[23] If a tradition were transmitted by a chain of transmitters who are surrounded by a set of strong *qarāʾin*, the probability that this tradition is authentic is raised significantly. The weight that *qarāʾin* lend to Prophetic traditions derives not only from the fact that the *qarāʾin* simply surround the tradition with supportive and authenticating evidence but also from their being a source of knowledge in themselves. In fact, a group of jurists went as far as to argue that *qarāʾin* can, in their aggregation, yield certain knowledge even when they accompany weak traditions.[24] It suffices here to give one example. When we observe a mother nursing her child, we do not really see the milk reaching the stomach of the child. Our knowledge of this is only supposed. But we become certain of the fact that the child is taking the milk merely by noticing that the throat of the child is showing a movement peculiar to suckling; that he makes a certain sound also peculiar to that activity; that he stopped crying; that he has not eaten for a number of hours; that the woman feeding him, his mother, is in the period of nursing; that sucking the breast of the mother is an infantile instinct; that after having done with his mother the child has become thoroughly satisfied.[25]

The certainty of knowledge generated by *qarāʾin* may well have been the underlying cause for an established controversy concerning whether or not a solitary tradition (*khabar āḥād*) can yield certain knowledge of the information it conveys. A number of jurists insisted that an *āḥād* tradition may lead to certainty only if accompanied by strong *qarāʾin*. If a single person tells us, for instance, that the son of a king died we will be certain of his death once we take into account the *qarāʾin* relevant to the tradition we heard. The first *qarīna* is our knowledge that the son had for sometime been afflicted with a fatal disease. But contemporaneous *qarāʾin*, such as wailing and crying of relatives, the marching of a funeral procession, the improper appearance in public of the female relatives as well as the king himself, the marching in the funeral of the king and his entourage, including viziers and high-ranking officers, can only lead to certain knowledge of the son's death.[26] The majority of jurists, however, rejected the view that an *āḥād* tradition can lead to certainty in conjunction with *qarā'in.*[27] The chief argument adduced in support of this view was that even four witnesses, whose personal integrity (*ʿadāla*) is proven in a court of law to be beyond impeachment, fall short of confirming beyond any doubt a claim of committing adultery. Only a number of transmissions larger than four and enhanced by strong *qarā'in al-aḥwāl* can lead to certainty. But this type of tradition, commonly known as the *mutawātir*, does not necessarily engender certain knowledge in all minds exposed to it. One intellect may reach certitude upon hearing a tradition transmitted a certain number of times, while another intellect may not reach such knowledge even though it was exposed to the same number of transmissions. The reason for this is that the first intellect would be familiar with certain relevant *qarā'in* which are unknown to the second.[28]

The certitude imparted by the *mutawātir* may sometimes be the result not of meeting the strictly formal conditions of the *tawātur*, but rather the outcome of an interplay between highly probable traditions—i.e., traditions stronger than the common *āḥād* but weaker than the consummate *mutawātir*—and an adequate set of *qarā'in*. *Qarā'in* may thus be substitutes for instances of transmission, strengthening a tradition to a degree of certainty.[29] Qarāfī, for one, admitted the conclusiveness of such a tradition, but refused to give it the designation "*mutawātir.*" He simply did not know what it was technically called.[30]

Qarā'in, on the other hand, may derive from indirect textual statements bearing upon the issue under discussion. A prominent case in point is the authoritativeness of consensus which was partly established by means of a variety of Quranic verses and prophetic traditions bearing indirectly upon the theme of the infallibility of the community, but lending support to the more direct traditions which explicitly state this infallibility.[31] *Qarā'in* then are not restricted to any one type; they may be circumstantial, rational or even textual.[32]

IV

In positive and substantive law, *qarāʾin* play an equally varied and crucial role. Consider for example the case in which a dispute arises as to whether a certain commodity was bartered for another commodity or sold for a price. If the seller says that he received a price for the commodity, then his word is admitted in a court of law, since the accepted mode of sale is by payment, not barter. The customary practice here is in itself evidence bearing upon the truthfulness of the seller (*fal-qawlu qawlu al-bāʾiʿi li-quwwati qarīnati ṣidqihi*).[33] Any context, be it a given or presumed set of facts underlying a particular situation, or any circumstantial evidence affecting a matter under consideration, is considered a *qarīna*; when it bears upon truthfulness it is *qarīnat al-ṣidq*, and when it has to do with a price it would be *qarīnat al-tasʿīr*; if the matter entails preference, say a male over a female as a witness in a court of law, it would be *qarīnat al-tafḍīl*, etc.[34]

Qarāʾin may also appear as non-linguistic, "rational" factors, determining the scope of the application of the law. The existence of *al-qarāʾin al-ʿaqliyya* as a permanent guiding principle in the mind of the jurist dictates, for instance, that such persons as the mentally handicapped and minors are not subject to the generally applicable provisions of the law.[35]

V

The pervasive effect of *qarāʾin* in legal theory confirms the multi-faceted approaches to the evaluation or solution of problems of jurisprudence, be they relative to the textual interpretation of a divine command or to the epistemic assessment of a Prophetic tradition. A text may stand subject to varying interpretations by different jurists by virtue of the fact that each interpreter comes to the text with a different idea of what the relevant *qarāʾin* are, and surely, the meaning of the text is presumed to be established according to the *qarāʾin* preconceived by each interpreter. Similarly, the epistemic value of legal precepts are determined by the mode and circumstances of the transmission of Prophetic traditions which are in turn largely affected by the strength and number of *qarāʾin* surrounding them. The absence from legal theory of a control for defining what the *qarāʾin* can and should be in each case leaves the door open—at least theoretically—to a significant latitude in the textual interpretation of the divine decree and in the epistemic assessment of the most substantive source of law, the Sunna. Although the interpretative latitude brings with it the implication that the law may have as many interpretations as its interpreters, reality allowed for a rich diversity albeit within relatively narrow boundaries; differences among schools in methodological constructions and positive legal formulations remained minimal at best. On the other hand, the *qarāʾin* played one of the most important, if not a crucial role in creating remarkably diverse epistemic structures underlying legal theories. The line between the probable and the certain within the spectrum of the legal schools remained as elusive as ever.

[1] Muḥammad b. ʿAlī al-Tahānawī, *Kashshāf Iṣṭilāḥāt al-Funūn*, 2 vols. (Calcutta: W. N. Leeds' Press, 1862), II, p. 1228, s.v. "*qarīna.*" An extremely laconic definition may also be found in the equally authoritative dictionary of ʿAbd al-Nabī al-Aḥmadnagarī, *Jāmiʿ al-ʿUlūm fī Iṣṭilāḥat al-Funūn al-Mulaqqab bi-Dustūr al-ʿUlamāʾ*, 4 vols. (Beirut: Muʾassasat al-Aʿlamī lil-Maṭbūʿāt, 1975), III, p. 64.

[2] Jamāl al-Dīn Muḥammad Ibn Manẓūr, *Lisān al-ʿArab*, 15 vols. (Beirut: Dār Ṣādir, 1972), XII, pp. 331–42, especially 336b.

[3] Tahānawī, op. cit., II, pp. 1228, 1229, s.v. *iqtirān*. For the syllogistic moods see Ibn Abī al-Ṣalt al-Dānī, *Taqwīm al-Dhihn*, ed. & trans. C. G. Palencia (Madrid: n.p., 1915), pp. 22 ff.

[4] Fakhr al-Dīn al-Rāzī, *al-Maḥṣūl fī ᶜIlm Uṣūl al-Fiqh*, ed. T. J. F. al-ᶜUlwānī, 2 vols., 6 parts. (Riyāḍ: The Islamic University of Muḥammad b. Suᶜūd Press, 1979–81), I, i, 461; Sayf al-Dīn al-Āmidī, *al-Iḥkām fī Uṣūl al-Aḥkām*, 3 vols. (Cairo: ᶜAlī Ṣubayḥ, 1968), I, p. 34 (l. 5 from bottom).

[5] Āmidī, op. cit., II, pp. 66, 107–108.

[6] Muḥammad b. ᶜAlī al-Sakkākī, *Miftāḥ al-ᶜUlūm* (Cairo: al-Maṭbaᶜa al-Adabiyya, 1317 H.), pp. 192 ff., 204; Ghazālī, *al-Mustaṣfā min ᶜIlm al-Uṣūl*, 2 vols. (Cairo: Būlāq, 1324 H.), I, 360.

[7] Abū al-Ḥusayn al-Baṣrī, *al-Muᶜtamad fī Uṣūl al-Fiqh*, ed. M. Hamidullah et al., 2 vols. (Damas: Institut Français de Damas, 1964–1965), II, p. 910; Āmidī, op. cit., I, pp. 24 (ll. 9–10), 26 (l. 5), 34; Rāzī, op. cit., I, pp. i, 403, 481, 498; Abū Yaᶜlā b. al-Ḥusayn al-Farrāʾ al-Baghdādī, *al-ᶜUdda fī Uṣūl al-Fiqh*, ed. Aḥmad al-Mubārakī, 3 vols. (Beirut: Muʾassasat al-Risāla, 1980), I, p. 242.

[8] Muḥibbullāh Ibn ᶜAbd al-Shakūr, *Musallam al-Thubūt*, a commentary on Muḥammad b. Niẓām al-Dīn al-Anṣārī's *Fawātiḥ al-Raḥamūt*, 2 vols. (Cairo: Būlāq, 1322 H.), I, p. 203; Āmidī, op. cit., I, p. 17.

[9] Rāzī, op. cit., I, i, 386–87, 493, 495. Rāzī reports that Shāfiᶜī and Abū Bakr al-Bāqillānī held the view that when a homonym is divested of its *al-qarāʾin al-mukhaṣṣiṣa* it must be taken to encompass all of its homonymous meanings. Ibid., p. 380.

[10] Āmidī, op. cit., II, pp. 14, 31 (ll. 21–23), 34.

[11] Ibid., II, p. 22; Ḥasan b. Zayn al-Shahīd al-Thānī, *Maᶜālim al-Uṣūl*, ed. Mehdi Mohaghegh (Tehran: Sherkat-e Enteshārāt-e Elmī va Farhangī, 1364 H.), p. 60.

[12] Āmidī, op. cit., II, pp. 22 (ll. 12–22), 27 (ll. 12–15); Sakkākī, op. cit., pp. 192, 198 (l.19). The opposite of *qarīna māniᶜa* is *qarīna ṣārifa*.

[13] Māwardī, *Adab al-Qāḍī*, ed. M. H. Sarḥān, 2 vols. (Baghdād: Maṭbaʿat al-Irshād, 1971), I, p. 278; Ghazālī, *Mustaṣfā*, I, pp. 419–20, 429–30; Muwaffaq al-Dīn Ibn Qudāma, *Rawḍat al-Nāẓir wa-Jannat al-Munāẓir* (Beirut: Dār al-Kitāb al-ʿArabī, 1981), p. 170.

[14] Ibn ʿAbd al-Shakūr, op. cit., I, pp. 380 (ll. 15–19, 25), 283 (l. 26); Ghazālī, op. cit., I, pp. 350, 355; Ibn Qudāma, op. cit., p. 164.

[15] Ghazālī, op. cit., I, pp. 390–92; Ibn Qudāma, op. cit., p. 158.

[16] Farrāʾ, op. cit., I, pp. 221–22.

[17] Ghazālī, op. cit., I, p. 406. See also idem., *al-Mankhūl min Taʿlīqāt al-Uṣūl*, ed. M. Ḥ. Haytū (Damascus: n. p., 1970), p. 51.

[18] Sulaymān Ibn Khalaf al-Bājī, *al-Ḥudūd fī al-Uṣūl*, ed. Nazīh Ḥammād (Beirut and Homs: Muʾassasat al-Zuʿbī, 1973), p. 38.

[19] Farrāʾ, op. cit., p. 245 (l. 16); Abū al-Walīd al-Bājī, *al-Minhāj fī Tartīb al-Ḥijāj*, ed. Abdel Magid Turki (Paris: G.-P. Maisonneuve et Larose, 1978), p. 17 (l. 5); Ibn Qudāma, op. cit., p. 157 (ll. 19–20).

[20] Shihāb al-Dīn Ibn Idrīs al-Qarāfī, *Sharḥ Tanqīḥ al-Fuṣūl*, ed. T. ʿAbd al-Raʾūf Saʿd (Cairo: Dār al-Fikr, 1973), pp. 354–55.

[21] Ghazālī, *Mankhūl*, pp. 46–47, 51.

[22] Imām al-Ḥaramayn al-Juwaynī, *al-Burhān fī Uṣūl al-Fiqh*, ed. ʿAbd al-ʿAẓīm Dīb, 2 vols. (Cairo: Dār al-Anṣār, 1979), I, p. 131, par. 50.

[23] Āmidī, op. cit., I, p. 232 (l. 9); Abū al-Barakāt Ḥāfiz al-Dīn al-Nasafī, *Kashf al-Asrār*, 2 vols. (Cairo: Būlāq, 1316 H.), II, pp. 12–13; al-Muḥaqqiq al-Ḥillī, *Maʿārij al-Uṣūl*, ed. M. Ḥ. Raḍwī (Qum: Maṭba ʿat Sayyid al-Shuhadāʾ, 1403 H.), p. 148.

[24] Ghazālī, *Mustaṣfā*, I, p. 135 (l. 8); Ibn Quḍāma, op. cit., p. 87 (ll. 5–6). In his *al-Mankhūl*, 237, 238, Ghazālī was prepared to say that it is the *qarāʾin* surrounding the tradition

which constitute the proof of truthfulness and authenticity, not the language or the content of the traditions themselves.

[25] Ibn Qudāma, op. cit., pp. 87–88.

[26] Muṣṭafā al-Iᶜtimādī al-Tabrīzī, *Sharḥ Maᶜālim al-Dīn fī al-Uṣūl* (Qum: Kitāb-ī Furūshī Muṣṭafāwī, 1377 H.), pp. 295f.

[27] On the parties to this dispute see Abū Bakr al-Sarakhsī, *Uṣūl*, ed. Abū al-Wafā᾽ al-Afghānī, 2 vols. (Cairo: Dār al-Kitāb al-ᶜArabī, 1372 H.), I, p. 330; Qarāfī, op. cit., pp. 354f.; Āmidī, op. cit., I, pp. 234, 237, 238; Ibn Qudāma, op. cit., p. 92; Kamāl al-Dīn Ibn al-Humām, *al-Taḥrīr fī Uṣūl al-Fiqh* (Cairo: Muṣṭafā Bābī al-Ḥalabī, 1351 H.), p. 331; Ḥillī, op. cit., p. 141; Kamāl al-Dīn al-Anbārī, *Lumaᶜ al-Adilla fī Uṣūl al-Naḥw*, ed. Attia Amer (Stockholm: Almqvist & Wiksell, 1963), p. 34.

[28] Ibn Qudāma, op. cit., p. 87 (ll. 3–6); Ghazālī, *Mustaṣfā*, I, p. 135 (ll. 4–6); Āmidī, op. cit., I, pp. 229, 230 (ll. 1–3); Qarāfī, op. cit., p. 352 (ll. 12–15). For a detailed analysis of *tawātur* knowledge and the element of subjectivity in it see W. B. Hallaq, "On Inductive Corroboration, Probability and Certainty in Sunni Legal Thought" (forthcoming).

[29] Āmidī, op. cit., I, p. 238.

[30] Qarāfī, op. cit., pp. 349 (ll. 12–14), 357.

[31] See W. B. Hallaq, "On the Authoritativeness of Sunni Consensus," *International Journal of Middle East Studies*, 18, 4 (1986), pp. 441ff.

[32] Baṣrī, op. cit., II, pp. 912–20, especially 913 (ll. 10–11).

[33] Burhān al-Dīn Muḥammad Ibn Farḥūn, *Tabṣirat al-Ḥukkām fī Uṣūl al-Aqḍiya wa-Manāhij al-Aḥkām*, 2 vols. (Cairo: Dār al-Kutub al-ᶜIlmiyya, 1301 H.), II, p. 250.

[34] Ghazālī, *Miᶜyār al-ᶜIlm fī Fann al-Manṭiq*, ed. Sulaymān Dunyā (Cairo: Dār al-Maᶜārif, 1961), p. 75. On the general uses of *qarā᾽in* in positive law see Aḥmad b. Yaḥyā al-Wansharīsī, *al-Miᶜyār al-Muᶜrib*, ed. M. Ḥajjī (Beirut: Dār al-Gharb al-Islāmī, 1981), III, pp. 213–14, passim.

[35] Āmidī, op. cit., II, p. 77.

XI

THE PRIMACY OF THE QUR᾿ĀN IN SHĀṬIBĪ'S LEGAL THEORY

I

A noticeable advance in recent Islamicist scholarship has been the gradual disclosure of the connection between the highly formal literary output in medieval Islam and the social setting or the "worldliness" underlying and effecting such output. Behind the morbid formality of annalistic historical writing, theology, juristic political theory, law and other genres, there lies a close link between the strikingly impersonal style and seemingly monolithic, repetitive content, on the one hand, and the particular reality of the author's world on the other. The deceptively detached character of exposition ought not conceal the author's individuating imprint on his work. By virtue of this imprint, the work, notwithstanding all appearances of impervious formality, must, in some way, display a distinctive character. The clearer the makeup of the author, of his audience and society, the more sharply defined the particular relevance of his theory, argument or narrative to a given setting becomes.

Islamic legal theory represents one such genre where formality of method and style of presentation seem salient. In fact, there certainly exists the claim that in addition to that formality, if not partly because of it, this theory, which represents in effect the collective product of successive generations of jurists, is so uniform that its treatment as a single mode of expression would be perfectly justified. In other words, since works of legal theory are uniform, one work would represent this collective product as accurately as any other.[1] But to biur the distinctions between one theory and another, between one author and another, constitutes no less than a total dismissal of any subtle appreciation of the social, epistemological and other assump-

[1] This attitude is quite prevalent among students of Islamic law. See, for example, N.J. Coulson, *A History of Islamic Law* (Edinburgh, 1964), 84, who seems to echo statements made earlier by H.A.R. Gibb in his *Mohammedanism* (New York, 1962), 104. For a more direct statement, however, see Bernard Weiss, "Knowledge of the Past: The Theory of *Tawātur* According to Ghazālī," *SI*, 61 (1985), 85 (ll. 13–16). The attitudes of Middle Eastern scholars writing in Arabic are no different.

tions of individual authors, and in consequence to be blinded to the distinctive mode, substance, and most importantly, purpose of their discourses.

However, it must be at once admitted that works of *uṣūl al-fiqh* tend to conform to varying patterns, thus creating quite distinct and diverse groups of theories. Individual works belonging to a particular group manifest, it is true, a certain degree of similarity. But this is far from arguing that the differences between works within a given group are not worth our while, or that differences between the groups themselves are less than extraordinary. Among such groups is one that defies any particular legal or theological affiliation, and has members ranging from the fifth/eleventh century Juwaynī[2] and Ghazālī[3] to the seventh/thirteenth century Āmidī,[4] Ibn Qudāma[5] and Ibn al-Ḥājib.[6] While the first three were Shāfiᶜī-Ashᶜarīs and Ibn Qudāma was an ardent Ḥanbalī, the last was a Mālikī scholar whose works have attracted an unusual number of commentaries by major and minor jurists from various legal and theological schools.[7] All these jurists, particularly the latter ones, were influenced, directly or indirectly, by an earlier brand of *uṣūl al-fiqh* which found its clearest manifestation in the work of the Ḥanafī-Muᶜtazilī thinker Abū al-Ḥusayn al-Baṣrī.[8]

Though these works share a common denominator—or at least they are said to do so[9]—differences between them in style, approach and content are readily discernible. Even if we ignore the social factors which enter into play in the scheme of the jurist's theory, we must account for the far-reaching impact of his theological affiliation

---

[2] Imām al-Ḥaramayn al-Juwaynī, *al-Burhān fī uṣūl al-fiqh*, ed. ᶜAbd al-ᶜAẓīm Dīb, 2 vols. (Cairo, 1400/1980).

[3] Abū Ḥāmid al-Ghazālī, *al-Mustaṣfā min ᶜilm al-uṣūl*, 2 vols. (Cairo, 1322/1904–05); *idem*, *al-Mankhūl min taᶜlīqāt al-uṣūl*, ed. M.Ḥ. Haytū (Damascus, 1970).

[4] Sayf al-Dīn al-Āmidī, *al-Iḥkām fī uṣūl al-aḥkām*, 3 vols. (Cairo, 1968).

[5] Muwaffaq al-Dīn Ibn Qudāma, *Rawḍat al-nāẓir wa-junnat al-munāẓir*, ed. Sayf al-Dīn al-Kātib (Beirut, 1981).

[6] Jamāl al-Dīn Ibn al-Ḥājib, *Muntahā al-wuṣūl wal-amal fī ᶜilmay al-uṣūl wal-jadal*, ed. M. Badr al-Dīn al-Naᶜsānī (Cairo, 1326/1908).

[7] Muḥammad b. Ibrāhīm al-Yamānī, *Īthār al-ḥaqq ᶜalā al-khalq* (Cairo, 1318/1900–01), 200, remarks that Ibn al-Ḥājib's *Mukhtaṣar* (the abridgement of *Muntahā al-wuṣūl*) attracted seventy commentaries. Yamānī died nearly two centuries after Ibn al-Ḥājib.

[8] Abū al-Ḥusayn al-Baṣrī, *al-Muᶜtamad fī uṣūl al-fiqh*, ed. Muhammad Hamidullah, *et al.*, 2 vols. (Damas, 1964–1965).

[9] See the statement of Ibn Khaldūn, *The Muqaddimah*, trans. Fr. Rosenthal, 3 vols. (London, 1967), III, 28 ff.; Nicholas P. Aghnides, *Mohammedan Theories of Finance* (New York, 1916), 173–175 (nos. 3, 8, 10, 11).

upon the epistemological assumptions and theologically-based premises of his discourse. But differences aside, these works, subsumed under a more or less distinct group, vary significantly from other groups and still other individual works. Sarakhsī's work,[10] for example, represents one group while Ibn ᶜAbd al-Salām[11] and Shāṭibī[12] belong to yet another.

It must then be conceded that uniformity in *uṣūl al-fiqh* cannot be taken for granted. Once we admit that two theories differ in one or more respects, we must account, as a matter of necessity, for the claim of similarity with regard to other related aspects within both theories. In other words, the high level of interrelatedness of arguments within each theory poses the problem of how, if two theories differ, say concerning the epistemological status of consensus (*ijmāᶜ*), they resolve the problems created by such difference in other parts of their theories. Methodologically, this is a fundamental problem. We shall encounter it in Shāṭibī's theory about the Qurʾān, and shall assess, by means of comparison with the group of theories expounded by Ghazālī, Āmidī and others, the ramifications of Shāṭibī's particular attitude to the Qurʾān on the rest of his theory.

II

The most salient characteristic of Shāṭibī's particular attitude to the Qurʾān is that he views this text as an integral whole. In this, as we shall see, he came closer to the doctrine of the exegetes than to that of fellow legal scholars. For many other *uṣūlists*, the Qurʾān represents a body of legal language to be interpreted as commands, prohibitions, tropes, equivocations, univocalities, etc. After setting forth the meaning of the basic terms and expounding the logical and legal categories to be used in expounding the theory, legal works such as those of Ghazālī, Āmidī or Ibn al-Ḥājib would enumerate the four recognized sources of the law, and then proceed to establish the

---

[10] Shams al-Dīn al-Sarakhsī, *Uṣūl*, 2 vols. (Cairo, 1327/1909–10).

[11] ᶜIzz al-Dīn ᶜAbd al-ᶜAzīz Ibn ᶜAbd al-Salām, *Qawāᶜid al-aḥkām fī maṣāliḥ al-anām*, 2 vols. (Cairo, n.d.).

[12] Abū Isḥāq al-Shāṭibī, *al-Muwāfaqāt fī uṣūl al-aḥkām*, ed. M. ᶜAbd al-Ḥamīd, 4 vols. (Cairo, 1970). While both Ibn ᶜAbd al-Salām and Shāṭibī premise their theories on the primacy of public interest (*maṣlaḥa*), their methodologies as well as the structure of their theories differ significantly from each other. For a survey of the Granadan socio-economic background around the era of Shāṭibī and on his legal theory in general see Khalid Masud, *Islamic Legal Philosophy* (Islamabad, 1977). This work originated as a McGill doctoral dissertation written under the supervision of Charles Adams.

authenticity of the text of the Qurʾān insofar as its transmission is concerned.[13] Beyond this, the Qurʾān is presented as no more than a body of legal language from which particular legal rulings are derived. The theory of abrogation (*naskh*) in the works of these *uṣūlists* treats the Qurʾān no differently; apart from the discussion of what statement repeals which, there is a minimal reference to the importance of the chronological order in which the text was revealed.[14] In sum, the Qurʾān—and for that matter the Sunna—simply constitutes an aggregate body of legal commands on the basis of which cases of positive law are decided.

As we shall see later, Shāṭibī's concept of the Qurʾānic text transcends these boundaries. But to delimit his concept, Shāṭibī lays down a number of premises, the most elementary of which concerns the comprehensibility of the Qurʾānic language. Notwithstanding its miraculous and inimitable nature (*iʿjāz*), this language is not beyond the apprehension of those who are adept at the generally established usages of the Arabic language. For should it be beyond their apprehension, the divine obligation to abide by God's law would be absurd. This amounts to charging people with a duty they obviously cannot fulfill, a proposition which runs against the nature of religious obligation.[15]

That the language of the Qurʾān is comprehensible constitutes no guarantee that the jurist-exegete will necessarily understand the precise meaning and intent of the text's language. A word or a sentence may have a meaning that seems intelligible to the interpreter, but, it will be asked, is it the meaning intended by God? To ensure that the real meaning and intent are understood, Shāṭibī emphasizes the necessity of exploring the reasons and circumstances of revelation, *asbāb al-tanzīl*.[16] An interrogative statement in the text, for instance, may have one of several functions; it may, among other things, sanction a matter or reproach an audience. Only when the circumstances in which the particular verse encompassing this interrogation is revealed are known, is it possible to come closer to the

---

[13] Ibn Qudāma, *Rawḍa*, 60–62; Ibn al-Ḥājib, *Muntahā*, 33–34; Ghazālī, *Mustaṣfā*, I, 100–101. Abū al-Ḥusayn al-Baṣrī, *Muʿtamad*, I, 13–14, does not even mention the sources but begins directly with the exposition of linguistic categories. See also Abū ʿAlī al-Shāshī, *Uṣūl*, (Beirut, 1982), 13 ff. and Abū Isḥāq Ibrāhīm al-Shīrāzī, *al-Lumaʿ fī uṣūl al-fiqh*, ed. M. Badr al-Dīn al-Naʿsānī (Cairo, 1326/1908), 4 ff.

[14] See, e.g., Ibn Qudāma, *Rawḍa*, 77–78.

[15] Shāṭibī, *Muwāfaqāt*, III, 224. The argument is obviously based on the commonly accepted premise that "*taklīf mā lā yuṭāq*," charging a Muslim with an obligation he or she is clearly incapable of fulfilling, is untenable.

[16] *Ibid.*, III, 225 ff.

real purpose of the question. The second and equally important requirement, which together with the first assists in disclosing the intention of the Lawgiver, is knowledge of the customs and linguistic conventions prevalent among the Arabs during the time of revelation.[17] God has spoken to the Arabs in the language they understand with reference to a reality which was specifically theirs, and since both language and reality may—and Shāṭibī implies that they do—differ from later usages and realities, the jurist-exegete must thoroughly acquaint himself with them.

Other *uṣūlists* seem to lay very little stress on such requirements, satisfying themselves with the general assumption that any part of speech must, in order to be properly construed, be viewed within its own context, a context determined by what they coined as *qarāʾin al-aḥwāl*.[18] Though *qarāʾin al-aḥwāl* include, among other things, the circumstances under which a particular verse was revealed and the currently surrounding social and linguistic conventions, these *uṣūlists* clearly fail to articulate the exact ingredients which go into the making of any hermeneutical act. That Shāṭibī did articulate such ingredients in the framework of his theory[19] is, as we shall see later, quite significant.

A thorough familiarity with the circumstantial context of revelation and the linguistic conventions prevalent in that context merely guarantees a sound understanding of the apparent meaning (*ẓāhir*) of the Qurʾānic language. Hermeneutically, this is already a step in the right direction, for to establish the outward meaning of a text in accordance with the accepted rules of linguistic and literary usages constitutes a prerequisite for any attempt at a deeper level of interpretation. By seeking this deeper level, the *bāṭin*, one transcends the immediate and perhaps superficial meaning of the text in order to reach the real intent, *maqṣūd*, of the Lawgiver. It is not a symbolic but a rather perceptive interpretation. Whereas the *ẓāhir* meaning of S. V:3 ("Today I have perfected your Religion for you") is the actual

---

[17] *Ibid.*, II, 44 ff., 55 ff.; III, 229–230; *idem*, *Iʿtiṣām*, ed. Muḥammad Rashīd Riḍā, 2 vols. (Cairo, 1332/1913/14), II, 256 ff.

[18] See Wael Hallaq, "Notes on the Term *Qarīna* in Islamic Legal Discourse," *JAOS*, 108 (1988), 475–480.

[19] *Asbāb al-nuzūl* did, of course, constitute part of the field of Qurʾānic exegesis. In fact, Shāṭibī's argument for the necessity of *asbāb al-nuzūl* for an adequate understanding of the legal language has a long-established precedent in that field. See, e.g., Badr al-Dīn Muḥammad b. ʿAbd Allāh al-Zarkashī, *al-Burhān fī ʿulūm al-Qurʾān*, ed. M. Abū al-Faḍl Ibrāhīm, 4 vols. (Cairo, 1972), I, 22, who holds that one of the benefits of *ʿilm al-nuzūl* is the discovery of the rationale (*al-ḥikma al-bāʿitha*) behind divine legislation of legal rulings (*tashrīʿ al-ḥukm*).

completion of Islamic revelation, the *bāṭin* meaning is to note the approaching death of the Prophet. After all, he was sent to deliver a message, and once the task was completed, he had no reason to stay. The fact that the Prophet departed from this world eighty-one days after the final revelation confirms, Shāṭibī insists, the validity of this interpretation.[20]

But this deeper level of exegesis is, in Shāṭibī's thought, imbued with a pietistic element. To understand the intent of God is one thing, to be wholeheartedly convinced of it is another. The knowledge of the *bāṭin* is both. It is on such interpretative grounds that Shāṭibī spurns legal stratagems (*ḥiyal*) which are intended to circumvent the divinely prescribed law. Only those who have not perfectly understood the intent of the Lawgiver try to, and indeed do, resort to the manipulation of the law by means of such stratagems;[21] the more one penetrates the *bāṭin* of the text, the more guided and pious he is deemed.[22]

Shāṭibī is quick to dissociate this notion of *bāṭin* from other sectarian notions,[23] arguing that what is interpreted on the basis of his notion of *bāṭin* to be the intent of God is not open to doubt.[24] To ensure that a far-fetched interpretation, like that of the Ismāʿīlīs, is avoided, the standard rules of the Arabic language and grammar must be closely adhered to, and no meaning beyond what the language dictates should be inferred. Furthermore, any interpretation of the *bāṭin* must not only find corroboration from other textual citations, but must not run counter to another accepted interpretation.[25] With all these safeguards, and with the absence of such hermeneutical principles from other *uṣūl al-fiqh* works, Shāṭibī is clearly at pains in trying to pin down a set of criteria for what is a novel *uṣūlī* system of linguistic interpretation. While pressing for a particular interpretational approach—which will yield, to be sure, the results he is seeking—and adducing an unusual number of examples[26] illustrating instances of faulty (i.e., sectarian) interpretation, Shāṭibī is especially cautious not to transgress the hermeneutical ways of orthodoxy.

The much spurned interpretational extremities are the result not

---

[20] Shāṭibī, *Muwāfaqāt*, III, 255 (ll. 14–15), 256, 264.

[21] *Ibid.*, III, 260 (ll. 3–5).

[22] *Ibid.*, III, 260 (ll. 20–22).

[23] *Ibid.*, III, 254–255; M. Hodgson, '*Bāṭiniyya*,' *EI*², I, 1098 f.

[24] Shāṭibī, *Muwāfaqāt*, III, 255 (ll. 2–3).

[25] *Ibid.*, III, 264.

[26] *Ibid.*, III, 263 (l.-2), where he himself notes the inordinate number of examples he gives in this *Question*.

only of the lack of strict application of linguistic rules and conventions prevalent during the time of revelation, but also of the absence of a comprehensive approach to the larger context of the Qur˒ānic passage in question. Extremist interpretations for Shāṭibī stand opposite to reasonable, moderate, and middle-of-the-road interpretations. The latter, being the ultimate aim of our jurist, may be achieved by examining the meaning of the Qur˒ānic passage under consideration in light of the general theme of the verses which precede and follow it. Referring to the commonly accepted view in the field of Qur˒ānic commentary that the Qur˒ān often deals with an issue or a set of related issues in more than one place, Shāṭibī argues the need for reviewing all the relevant verses when extracting a legal ruling from the text. It is often the case, he says, that one or more verses explicate an otherwise vague verse. If an adequate understanding of one part depends on another part, then the Qur˒ān is interrelated in a number of ways; a part may introduce, confirm, clarify, or complement another.[27]

That the Qur˒ānic text represents a closely interrelated and complete whole[28] means that for a particular verse to be properly understood it must be viewed not only in light of its general textual context but also mainly with reference to the verses which precede it in time. The later parts in the text must thus be explained in terms of the earlier parts, just as the entire Medinese revelation must, to be properly understood, be viewed in light of the Meccan Qur˒ānic phase. And within the Medinese phase—and for that matter the Meccan—the latter verses are to be interpreted only after a full consideration of what came down earlier.[29] The Meccan Sūra of the Cattle illustrates this general principle. On the basis of this Sūra, wherein the foundations of faith and religion were laid down, the theologians elaborated their system, beginning with the affirmation of the Necessary Existent down to the last issue ordinarily discussed by them, the Imāma. Similarly, the Sūra provides the general foundations (*kulliyyāt*) of the law. Setting aside any relevant part of it

---

[27] *Ibid.*, III, 276 ff., 279–280, 284.

[28] Here, as elsewhere, Shāṭibī draws upon notions already well established in the science of Qur˒ānic exegesis. It seems that his ideas in this regard derive, *mutatis mutandis*, from *ᶜilm al-munāsaba*, an area of exegesis treating of the verses' interrelatedness and unity of meaning. See, e.g., Zarkashī, *Burhān*, I, 35 ff. According to Jalāl al-Dīn al-Suyūṭī, *Muᶜtarak al-aqrān fī iᶜjāz al-Qur˒ān*, ed. ᶜAlī Bajāwī, 2 vols. (Cairo, 1969), I, 54 ff., the element of *munāsaba* is one of the proofs for the miraculousness (*iᶜjāz*) of the Qur˒ān.

[29] Shāṭibī, *Muwāfaqāt*, III, 274 (ll. 5–9).

may demolish one of these foundations or even damage the entirety of the legal system (*niẓām al-sharīʿa*).[30] Now, when the Prophet emigrated to Medina, the Sūra of the Cow was revealed in order to lay down the details and to explicate the general principles in the Sūra of the Cattle. Though some of these details appeared elsewhere, here are found the specific laws of rituals, diet, crime, commercial transactions, marriage, etc. The universal principles (*uṣūl kulliyya*) established in the Cattle concerning the preservation of one's religion, life, mind, offspring and property are all confirmed in the Sūra of the Cow. Thus what is revealed in Medina subsequent to the latter, must be viewed in its light. The importance of chronology here can hardly be exaggerated.[31]

III

Most *uṣūlists* are willing to subscribe to little of what Shāṭibī has so far asserted, and when they do, it is only with many qualifications. As far as I know, no other *uṣūlist* placed such heavy emphasis on the chronological sequence and interrelatedness of verses in Qurʾānic hermeneutics. But while this may not constitute the most serious difference between Shāṭibī and these *uṣūlists*, the implications which the former drew from it and the thesis which he advanced on the grounds of these implications certainly drive a sizable wedge between his theory and theirs.

That the later Sūras and verses explain what precedes them in revelation leads to a certain hierarchy in the Qurʾān with the very early Sūras being the most comprehensive. Even if a Medinese verse appears to be universal or general, there must always exist a more universal verse revealed earlier in time. And even if it were indeed universal, it would only be a supplement to earlier universal verses.[32] The ultimate reference would then be the Meccan revelation, the earliest in point of time.[33]

As might be expected, the implications of this view are dramatic, and Shāṭibī does not hesitate to state them boldly. Within the limits of the Qurʾān, the general rule is that the verses revealed at the outset of the Prophet's career lay down the most general and universal legal principles—i.e., protection of the right to religion, life, mind, progeny and property. Later revelations may complement these principles,

---

[30] *Ibid.*, III, 274 (ll.14–18).
[31] *Ibid.*, III, 274–276.
[32] *Ibid.*, III, 29.
[33] *Ibid.*, III, 70–71.

but in the main they provide explanations and details of preceding revelations. It is for this reason that the Medinese Sūras are, in relation to the Meccan, less universal, often providing legal rulings concerning points of detail.

Whether all the details were provided in the Qurʾān or not, God perfected for Muslims their religion once the entirety of the Qurʾānic subject matter was revealed. Citing the verse "Today I have perfected your Religion for you," Shāṭibī argues that the Qurʾān contains all the fundaments of faith, spiritual and practical; it encompasses all things, and, conversely, nothing needed in religion stands outside its teaching.[34] The logical conclusion of this premise represents no less than a complete relegation of the Prophetic Sunna to a secondary status, and Shāṭibī, to be sure, does reach this very conclusion. But though the Qurʾān lays the foundations of law and religion, no rulings ought to be extracted from it without consulting the Sunna, because the latter, just like the Medinese revelations, provides explanations and details for the Qurʾān. Nonetheless, Shāṭibī affirms the completeness and self-sufficiency of the latter and, in consequence, rejects the view that the Sunna offers any substantive addition to the Qurʾān.[35]

The roles that Shāṭibī assigns to the Qurʾān and the Sunna, and their hierarchy in his system, have, insofar as I know, no precedent in *uṣūl al-fiqh*. He does agree with other jurists that God made it an obligation upon Muslims to consider as authoritative and binding the words of the Prophet.[36] But this is different from arguing that there is essentially nothing in the Sunna that is not found in the Qurʾān—a view unacceptable to the great majority, if not all, scholars.[37] Undoubtedly, this is an immensely important position, having considerable ramifications for virtually all other arguments in Shāṭibī's theory. No less important than the dimensions of these effects is the defense and justification of this position. How he justified

[34] *Ibid.*, III, 242–243, 244 (ll. 4–5).

[35] *Ibid.*, III, 243–244; IV, 9 (ll. 2–5).

[36] *Ibid.*, III, 25 (ll. 14–23). Muḥammad b. Aḥmad al-Anṣārī al-Qurṭubī, *al-Jāmiʿ li-aḥkām al-Qurʾān*, 20 vols. (?) (Cairo, 1933), I, 32. See also Muḥammad Ibn Idrīs al-Shāfiʿī, *Risāla*, ed. M. Kīlānī (Cairo, 1969), pars. 569–571, although he is reported to have held the view that the entire Sunna is an explanation of the Qurʾān. See Zarkashī, *Burhān*, I, 6 (ll. 5–6).

[37] Cf. Shāfiʿī, *Risālā*, par. 571; Qurṭubī, *Jāmiʿ*, I, 33–34. As far as I know, the Sunna as an independent source of law is ordinarily taken for granted by other *uṣūlists*, and the issue of whether it contains legal subject matter that may not be found in the Qurʾān does not seem to arise. For a standard treatment see Ibn al-Ḥājib, *Muntahā al-wuṣūl*, 33 ff.

it will be our concern in the remaining part of this section. Why, on the other hand, did he hold such a position and what was its significance to his overall agenda are questions to be addressed in the final section.

Before proceeding with his argument for the primacy of the Qur'ān over the Sunna, Shāṭibī asserts the more basic point that in the *mujtahid's* legal reasoning about individual legal cases the Qur'ān merits attention before the Sunna. That the Sunna should be demoted to a second position is the result of the higher degree of certitude the Qur'ān enjoys. Insofar as authenticity enters into the criteria determining the epistemological status of the two sources, the entirety of the Qur'ān as a text, as well as its individual verses, is deemed certain; but whereas it is true that the Sunna as a source of law is on the whole certain, the great majority of prophetic traditions are probable.[38] From the perspective of certitude the Qur'ān thus provides the first and most solid basis for legal reasoning. Furthermore, even if one grants that the Sunna contains material not within the compass of the Qur'ān, the *mujtahid* must, at any rate, first look in the Qur'ān in order to ascertain that it indeed provides no answer. But since in reality the Sunna merely explains the Qur'ān, one must examine the text before examining the "commentary" on it; without the commentary a text remains viable, but without the text, the commentary is meaningless if not impossible.[39] Further to bolster his argument Shāṭibī marshals a number of traditions to the effect that the Qur'ān reigns supreme.[40]

As this position is not merely a marginal novelty but rather signifies a total departure from the view of the great majority of scholars on this matter, Shāṭibī obviously cannot content himself with such a relatively simple refutation: The arguments of this majority must be confuted one by one, and in detail.

According to the great majority of scholars, when the Qur'ān is ambiguous on a particular matter, the Sunna, with its highly detailed content, intervenes to determine the specific intent of the Lawgiver. The Sunna functions in a similar manner whenever the Qur'ān fails to address any problem with exactitude and clarity. A case in point is the Qur'ānic injunction to cut off the hand of thieves. The Sunna

---

[38] Shāṭibī, *Muwāfaqāt*, IV, 5. Elsewhere, Shāṭibī argues that discussions concerning the certainty of *tawātur* traditions are mostly hypothetical, since it is unlikely to find such traditions surviving in their *tawātur* form until such later time when a hitherto unsolved legal case (*wāqiʿa*) occurs. *Ibid.*, IV, 8 (11. 19–21). See also note 72 below.

[39] *Ibid.*, IV, 5.

[40] *Ibid.*, IV, 5–6.

delimited the Qur'ānic meaning by decreeing that this punishment should be meted out only when there is break and entry and the value of the stolen goods exceeds a certain prescribed amount. Likewise, the unconditional Qur'ānic permission for matrimony was narrowed in scope by precluding the marriage of the maternal and paternal aunt of one's wife. A good number of rules related to prayers, alms-tax, fasting, ablution, pilgrimage, hunting, and other liturgic and mundane matters have also been legislated by the Sunna on the basis of the Qur'ān. While the Qur'ān made it, in succinct terms, a duty upon Muslims to perform prayer, the Sunna set forth the times of prayer each day, the manner of their performance, and other minute but nonetheless substantive specifications.[41] Shāṭibī does accept the authority of the Sunna, but only insofar as it complements the Qur'ān. The Sunna, he argues, merely expresses and articulates the intention of the Qur'ān; for after all, God, addressing his Prophet, has said: "We have sent down to you the Remembrance that you may explain to mankind what had been revealed for them" (S. XVI:44). Thus, when the Sunna qualifies the Qur'ān in such matters as the thief's punishment it is simply stating what the Qur'ān meant to say. If a jurist establishes the exact meaning of a verse, we cannot say, Shāṭibī analogically argues, that the ruling based on that verse stems from the authority of the jurist himself.[42] He, like the Sunna, functions only as an interpreter of what is ultimately the very word of God.

When the two sources present the jurist with two different or contradictory pieces of evidence, and when one piece enjoys the same degree of certainty as the other, thus precluding the possibility of one repealing another, the common practice has been to choose the evidence that is more agreeable (*ashal*, *aqrab*), even though it may not be Qur'ānic. In this practice Shāṭibī sees no problem, because the evidence in the Sunna represents, in the final analysis, an explanation or reformulation of a general Qur'ānic injunction. Put differently, the evidential competition is not between the Qur'ān and the Sunna, but ultimately between two different or seemingly contradictory statements within the Qur'ān.[43]

This argument further underscores Shāṭibī's underlying assumption that the Qur'ān contains the essence of the Sharīʿa, and that anything else represents, so to speak, a footnote to the self-sufficient Book. The hypothetical opponents of this view adduce a number of

---

41 *Ibid.*, IV, 7, 18–19. See also Qurṭubī, *al-Jāmiʿ*, I, 33.
42 Shāṭibī, *Muwāfaqāt*, IV, 7–8.
43 *Ibid.*, IV, 7, 8 (ll. 13–17).

verses to the effect that the Prophet's Sunna constitutes a source of authority equal to that of the Qur'ān. Sūra IV:59, for example, states: "O believers, obey God, and obey the Messenger and those in authority amongst you. If you should quarrel on anything, refer it to God and the Messenger, if you believe in God and the Last Day"; and Sūra V:92 reasserts: "Obey God and obey the Messenger, and beware!" The tenor of enjoining obedience to the Prophet would be pointless, the opponents say, should the Prophet's statements and commands be mere repetitions of those in the Qur'ān. The specific directive to bow to the Prophet's authority clearly indicates that the Prophet did introduce injunctions unspecified by the Qur'ān. Such directives as those in S. LIX:7: "Whatever the Messenger gives you, take; and whatever he forbids you, give up," empower the Prophet to decide in matters that expand on the Word of God and, *ipso facto*, add to it.[44] Needless to say, the traditions fully corroborate the Qur'ān on this score and add the prophetic condemnation of those who make the Book their sole reference.[45]

Facing no choice but to admit the foregoing textual evidence, Shāṭibī concedes that the validity of the texts adduced cannot be disputed, though he does not see how this evidence confutes his position. When the Sunna renders clear a verse pertaining to a legal ruling, the said ruling would be ultimately grounded in the Qur'ān, not the Sunna. Both God and his Messenger presumably bestowed on the case a certain authority. In conforming to, or violating the established ruling, the Muslim individual would be, respectively, obeying or disobeying God as well as the Prophet. Distinguishing between the two sanctioning authorities does not entail differentiating between two different rulings.[46] In other words, when the Qur'ān calls upon the believers to obey God and the Prophet, the import of the command relates to their authority as two distinct sanctioning powers, although the Prophet's authority derives, in the final analysis, from that of God. Since, Shāṭibī argues, the separation of these two authorities does not necessarily involve distinguishing between two different rulings belonging to a single case, then there would be no proof that the Sunna contains material not within the compass of the Qur'ān.

---

[44] The opponents produce three more verses: "But no, by thy Lord! they will not believe till they make thee the judge regarding the disputes among them" (IV:65); "Let those who go against His command beware, lest trial befall them" (XXIV:63); "Whosoever obeys the Messenger, thereby obeys God" (IV:80). See *ibid.*, IV, 9–10.

[45] *Ibid.*, IV, 10–11.

[46] *Ibid.*, IV, 13–14.

Having introduced traditions in condemnation of those who set aside the Sunna, Shāṭibī's hypothetical opponents assert that the interpretation of the Qurʾān without reference to the explicative Sunna not only leads to heretical doctrines but such interpretative approach has also been specifically forbidden by the Qurʾān itself. Far from enjoining the rejection of traditions whose legal import is not found in the Qurʾān, God has ordered Muslims to adhere to the Prophet and take him as the highest example. In fact, the opponents say, there is nothing in God's Book to give us reason to think that even traditions different from the Qurʾān are to be avoided. Now, while Shāṭibī admits that abandoning the Sunna altogether is conducive to heresy, he rejects individual traditions which agree neither with the Qurʾān nor with the overall body of the Sunna;[47] the reasoning here being that since the Sunna cannot conceivably contradict the Qurʾān, no individual tradition may be accepted unless it is in agreement with this primary source. And if it is in agreement, there would be nothing in the Sunna which is not approved by, and thus accounted for in the Qurʾān.

All these arguments and counter-arguments are launched on such a general level that they address none of the positive legal cases whose rulings, the opponents say, derive exclusively from the Sunna. The prohibition on marrying the paternal and maternal aunt of one's wife; the prohibition on eating the meat of donkeys and certain kinds of predatory animals; the ruling that capital punishment must not be meted out to a Muslim who kills a non-Muslim, etc., are all examples of laws provided for by the Sunna alone.[48]

Analogous to the *mujtahid* who must often choose between two pieces of legal evidence relevant to the case in hand, the Sunna preponderates one Qurʾānic injunction over another when applying its judgment to a particular legal case not specifically stated in the Qurʾān. In the latter, for example, God permitted in general terms the consumption of good foods and forbade the putrid ones, without, however, defining the status of many kinds of them. The Sunna then came to decide each kind in accordance with the principles regulated in the Qurʾān. In other words, the Sunna subsumed certain foods under one Qurʾānic legal norm or the other. Among these were the prohibitions concerning the consumption of the meat of donkeys and certain predatory animals. Similarly, God prohibited inebriants and permitted other non-alcoholic beverages such as milk. The rationale

---

47 *Ibid.*, IV, 11–13, 14–16.
48 *Ibid.*, IV, 11. See also Qurṭubī, *al-Jāmiʿ*, I, 34.

behind the prohibition was the effect of alcohol on the mind in that it distracts the Muslim from the worship of his Lord, let alone its negative social effects. Again, the Sunna interfered here to determine to which of the two categories date-wine and other semi-intoxicating beverages belong. On the basis of the principle extracted from the Qur'ān, all beverages, whether containing high or significantly low percentage of alcohol, were prohibited. And on these grounds, the Sunna articulated the classic dictum that any beverage which inebriates when consumed in large quantities is prohibited even in small quantities.[49] Although the Sunna does provide specific rules and even some legal maxims, this should not mean, Shāṭibī insists, that these have less grounding in the Qur'ān. In fact, their roots ultimately lay there.

Another category of prophetic rules which supply the detail for laconic Qur'ānic injunctions appears to be inferred by means of *qiyās*. Shāṭibī argues that it matters little to us whether the Prophet in fact arrived at these rules through revelation or intellectual reflection and *qiyās*, because insofar as we humans can perceive, he seems to have resorted to the latter. The law pertaining to the marriage of the aunt of one's wife represents an excellent case in point. The Qur'ān prohibited the marriage of the woman together with her daughter as a second wife, even if the husband divorces the mother before concluding the marriage of the daughter. The marriage of two sisters was prohibited as well. Analogically, the Prophet rendered the marriage of a woman together with her maternal or paternal aunt forbidden. The Prophet's statement which he made upon deciding in this type of marriage—namely, "If you do so [*viz.*, marry your wives' aunts] you shall put an end to your own offspring"—is reminiscent, Shāṭibī says, of the mode of legal reasoning used in *qiyās*.[50] The admission of oaths as evidence in the law of procedure is another product of prophetic *qiyās*. Sūra II:282 states: "And call to witness, from among your men, two witnesses; and if the two be not men, then a man and two women." In spite of the fact that women are inferior to men, he says, the acceptance of their testimony in the Qur'ān clearly indicates that when a male witness is not available, a substitute would be admissible. Like women, oaths can supplement the testimony of one male witness when other male witnesses are not to be found.[51]

---

[49] Shāṭibī, *Muwāfaqāt*, IV, 23–24. The Arabic maxim is: "*mā askara kathīruhu fa-qalīluhu ḥarām.*"

[50] *Ibid.*, IV, 27, 28 (ll. 16 ff.)

[51] *Ibid.*, IV, 30–31.

In line with this analogical procedure the Sunna determined the punishment of a Muslim who kills a non-Muslim. On the basis of S. IV:141, "God will not grant the unbelievers any way over the believers," and, to a lesser extent, S. LIX:20, "Not equal are the inhabitants of the Fire and the inhabitants of Paradise," the status of Muslims is known to be decidedly higher than that of non-Muslims, and therefore the Muslim's punishment for killing a non-Muslim should be less than death.[52]

Having accounted for cases presumed by his opponents to be significant material additions to the Qur᾽ān, Shāṭibī moves on to a higher level of analysis. On this level he not only attempts to enhance further the thesis that the Qur᾽ān encompasses, among other things, all matters of legal obligation, but also alludes to some of the reasons underlying the formulation of this thesis.

The Sunna may, it is true, contain some legal subject matter which is found neither in a laconic Qur᾽ānic statement nor even in an ambiguous or indirect one. Such subject matter, nonetheless, has its origins in the Qur᾽ān. It is Shāṭibī's fundamental assumption that each Qur᾽ānic verse or statement possesses multifaceted meanings, some direct and others indirect. While a verse may exist in its own particular context and may appear to have an immediate, obvious meaning, this very verse may, at the same time, manifest another meaning which is identical to meanings found in other verses. To put it differently, a group of verses in the Qur᾽ān may all have in common one theme which happens to be subsidiary to the main meaning in each verse. The inductive corroboration of one verse by the others lends the common theme a certain authority which could reach the degree of certitude.[53] Whereas this theme remains hidden in the linguistic terrains of the Qur᾽ān, the Sunna unfolds it in the form of a prophetic tradition.[54] The result of one such case of corroboration in the Qur᾽ān is the prophetic report "No injury and no counter-injury in Islam."[55]

As a general rule, however, the Qur᾽ān provides what Shāṭibī

[52] *Ibid.*, IV, 35–36.

[53] Further on this and on the importance of inductive corroboration in the theories of Shāṭibī and other *uṣūlists* see my article "On Inductive Corroboration, Probability and Certainty in Sunnī Legal Thought." N. Heer, ed., *Islamic Law and Jurisprudence: Studies in Honor of Farhat J. Ziadeh* (Seattle, forthcoming).

[54] Shāṭibī, *Muwāfaqāt*, IV, 32.

[55] For a detailed discussion of this tradition see *ibid.*, III, 9–10; M.H. Kerr, *Islamic Reform* (Berkeley and Los Angeles, 1966), pp. 97 ff.; see also Jamāl al-Dīn Ibn Manẓūr, *Lisān al-ᶜArab*, 15 vols. (Beirut, 1972), IV, 482.

characterizes as the most important foundation of the Sharīʿa; namely, the principle governing the interests of people. For after all, the entire enterprise of the Sharīʿa was instituted in the interests of Muslims, whether these interests pertain to this life or to life in the hereafter.[56] In order to safeguard these interests the Sharīʿa seeks to achieve three goals (*maqāṣid*): namely, that which is indispensable (*ḍarūriyyāt*), necessary (*ḥājiyyāt*) and beneficial (*taḥsīniyyāt*). Without the first category, which presupposes the protection of one's religion, life, offspring, property and mind, secular as well as religious existence can never be orderly, and at worst, it is impossible. The other two categories, on the other hand, make the implementation of the law possible by mitigating harsh requirements and reducing legal demands. The Sharīʿa, Shāṭibī relentlessly asserts, rests squarely on these three general principles,[57] principles stipulated in the Qurʾān and articulated in the Sunna.

Any particular detail found only in the Sunna is nothing but an extension of an all-embracing Qurʾānic principle; the contrast here is between the Qurʾānic *taʾṣīl*, laying down the foundations, and *tafṣīl*, the explication of the foundations by extending their law to particular cases.[58] All five sub-categories of *ḍarūriyyāt* are prescribed by the Qurʾān and then further expounded by the Sunna. The Qurʾān enjoins belief in Islam, threatens those who reject it, prescribes *jihād* against them, etc. The legislation with regard to marriage, procreation, subsistence, and other similar matters is designed to protect life and its continuity. So are the laws regarding fornication, the validating conditions of marriage, divorce and other forms of marital dissolution. Laws dealing with crime, hunting and diet are also intended for the maintenance of orderly life. Similarly, the Qurʾān provided general legal principles aiming at the protection of property. However, the last sub-category, the mind, though briefly taken into consideration in the Qurʾān, is subject to no general principles. The laws governing this area are left for the *mujtahid* to articulate. The Sunna, on the other hand, follows suit in neglecting to establish laws relative to the mind—a fact which Shāṭibī finds quite convenient for making the point that the Sunna leaves out whatever the Qurʾān omits. In the same vein, the principles governing the other two categories of *ḥājiyyāt* and *taḥsīniyyāt* and their sub-categories are stated in the Qurʾān, with their minute details found in the Sunna.[59]

---

56 Shāṭibī, *Muwāfaqāt*, II, 3–4.
57 *Ibid.*, II, 4–6.
58 *Ibid.*, IV, 20 (ll. 4–7).
59 *Ibid.*, IV, 21–22.

IV

Shāṭibī's insistence on the primacy of the Qur'ān over the Sunna—a stance heralding a departure from the established *uṣūl al-fiqh* theory—must be explained in light of the results which his theory proposes to achieve. Shāṭibī, however, makes no effort at drawing any conclusions from his thesis on the Qur'ān. Nor does he speak of the significance or ultimate purpose of the views he propounds. He establishes the place of the Qur'ān in relation to Sunna and moves on to treat other issues not necessarily of direct relevance to what he has just finished expounding. But the clues to understanding the significance of Shāṭibī's peculiar hierarchization of the material sources of Sharīʿa are found in the earlier parts of the book, where he lays down the epistemological and juridical principles of his theory.

The two most important components of this theory are the juridical principle of public good and the logical method of induction. Public good represents the end of Shāṭibī's theoretical enterprise, and induction, its means. Shāṭibī considered the purpose of the Sharīʿa to be primarily the protection of the five sub-categories of *ḍarūriyyāt*, as well as the promotion of *ḥājiyyāt* and *taḥsīniyyāt*. The admission in law of the *ʿarāyā* contract[60] which involves risk, and the reduction of ritual obligations under circumstances of hardship and illness, are two examples of relaxing the law when the need to accommodate reality arises. These mitigated laws are absolutely needed (*ḥājiyyāt*) in order to make life and legal practice of Muslims tolerable. The recommendations to free slaves, to perform ablution before prayer, to be charitable to the poor, etc., are not needed to such an extent that without them the law becomes inoperable—as is the case in the first two categories, the *ḍarūriyyāt* and *ḥājiyyāt*—but they certainly improve (hence the term *taḥsīniyyāt*) the character of the Sharīʿa.[61]

The authoritativeness (*ḥujjiyya*) of the principles of public good has no basis in any single conclusive (*qaṭʿī*) statement in the Qur'ān or the Sunna, but rather derives from an inductive survey of revelation. In fact, a number of jurisprudential institutions, such as consensus, *qiyās* and *istiḥsān*, were proven to be authoritative by means of such induction.[62] For example, there exists no explicit Qur'ānic verse or

[60] *ʿArāyā* is a type of contract in which unripe dates on the palm tree are bartered against their calculated value in edible dried dates. Although Islamic law does not allow the element of risk (*gharar*) in contractual transactions, the *ʿarāyā* contract was recognized despite the uncertainty it entails.

[61] *Ibid.*, II, 4–6.

[62] *Ibid.*, I, 15–16.

a highly reliable tradition (*khabar mutawātir*) that explicitly states the infallibility of the Muslim Community. Alternatively, the authoritativeness of consensus had to be founded upon verses, traditions and other circumstantial evidence which were individually inconclusive but which have in common the indubitable theme of the inerrancy of the Muslim community.[63] In other words, Shāṭibī argues that the Sharīᶜa consists of universal principles (*kulliyyāt*) whose authority is based on a multitude of probable instances or particular statements (*juzʾiyyāt*) which corroborate one another to the degree of absolute certainty.

The three universals of *ḍarūriyyāt*, *ḥājiyyāt* and *taḥsīniyyāt*, for the realization of which the Sharīᶜa was decreed, are all grounded in their perfect form (*ᶜalā al-kamāl*) in the Qurʾān.[64] "Perfect form" does not necessarily imply a single, explicit Qurʾānic passage defining and enjoining in precise and specific terms the three *maqāṣid*. Rather, a *sufficient* number of Qurʾānic verses are found by induction to possess in common one *maᶜnā*, namely, that these are the aims for the attainment of which God revealed his law. Once these principles (*maᶜānī*) have been established as *kulliyyāt*, they acquire, on account of their certitude, the status of irrevocability,[65] and thus become a regulating force in Sharīᶜa. Given that God would not reveal contradictory *kulliyyāt*, as this would render the Sharīᶜa paradoxical, let alone absurd, the problem that arises is the relation between a *kulliyya* and a non-conforming particular (*juzʾī*).

Since a conclusive universal cannot be reached without the enumeration of all the members (particulars) belonging to its class, there can be no particular instance which is relevant, yet at the same time contrary, to the universal. For if it were relevant and were not taken into consideration in inductive enumeration, then the universal is merely a pseudo-universal, and therefore revocable.[66] But what if a diverging particular surfaces only after a universal has been established on the basis of a multitude of other supporting particulars? One might argue that in legal matters it is normative to establish general principles on the basis of the great majority, but not necessarily all, of the extractable legal evidence. And once the five sub-categories of *ḍarūriyyāt* are established as universals according to

63 See W.B. Hallaq, "On the Authoritativeness of Sunni Consensus," *IJMES*, 18 (1986), 427–454.

64 Shāṭibī, *Muwāfaqāt*, III, 243 (ll. 4–5).

65 *Ibid.*, I, 11 (ll. 13–18).

66 *Ibid.*, III, 5.

which all law must be interpreted, then any particular, hitherto not considered, must be either subsumed under the five *ḍarūriyyāt* or, if it is a non-conforming particular, must be left out. Shāṭibī generally accepts this methodology but finds that it is of crucial importance to account for non-conforming particulars. The assumptions on which the *ᶜarāyā* contract is based, for example, stand in sharp contrast to the standard contractual principles of Sharīᶜa, and yet it is deemed a valid form of contract. This exception, as one of a great many, constitutes in fact another *kulliyya* which is the second category of *maṣāliḥ*, the *ḥājiyyāt*. For, after all, the function of this last universal category is to mitigate the harshness of the first. The emergence of a *kulliyya*, it will be noted, is the result of the existence of a number of exceptions *sufficient* to produce another *kulliyya*. Thus, failing to account, both qualitatively and quantitatively, for exceptions will lead to the obliteration of the second as well as the third of the Sharᶜī *kulliyyāt*.[67] Setting aside the particulars which do not conform to a *kulliyya*, particularly when they are numerous, will neither serve the interests of man, nor be faithful to the intent of the law, for the Lawgiver could not have decreed them in vain.

Having endorsed these as *kulliyyāt*, Shāṭibī is willing to reject any particular which contradicts them. But how does this assertion square with his previous argument that non-conforming particulars should be accounted for? The three *kulliyyāt*, Shāṭibī reasserts, represent, after all, the *raison d'être* of the law, and therefore there should be no particular which stands in opposition to them. If there appears to be a particular contravening a given *kulliyya* then the particular must have been revealed to protect another general legal principle or to undergird another aspect of the same *kulliyya*. Capital punishment, a particular, surely contradicts the sub-category of *ḍarūriyyāt* which calls for the protection of life. Although killing the murderer is in and by itself an act violating this principle, it is at once necessary to maintain that very principle; a soul is killed in order to protect another. Shāṭibī insists that no isolated particular can undermine the Sharᶜī *kulliyyāt*, particularly the *ḍarūriyyāt*, *ḥājiyyāt* and *taḥsīniyyāt*.[68] "In Sharīᶜa" he says, "the great majority of particulars [constituting a *kulliyya*] are considered tantamount to a conclusive general, since the instances diverging from a *kulliyya* cannot constitute another *kulliyya* which can then compete with the first established *kulliyya*."[69]

---

[67] *Ibid.*, III, 6–7.
[68] *Ibid.*, II, 42 (ll. 17–20), 43–44.
[69] *Ibid.*, II, 37 (ll. 6–7).

They cannot constitute another *kulliyya* because they can only be isolated exceptions. His assertive and frequent statements concerning the conclusiveness and irrevocability of *kulliyyāt*, and the total inability of non-conforming *juzʾiyyāt* to alter them,[70] clearly indicate that for Shāṭibī only universals count.

By adopting this epistemology Shāṭibī's purpose in relegating the Sunna to a mere elaborate footnote to the Qurʾān becomes easier to understand. His insistence upon the all-inclusiveness of the Qurʾān, especially the comprehensive legal character of the early Meccan Sūras, is intended to argue that the Qurʾān alone provides the *kulliyyāt* of Sharīʿa, and since the Sunna only interprets the Qurʾān and provides details that are not specified in the Book, everything in the Sunna represents mere particulars that must correspond with the Qurʾānic *kulliyyāt*. This is precisely why he rejects all traditions not in harmony with the Qurʾān.[71]

The unqualified certitude of the Qurʾānic text in general and the individual verses in particular present yet another argument in favor of Shāṭibī's theory. The uncertainty surrounding the solitary prophetic traditions, and the virtual absence of the *mutawātir* traditions,[72] render the Sunna epistemologically inferior to the Qurʾān. When a tradition, assumed by Shāṭibī to be a *juzʾī*, contradicts a Qurʾānic *kulliyya* it is immediately dismissed. Conversely, if a tradition is upheld it would be by virtue of its support of a Qurʾānic statement, either by way of clarifying an ambiguity or by stipulating the details of a categorical Qurʾānic command.

It is the Meccan text then that contains the *kulliyyāt* of Sharīʿa, and in effect the *indisputable* crux of the law.[73] In a separate discussion, Shāṭibī demonstrates that the Meccan verses are almost exclusively concerned with both obedience to God and human welfare under His guidance.[74] Thus the reduction of the substantive sources of Sharīʿa to the Qurʾān—nay, to the Meccan revelation—gives Shāṭibī an edge over the established legal theory in propounding an idea of

---

[70] See, e.g., *ibid.*, I, 119 (*al-kulliyyatu idhā ʿāraḍahā al-juzʾiyyu fa-lā athara lil-juzʾiyyi*), II, 36 (*al-kulliyyātu . . . lā yarfaʿuhā takhallufu āḥādi al-juzʾiyyāti*), III, 7 (*al-kulliyyu lā yankharimu bi-juzʾiyyin*).

[71] *Ibid.*, IV, 16 (1.–3).

[72] On at least two separate occasions (*Muwāfaqāt*, II, 34; IV, 8) Shāṭibī remarks that with the lapse of time the *mutawātir* traditions have become so few that they are on the verge of extinction. See note 38 above.

[73] To the issue of the absence of contradictions within the Qurʾān as well as to the matter of its certainty, Shāṭibī devotes a lengthy discussion. See *ibid.*, IV, 201 ff.; see also *al-Iʿtiṣām*, II, 265–267.

[74] Shāṭibī, *Muwāfaqāt*, IV, 153 ff.

Sharīᶜa based on the most solid textual foundations in Islam, while at once advocating the interests of man as no less worthy than the interests of the Lord.[75] The link that Shāṭibī forged between the highest type of textual certitude and the idea of "humanistic" law—expressed in his theory of *maqāṣid*—is of crucial importance for his enterprise. The emphasis on human exigency as the perfect counterpart of spiritual obedience represents a risky departure from mainstream legal Sunnism and therefore requires the most incisive backing. When Shāṭibī demonstrates, within the framework of a highly structured theory of legal induction, that the Meccan revelation with its conclusive and irrefutable universals upholds the interests of man, the opponents cannot but stand disarmed.

Furthermore, in espousing a theory of law that stresses the mundane interests of society while maintaining a strong link with the divine decree, Shāṭibī was attempting to address what he seems to have considered a problematic issue of his day. Throughout his writings he advocates the simplification of the law and relentlessly battles the intricate formulations and abstractions of the then existing legal theory.[76] The prevalence of this abstract, highly theological theory appears to be causally linked with a serious problem which Shāṭibī thought to have plagued his Andalusian society. His two surviving works repeatedly testify to his staunch and elaborate opposition to the legal practices of this society, a society that, to his mind, unperturbedly evaded and manipulated God's law.[77] The practice of *ḥiyal*, of arbitrary eclecticism of the four schools' positive legal doctrines, as well as the virtual abandonment of the law is seen as an outcome not only of the abstract character of legal theory, but also of its highly theological, non-humanistic outlook.[78] In other words,

---

[75] *Ibid.*, IV, 155 (ll. 15–16).

[76] See *ibid.*, I, 25–27; II, 59, 62, where he argues that law, legal obligations and legal rights must not be incomprehensible to the generality of people. The Qurʾān and the Sunna are written in clear Arabic that is understood by all those who know the Arabic language (II, 55 ff.). Furthermore, Shāṭibī devotes lengthy sections (I, 17 ff.) attempting to divest *uṣūl al-fiqh* from all discussions that have no immediate bearing on positive law, thereby excluding from law any logical, theological or philosophical material. Significantly, the text of the Qurʾān was to be particularly protected from engaging in such useless sophistry (II, 55).

[77] Shāṭibī, *Iᶜtiṣām*, I, 9–10, 11–12, passim. See also next note.

[78] For statements on such practices see Shāṭibī, *Muwāfaqāt*, IV, 85, 93–94, 96, passim. In fact, Shāṭibī wrote his *Iᶜtiṣām* in order to rebut a number of accusations levelled against him by what seems to be a Granadan group of scholars. One of these accusations (I, 11) alleged that Shāṭibī was too fastidious and overly strict in demanding an unmitigated application of the law. To this allegation he replied that his is the mainstream doctrine (*mashhūr al-madhhab*) while his opponents' legal views compromise God's decree in favor of a law motivated by pure personal interests.

the failure of the existing theory to develop an understanding of the law's protection of worldly matters, and the abstractionist discourse that the jurists employed in expounding their jurisprudence has alienated Muslims from the Sharīᶜa. This is precisely why Shāṭibī stresses, time and again, that Islam and Islamic law are no different from their founder who was a *nabiyyun ummiyyun*, an unlettered Prophet.[79] The fundamental legal obligations incumbent upon all Muslims, as well as their rights are, as set forth in the Meccan Sūras, comprehensible to people of every walk of life.[80] By assigning to these Sūras, which allot to the wordly existence its fair share of rights and privileges, a major role in his theory, Shāṭibī was bidding his fellow Muslims to return to the proper practice of God's law, a law that is heedful of human need and welfare.

That the worldliness underlying Shāṭibī's theory was responsible for a unique attitude towards the role of the Qurʾān in legal theory poses an even more important question than the fact that Shāṭibī increased the substantive legal contribution of the Qurʾān at the expense of the Sunna. Such a novel view of the Qurʾān is bound to effect, within a highly structured theory, a set of doctrines which are as peculiar to Shāṭibī as they are different from those of other jurists. The sum total of these views comes, in the final analysis, to no less than a theory that appropriates as its own a given set of motives, starting points as well as an individuating system that regulates its own mode of discourse. By its very theoretical nature, this discourse serves to dissociate the theory from the particular reality that produced it, a reality that may well present itself on an epistemological, theological, social or simply material level. To what extent can the theory reveal its own worldliness, or the worldliness reveal the intricacies of the formality of legal discourse are questions whose answers must be sought in the dialectical relationship between the text and the author's world. Without bringing the latter into close scrutiny, this relationship, which is indispensable for a more adequate understanding of Islamic legal theory, can have no existence.

---

[79] *Ibid.*, I, 22, 25; II, 48 ff.
[80] *Ibid.*, IV, 153–154, and see note 76 above.

XII

UṢŪL AL-FIQH: BEYOND TRADITION[1]

I

Anyone who ever takes the intellectual history of religion seriously is bound to deal with the notion of originality either directly or obliquely. And perhaps more than any other religion, the originality of Islam, of its intellectual history, of its scripture, and even of its founder, has long stood at the centre of Western scholarly discourse. That the textual foundations as well as the originator of this religion were studied, and indeed questioned, in terms of originality need hardly be stressed. The Prophet's originality was often doubted, and the Qur'ān was seen as no more than a poor reproduction and disorderly imitation of earlier monotheistic scriptures. The attribute of imitation, as a binary opposite of originality, was thus attached, if not made inherent, to Islam from its moment of birth.

In the rest of its history, Islam was to receive the same indictment. Its intellectual history, like virtually all other facets of its life, was predominantly perceived in orientalist discourse in terms of influences, debts, borrowings—terms that persistently negate the quality of originality. Speaking of borrowing, a prominent orientalist declared that 'No cultural history lends itself better to studying this [phenomenon of borrowing] than does that of the Muslim peoples.'[2] The possible debt of Islam to other religions and cultures has often been deemed not as a hypothesis to be proved or disproved, but rather as an established fact only to be taken for granted. Evidence thus becomes unnecessary, and indeed superfluous. In his discussion of the 'sources of Islamic civilization', and of Islam's indebtedness to other legal systems, von Grunebaum was able to announce with resounding confidence: 'It is, I

[1] A summary of this paper was presented at the University of Manchester as part of a conference entitled 'Law and its Interpretation in Judaism and Islam', 23–5 September 1991.

[2] Brunschvig, 'Perspectives', 59.

Journal of Islamic Studies 3:2 (1992) pp. 172–202.

believe, only our lack of familiarity with Sassanian law which prevents us from uncovering its traces in the *fiqh*.'[3] Accordingly, foreign influences on Islamic civilization are certainly out there; the only problem is that we cannot always identify them!

Even the formidable growth and developments during the first three Islamic centuries, recognized as relatively impressive by Islamicists, are none the less not credited as achievements comparable with those of other cultures. Islam in the second/eighth and third/ninth centuries was, Brunschvig maintains, 'a system that had grown very substantial in various directions.... During this fruitful formative period, Islam was already—it is undeniable—a powerful factor; but this factor, whatever originality it had in some points and in its texture as a whole, still resulted from multiple components drawn heavily on older civilizations.'[4] Whatever 'texture' means here, and wherever those 'points' are, the verdict is clear: the originality of what is thought to be the best centuries of Islamic cultural and intellectual contribution is seriously marred (if not negated altogether) by Islam's penchant for appropriating from other cultures. 'To borrow a well-expressed formula', Brunschvig continues, Muslims '"turned in a horizontal spiral around their techniques". It was the same for their thinking. It is well known today that "proliferating detail" characterizes civilizations that are moving their feet in one spot but not going beyond themselves.' He advises us that this 'failure to go beyond oneself' or 'stagnation or stiffening of the joints in Islamic history' (generally characterized as ankylose)[5] must be studied.[6] It is curious, to say the least, that rendering a judgement on the 'stagnation' of Islamic culture was possible despite the acknowledged fact that the phenomenon still awaits further study and thus is not within the realm of established knowledge.[7] As we have noted earlier, discourse on things Islamic does not take the form of a hypothesis whose truth or falsehood is to be tested, but rather of a postulate, only to be posited, affirmed, and reaffirmed, whatever its true epistemic value. More curious, if not astonishing, is the daring generality and universality of the judgement, for it offers neither distinctions nor exceptions. It is categorical, yet it is confident.

Thus discourse on Islam and Muslims took the form of assertions,

[3] See his 'Sources of Islamic Civilization', 37.

[4] Brunschvig, 'Perspectives', 53. It is significant that before it was published in *Unity and Variety in Muslim Civilization* in 1955, Brunschvig's 'Perspectives' constituted the inaugurating article of the prestigious journal *Studia Islamica* (1 (1953), 5–18).

[5] See, e.g., the articles of Gardet and Schacht in *Classicisme et déclin culturel*, 93 ff., 141 ff.

[6] Brunschvig, 'Perspectives', 58.

[7] Note, for instance, the characteristic spirit in which *Classicisme et déclin culturel* was written.

judgements, and postulates concerning not only originality and, more accurately, the lack of it, but also the intellectual inadequacy of Muslims to aspire to any form of genuine originality. Brunschvig, to be sure, was not alone in upholding these views of Islam. In fact he expressed, more or less, the mean of orientalist discourse on a variety of things Islamic. In theology and dialectical method Muslims are thought to be no more than the appropriators of what once belonged to their non-Muslim predecessors; in philosophy they not only failed to produce their own system, but theirs was a 'mediocre assimilation' of Greek philosophical ideas.[8] Nearly all branches of knowledge in Islam were subject to the same judgement. And the *Sharīʿa* was by no means an exception.

Orientalist commentary on the history of *Sharīʿa* may be characterized as a subcategory of the broader commentary on the history of Islam as a whole. This commentary reduces Islamic history to a short-lived upsurge of a body politic accompanied by some sort of a civilization, followed by an endless process of widespread decline. Against this long and persistent decline, the rather brief rise at the outset would seem an anomaly, and thus an exception to the general rule which is deterioration, decay, and stagnation. In introducing his book *Women in Muslim Family Law*, J. L. Esposito reproduces the received wisdom on Islamic legal history which, we have noted, stands in orientalist perception as a subcategory of Islam's general history. The 'dynamism of legal development', Esposito tells us, was 'stifled' after the fourth/tenth century, and what remained was a 'static Muslim society and law in the medieval period'.[9] Esposito's knowledge of dynamism in the early Islamic legal system comes mainly from the excellent findings of Schacht, and perhaps to a lesser extent from the more limited studies of Goldziher and, ironically, Brunschvig. But credible evidence for a static Muslim society in the medieval period is not proffered, nor can one observe any significant, respectable research in support of this statement. Esposito's evidence includes closing the gate of *ijtihād*, political decay, and the Mongol invasion. I do not wish here to venture a refutation of these widespread claims, though one can now easily maintain either that such evidence is mythical, as is the case with the closure of the gate of *ijtihād*,[10] or that a *necessary connection* between the facts purportedly constituting evidence and the supposed facts of categorical decline and a static Muslim society has not thus far been established.

It is rather curious that Esposito was speaking here with full authority

[8] See J. Duchesne-Guillemin's remarks in the introduction to *Unity and Variety*, 6.

[9] Esposito, *Women*, 10, 12.

[10] See Hallaq, 'Was the Gate of Ijtihad Closed?', 3–41; and 'On the Origins of the Controversy about the Existence of Mujtahids', 129–41.

although his scholarly expertise lies elsewhere. This authority, as is well known, finds its roots early in European studies of the Orient, an authority that has been anchored in sets of assumptions the greatest bulk of which have not been adequately demonstrated. A central set of these assumptions revolves around the idea of a massive decline due to rigidity, lack of imagination, a penchant for repetition, an inherent Arab conservatism, and a host of qualities that essentially run counter to originality.[11] Explicit statements, intimations, and latent assumptions of this idea are quite abundant in orientalist writings and can be multiplied at will. Snouck Hurgronje, whose scholarly legacy still persists among living students of Islamic law, was writing also within the *sunna* of orientalism when he spoke of this decline and of its alleged accompanying symptoms. One such symptom that is relevant to our present concern is what he saw as the incredulously monolithic nature of Islamic law. Of this Hurgronje wrote:

> [I]t may be said without exaggeration that no modern science shows such a surprising unity of method as the Muslim *fiqh*. Differences in the character and in the education of the persons who devoted themselves to this science, and the various needs of countries and peoples, could not fail to bring about variations; by the beginning of the second century people were speaking of the *fiqh* of A or of B, the *fiqh* of Medina, Syria, or Iraq. Nevertheless all this did not imply variations of any importance because the principle was everywhere the same.
>
> It is true that eminent Muslim scholars ... wrote books in order to refute one another ... [B]ut all this does not prevent us from recognising that polemics did not touch essential points.[12]

Of course, neither Hurgronje nor anyone else by his time had conducted any sort of comprehensive or near-comprehensive research to substantiate these statements. Hurgronje was simply relaying his impressions of a rather select legal literature that he encountered and that was available to him. His sparse documentation of what he wrote on the history of *Sharīʿa* is sufficient indication of his generalist approach.

Over a century later, Hurgronje's thought on the subject remains in full force among younger scholars, with, alas, the same impressionistic support.[13] The position of the majority of today's Islamicists is predominantly this: that Islamic law was laid down in the first three or four centuries of Islam; that legal creativity was exhausted immediately

[11] See, e.g., Vesey-Fitzgerald, 'Nature and Sources', 106: Esposito, *Women*, 10–12.

[12] Snouck Hurgronje, *Selected Works*, 279.

[13] Note that Schacht, with his magisterial authority, stamped Hurgronje's writings on Islamic law with approval: '[T]he writings of Snouck Hurgronje are fundamental for a correct understanding of the nature of Islamic law.' *Introduction*, 216.

thereafter; and that new ideas and principles have not evolved since then. The entire legal literature of Islam after the third-fourth/ninth-tenth centuries is thus reduced to virtual nothingness. As recently as 1987 Patricia Crone was able to write, again basing herself on nothing but impressionistic evidence in a long orientalist tradition, that 'In practical terms ... any legal work composed between 800 and 1800 may be cited as evidence of classical doctrine.'[14] Crone couples the unforgivably rash and unsubstantiated statements of Hurgronje with another shortcoming of which Hurgronje was innocent: to Crone there are now available works of excellent scholarship, such as those of Chehata[15] and Meron,[16] which instruct us carefully to reconsider the archaic beliefs promulgated by Hurgronje and his like. But Crone here still labours under an ideology that has thus far proved immune to the sound and highly promising scholarship in the field.

Crone's aforementioned statement amounts to an assertion that legal works written throughout the millennium after AD 800 are identical, and can therefore be isolated from a particular context of time and place. When common sense dictates that some sort of change throughout the centuries was inevitable, as Schacht seems to have assumed, the occurrence of change and development is finally admitted but given such a marginal import that it disappears into oblivion when compared with what is seen as the massive stagnation and 'ankylose'. 'Even during the period of *taḳlīd*', Schacht tells us, 'Islamic law was not lacking in manifestations of original thought in which the several schools competed with and influenced one another. But this original thought could express itself freely in nothing more than abstract systematic constructions which affected neither the established decisions of positive law nor the classical doctrine of the *uṣūl al-fiqh*.'[17] It is instructive to note here that despite the total absence of research on the 'period of *taḳlīd*', Schacht, who in this statement faithfully follows in the footsteps of Hurgronje, could still pass this definitive judgement.

II

The insidiously prevalent view of decay, 'ankylose', and intellectual rigidity is completely antithetical to variety, difference, originality. Most importantly, it negates from Islamic history the notion of individuality

[14] See her *Roman, Provincial and Islamic Law*, 19.

[15] *Études de droit musulman*.

[16] 'The Development of Legal Thought', 73–118.

[17] Schacht, *Introduction*, 71–2.

and individual human experience. Accepting the perfect interchangeability of a ninth-century text with that of a nineteenth-century one would amount to reducing the texts and their authors to a single experience, to a single act of writing, to a single mind. The implications of such an attitude are immeasurably grave, for it obscures the cultural and social factors that may, and quite often do, unravel the individuality of human intellectual experience which constitutes, together with a multiplicity of cognate yet different experiences, that culture and society.

Both substantively and methodologically, the study of originality as an activity in intellectual history, and in our case in Islamic legal theory, is of great significance: substantively, because a conscious effort at seeking to locate any activity of originality expands for us the range of variety, and thus the multiple forms of discourse in legal thought; methodologically, because such an expansion can have no place if the possibility of originality's existence is excluded from the bag of assumptions with which the modern scholar approaches legal theory.

Uṣūl al-fiqh as a theoretical activity that lays claim to a particular reality demands our attention on two distinct levels of enquiry. The first level is the system of interpretation and the sets of principles and precepts that determine the deontic values of external reality. Here it cannot be assumed that Islamic legal theory as a hermeneutical, logical, and ultimately juridical system is disconnected from actual reality and positive law. But more on this later. The second level of enquiry addresses, on the one hand, the direct and oblique relationships between legal theory and positive law, and, on the other, the concrete human circumstances of the individual author and their role in shaping his abstract and theoretical production. The connection between the aggregate of these circumstances—an aggregate that has been called worldliness—and the author's theoretical formulations differs from the first level of enquiry in that its causes are not exclusively juridical. While the dynamics between legal theory and positive law, and in turn between positive legal doctrine and society—which is the locus of the law—are purely juridical, the dynamics of worldliness, i.e. the connection between the world of the legal theoretician as author and his theoretical production, belong to things textual. It is these types of dynamics that force to the forefront not only the subtle imprints of individuality on legal contents, but the more obvious uniqueness of the author's intellectual make-up as reflected in his text.

Thus worldliness is here defined as the aggregate of the components of reality surrounding and affecting, directly or indirectly, consciously or subconsciously, the thinking processes and hence the intellectual production of the *uṣūlī*. I said intellectual in order to bring to prominence the crucial constituents of a theoretic that do not squarely belong to positive legal doctrine but which must constitute an integral part of evaluating legal literature by the historian of ideas. However, if legal, quasi-legal, and purely ideational components of legal theory are all brought under scrutiny, it can be maintained that juridico-social reality constitutes the most obvious element of worldliness. But also of considerable importance is obviously a multiplicity of subsidiary factors that enter into the complex process of textual production. A significant determinant giving, among many other things, orientation and direction to the legal theoretical text is the intellectual traditions upon which the author draws. Legal theoreticians, steeped in Greek philosophy and logic, or theology, or mysticism, are bound to be affected by both the methods and the substantive assumptions prevalent in these fields of enquiry, with this having an impact on their particular perception of legal theory. Finally, the audience of the *uṣūlī* partakes in his worldliness, for it directs and colours his mode of argumentation which constantly assumes the existence of an intellectual contact with that audience.

These factors which we have subsumed under the above-mentioned levels of enquiry have been largely ignored. If it is agreed that the study of originality constitutes a legitimate path of enquiry into intellectual history in general, and into *uṣūl al-fiqh* in particular, then these factors must be present in all thinking about the subject. Originality as a quality that occurs in our minds is partly the substitution of an activity, in this case a textual activity, that succeeds in overshadowing, if not pushing aside, other mental activities. Such a quality cannot claim universal presence, nor, therefore, can it even demand the critical attention of the scholar, if these factors are suppressed or deemed irrelevant in our enquiries.

III

Like any system of interpretation, *uṣūl al-fiqh* starts from given or self-evident premises. The decisive fact about these premises is that, while they are humanly conceived, they must strive to express what is thought by the *human mind* to be God's law. In short, they are bound by the unalterable proposition of the divine origins of the law. This basic but crucial fact restricts, on the one hand, the range of possible interpretations, yet allows, on the other, a wide spectrum of interpretative possibilities within the divine limitations of the law. Marxism and empiricism provide two, out of many, analogous examples of philosophies that allow for significantly divergent interpretations while simultaneously setting a boundary beyond which the committed philosopher simply cannot go. Hume, Berkeley, and Locke, for instance, afford us three empiricist philosophical systems; yet they are widely different from each other. Shāfiʿī, Sarakhsī, Ghazālī, and Shāṭibī, among others, present us with equally divergent legal theories that assume the common denominator of a divine command. If we are justified, and we surely are, in studying the three British philosophers as authors of distinct and unique empiricist philosophies, we are equally justified in viewing the four Muslim doctors as proponents of theories that are so different from each other as to constitute four widely variant interpretations of the means to arriving at God's law.

In principle then one cannot speak of *uṣūl al-fiqh* as a single, uniform phenomenon, for one must account for the differences that exist between one *uṣūl* theory and another. The differences manifest themselves as distinct interpretations that may be placed on a wide spectrum whose extreme ends represent uncompromising literalism and liberal pragmatism. Ibn Ḥazm, for instance, belongs to the former while Ṭūfī[18] and Shāṭibī belong to the latter. Between these two extremes stands a whole range of theorists, each armed with what he thinks to be the tools necessary for his task. And these changed from one theorist to another.

The most obvious indication of the differentials between theories is the fact of the controversial contents of *uṣūl al-fiqh*. A mere perusal of the contents of works produced even in a single century reveals considerable differences. A review of the jurists' production throughout a millennium discloses astonishing opinions of what the subject-matter of this discipline is or should be. It is well known that Ghazālī criticized those legal theorists who, he thought, went to excesses in treating issues of theology, positive law, and grammar in *uṣūl al-fiqh*.[19] Shāṭibī also put forth a similar criticism, limiting his theory to issues that were clearly intended to serve his particular purposes.[20] There was nothing throughout the jurists' writings to indicate that the subject-matter of *uṣūl al-fiqh* was either fixed or well defined. A survey of a randomly selected topic, *al-ʿazīma wal-rukhṣa*,[21] reveals that it was discussed in a number

[18] In his *Sharḥ al-Arbaʿīn al-Nawawiyya*.

[19] Ghazālī, *Mustaṣfā*, i. 9–10; see also Makdisi, 'Juridical Theology', 34–5, for a discussion of the contents of *uṣūl al-fiqh*.

[20] Shāṭibī, *Muwāfaqāt*, i. 17–18.

[21] *ʿAzīma* is the binding force of a ruling without consideration for mitigation due, e.g., to hardship. *Rukhṣa* represents the mitigation or the setting aside of legal rulings in favour of more lenient ones due to such hardship. See Ibn Qudāma, *Rawḍa*, 58; Shāṭibī, *Muwāfaqāt*, i. 204–45, ii. 84–119.

of works,[22] but was left out altogether in the works of Ibn al-Ḥājib,[23] Bājī,[24] Shīrāzī,[25] Juwaynī,[26] and Tilimsānī.[27] The inclusion or exclusion of Greek logic is another well-attested matter.[28] The discussions of legal prepositions (*ḥurūf*), Kalām theories of knowledge, the auxiliary sources of the law, and an array of other topics, were incorporated or excluded at will, and could never, as such, affect the credibility and quality of a work.

In the same vein, the arrangement of material in the works of *uṣūl* varied according to authors, with certain arrangements generating at times criticism by fellow jurists. Some jurists began by an exposition of the legal norms (*aḥkām*), to be followed by the four sources of the law, the controversial sources, legal language, *qiyās, ijtihād, taqlīd*, and finally *tarjīḥ* (preponderance). Others, who objected to this arrangement,[29] preferred to begin by an exposition and analysis of the legal language, and then proceeded to other issues, their reasoning being that all things are dependent on the language of the *Sharīʿa* and a proper discussion of this language paves the ground for the rest of the topics in the book. Yet others chose to begin with logic, or a theory of knowledge, thereafter taking up the legal norms, the four sources, legal language, and so on.[30] Ṭūfī gave a lengthy analysis of at least six distinct methods (*ṭuruq*) of arrangement which belonged to Ghazālī, Shīrāzī, al-Fakhr al-Rāzī, Qarāfī, Ibn al-Ṣayqal, and Āmidī. Having discussed these, he then offered a method of his own.[31] And Ghazālī himself declared his own method in *al-Mustaṣfā* to be unique.[32]

The choice of contents and of their arrangement was combined with emphasis or de-emphasis of certain issues selected to be included in the theory. The various degrees of importance given to *istiḥsān* and *istiṣlāḥ* in the various works are an obvious case in point. Other issues were the subject of such an expanded and specialized enquiry that they resulted in independent treatises of a highly individualistic nature. Ibn Taymiyya's *Mas'alat al-Istiḥsān* and Ghazālī's monumental *Shifāʾ al-Ghalīl* represent two instances.

The choice of particular contents, the method of their arrangement, and the extent to which these contents are explicated are but three

[22] In addition to sources cited in the previous note, see Sarakhsī, *Uṣūl*, i. 117, 303; Ghazālī, *Mustaṣfā*, i. 98; Ibn al-Laḥḥām, *Qawāʿid*, 114; Taftāzānī, *Ḥāshiya*, ii. 8; Āmidī, *Iḥkām*, i. 101.

[23] *Muntahā al-Wuṣūl wal-Amal.* [24] *Iḥkām al-Fuṣūl.* [25] *Tabṣira.*

[26] *Burhān.* [27] *Miftāḥ al-Wuṣūl.*

[28] See Hallaq, 'Logic, Formal Arguments', 321–35.

[29] e.g. Ṭūfī, *Sharḥ al-Rawḍa*, i. 97–8.

[30] e.g. Ibn al-Ḥājib, *Muntahā al-Wuṣūl wal-Amal.*

[31] Ṭūfī, *Sharḥ*, i. 101–6; for his own method, see 107–8.

[32] *Mustaṣfā*, i. 4 (l. 7).

symptoms of a more fundamental variety of doctrine with which one must deal if a serious study of *uṣūl al-fiqh* is to be undertaken. Dismissing these differences as ornamental, superficial, or irrelevant amounts to a deliberate disregard of some of the crucial means to a successful diagnosis of what the individual treatise of *uṣūl al-fiqh* is all about.

IV

We have spoken earlier of the components of worldliness which compete in producing the text. The competition, whose locus is the mind of the author, takes various forms, and each form produces a different result. At times the competition leads to a synthesis of the entirety of the components, namely, to a state of equilibrium in which all the components exercise influence and receive proportionate representation. At others, and this seems to be more frequent, it leads to the dominance of one or more components over the others, in which case the text becomes partly subservient to the imperatives of the overriding component(s). I said 'partly' because the text can never be wholly geared towards the service of these imperatives. After all, the divine components of the law, coupled with the sheer authority of tradition within the discipline, are weighty and powerful constants in any competition.

Be that as it may, a significant component of the worldliness of any legal theory is the juridical reality of the social and political order. In the light of the findings of recent scholarship, we now have no good reason to assume any appreciable gulf between the social realities of Islam and the variant interpretations of the law. Modern research has shown that the *Sharīʿa* remained to a significant degree the supreme law, even in those areas of legal practice which have for long been assumed to have lain outside the domain of the *Sharīʿa*—e.g. penal, commercial, and land law. In land law and land taxation and rent B. Johansen has shown that legal practice is in conformity with the *Sharīʿa* and that the jurists were not hesitant to reinterpret the religious law in order to address the exigencies arising in their societies.[33] Brunschvig has also convincingly shown that the variety of positive legal doctrines is closely connected with the sociological matrix from which these doctrines emerged.[34] Other studies of legal practices throughout selected epochs and locales of Islamdom have similarly pointed to the connect-

[33] Johansen, *Islamic Law on Land Tax*, especially 124–5.
[34] See his 'Considérations', 61–73.

edness of social realities and judicial doctrines,[35] notwithstanding the partial supplementation of religious law by the state. In a detailed study of Muslim commercial law—a law that has until recently been supposed to have little relevance to actual practice—Udovitch has shown how much awareness the medieval lawyers demonstrated in their writings about commercial law and partnership. The 'jurists' discussion of commercial matters', he argues, 'was based on a fairly clear and accurate understanding of the economic realities of their environment, and a consciousness of the likely effects of their promulgations on the conduct of economic life'.[36] Udovitch concluded that Islamic partnership and commercial law represents 'an instance of the logic of practical reality interacting with the theoretical edifice of Islamic law and achieving an equilibrium that eminently satisfied the requirements of both theory and practice'.[37] It is to be noticed here that the reference to 'theory' includes positive law as a theoretical exposition of what the law should be. In any case, it is undeniable that recent specialized studies of this matter increasingly and consistently point in the direction of a close link between positive law and socio-economic, political, and other realities.[38]

Even more undeniable is the inextricable relationship between positive
* law and legal theory. The fifth/eleventh-century Shams al-Dīn al-Sarakhsī composed a highly original work on legal theory, and this was for the explicit purpose of explaining the methodology on the basis of which he elaborated his positive legal system.[39] A close examination of his *Uṣūl* reveals its careful and constant attention to positive law and legal practice. The book is almost single-mindedly legalistic, and the persistent reference to *furūʿ* cases betrays the affinity between the positive rulings of Sarakhsī and his methodology and theory of legal interpretation. In their legal theories Abū Zayd al-Dabbūsī and Sarakhsī's contemporary, Pazdawī, have also given a great deal of attention to the legal practices of their day.[40] Qarāfī has also linked his positive law as expounded in *al-Dhakhīra* with his theory of law which he laid down

* [35] We are referring to studies conducted, among others, by B. Johansen, R. C. Jennings, U. Heyd, H. R. Idris, A. L. Udovitch, David Powers, G. Nahal, D. P. Little, Huda Lutfi, D. Crecelius, H. Gerber, and J. Mandaville.

[36] Udovitch, 'The "Law Merchant"', 119, 116 f. Udovitch's main contribution in this area is his *Partnership and Profit in Medieval Islam*.

[37] 'The "Law Merchant"', 130.

* [38] Wansharīsī's *al-Miʿyār al-Mughrib* is, among others, an eloquent testimony for this link.

[39] Sarakhsī, *Uṣūl*, i. 10.

[40] For Dabbūsī, see his *Ta'sīs al-Naẓar*, as well as Ghazālī's references to him in *Shifā' al-Ghalīl*, *passim*. For Pazdawī's theory, see his *Uṣūl*.

in *Tanqīḥ al-Fuṣūl*,[41] making the latter the methodological prolegomenon to the former.

That positive law and legal theory were interconnected is shown by the qualifications necessary for a jurist to become adept as an *uṣūlī*. Some legal theorists deemed an adequate proficiency in positive law indispensable for the successful *uṣūlī*, and failure to fulfil this requirement meant a major deficiency in one's knowledge of legal theory.[42] In fact, it was universally agreed that the *raison d'être* and sole purpose of *uṣūl al-fiqh* is the formulation of positive law. And this finds expression in the literature of *adab al-qaḍā'* where theory and practice meet. In his work *Adab al-Qāḍī*, for instance, Māwardī allocates about 350 out of a total of 1400 pages for a comprehensive exposition of *uṣūl al-fiqh*, for he thought it necessary for *qāḍī*s and *muftī*s to be able to practise *ijtihād*, which cannot be carried out without a proficient knowledge of *uṣūl*.[43] The requirement that *muftī*s and *qāḍī*s be able to practise *ijtihād* through the prescribed theory of *uṣūl* was stipulated in as early a theory as that of Shāfi'ī.[44] The two sciences of *uṣūl* and *furū'* became formally interdependent and were later merged into one area of specialization. In the fifth/eleventh, and particularly the seventh/thirteenth, century a new branch of legal science, which we may label as *takhrīj*, made an appearance. The declared purpose of this science, hitherto unstudied, was to bring under close scrutiny specific principles of legal methodology and theory together with cases of positive law that *derive* therefrom (hence the term *takhrīj*). Zinjānī's *Takhrīj*, Isnawī's *Tamhīd*, and Tilimsānī's *Miftāḥ* are three prominent representatives of this genre.[45]

As a matter of principle and methodology then *uṣūl al-fiqh* could never be severed from *furū'*. And in certain works of legal theory, such as that of Sarakhsī, the competing components of worldliness have given way to the overriding demands of juridical reality in the external world. But the dominant component or components of worldliness may originate not in concrete juridical reality but rather in a non-legal field of discourse which may exercise influence upon the legal theorist's modes of thought. Among the intellectual traditions that left an indelible mark on a number of *uṣūl* works are theology, philology, dialectic,

[41] See his *Sharḥ Tanqīḥ al-Fuṣūl*, 2. Further on his *Tanqīḥ* and *Sharḥ*, see below, section VI.

[42] See, e.g., Ibn al-Farrā', *'Udda*, i. 70; Sarakhsī, *Uṣūl*, i. 10.

[43] Māwardī, *Adab*, i. 636–7.

[44] See his *al-Umm* (*Bāb Ibṭāl al-Istiḥsān*), vii. 274. See also Hallaq, '*Iftā'* and *Ijtihād* in Sunnī Legal Theory'.

[45] Other works that may be considered to belong to this branch of legal knowledge are Shīrāzī's *Tabṣira* and Ibn al-Laḥḥām's *al-Qawā'id wal-Fawā'id*. See also the editor's introduction to Isnawī's *Tamhīd*, 15 ff.

logic, and, to a lesser degree, mysticism. The substantive involvement of *uṣūl al-fiqh* in the arena of Kalām is well documented.[46] The works of Ghazālī, Ibn al-Ḥājib, and Anṣārī afford us other examples of the incorporation of logic into *uṣūl al-fiqh*, although the precise effects and implications of such incorporation still await detailed study.[47] The *uṣūl* works of Bājī, Ibn 'Aqīl, and Ibn al-Ḥājib also present us with examples of theories deeply affected by dialectic (*jadal*); and *Qawā'id al-Aḥkām* of Ibn 'Abd al-Salām reflects, among other things, mystical as well as contemporary political influences. In the sphere of language and philology, *uṣūl al-fiqh* was more than a recipient of the contributions made by the specialists in the respective fields. It is not without good reason that Zarkashī remarked that 'the scholars of *uṣūl al-fiqh* have made a close study of certain matters in the language of the Arabs not achieved by the grammarians or the philologists.'[48]

Now, although these intellectual traditions constitute a component of worldliness which competes with that of juridical reality and positive law, the two components are not mutually exclusive, for they often provide ideological support for each other at different stages of theory. One cannot overstress the multifaceted nature of *uṣūl al-fiqh* which comprises what is equivalent in Western jurisprudence to legal theory, legal methodology, interpretation, and, more importantly in this context, legal philosophy. In works where the two aforementioned components are equal competitors, it is quite conceivable, as is in fact often the case, that these components may sustain aspects of theory, methodology, and/or philosophy. For example, the question of *sharā'i' man qablanā* (namely, laws governing nations before the advent of the Islamic revelation) can be profitably sustained on the level of legal philosophy by deploying an array of arguments emanating from the field of theology without there being a necessary connection, or contradiction, between the doctrine held with regard to this question and other doctrines in the same work pertaining to the methodology of positive law as strictly so defined. An indication of the absence of such a necessary connection is the exclusion of the discussion of *sharā'i' man qablanā* from certain *uṣūl* works, notably Shāṭibī's *Muwāfaqāt*. In the case of this work, the component of juridical reality is ever paramount, and that of the intellectual traditions is fully controlled and creatively placed in the service of the methodological considerations of the work. But in the discussion of more involved issues, the two components

[46] See the writings of G. Makdisi, especially 'Ash'arī and Ash'arites', 44 ff., 64 ff., 34 ff. See also Rāzī's *Muḥaṣṣal*, 269–70, 296, *passim*.

[47] For an attempt in this direction, see, e.g., Hallaq, 'Logic, Formal Arguments', 315–58.

[48] Cited in G. Makdisi, 'Juridical Theology', 39.

operated with equally competing force. The elaborate doctrines of *'illa* and *ta'līl* (causation) in the *Uṣūl* of Sarakhsī and the *Shifā'* of Ghazālī offer two examples of the conflict between the two components. Here, theological considerations were reconciled with purely legal exigencies.

The synthesis of the various components in one and the same work is thus to be expected. Ibn 'Abd al-Salām's *Qawā'id al-Aḥkām* brings into prominence not only the imaginative and original uses into which old and familiar *uṣūl* concepts and doctrines are put, but the unique manner in which the author chose to deal with a legal theoretic. The first striking, and somewhat uncommon, feature in this work is the Ṣūfī presence in it: Ibn 'Abd al-Salām was a declared mystic.[49] Second, the author includes metaphysical discussions indirectly relevant to his text.[50] Third, through purely legal devices the author engages himself in defining political concepts as well as outlining the political obligations of the sovereign. This should be of no surprise since he, together with Ibn al-Ḥājib, clashed with the Syrian political authorities, a clash that resulted in their exile to Egypt.[51] Fourth, Ibn 'Abd al-Salām gives weight to the role of custom (*'urf, 'āda*) and societal practices in both theoretical and positive legal considerations. Fifth, there seems to be a deliberate attempt to exclude from *Qawā'id* a number of *uṣūl* issues that are normally taken up by legal theorists. Now, all elements of the work, however variegated in content and focus they may seem, are remarkably well integrated into one theoretical whole. Ibn 'Abd al-Salām's treatise provides an example, by no means singular, of a synthesis of several competing components that variably derive from political reality, juridical practices, positive and customary law, Ṣūfī experience, metaphysics, and other, perhaps less important elements, which may be unravelled upon a closer examination of the author and his work.

When we speak of 'author' the intention is not limited to identifying a mere agent of writing who *happened* to be acting in an indistinguishable framework of time and place. Rather an author, every author, is the depository of a unique combination of experiences that find their genesis and momentum in what we have called the components of worldliness. But although these are the most salient ingredients in effecting *uṣūl* theories, there may be added a number of subsidiary components affecting the ultimate subject-matter and form of the text. We shall touch upon only one or two examples of such subsidiary components in order to make our point.

It is well known that *uṣūl al-fiqh* ranked rather high on the educational syllabus of the *madrasa*, and this had considerable consequences

[49] Subkī, *Ṭabaqāt al-Shāfi'iyya*, v. 83.
[50] *Qawā'id*, 168–74.
[51] Subkī, *Ṭabaqāt al-Shāfi'iyya*, v. 81.

on the overall genre of legal theory. One of the most central facts about the life of *uṣūl al-fiqh* as a science is that while, if not because, it was the theoretical underpinning of the actual legal experiences of Islamic societies, it occupied a paramount place among academic subjects. Thus, along with the components we have thus far mentioned, the pedagogical and didactic side of many *uṣūl* works must never be underestimated. A good number of these works originated either as textbooks intended for teaching students, or as lecture notes (*taʿlīqāt*) taken down by students on the authority of their teachers. In either case, the element of the pedagogical background of a text cannot be ignored or even marginalized. It is simply a crucial fact in our study and evaluation of the text.

Once a treatise is identified as pedagogical, it cannot be judged in isolation from other, usually larger, works by the same author/professor. For it was the norm that educational textbooks and manuals constituted abridgements of longer works that expressed *particular* doctrines of *individual* authors. A survey of these textbooks might give the impression that they are generic in their treatment of the subject-matter. And this may well be true. But textbooks conveyed only the 'minimum' doctrine whose 'maximum' (or perhaps 'optimum') lies in complete and comprehensive works which were, more often than not, composed prior to the textbooks. These latter were employed as guiding lines by the professor whose commentary and explanation in the seminar provided the students with the full analytical range of the text. A textbook, therefore, without the professor's oral commentary—which was at any rate indispensable in the classroom—or without the comprehensive work, can hardly be expected to reflect either the calibre or the originality of its author.

A collateral index of the originality of the professor's text and his annotation of it is provided by the notes (*taʿlīqas*) taken down by students. The *taʿlīqas* were not without originality, and, as has been shown, they reflected a wide variety of doctrines.[52] At times the students gave a faithful account of the professor's series of lectures, but at other times they reformulated and even criticized the teacher's doctrine. A well-known example in point is Ghazālī's notes, published as *al-Mankhūl min Taʿlīqāt al-Uṣūl*, where he often disagrees with his teacher al-Juwaynī and offers his own views.[53]

Thus the audience as the final destination of the *uṣūlī*'s discourse

[52] G. Makdisi, *Rise of Colleges*, 122.

[53] It is worth noting that Juwaynī's *uṣūl* theory as expressed in *al-Burhān* was not lacking in originality. Subkī, for instance, maintained that 'in *al-Burhān* Juwaynī followed the footsteps of no one, and I call this work of his the puzzle of the nation [*lughz al-umma*]', *Ṭabaqāt*, v. 192.

partakes in shaping the text. The pedagogical treatise, unless dedicated to dialectic (*jadal*), tends to be less polemical and argumentative than a treatise written with a view to establishing one's own scholarly credibility and originality among one's peers. The presence of argumentation and detailed lines of reasoning was fundamental in the explication of an original idea, and what Muslim jurists knew as *taḥqīq al-adilla* (the verification of legal proofs) was indispensable to any attempt to establish oneself as an independent authority, with a distinct *ṭarīqa* in the field. Āmidī, for example, tells us that he wrote his large work *al-Iḥkām fī Uṣūl al-Aḥkām* to advocate and prove the truthfulness of what he thought to be the correct views, and, conversely, to refute what he deemed false.[54] This work, however, proved to be quite difficult for students, so he abridged it by eliminating complicated arguments and lines of reasoning, and by retaining the basic doctrines (*qawā'id*) propounded in the unabridged text.[55] Āmidī's younger contemporary, Ibn al-Ḥājib, went further: he is said to have abridged Āmidī's *Iḥkām* in his *Muntahā al-Wuṣūl* and thereafter he abridged the abridgement in *Mukhtaṣar al-Muntahā* for the 'benefit of the intelligent student'.[56] For the same pedagogical purposes Ṣafī al-Dīn al-Baghdādī abridged his *Taḥqīq al-Amal* by removing detailed lines of argument and keeping only the essentials of theory.[57]

On the non-pedagogical level, one may give the example of how two (or more) texts by the same author differ precisely because they are directed at different audiences. In his *Iḥkām al-Fuṣūl*, for instance, the Mālikī jurist Bājī gave a detailed and systematic exposition of the Madinese consensus (*ijmā' ahl al-Madīna*), which comprised two types of consensus. This work was clearly directed at an *uṣūlī* audience not particularly interested in scholarly disputation. But in his *Minhāj*, a dialectical *uṣūl* work, Bājī ostensibly thought it more defensible to drop one type of the Madinese consensus and retain the other.[58]

V

The foregoing makes it abundantly clear that no adequate study of *uṣūl al-fiqh* can be undertaken without taking into consideration the effects that the components of worldliness, severally or aggregately, have on the text. With such a consideration there should be coupled a set of assumptions allowing for the possibilities of variety, development, and

[54] See his *Muntahā al-Sūl*, 3, ll. 2–3.
[55] Ibid. 3.
[56] *Mukhtaṣar*, 2, ll. 3–6.
[57] See the abridgement *Qawā'id al-Uṣūl wa-Ma'āqid al-Fuṣūl*, 82.
[58] See the editor's introduction to Bājī's *Iḥkām*, 129 f.

originality. It is simply wrong to omit from one's consideration the fact of geographical disparity between, say, Andalusia and Persia, or for that matter between Baghdad and Damascus. It would be equally and flagrantly wrong to suppress the assumption that two jurists separated by six or seven centuries ought to be driven apart by a multiplicity of doctrinal, substantive, structural, organizational, and stylistic differences. It would be utterly unreasonable to underestimate the developments occurring between an eighth-century Egyptian theory and another belonging to fourteenth-century Andalusia. A comparative study of Shāfiʿī's and Shāṭibī's theories affords us perhaps the best rebuttal of the dogmatic view insisting on the morbidly uniform and monolithic nature of *uṣūl al-fiqh*.[59]

In the remainder of this section I shall indicate possible areas of research that may profit from the application of a methodology that does not a priori preclude the possibility of originality in legal theory. I shall limit my remarks to two broad examples, one relating to three works by the same author, the other to a number of commentaries by different commentators.

The three works are by Ghazālī who affords us a case study not only of the uniqueness of his own discourse on legal theory but also of the significant changes and developments within his writings on the subject. We have already seen the role of the audience in determining and creating differences in the contents of Bājī's two works. The audience in Ghazālī's case is but one among a number of elements that interacted in producing his discourse. The tumultuous events during the last two or three decades of his life were sufficient to guarantee a variegated outlook at the intellectual consistency of religious and non-religious disciplines. In legal theory *al-Mankhūl* was the first treatise Ghazālī wrote, and being a *taʿlīqa*, it was ineluctably influenced by the teachings of his professor Juwaynī. We know of at least three other major works by Ghazālī on legal theory: *Shifāʾ al-Ghalīl*, *Mustaṣfā*, and *Tahdhīb al-Uṣūl*. Unfortunately, the latter is lost and seems to have been the most comprehensive and detailed of his *uṣūl* treatises.[60] In *Shifāʾ al-Ghalīl*, which he wrote probably before *Tahdhīb* but certainly after *Mankhūl*, he expounds one of the most thorough and original theories of legal causation, to which he in fact dedicated the entire work. A general comparison between the three works, *Mankhūl*, *Shifāʾ*, and *Mustaṣfā*, reveals substantial differences in Ghazālī's views on *taʿlīl*. On various

[59] In addition to the sources quoted under section I above, see Lambton, *State and Government*, 4; M. Bernand, 'Ḳiyās', 241a, declares that 'With the elaboration of the science of the *uṣūl al-fiḳh*, the concepts are *defined* and *fixed*' (italics mine).

[60] See Ghazālī's description of the treatise in *Mustaṣfā*, i. 4; and Hourani, 'Revised Chronology', 292.

aspects of *uṣūl*, not dealt with in *Shifā'*, the early *Mankhūl* differs considerably from *Mustaṣfā*, a work he wrote about two years before his death.[61]

In the opening pages of *Shifā'*,[62] Ghazālī boasts that the treatise contains marvels of scholarship and the quintessence of knowledge. To understand and appreciate the book, Ghazālī bids the reader rid himself of erstwhile beliefs and familiar ways of thinking, for old habits of thought hinder sound apprehension. The 'reader must fulfil the prerequisite of being thirsty for understanding secrets that have not been unravelled in [existing] writings, and he must be eager to grasp truths unknown to people'.[63] These remarks should by no means be taken as self-vaunting. Ghazālī is preparing the reader for what is to come, namely, a theory of legal reasoning and causation that manifests a great deal of ingenuity. An adequate study of this treatise will certainly take us beyond the bounds of this essay, but it suffices in order to make our point to refer to his discussion of *munāsaba* (relevancy)[64] where he introduces the issue of *maṣlaḥa* (public interest) as a central element in reasoning about legal cases.[65] Significantly, he allots to this matter over 120 pages out of a total of about 600 pages.[66] More significant is the fact that his theory of *munāsaba* and *maṣlaḥa* is underscored by a strong tendency towards reason as the basis of determining public interest which ultimately enters into the legal norms of the *Sharī'a*. In fact, his bold tendency towards reason was so obvious that he felt compelled, on more than one occasion, explicitly to dissociate himself from Mu'tazilism.[67]

It is indeed a long leap between Ghazālī's theory of *munāsaba* in *Shifā'* and that which he expounded later in *Mustaṣfā*,[68] where he is clearly less imaginative and more conservative. His conservatism in this work seems to run through the entire gamut of legal theory. It is instructive that under the category of *munāsaba* in *Shifā'* he offers a lengthy discussion of the issue of *maṣlaḥa* and *ri'āyat al-maqāṣid* (upholding the aims of the law), thus adopting *maṣlaḥa* as a formally legitimate principle. In *Mustaṣfā*, on the other hand, he not only abandons reason as a major source of defining *maṣlaḥa*, but by refusing to discuss it under *munāsaba* and by relegating it to the chapter on

[61] Hourani, 'Revised Chronology', 301–2. [62] *Shifā'*, 4–8. [63] Ibid. 8.

[64] The relevance of a property as a legal cause (*'illa*) is said by some jurists, including Ghazālī, to be a legitimate method of establishing the cause of a legal ruling. However, some jurists, such as Dabbūsī, argued that this method is highly subjective and arbitrary. But Ghazālī maintained that the method can be justified on objective and rational grounds. See his *Shifā'*, 142–3.

[65] Cf. Brunschvig. 'Valeur et fondement', 375 ff. [66] See *Shifā'*, 142–266.

[67] Ibid. 163 (l. 1), 204–5. [68] *Mustaṣfā*, ii. 296–306.

istiṣlāḥ,[69] where the principle is considered controversial, he reduced a major avenue of reasoning to the domain of controversial legitimacy. If we were to locate Ghazālī on the aforementioned spectrum whose two extreme ends are uncompromising literalism and liberal pragmatism, we would argue that in *Shifā'* he may be placed closer to the latter, whereas in *Mustaṣfā* he strongly tilted towards the former.

Why did Ghazālī change his position? Although Ghazālī's biography and checkered career are relatively well known to us, they are not quite sufficient to explain fully the differences in the two works. A thorough study of the contents of his legal works and a detailed chronological account of his personal and professional experience are needed before any such explanation is attempted. However, we may tentatively venture to explain the differences in terms of the varying components of worldliness behind the two texts. Ghazālī wrote *Shifā'* in an early period of his scholarly career, but certainly at a time when he was mature enough not to be directly influenced by Juwaynī, or for that matter by anyone else. It is clear from his treatment that he was familiar with an extraordinary range of scholarly legal writings on the subject. We know that at this phase of his career he taught law in Baghdad, issued *fatwā*s, and was intensely involved in the study of the legal sciences, as evinced in the many juridical works he composed early on in his life.[70] These works also included a number of treatises on positive law and juridical dialectic. We also know that at this time, but also earlier, Ghazālī became quite interested in the rational sciences and the rational movements in Islam. His serious preoccupation with positive law, on both the pedagogic and the practical levels, as well as his avid interest in a variety of rational disciplines, each constituted a necessary condition which together were sufficient to produce *Shifā'* and the theory of *munāsaba* he expounded there. But both conditions were absent towards the end of his life, when he wrote *Mustaṣfā*.

After his spiritual crisis in Palestine and Syria, rationality seems to have failed Ghazālī, and the mundane affairs of the world concerned him least. In *Mustaṣfā*, a work that was written in the same period as *Iḥyā' 'Ulūm al-Dīn*, there is a marked retreat to fearsome piety. The *Mustaṣfā* was little more than a manual for teaching law,[71] in which Ghazālī safely stated the 'minimum' doctrine without risking what might be taken as daring, innovative, or controversial. The pragmatism and the attention to *maṣlaḥa* that characterized *Shifā'* are entirely absent from *Mustaṣfā*. Yet the latter remains uniquely Ghazālian in its choice

[69] Ibid. ii. 297, l. 3.

[70] See Subkī, *Ṭabaqāt al-Shāfi'iyya*, iv. 104 ff.; Hourani, 'Revised Chronology', 292.

[71] He himself acknowledged that the treatise was intended for students. See *Mustaṣfā*, i. 4.

of subject-matter, treatment, style, and the logical prolegomenon which became its hallmark.

This instance of variety in Ghazālī's theoretical treatises on law is by no means exceptional. It may be found in the works of several other jurists, beginning with Shāfi'ī, whose 'Old' and 'New' doctrines are well known, down to Ṭūfī, whose *Sharḥ Mukhtaṣar al-Rawḍa* shares virtually nothing with his theory of *maṣlaḥa* which he expounded in *Sharḥ al-Arba'īn al-Nawawiyya*.

Variety, and indeed originality, find expression not only in the jurists' very own works but also elsewhere where they are least expected. The conventional view has it that commentaries, super-commentaries, and super-glosses on juridical works betray a slavish commitment to the ideas propounded by the original author, and thus what is offered by the commentators is nothing more than hair-splitting motivated by a single-minded concern for the merely trivial minutiae of legal doctrine.[72] Again, this has long been the prevalent view among orientalists despite the glaring fact that no study whatsoever has been conducted to trace down systematically the developments of doctrine in these commentaries and super-commentaries. Even a preliminary assessment of this literature reveals enough facts and information as to render the traditional view invalid.

While commentaries must have been a conceivable avenue for the less imaginative and ambitious jurists to publish their traditional knowledge, they also constituted another avenue for jurists of a higher calibre to put forth distinctly original ideas. Perhaps the foremost and most immediate act of originality in the work of these latter commentators is that, unlike the former, they managed to inject themselves between the original text and the reader, only to assert, as a constant reminder, that their presence is essential and that nothing, in effect, can reach the reader except through them. This kind of commentary allows the text to be connected with its audience only after having the commentator bestow on it his own colour and after filtering it through his 'ideological' screen. Nor is this all. The commentator in this genre has generally proved to be uncommitted to the substance, arrangement, and orientation of the original work and its author. The commentators had their own agenda which was, more often than not, independent of the original work.

One can distinguish at least six types of commentary on *uṣūl al-fiqh* works, and, except for one, they are distinctly individualistic. The

[72] See, e.g., Coulson, *History of Islamic Law*, 84; Gibb, *Mohammedanism*, 104: 'Since the formal legal doctrines and definitions of the [juridical] schools remained substantially unchanged through all the later centuries, there is little to be gained by tracing down and discussing their formidable output of juristic works.'

exception belongs to the type concerned with annotating the lexical connotation of words and concepts used by the original author or, if it is a super-commentary, by the first commentator. In this there is very little, if any, originality and innovation worth mentioning. The second type is a commentary that explicates undeveloped concepts, expands in detail on the original text's terse language, and clarifies its ambiguities. One of the many examples of this type is Ibn 'Abd al-Shakūr's *Musallam al-Thubūt*, a commentary on the abridgement entitled *Fawātiḥ al-Raḥamūt* by Anṣārī; another is Shīrāzī's *Sharḥ al-Luma'*, a commentary on an earlier work by the same author. What separates this type from two other kinds of commentary is the commentator's concern for bringing out in detail what he thinks to be the intended meanings and ideas of the original author, without being avidly committed to defend or refute them, as is the case with the third and fourth types in our classification. Such commentaries seem to have been especially written, as their authors would at times openly admit,[73] with a view to rebutting criticism directed at a particular text or author, or refuting doctrines in the *uṣūl* work which is the object of their commentary. Both al-'Aḍud al-Ījī and Taftāzānī wrote, respectively, a commentary and a super-commentary on Ibn al-Ḥājib's *Mukhtaṣar* primarily in defence, but also in explanation, of the work against the disdain directed at it by anonymous opponents.[74] 'Abbādī also composed his *al-Āyāt al-Bayyināt* as a super-commentary on Maḥallī's commentary on *Jam' al-Jawāmi'* of Subkī with the explicit purpose of defending Maḥallī and Subkī against the attacks of the adversaries.[75] On the other hand, Māzirī and Anbārī have each commented on Juwaynī's *Burhān* in a reportedly critical vein.[76] Likewise, Aṣfahānī's *Bayān al-Mukhtaṣar*, a commentary on Ibn al-Ḥājib's aforementioned work, is replete with criticism of Ibn al-Ḥājib's theory.

The fifth type of commentary has as its main concern the synthesis of doctrines belonging to different legal schools or jurists. Anṣārī's and Ibn 'Abd al-Shakūr's commentaries, for instance, represent an attempt at bringing into one coherent whole the Shāfi'ī and Ḥanafī theories of law,[77] whereas Bukhārī's commentary on Pazdawī's *Uṣūl* is an example of a synthesis of different doctrines held by a number of jurists.[78] Finally,

[73] See, e.g., sources cited in the next two notes.

[74] See Ījī, *Sharḥ*, i. 5; Taftāzānī, *Ḥāshiya*, i. 3.

[75] 'Abbādī, *Āyāt*, i. 2–3. See also below, n. 90.

[76] Aghnides, *Mohammedan Theories*, 174.

[77] See Ibn 'Abd al-Shakūr, *Musallam*, i. 7 (l. 14).

[78] It is also worthy of note that certain non-commentative works had as their goal the synthesis of two schools of legal thought. See, for instance, Shāṭibī's *Muwāfaqāt* (i. 8), declared by its author to be a work bringing together the teachings of Ibn al-Qāsim and those of Abū Ḥanīfa.

the sixth type is a commentary on an abridgement where both the abridgement and the commentary on it are undertaken by the same jurist. Qarāfī's commentary on his own abridgement of Rāzī's *Maḥṣūl*, and Ṭūfī's commentary on *al-Bulbul*, an abridgement he made of Ibn Qudāma's *Rawḍa*, are two cases in point.

Now, with the exception of the first type, commentaries seem to manifest greater or lesser degrees of innovation and originality, not unlike the varying degrees of originality exhibited by the authors upon whose texts these commentaries were written. And like these authors, the commentators were subject to the similar influences brought about by the components of worldliness. A significant indication of the commentators' contribution to recreating and refashioning the original text lies in a comparison between commentaries on the same text. In the case of Ibn al-Ḥājib's *Mukhtaṣar*, which attracted seventy commentaries in a span of a mere two centuries after its author's death,[79] it would be utterly unreasonable to assume that all these commentaries, some of which are by leading jurists and theologians, are nothing but the rehashing of the same themes. In fact, even a preliminary comparison between Ījī's *Sharḥ* (and Taftāzānī's super-commentary) on the one hand, and Aṣfahānī's *Bayān* on the other, discloses such vast differences between these works that the only common ground they share seems to be reducible to their point of departure, namely, the *Mukhtaṣar*.

Nor should one assume that the abridgements (*mukhtaṣarāt*) which constituted the bases of commentaries are completely faithful to the original works from which they were abstracted. In abridging larger works, jurists took liberties in selecting certain materials and in rearranging them, and when they wrote commentaries on their own abridgements they took even more liberties in determining what is or is not important, and emphasized or de-emphasized issues as they deemed fit. The result of this process of sifting, selecting, and augmenting was that the original, unabridged text had little in common with the final commentary. Consider the case of Qarāfī who abridged Rāzī's *Maḥṣūl* under the title *Tanqīḥ al-Fuṣūl fī Ikhtiṣār al-Maḥṣūl*.[80] Qarāfī declared that in the abridgement 'there are hidden meanings that can by no means be understood except by me, since I have not taken them from anyone else'.[81] To explain these meanings, he wrote a *Sharḥ* on the *Tanqīḥ*, resulting in a work that is vastly different from Rāzī's *Maḥṣūl*. Between the freedoms Qarāfī exercised in abridging the original work and his independence in writing the commentary, his *Sharḥ Tanqīḥ al-Fuṣūl* certainly deserves to be studied as a work entirely of his own

[79] Yamānī, *Īthār al-Ḥaqq*, 200.
[80] He again abridged this abridgement under the title *Mukhtaṣar Tanqīḥ al-Fuṣūl*.
[81] *Sharḥ Tanqīḥ al-Fuṣūl*, 2.

creation. So was Ṭūfī's commentary on his own abridgement of Ibn Qudāma's *Rawḍa*, which is said to be an abridgement of Ghazālī's *Mustaṣfā*.[82] Ṭūfī's *Sharḥ* drastically differs from both Ibn Qudāma's and Ghazālī's works. In the abridgement and the commentary on it, Ṭūfī claimed he exercised his own *ijtihād*, and in the latter he explicitly maintained that he expressed unique views not to be found elsewhere.[83] In the substance of doctrines in the *Sharḥ*, in the arrangement of the subject-matter, and in the lines of reasoning leading to the elaboration of the theory, he argued that he followed his own methods and no one else's.[84]

We are obviously under no obligation to take the jurists' evaluation of their own contributions at face value. But such descriptions acquire an added significance when even a preliminary study of the jurists' works, whether commentative or not, reveals the ingenuity and individualistic imprint of their discourse. Qarāfī's and Ṭūfī's commentaries, among many others, may be said without the slightest hesitation to be as independent-minded as any other 'original' work. It would certainly not be an exaggeration to say that the use of abridgements as the basis of expanded works represents more a pretext than a genuine need for a text to the substance and framework of which the jurists were committed.[85] This, of course, raises the question of why these jurists opted to comment on abridgements of already existing works rather than compose treatises entirely of their own. A complete answer must await further research, but we may tentatively argue that while some theorists were indeed limited in their commentaries to the main ideas expressed in the text upon which they were commenting, others found in well-accepted and highly authoritative abridgements a means through which their works, which have only the semblance of commentaries, would gain immediate recognition and acceptance. The attribution and association of a work/commentary with a distinguished text would guarantee its ultimate, if not immediate, success and absolve it from the initial burden of proving itself.

[82] Ṭūfī, *Sharḥ*, i. 98. Yet another example is Ibn al-Najjār's commentary on his own abridgement of 'Alā' al-Dīn al-Mirdāwī's *Taḥrīr*, entitled *Sharḥ al-Kawkab al-Munīr* (i. 21, 29).

[83] Ṭūfī, *Sharḥ*, iii. 750.

[84] Ibid. i. 95, 97–8; iii. 750, 751.

[85] It is remarkable, for instance, that Shīrāzī chose to write a large work of *uṣūl* by way of commenting on his own *Luma'*. *Sharḥ al-Luma'*, however, could stand as an entirely original (viz. non-commentative) work, and some bibliographers have indeed thought it so and have given it another title, i.e. *al-Wuṣūl ilā Ma'rifat al-Uṣūl* (see editor's introduction to *Sharḥ al-Luma'*, 57). Another interesting case is that of 'Abbādī who commented on Maḥallī's commentary on Juwaynī's *Waraqāt*, this having the dubious distinction of being the shortest treatise on *uṣūl* we know. The choice of the *Waraqāt* as the object of a commentary is curious since the treatise barely states the

VI

Admitting the legitimacy of the relationship between the author and his worldliness, as well as the resultant products of this relationship, would necessarily mean that variety and originality are qualities whose *possible* existence must be presumed until proved otherwise. To preclude their existence a priori would be methodologically wrong.

The problematics of the now dominant methodology lie precisely in its controlling assumption that the law is immutable, this having the necessary consequence that it is rigid and thus monolithic. This archaic approach accounts, among other things, for the fact that thus far there has been no single study which attempts to trace down the chronological development of concepts and doctrines within *uṣūl al-fiqh*. If the underlying assumption insists on a monolithic and immutable legal history, then any curiosity about an intellectually vigorous development in this literature is crushed before its birth.

Chronological conceptual developments within *uṣūl* went hand in hand with the extent of variety and originality we have been discussing. The science of legal theory attracted the best minds, and their ingenious contributions over the centuries could not but result in significant developments. To acknowledge the inventiveness of Shāfiʿī, Ibn Surayj, Dabbūsī, Bāqillānī, Baṣrī, Juwaynī, Ghazālī, Ibn ʿAqīl, Rāzī, Ibn Taymiyya, Shāṭibī, and a dozen others, and still refuse the proposition that, methodologically, significant developments must be considered in the bag of our assumptions, would amount to blind obstinacy.

This is certainly not a far-fetched argument, for it has a firm foundation in *uṣūl al-fiqh*'s history. Even in the relatively scarce primary literature thus far published one can detect important doctrinal developments. Consider, for instance, the development of discourse concerning the requirement that a *muftī* must be a *mujtahid*, a development that reflects the adaptation of legal theory to the exigencies of juridical practices.[86] Another instance is the problem of the authoritative basis of consensus which posed serious difficulties and challenged the jurists' imagination. The problem was debated in as early a period as that of Shāfiʿī, if not before, and until the beginning of the fifth/eleventh century it remained unresolved. It was only during the next three centuries that a solution was found, and only then was the problem finally put to

outline of *uṣūl* (it consists of about 1600 words). Be that as it may, ʿAbbādī later abridged his long commentary (*sharḥ kabīr*) on Maḥallī. It is not inconceivable that the shorter commentary could serve as the text of another commentary, and this latter may be considerably different from ʿAbbādī's long commentary.

[86] This issue has been studied in some detail. See Hallaq, '*Iftā*' and *Ijtihād* in Sunnī Legal Theory'.

rest.[87] But the solution would have been unattainable had it not been for concurrent and concomitant developments which armed the jurists with tools that enabled them to reach a solution. The central device that was brought to bear upon the authoritativeness of consensus was the thematic *tawātur* in prophetic traditions (*tawātur ma'nawī*),[88] and this in turn would not have been developed had it not been for elaborating a theory of induction which reached a high level of sophistication by the eighth/fourteenth century.

The theory of public interest (*maṣlaḥa, istiṣlāḥ*) represents another area of the law that witnessed a great deal of development. It now hardly needs arguing that Ghazālī's concept of *maṣlaḥa* expounded in *Shifā'* was an outstanding advance over previous concepts. Yet, Ghazālī's writings on this issue would seem unimpressive when compared with the monumental achievement of Shāṭibī in his *Muwāfaqāt*, a work entirely based on a unique and creative marriage between a notion of induction and the doctrine of *maṣlaḥa*.[89] Although Shāṭibī seems to have assimilated in his work the views Ghazālī expressed in his *Shifā'*, he took the theory of *maṣlaḥa* into unprecedented dimensions. Shāṭibī, however, would not have been able to produce his theory without having had at his disposal a rich variety of highly developed doctrines of law and legal logic. While it is undeniable that Shāṭibī's theory is the outcome of a process that began in the second/eighth century, it would not be an exaggeration to maintain that he was far more indebted to the contributions made during the three centuries that immediately preceded him than to the earlier period.

A development parallel to that of *istiṣlāḥ* is *istiḥsān* which did not culminate in a work of the weight and stature of *Muwāfaqāt*, yet succeeded in attracting some of the most complex and seminal arguments in the history of *uṣūl*. It is indeed a long way from the elementary notions of *istiḥsān*, as found in Abū Ḥanīfa and Shaybānī, to the theories on the subject propounded by Pazdawī,[90] Sarakhsī,[91] and, later on, Ibn Taymiyya who allocated to its treatment an independent treatise.[92] The broad outlines of the evolution of *istiḥsān* from the second/eighth-century arbitrary or semi-arbitrary mode of reasoning—severely attacked by Shāfi'ī—to a coherent and systematic doctrine during the fifth/eleventh century and thereafter are well known.[93] And like the

[87] See Hallaq, 'On the Authoritativeness of Sunni Consensus', 427–54.

[88] Ibid. Also see id., 'On Inductive Corroboration', 9–24.

[89] See, e.g., Hallaq, 'On Inductive Corroboration', 24–9; id., 'The Primacy of the Qur'ān', 84–90.

[90] *Uṣūl*, iv. 2–14, 32–43. [91] *Uṣūl*, ii. 199–215. [92] i.e. *Mas'alat al-Istiḥsān*.

[93] For a discussion and analysis of the main authors on *istiḥsān*, see J. Makdisi, 'Legal Logic', 73–85.

interconnected developments of *al-tawātur al-ma'nawī*, induction, and consensus, *istiḥsān* was capable of development only by virtue of the refinements that took place in the theory of causation (*ta'līl*)[94] which in its fifth/eleventh- or seventh/thirteenth-century form would have bewildered Shāfi'ī.

VII

Acknowledging these developments, and, more importantly, acknowledging the possibility of their existence throughout the history of *uṣūl al-fiqh*, has serious implications for our methodology. For it not only sheds the myth of a monolithic Islamic legal theory, but calls upon those who still adopt such a myth to re-evaluate the basic assumptions and starting-points of their thinking on the subject. The theory of an individual jurist cannot any more be taken to represent an anonymous collectivity called *uṣūl al-fiqh*; there is simply no such thing. Can any one theory equally represent the contributions of Shāfi'ī, Sarakhsī, Ghazālī, Ṭūfī, and Shāṭibī? Can Ibn al-Ḥājib speak for Baṣrī, or, for that matter, for any of the leading figures of *uṣūl*? Shāfi'ī or Shāṭibī are no more representatives of *uṣūl al-fiqh* than William of Ockham or Berkeley of British empiricism. The contributions of the leading jurists cannot be treated as an indistinguishable mass, one speaking for the other, the other for one. A glance at biographical works instructs us that these jurists were individuals with a strong sense of their individuality. Each was the product of his own experience and of his own age, no less than we who write about them are the products of our own specifically social, religious, political, and ideological experiences and backgrounds. The worldliness underlying and affecting their discourse varied from one jurist to another, and changed with the constant changes of time. The fifth/eleventh-century *uṣūlist* Sam'ānī perhaps did not apprehend the prophetic quality of his words when he declared that the law is 'an ongoing science continuing with the passage of centuries and changing with the change of circumstances and conditions of men'.[95]

[94] For a preliminary attempt at tracing developments in *ta'līl* see Hallaq, 'The Development of Logical Stucture', 42–67.

[95] Cited in G. Makdisi, 'Juridical Theology', 36.

WORKS AND ARTICLES CITED

'Abbādī, Aḥmad b. Qāsim, *al-Āyāt al-Bayyināt 'alā Sharḥ Jam' al-Jawāmi'*, 4 vols. (Cairo: n.p., 1289/1872).

—, *Sharḥ 'alā Sharḥ al-Maḥallī 'alā al-Waraqāt*, printed on the margin of Shawkānī's *Irshād al-Fuḥūl* (Surabāyā: Sharikat Maktabat Aḥmad b. Sa'd b. Nabhān, n.d.).

Aghnides, N.P., *Mohammedan Theories of Finance* (New York: P.S. King & Son Ltd., 1916).

Āmidī, Sayf al-Dīn Abū al-Ḥasan, *al-Iḥkām fī Uṣūl al-Aḥkām*, 3 vols. (Cairo: Maṭba'at 'Alī Ṣubayḥ wa-Awlādih, 1387/1968).

—, *Muntahā al-Sūl fī 'Ilm al-Uṣūl* (Cairo: Maktabat Muḥammad 'Alī Ṣubayḥ, n.d.).

Anṣārī, Muḥammad b. Niẓām al-Dīn, *Fawātiḥ al-Raḥamūt*, 2 vols. (Cairo: al-Maṭba'a al-Amīriyya, 1324/1906).

Aṣfahānī, Shams al-Dīn Maḥmūd, *Bayān al-Mukhtaṣar*, ed. Muḥammad Maẓharbaqā, 2 vols. (Jadda: Dār al-Madanī, 1406/1986).

Baghdādī, Ṣafī al-Dīn b. 'Abd Allāh, *Qawā'id al-Uṣūl wa-Ma'āqid al-Fuṣūl*, in *Majmū' Mutūn Uṣūliyya* (Damascus: al-Maktaba al-Hāshimiyya, n.d.).

Bājī, Abū al-Walīd, *Iḥkām al-Fuṣūl fī Aḥkām al-Uṣūl*, ed. 'Abd al-Majīd Turkī (Beirut: Dār al-Gharb al-Islāmī, 1407/1986).

Bannānī, 'Abd al-Raḥmān, *Ḥāshiyat al-Bannānī 'alā Jam' al-Jawāmi'*, 2 vols. (Bombay: Molavi Mohammed B. Gulamrasul Surtis, 1970).

Baṣrī, Abū al-Ḥusayn Muḥammad b. 'Alī, *al-Mu'tamad fī Uṣūl al-Fiqh*, ed. M. Hamidullah *et al.*, 2 vols. (Damas: Institut Français, 1964–5).

Bernand, M., 'Ḳiyās', *Encyclopedia of Islam*, new edn. (Leiden: E. J. Brill, 1960-), v. 238–42.

Brunschvig, R., 'Considérations sociologiques sur le droit musulman ancien', *Studia Islamica*, 3 (1955), 61–73.

—, 'Perspectives', in G. E. von Grunebaum, ed., *Unity and Variety in Muslim Civilization* (Chicago and London: University of Chicago Press, 1955), 47–62. Also published in French under the same title in *Studia Islamica*, 1 (1953), 5–18.

—, 'Valeur et fondement du raisonnement juridique par analogie d'après al-Gazālī', in *Études d'islamologie*, vol. 2 (Paris: G.-P. Maisonneuve et Larose, 1976), 363–94.

Chehata, Chafik, *Études de droit musulman*, 2 vols. (Paris: Presses Universitaires de France, 1971–3).

Classicisme et déclin culturel dans l'histoire de l'Islam. Actes du symposium international d'histoire de la civilization musulmane, organisé par R. Brunschvig et G. E. von Grunebaum (Paris: G.-P. Maisonneuve, 1957).

Coulson, N.J., *A History of Islamic Law*, new edn. (Edinburgh: Edinburgh University Press, 1989).
Crone, Patricia, *Roman, Provincial and Islamic Law* (Cambridge: Cambridge University Press, 1987).
Dabbūsī, Abū Zayd 'Ubayd Allāh b. 'Umar, *Kitāb Ta'sīs al-Naẓar* (Cairo: al-Maṭba'a al-Adabiyya, n.d.).
Esposito, J. L., *Women in Muslim Family Law* (Syracuse: Syracuse University Press, 1982).
Ghazālī, Abū Ḥāmid, *al-Mankhūl min Ta'līqāt al-Uṣūl*, ed. M. Ḥ. Haytū (Damascus: Dār al-Fikr, 1400/1980).
—, *al-Mustaṣfā min 'Ilm al-Uṣūl*, 2 vols. (Cairo: al-Maṭba'a al-Amīriyya, 1324/1906).
—, *Shifā' al-Ghalīl fī Bayān al-Shabah wal-Mukhīl wa-Masālik al-Ta'līl*, ed. Ḥamd al-Kabīsī (Baghdād: Maṭba'at al-Irshād, 1390/1971).
Gibb, H. A. R., *Mohammedanism*, 2nd edn. (New York: Oxford University Press, 1962).
Grunebaum, Gustave E. von, 'Sources of Islamic Civilization', *Der Islam*, 46 (1970), 1–54.
—, ed., *Unity and Variety in Muslim Civilization* (Chicago and London: University of Chicago Press, 1955).
Hallaq, Wael B., 'The Development of Logical Structure in Sunni Legal Theory', *Der Islam*, 64 (1987), 42–67.
—, '*Iftā'* and *Ijtihād* in Sunnī Legal Theory: A Developmental Account', in D. Powers, B. Messick and M. Masud, eds., *Worldly Interpretation: Muftīs, Fatwās, and Muslim History* (forthcoming).
—, 'Logic, Formal Arguments and Formalization of Arguments in Sunnī Jurisprudence', *Arabica*, 37 (1990), 315–58.
—, 'On the Authoritativeness of Sunnī Consensus', *International Journal of Middle East Studies*, 18 (1986), 427–54.
—, 'On Inductive Corroboration, Probability and Certainty in Sunnī Legal Thought', in Nicholas Heer, ed., *Islamic Law and Jurisprudence: Studies in Honor of Farhat J. Ziadeh* (Seattle: University of Washington Press, 1990), 3–31.
—, 'On the Origins of the Controversy about the Existence of Mujtahids and the Gate of Ijtihad', *Studia Islamica*, 63 (1986), 129–41.
—, 'The Primacy of the Qur'ān in Shāṭibī's Legal Theory', in W. B. Hallaq and D. P. Little, eds., *Islamic Studies Presented to Charles J. Adams* (Leiden: E. J. Brill, 1991), 69–90.
—, 'Was the Gate of Ijtihad Closed?', *International Journal of Middle East Studies*, 16 (1984), 3–41.
Hourani, George, 'A Revised Chronology of Ghazālī's Writings', *Journal of the American Oriental Society*, 104 (1984), 289–302.

Ibn 'Abd al-Salām, 'Izz al-Dīn al-Sulamī, *Qawā'id al-Aḥkām fī Maṣāliḥ al-Anām*, 2 vols. (Cairo: Maṭba'at al-Istiqāma, n.d.).
Ibn 'Abd al-Shakūr, Muḥibb Allāh, *Musallam al-Thubūt: Sharḥ Fawātiḥ al-Raḥamūt*, 2 vols. (Cairo: al-Maṭba'a al-Amīriyya, 1324/1906).
Ibn al-Farrā', Abū Ya'lā al-Baghdādī, *al-'Udda fī Uṣūl al-Fiqh*, ed. Aḥmad al-Mubārakī, 3 vols. (Beirut: Mu'assasat al-Risāla, 1400/1980).
Ibn al-Ḥājib, 'Uthmān b. 'Umar b. Abī Bakr, *Mukhtaṣar al-Muntahā al-Uṣūlī* (Cairo: Maṭba'at Kurdistān, 1326/1908).
—, *Muntahā al-Wuṣūl wal-Amal fī 'Ilmay al-Uṣūl wal-Jadal* (Cairo: Maṭba'at al-Sa'āda, 1326/1908).
Ibn Ḥazm, Muḥammad 'Alī, *al-Iḥkām fī Uṣūl al-Aḥkām*, ed. Muḥammad 'Abd al-'Azīz, 8 vols. (Cairo: Maṭba'at al-Imtiyāz, 1398/1978).
Ibn al-Laḥḥām, 'Alī b. 'Abbās al-Ba'lī, *al-Qawā'id wal-Fawā'id al-Uṣūliyya*, ed. Muḥammad al-Fiqī (Beirut: Dār al-Kutub al-'Ilmiyya, 1403/1983).
Ibn al-Najjār, Muḥammad b. Aḥmad al-Futūḥī al-Ḥanbalī, *Sharḥ al-Kawkab al-Munīr*, ed. M. Zuḥaylī and N. Ḥammād, 3 vols. (Damascus: Dār al-Fikr, 1400/1980).
Ibn Qudāma, Muwaffaq al-Dīn, *Rawḍat al-Nāẓir wa-Junnat al-Munāẓir*, ed. Sayf al-Dīn al-Kātib (Beirut: Dār al-Kitāb al-'Arabī, 1401/1981).
Ibn Taymiyya, Taqī al-Dīn, *Mas'alat al-Istiḥsān* in G. Makdisi, 'Ibn Taimīya's Autograph Manuscript on *Istiḥsān*: Materials for the Study of Islamic Legal Thought', in G. Makdisi, ed., *Arabic and Islamic Studies in Honor of Hamilton A. R. Gibb* (Cambridge: Harvard University Press, 1965), 454–79.
Ījī, 'Aḍud al-Dīn, *Sharḥ Mukhtaṣar al-Muntahā al-Uṣūlī*, 2 vols. (Cairo: Maktabat al-Kulliyyāt al-Azhariyya, 1973).
Isnawī, Jamāl al-Dīn Ibn al-Ḥasan, *al-Tamhīd fī Takhrīj al-Furū' 'alā al-Uṣūl*, ed. Muḥammad Haytū (Beirut: Mu'assasat al-Risāla, 1400/1980).
Johansen, Baber, *The Islamic Law on Land Tax and Rent* (London: Croom Helm, 1988).
Jurjānī, al-Sharīf 'Alī b. Muḥammad, *al-Ta'rīfāt* (Cairo: Muṣṭafā Bābī al-Ḥalabī, 1357/1938).
Juwaynī, Imām al-Ḥaramayn, *al-Burhān fī Uṣūl al-Fiqh*, ed. 'Abd al-'Aẓīm Dīb, 2 vols. (Cairo: Dār al-Anṣār, 1400/1980).
—, *Waraqāt*. See 'Abbādī, *Sharḥ*.
Lambton, A. K. S., *State and Government in Medieval Islam* (Oxford: Oxford University Press, 1981).
* Maḥallī, Shams al-Dīn. See Bannānī and 'Abbādī.

Makdisi, George, 'Ash'arī and the Ash'arites in Islamic Religious History', *Studia Islamica*, 17 (1962), 37–80, and 18 (1963), 19–39.

—, 'The Juridical Theology of Shāfi'ī: Origins and Significance of *Uṣūl al-Fiqh*', *Studia Islamica*, 59 (1984), 5–47.

—, *The Rise of Colleges* (Edinburgh: Edinburgh University Press, 1981).

Makdisi, John, 'Legal Logic and Equity in Islamic Law', *American Journal of Comparative Law*, 33 (1985), 63–92.

Māwardī, Abū al-Ḥasan Muḥammad b. Ḥabīb, *Adab al-Qāḍī*, ed. Muḥyī Hilāl Sarḥān, 2 vols. (Baghdad: Maṭba'at al-Irshād, 1391/1971).

Meron, Y., 'The Development of Legal Thought in Hanafi Texts', *Studia Islamica*, 30 (1969), 73–118.

Pazdawī, 'Alī b. Muḥammad Ibn al-Ḥusayn, *Uṣūl*, printed on the margin of 'Alā' al-Dīn al-Bukhārī, *Kashf al-Asrār*, 4 vols., repr. (Beirut: Dār al-Kitāb al-'Arabī, 1394/1974).

Qarāfī, Shihāb al-Dīn Abū al-'Abbās, *Mukhtaṣar Tanqīḥ al-Fuṣūl fī al-Uṣūl* (Damascus: al-Maktaba al-Hāshimiyya, n.d.).

—, *Sharḥ Tanqīḥ al-Fuṣūl*, ed. Ṭāha Sa'd (Cairo: Maktabat al-Kulliyyāt al-Azhariyya, 1973).

Rāzī, Fakhr al-Dīn, *al-Maḥṣūl fī 'Ilm Uṣūl al-Fiqh*, ed. T. J. al-'Ulwānī, 2 vols., 6 pts. (Riyad: Islamic University of Muhammad b. Saud Press, 1979–81).

Sarakhsī, Muḥammad b. Aḥmad Abū Sahl, *Uṣūl*, ed. Abū al-Wafā al-Afghānī, 2 vols. (Beirut: Dār al-Ma'rifa, 1393/1973).

Schacht, J., *Introduction to Islamic Law* (Oxford: Clarendon Press, 1964).

Shāfi'ī, Muḥammad b. Idrīs, *al-Risāla*, ed. Muḥammad Kīlānī (Cairo: al-Bābī al-Ḥalabī, 1388/1969).

—, *al-Umm*, 7 vols. (Cairo: al-Maṭba'a al-Kubrā al-Amīriyya, 1325/1907).

Shāṭibī, Abū Isḥāq Ibrāhīm b. Mūsā, *al-Muwāfaqāt fī Uṣūl al-Aḥkām*, ed. Muḥyī al-Dīn 'Abd al-Ḥamīd, 4 vols. (Cairo: Maṭba'at 'Alī Ṣubayḥ, 1970).

Shīrāzī, Abū Isḥāq b. Ibrāhīm b. Yūsuf, *Sharḥ al-Luma'*, ed. 'Abd al-Majīd Turkī, 2 vols. (Beirut: Dār al-Gharb al-Islāmī, 1408/1988).

—, *al-Tabṣira fī Uṣūl al-Fiqh*, ed. M. H. Haytū (Damascus: Dār al-Fikr, 1403/1983).

Snouck Hurgronje, C., *Selected Works*, ed. G.-H. Bousquet and J. Schacht (Leiden: E. J. Brill, 1957).

Subkī, Tāj al-Dīn b. Taqī al-Dīn, *Jam' al-Jawāmi'*. See Bannānī.

—, *Ṭabaqāt al-Shāfi'iyya al-Kubrā*, 6 vols., repr. (Beirut: Dār al-Ma'rifa, n.d.).

Taftāzānī, Sa'd al-Dīn, *Ḥāshiya* (printed with Ījī's *Sharḥ*), 2 vols. (Cairo: Maktabat al-Kulliyyāt al-Azhariyya, 1973).

Tilimsānī, Muḥammad b. Aḥmad al-Sharīf, *Miftāḥ al-Wuṣūl fī 'Ilm al-Uṣūl* (= *Miftāḥ al-Wuṣūl ilā Binā' al-Furū' 'alā al-Uṣūl*) (Cairo: Maktabat al-Kulliyyāt al-Azhariyya, n.d.).

Ṭūfī, Najm al-Dīn Sulaymān b. Sa'īd, *Sharḥ al-Arba'īn al-Nawawiyya*, in Muṣṭafā Zayd, ed., *al-Maṣlaḥa fī al-Tashrī' al-Islāmī*, 2nd edn. (Cairo: Dār al-Fikr al-'Arabī, 1384/1964).

—, *Sharḥ Mukhtaṣar al-Rawḍa*, ed. 'Abd Allāh Turkī, 3 vols. (Beirut: Mu'assasat al-Risāla, 1407/1987).

Udovitch, A. L., 'The "Law Merchant" of the Medieval Islamic World', in G. E. von Grunebaum, ed., *Logic in Classical Islamic Culture* (Wiesbaden: Otto Harrassowitz, 1970), 113–30.

—, *Partnership and Profit in Medieval Islam* (Princeton: Princeton University Press, 1970).

Vesey-Fitzgerald, S. G., 'Nature and Sources of the Sharī'a', in M. Khadduri and H. J. Liebesny, eds., *Law in the Middle East* (Washington, D.C.: Middle East Institute, 1955), 85–112.

Wansharīsī, Aḥmad b. Yaḥyā, *al-Mi'yār al-Mughrib wal-Jāmi' al-Mu'rib 'an Fatāwī 'Ulamā' Ifrīqiyya wal-Andalus wal-Maghrib*, 13 vols. (Beirut: Dār al-Maghrib al-Islāmī, 1401/1981).

Yamānī, Muḥammad b. Ibrāhīm Ibn al-Wazīr, *Īthār al-Ḥaqq 'alā al-Khalq* (Cairo: n.p., 1318/1900).

Zinjānī, Shihāb al-Dīn Maḥmūd, *Takhrīj al-Furū' 'alā al-Uṣūl*, ed. Muḥammad Ṣāliḥ (Beirut: Mu'assasat al-Risāla, 1404/1984).

ADDENDA ET CORRIGENDA

p. 182, n. 35: now, see also Baber Johansen, 'Legal Literature and the Problem of Change: The Case of the Land Rent', in *Islam and Public Law*, ed. Chibli Mallat (London: Graham & Trotman, 1993): 29–47; Wael B. Hallaq, 'From *Fatwās* to *Furū'*: Growth and Change in Islamic Substantive Law', *Islamic Law and Society*, 1, 1 (1994): 29–65; id., 'Murder in Cordoba: *Ijtihād*, *Iftā'* and the Evolution of Substantive Law in Medieval Islam', *Acta Orientalia*, 55 (1994; forthcoming).

p. 182, n. 38: see Hallaq, 'From *Fatwās* to *Furū'*'.

p. 182, ll. 21–2: read Abū Bakr Ibn Sahl al-Sarakhsī not Shams al-Dīn.

p. 200, last line: read Jalāl al-Dīn al-Maḥallī not Shams al-Dīn.

INDEX OF ARABIC TERMS

In classifying entries no account is taken of the letter *'ayn* and the Arabic definite article *al-*.

GENERAL INDEX